THE WORLD ACCORDING TO

TRUMP

VOLUME I

DEMOCRATS, ELECTIONS, AND MORE

2017, 2018, 2019

ACTUAL QUOTES OF
PRESIDENT TRUMP BROKEN
DOWN AND CATEGORIZED BY
SUBJECT MATTER

THE WORLD ACCORDING TO TRUMP: VOLUME I - Democrats, Elections, and More (2017, 2018, 2019) in its current format, copyright © Arc Manor 2020.

ISBN: 978-1-64973-000-8

Arc Manor
P. O. Box 10339
Rockville, MD 20849-0339
www.ArcManor.com

These are the direct quotes of President Trump. We have made every effort to check accuracy and no quote is included without a direct reference to the source material. We apologize for any typos or mistakes inadvertently introduced into the compilation of a project as large as this (nearly 1,000 pages between the two volumes).

We have attempted to include all his direct quotes readily accessible, but due to the volume of material had to eliminate obvious repetitions. No attempt was made to correct original typos or usage for the sake of authenticity...all quotes are presented as they were originally referenced.

Contents

Democrats—2017 News Quotes

Response to a question from Bill O'Reilly of FOX News, February 7, 2017.
Source: https://www.foxnews.com/transcript/bill-oreillys-exclusive-interview-with-president-trump

"Yes. We are working very much right .now on the healthcare package. Which I think would be, it is moving along very well. We are trying to get our person Dr. Tom Price[1] approved, as you know, the Democrats are being purely political reasons."

Response to a question from Tucker Carlson of FOX News, March 15, 2017.
Source: https://www.youtube.com/watch?v=RYGH6ejacNO

"If I had the greatest bill in the history of the world, they [the Democrats] would not vote for us because they hate the Republicans. They probably hate me, but they hate the Republicans so badly that they cannot see straight. So, they will always vote against us. It's really a shame because and that's one of the problems that we have when people coming to my office, about lowering drug prices, lowering other things. The Democrats will always going to vote against us. It's been simmering for years. The hatred has been there for years. Not just with me. I mean, the hatred has been there for years. You know, when I was in Washington years ago, I would come in and Republicans would fight with the Democrats during the day and then you would see them after dinner at a restaurant and their families would be out. I mean, they get along. The hatred is so incredible. And honestly, it has been

---

1   At the time of the interview, Dr. Tom Price was a U.S. Congressman (R-Georgia) and a candidate for the position of Secretary of Health and Human Services.

1

like that for a long time. It has been like that through the [former U.S. President Barack] Obama years."

Response to a question from Tucker Carlson of FOX News, March 15, 2017.
Source: https://www.youtube.com/watch?v=RYGH6ejacNO

"Obamacare is a disaster. The premiums are going up. Numbers are as high as 116%. And by the way, this year will be the worst year of all.

"And I said the other day, they [the Democrats] criticized me.

"I said, 'Look, [former U.S. President Barack] Obama is gone. Smart guy. He put things on. '17 is going to be the worst year because he is gone.' He knew that was the year. I mean, you know, let him be out before it implodes.

"Obamacare is imploding. It is a disaster. And the Democrats know that.

"If we had the greatest healthcare bill ever in history, and we needed 8 votes from the Democrats to get us up to the 60 number that you would need? They would not vote for it. It's a very selfish thing. They are doing a very, very bad disservice to the country."

Response to a question from John Dickerson of CBS News, April 30, 2017.
Source: https://www.cbsnews.com/news/face-the-nation-transcript-april-30-2017-president-trump/

"I think the rules in Congress, and in particular the rules in the Senate, are unbelievably archaic and slow moving and, in many cases, unfair. In many cases, you're forced to make deals that are not the deal you'd make. You'd make a much different kind of a deal. You're forced into situations that you hate to be forced into. I also learned, and this is very sad, because we have a country that we have to take care of. The Democrats have been totally obstructionist. [U.S. Senate Minority Leader] Chuck Schumer has turned out to be a bad leader. He's a bad leader for the country. And the Democrats are extremely obstruction-ist. All they do is obstruct. All they do is delay. Even our Supreme Court justice, as you know, who I think is going to be outstanding, Justice [Neil] Gorsuch, I think that it was disgraceful the way they handled that. But, you know, I still have people, I'm waiting for them to be approved, our chief trade negotiator. We can't get these people through. [Dickerson interrupts; Trump continues.] They are obstructionists. And you know what that's hurting? It's hurting the country."

Response to a question from Maggie Haberman of *The New York Times*, July 19, 2017.
Source: https://www.nytimes.com/2017/07/19/us/politics/trump-interview-transcript.html

"I want to either get it done or not get it done. If we don't get it done, we are going to watch Obamacare go down the tubes, and we'll blame the Democrats. And at some point, they are going to come and say, 'You've got to help us.'"

Democrats—2017 Tweets

January 30. 2017

9:23 am[2]: Where was all the outrage from Democrats and the opposition party (the media) when our jobs were fleeing our country?

7:45 pm: The Democrats are delaying my cabinet picks for purely political reasons. They have nothing going but to obstruct. Now have an Obama A.G.

January 31, 2017

6:21 am: Nancy Pelosi and Fake Tears Chuck Schumer held a rally at the steps of The Supreme Court and mic did not work (a mess)-just like Dem party!

---

2   All Tweets are listed using the Eastern Time Zone, which is the same time zone as the White House in Washington, D.C.

6:27 am: When will the Democrats give us our Attorney General and rest of Cabinet! They should be ashamed of themselves! No wonder D.C. doesn't work!

February 7, 2017

8:04 pm: It is a disgrace that my full Cabinet is still not in place, the longest such delay in the history of our country. Obstruction by Democrats!

February 9, 2017

6:57 am: Sen. Richard Blumenthal, who never fought in Vietnam when he said for years he had (major lie), now misrepresents what Judge Gorsuch told him?

8:19 am: Chris Cuomo, in his interview with Sen. Blumenthal, never asked him about his long-term lie about his brave "service" in Vietnam. FAKE NEWS!

February 16, 2017

9:39 am: The Democrats had to come up with a story as to why they lost the election, and so badly (306), so they made up a story—RUSSIA. Fake news!

February 25, 2017

5:02 pm: Congratulations to Thomas Perez, who has just been named Chairman of the DNC. I could not be happier for him, or for the Republican Party!

February 26, 2017

6:33 am: The race for DNC Chairman was, of course, totally "rigged." Bernie's guy, like Bernie himself, never had a chance. Clinton demanded Perez!

March 2, 2017

9:22 pm to 9:38 pm: Jeff Sessions is an honest man. He did not say anything wrong. He could have stated his response more accurately, but it was clearly not…

…intentional. This whole narrative is a way of saving face for Democrats losing an election that everyone thought they were supposed…

…to win. The Democrats are overplaying their hand. They lost the election, and now they have lost their grip on reality. The real story…

…is all of the illegal leaks of classified and other information. It is a total "witch hunt!"

March 3, 2017

7:09 am: It is so pathetic that the Dems have still not approved my full Cabinet.

3:47 pm: I hear by demand a second investigation, after Schumer, of Pelosi for her close ties to Russia, and lying about it.

March 5, 2017

6:32 am: Is it true the DNC would not allow the FBI access to check server or other equipment after learning it was hacked? Can that be possible?

March 20, 2017

5:49 am: The Democrats made up and pushed the Russian story as an excuse for running a terrible campaign.Big advantage in Electoral College and lost!

March 26, 2017

7:21 am: Democrats are smiling in D.C. that the Freedom Caucus, with the help of Club For Growth and Heritage, have saved Planned Parenthood & Ocare!

April 18, 2017

5:38 am: Democrat Jon Ossoff would be a disaster in Congress. VERY weak on crime and illegal immigration, bad for jobs and wants higher taxes. Say NO

3:38 pm: Just learned that Jon @Ossoff, who is running for Congress in Georgia, doesn't even live in the district. Republicans, get out and vote!

April 19, 2017

7:43 am: Dems failed in Kansas and are now failing in Georgia. Great job Karen Handel! It is now Hollywood vs. Georgia on June 20th.

April 23, 2017

10:42 am: The Democrats don't want money from budget going to border wall despite the fact that it will stop drugs and very bad MS 13 gang members.

April 26, 2017

6:06 pm: Democrats are trying to bail out insurance companies from disastrous #ObamaCare, and Puerto Rico with your tax dollars. Sad!

April 27, 2017

6:30 am: The Democrats want to shut government if we don't bail out Puerto Rico and give billions to their insurance companies for OCare failure. NO!

9:37 am: I want to help our miners while the Democrats are blocking their healthcare.

9:38 am: Democrats jeopardizing the safety of our troops to bail out their donors from insurance companies. It is time to put #AmericaFirst

9:39 am: As families prepare for summer vacations in our National Parks—Democrats threaten to close them and shut down the government. Terrible!

April 20, 2017

7:09 am: The Democrats, without a leader, have become the party of obstruction.They are only interested in themselves and not in what's best for U.S.

May 9, 2017

9:42 pm: Cryin' Chuck Schumer stated recently, "I do not have confidence in him (James Comey) any longer." Then acts so indignant. #draintheswamp

May 10, 2017

7:24 am to 7:39 am[3]: Watching Senator Richard Blumenthal speak of Comey is a joke. "Richie" devised one of the greatest military frauds in U.S. history. For…

years, as a pol in Connecticut, Blumenthal would talk of his great bravery and conquests in Vietnam—except he was never there. When

caught, he cried like a baby and begged for forgiveness…and now he is judge & jury. He should be the one who is investigated for his acts.

2:32 pm: Dems have been complaining for months & months about Dir. Comey. Now that he has been fired they PRETEND to be aggrieved. Phony hypocrites!

May 31, 2017

5:37 am to 5:45 am: So now it is reported that the Democrats, who have excoriated Carter Page about Russia, don't want him to testify. He blows away their…

---

3   As of late 2017, Twitter allowed 280 characters per Tweet—double its previous 140-character limit. Sometimes, U.S. President Donald J. Trump writes consecutive Tweets on the same issue. The timing for multiple, consecutive Tweets will be reported in this manner (post time of the first Tweet in a series to post time for the last Tweet in a series) throughout this book.

…case against him & now wants to clear his name by showing "the false or misleading testimony by James Comey, John Brennan…" Witch Hunt!

June 11, 2017

7:49 am: The Democrats have no message, not on economics, not on taxes, not on jobs, not on failing #Obamacare. They are only OBSTRUCTIONISTS!

June 19, 2017

7:27 am: The Dems want to stop tax cuts, good healthcare and Border Security. Their ObamaCare is dead with 100% increases in P's. Vote now for Karen H

June 21, 2017

5:32 am: Democrats would do much better as a party if they got together with Republicans on Healthcare, Tax Cuts, Security. Obstruction doesn't work!

June 20, 2017

4:49 am: Democrat Jon Ossoff, who wants to raise your taxes to the highest level and is weak on crime and security, doesn't even live in district.

June 21, 2017

5:32 am: Democrats would do much better as a party if they got together with Republicans on Healthcare, Tax Cuts, Security. Obstruction doesn't work!

June 22, 2017

9:01 am: …Why did Democratic National Committee turn down the DHS offer to protect against hacks (long prior to election). It's all a big Dem HOAX!

9:08 am: …Why did the DNC REFUSE to turn over its Server to the FBI, and still hasn't? It's all a big Dem scam and excuse for losing the election!

9:15 am: I certainly hope the Democrats do not force Nancy P out. That would be very bad for the Republican Party—and please let Cryin' Chuck stay!

June 24, 2017

7:51 am: Democrats slam GOP healthcare proposal as Obamacare premiums & deductibles increase by over 100%. Remember keep your doctor, keep your plan?

June 26, 2017

7:30 am: The Democrats have become nothing but OBSTRUCTIONISTS, they have no policies or ideas. All they do is delay and complain. They own ObamaCare!

June 27, 2017

5:22 pm: With ZERO Democrats to help, and a failed, expensive and dangerous ObamaCare as the Dems legacy, the Republican Senators are working hard

June 28, 2017

4:26 pm: Democrats purposely misstated Medicaid under new Senate bill—actually goes up. https://t.co/necCt4K6UH

July 7, 2017

2:40 am: Everyone here is talking about why John Podesta refused to give the DNC server to the FBI and the CIA. Disgraceful!

July 24, 2017

5:52 am: After 1 year of investigation with Zero evidence being found, Chuck Schumer just stated that "Democrats should blame ourselves, not Russia.

8:12 am: Sleazy Adam Schiff, the totally biased Congressman looking into "Russia," spends all of his time on television pushing the Dem loss excuse!

August 3, 2017

7:18 am: Our relationship with Russia is at an all-time & very dangerous low. You can thank Congress, the same people that can't even give us HCare!

August 7, 2017

6:47 am: Interesting to watch Senator Richard Blumenthal of Connecticut talking about hoax Russian collusion when he was a phony Vietnam con artist!

6:52 am: to 7:01 am: Never in U.S.history has anyone lied or defrauded voters like Senator Richard Blumenthal. He told stories about his Vietnam battles and…

.conquests, how brave he was, and it was all a lie. He cried like a baby and begged for forgiveness like a child. Now he judges collusion?

3:48 pm: I think Senator Blumenthal should take a nice long vacation in Vietnam, where he lied about his service, so he can at least say he was there.

August 14, 2017

5:54 am: The Obstructionist Democrats have given us (or not fixed) some of the worst trade deals in World History. I am changing that fast!

August 18, 2017

7:55 am: The Obstructionist Democrats make Security for our country very difficult. They use the courts and associated delay at all times. Must stop!

September 23, 2017

5:20 pm: Democrats are laughingly saying that McCain had a "moment of courage." Tell that to the people of Arizona who were deceived. 116% increase!

September 30, 2017

6:19 am: The Mayor of San Juan, who was very complimentary only a few days ago, has now been told by the Democrats that you must be nasty to Trump.

October 5, 2017

8:58 pm: Ralph Northam,who is running for Governor of Virginia,is fighting for the violent MS-13 killer gangs & sanctuary cities. Vote Ed Gillespie!

October 7, 2017

7:00 am: Late Night host are dealing with the Democrats for their very "unfunny" & repetitive material, always anti-Trump! Should we get Equal Time?

October 11, 2017

5:36 am: The Democrats want MASSIVE tax increases & soft, crime producing borders.The Republicans want the biggest tax cut in history & the WALL!

October 13, 2017

4:36 am: The Democrats ObamaCare is imploding. Massive subsidy payments to their pet insurance companies has stopped. Dems should call me to fix!

6:51 am: Hard to believe that the Democrats, who have gone so far LEFT that they are no longer recognizable, are fighting so hard for Sanctuary crime

October 16, 2017

7:21 am: The Democrats only want to increase taxes and obstruct. That's all they are good at!

7:49 am: Dem Senator Schumer hated the Iran deal made by President Obama, but now that I am involved, he is OK with it. Tell that to Israel, Chuck!

October 18, 2017

5:38 am: The Democrats will only vote for Tax Increases. Hopefully, all Senate Republicans will vote for the largest Tax Cuts in U.S. history.

6:25 am: Democrat Congresswoman totally fabricated what I said to the wife of a soldier who died in action (and I have proof). Sad!

1:20 pm: It was an honor to welcome Republican and Democratic members of the Senate Finance Committee to the @WhiteHouse today. #TaxReform https://t.co/ge4Xic9fId

October 21, 2017

7:07 am: I hope the Fake News Media keeps talking about Wacky Congresswoman Wilson in that she, as a representative, is killing the Democrat Party!

October 27, 2017

5:58 am: Wacky & totally unhinged Tom Steyer, who has been fighting me and my Make America Great Again agenda from beginning, never wins elections!

October 28, 2017

7:28 am: Just read the nice remarks by President Jimmy Carter about me and how badly I am treated by the press (Fake News). Thank you Mr. President!

October 31, 2017

9:06 am to 9:10 am: The biggest story yesterday, the one that has the Dems in a dither, is Podesta running from his firm. What he know about Crooked Dems is...

...earth shattering. He and his brother could Drain The Swamp, which would be yet another campaign promise fulfilled. Fake News weak!

November 3, 2017

6:55 am: Pocahontas just stated that the Democrats, lead by the legendary Crooked Hillary Clinton, rigged the Primaries! Lets go FBI & Justice Dept.

November 6, 2017

4:12 pm: The state of Virginia economy, under Democrat rule, has been terrible. If you vote Ed Gillespie tomorrow, it will come roaring back!

November 7, 2017

5:53 am: Ralph Northam will allow crime to be rampant in Virginia. He's weak on crime, weak on our GREAT VETS, Anti-Second Amendment...

...and has been horrible on Virginia economy. Vote @EdWGillespie today!

November 16, 2017

10:06 pm to 10:15 pm: The Al Frankenstien picture is really bad, speaks a thousand words. Where do his hands go in pictures 2, 3, 4, 5 & 6 while she sleeps? ...

...And to think that just last week he was lecturing anyone who would listen about sexual harassment and respect for women. Lesley Stahl tape?

November 17, 2017

6:00 am: If Democrats were not such obstructionists and understood the power of lower taxes, we would be able to get many of their ideas into Bill!

November 26, 2017

4:29 pm: Since the first day I took office, all you hear is the phony Democrat excuse for losing the election, Russia, Russia, Russia. Despite this I have the economy booming and have possibly done more than any 10 month President. MAKE AMERICA GREAT AGAIN!

November 28, 2017

9:17 am: Meeting with "Chuck and Nancy" today about keeping government open and working. Problem is they want illegal immigrants flooding into our Country unchecked, are weak on Crime and want to substantially RAISE Taxes. I don't see a deal!

December 4, 2017

6:17 am: Democrats refusal to give even one vote for massive Tax Cuts is why we need Republican Roy Moore to win in Alabama. We need his vote on stopping crime, illegal immigration, Border Wall, Military, Pro Life, V.A., Judges 2nd Amendment and more. No to Jones, a Pelosi/Schumer Puppet!

December 12, 2017

8:03 am: Lightweight Senator Kirsten Gillibrand, a total flunky for Chuck Schumer and someone who would come to my office "begging" for campaign contributions not so long ago (and would do anything for them), is now in the ring fighting against Trump. Very disloyal to Bill & Crooked-USED!

9:09 am: The people of Alabama will do the right thing. Doug Jones is Pro-Abortion, weak on Crime, Military and Illegal Immigration, Bad for Gun Owners and Veterans and against the WALL. Jones is a Pelosi/Schumer Puppet. Roy Moore will always vote with us. VOTE ROY MOORE!

11:08 pm: Congratulations to Doug Jones on a hard fought victory. The write-in votes played a very big factor, but a win is a win. The people of Alabama are great, and the Republicans will have another shot at this seat in a very short period of time. It never ends!

December 21, 2017

9:52 am: House Democrats want a SHUTDOWN for the holidays in order to distract from the very popular, just passed, Tax Cuts. House Republicans, don't let this happen. Pass the C.R. TODAY and keep our Government OPEN!

December 22, 2017

8:05 am: At some point, and for the good of the country, I predict we will start working with the Democrats in a Bipartisan fashion. Infrastructure would be a perfect place to start. After having foolishly spent $7 trillion in the Middle East, it is time to start rebuilding our country!

December 29, 2017

8:16 am: The Democrats have been told, and fully understand, that there can be no DACA without the desperately needed WALL at the Southern Border and an END to the horrible Chain Migration & ridiculous Lottery System of Immigration etc. We must protect our Country at all cost!

December 31, 2017

8:36 am: Why would smart voters want to put Democrats in Congress in 2018 Election when their policies will totally kill the great wealth created during the months since the Election. People are much better off now not to mention ISIS, VA, Judges, Strong Border, 2nd A, Tax Cuts & more?

Democrats—2018 News Quotes

Response to a question from an unidentified reporter before a dinner with then-House Majority Leader Kevin McCarthy at the Trump International Golf Club in Palm Beach, Florida, January 14, 2018.

Source: https://www.whitehouse.gov/briefings-statements/
remarks-president-trump-dinner-house-majority-leader-kevin-mccarthy-palm-beach-fl/

"I think you have a lot of sticking points, but they're all Democrat sticking points, because we are ready, willing, and able to make a deal, but they don't want to. They don't want security at the border. We have people pouring in. They don't want security at the border, and they don't want to stop drugs. And they want to take money away from our military, which we cannot do. So those are some of the sticking points."

Response to a question from an unidentified reporter before a dinner with then-House Majority Leader Kevin McCarthy at the Trump International Golf Club in Palm Beach, Florida, January 14, 2018.

Source: https://www.whitehouse.gov/briefings-statements/
remarks-president-trump-dinner-house-majority-leader-kevin-mccarthy-palm-beach-fl/

"Well, we're ready, willing, and able to make a deal on DACA, but I don't think the Democrats want to make a deal. And the folks from DACA should know the Democrats are the ones that aren't going to make a deal."

Remarks before meetings at the Pentagon, January 18, 2018.
Source: https://www.whitehouse.gov/briefings-statements/
remarks-president-trump-meetings-pentagon/

"Thank you, everybody. We're just here to support the General and all of the generals. We're here to support our country's military.

"If the country shuts down, which could very well be, the budget should be handled a lot differently than it's been handled over the last long period of time, many years.

"But if for any reason it shuts down, the worst thing is what happens to our military. We're rebuilding our military, we're making us—We're bringing it to a level that it's never been at. And the worst thing is for our military; we don't want that to happen. I'm here to support our military.

"Our military has to be the best in the world, by far. And as you know, it's been depleted over the last long period of time. And when we finish, there won't be anything like it. We need that now almost more than at any time in the past.

"So, I'm here for our military; I'm here to support our great, great, and very powerful military. And we're going to keep it that way, but we're going to make it much better and that's what we're doing.

"It also means jobs. You see what's happening with respect to jobs. You see what happened yesterday—Apple, and now it was just announced that they're giving each employee a lot of money.

"So, our tax cuts and our tax reform has turned out to be far greater than anybody ever anticipated, and I'm sure the Democrats would like to blunt that by shutting down government.

"But again, the group that loses big would be the military. And we're never letting our military lose at any point. We're going to fund our military. We're going to have a military like we've never had before because we just about, just about never needed our military more than now."

17

Response to a question from Margaret Brennan of CBS News, February 1, 2018.

Source: https://www.cbsnews.com/news/
donald-trump-interview-face-the-nation-margaret-brennan-today-2019-02-01/

"Well, I think that she [Speaker of the House Nancy Pelosi] was very rigid, which I would expect, but I think she's very bad for our country.

"She knows that you need a barrier. She knows that we need border security. She wanted to win a political point. I happen to think it's very bad politics because basically, she wants open borders. She doesn't mind human trafficking, or she wouldn't do this."

After then-Florida gubernatorial candidate Ron DeSantis[4] introduced Trump at a rally in Tampa, Florida, July 31, 2018.

Source: https://www.tampabay.com/florida-politics/buzz/2018/08/01/
heres-a-full-transcript-of-president-trumps-speech-from-his-tampa-rally/

"Earlier today I also spent time with your current governor, one of our nation's truly great leaders, Rick Scott. As you know, Rick is running to replace liberal Democrat, Schumer-controlled, Nancy Pelosi-controlled—[Audience boos.]

"And the new star of the Democrat Party, Maxine Waters.

"Name is Bill Nelson[5], and you know I live a lot of time in Florida. The only time I see Bill Nelson is five months before every election.

"And after a while you forget, who's the senator? But around five months you see him at parties and you see him around and we have to be careful, because we have to make sure that Rick Scott wins and wins big.

"Bill Nelson voted for Obamacare, which has been a totally disastrous situation.

---

4   DeSantis went on to become the governor of Florida.

5   At the time of the rally, Democrat Bill Nelson was a U.S. senator. He was defeated by Republican Rick Scott in the 2018 election. At the time of the rally, Scott was the governor of Florida.

"And we got rid of the individual mandate, the most unpopular aspect and most of Obamacare will be gone very soon. In fact, it was gone until one gentleman decided at 2:00 in the morning—[Audience boos.]

"Remember? Thank you very much, we appreciate it. And he voted against tax cuts, and he wants to go in there and raise your taxes. Tell me, is that good politics? I don't think so. Bill Nelson voted in favor of sanctuary cities.

"He opposed Kate's Law. Bill Nelson puts criminal aliens before American citizens, which is why it's time to vote Bill Nelson out of office. That's what's going to happen.

"And we have two unbelievable people, Ron DeSantis, Rick Scott, fighting for Florida. They always will. And fighting to make America great again. That's what they're doing.

"That's what they're doing."

Remarks at a rally in Tampa, Florida, July 31, 2018.
Source: https://www.tampabay.com/florida-politics/buzz/2018/08/01/
heres-a-full-transcript-of-president-trumps-speech-from-his-tampa-rally/

"Democrats want to raise your taxes. They want to destroy your jobs.

"They want to crush our industries with crippling regulations, and you know the stock market is up almost 40% since that great November day. Your 401Ks are doing very well. 401Ks."

Remarks at a rally in Tampa, Florida, July 31, 2018.
Source: https://www.tampabay.com/florida-politics/buzz/2018/08/01/
heres-a-full-transcript-of-president-trumps-speech-from-his-tampa-rally/

"Republicans want strong borders and no crime; Democrats want open borders, which equals massive crime. And on top of that, the Democrats—Nancy Pelosi, the whole group, Maxine [Waters]. Maxine. She likes me a lot. She likes me a lot.

"They've launched outrageous attacks on our incredible law enforcement officers, and on ICE and our Border Patrol, can you believe it?

"People that keep us safe. Their new platform, what they want to do—The Democrat Party, they want to abolish ICE. So in other words, they want to let MS-13 rule our country. That's not going to happen.

"Every day, the brave men and women of ICE are liberating communities and towns from savage gangs like MS-13 that are occupying our country like another nation would.

"We want maximum border security and respect for our heroes, ICE, Border Patrol, and law enforcement."

Remarks at a rally in Tampa, Florida, July 31, 2018.
Source: https://www.tampabay.com/florida-politics/buzz/2018/08/01/
heres-a-full-transcript-of-president-trumps-speech-from-his-tampa-rally/

"In some states, Democrats are even trying to give illegal immigrants the right to vote. They want to give them the right to vote.

"Yeah, what about all of those people that are waiting in line for 7, 8, 9, 10 years trying to get into our country? They don't have the right to vote. We believe that only American citizens should vote in American elections, which is why the time has come for voter ID like everything else, voter ID.

"You know, if you go out and you want to buy groceries, you need a picture on a card; you need ID. You go out and you want to buy anything, you need ID and you need your picture. In this country, the only time you don't need it in many cases is when you want to vote for a president, when you want to vote for a senator, when you want to vote for a governor or a congressman. It's crazy. It's crazy."

Remarks at a rally in Tampa, Florida, July 31, 2018.
Source: https://www.tampabay.com/florida-politics/buzz/2018/08/01/
heres-a-full-transcript-of-president-trumps-speech-from-his-tampa-rally/

"Look at Judge [Brett] Kavanaugh. This is a great, great, highly respected man. And the good news is the Republicans, I believe, are close to 100%, which is what we need. But so far, the Democrats haven't given us any votes, and that's because they will do anything they can to not help the Trump agenda, even though they know it's wrong.

"And Brett Kavanaugh, highest education, best grades, best tests, best everything. They thought 15 years ago he was going to be a Supreme Court judge. Look at Justice [Neil] Gorsuch, how good is he? How good is he? So we're getting them through. But it's not easy, because they really are. You know, their term that they use is 'resist.' It's actually resist and obstruct. Whatever they can do to resist and obstruct. And frankly, they're lousy politicians. They have horrible policy. The one thing they're good at, they stick together and they obstruct. And it's unfortunate.

"You know, we have almost 400 people trying to get into government, many of whom have left their jobs and the Democrats are holding them up with maximum delay. They're holding them up, not allowing these great people to serve their country. It's a disgrace. That's [Senate Minority Leader] Chuck Schumer, and it's a disgrace. It's a disgrace. But we'll get that Supreme Court judge, and that's the big one. That's the big one."

Response to an unidentified reporter's question after Trump's remarks at the Signing Ceremony for H.R. 390, Iraq and Syria Genocide Relief and Accountability Act of 2018, December 11, 2018.

Source: https://www.whitehouse.gov/briefings-statements/remarks-president-trump-signing-ceremony-h-r-390-iraq-syria-genocide-relief-accountability-act-2018/

"We've made tremendous strides on the farm bill, and we're working on your border security. You know, Republicans want very strong border security. And honestly, the Democrats, or most of them—It's hard to believe, but most of them want open borders, and that leads to crime and leads to other problems.

"And, you know, one of the problems that people don't talk about. You have a tremendous medical problem coming into a country—Communicable disease, tremendous problems. People don't want to talk about it. I don't like talking about it. But these are the difficulties of what they want to do.

"So, we want strong borders. We want people coming into our country legally, through a process. We want people that are going to love and help our country. And I don't think they feel the same way, or maybe they just don't want us to get a vote. You know, it could be that too. Because it's hard to believe that they don't want some form of protection."

Democrats—2018 Tweets

January 2, 2018

10:16 am: Democrats are doing nothing for DACA—just interested in politics. DACA activists and Hispanics will go hard against Dems, will start "falling in love" with Republicans and their President! We are about RESULTS.

January 4, 2018

6:02 am: Many mostly Democrat States refused to hand over data from the 2016 Election to the Commission On Voter Fraud. They fought hard that the Commission not see their records or methods because they know that many people are voting illegally. System is rigged, must go to Voter I.D.

January 11, 2018

6:33 am: Disproven and paid for by Democrats "Dossier used to spy on Trump Campaign. Did FBI use Intel tool to influence the Election?" @foxandfriends Did Dems or Clinton also pay Russians? Where are hidden and smashed DNC servers? Where are Crooked Hillary Emails? What a mess!

10:01 pm: Democrat Dianne Feinstein should never have released secret committee testimony to the public without authorization. Very disrespectful to committee members and possibly illegal. She blamed her poor decision on the fact she had a cold—a first!

January 12, 2018

7:20 am: ...Because of the Democrats not being interested in life and safety, DACA has now taken a big step backwards. The Dems will threaten "shutdown," but what they are really doing is shutting down our military, at a time we need it most. Get smart, MAKE AMERICA GREAT AGAIN!

8:50 am: Sadly, Democrats want to stop paying our troops and government workers in order to give a sweetheart deal, not a fair deal, for DACA. Take care of our Military, and our Country, FIRST!

8:48 am: Never said anything derogatory about Haitians other than Haiti is, obviously, a very poor and troubled country. Never said "take them out." Made up by Dems. I have a wonderful relationship with Haitians. Probably should record future meetings—unfortunately, no trust!

January 13, 2018

8:14 am: The Democrats are all talk and no action. They are doing nothing to fix DACA. Great opportunity missed. Too bad!

9:20 am: I don't believe the Democrats really want to see a deal on DACA. They are all talk and no action. This is the time but, day by day, they are blowing the one great opportunity they have. Too bad!

January 14, 2018

8:09 am: DACA is probably dead because the Democrats don't really want it, they just want to talk and take desperately needed money away from our Military.

January 15, 2018

7:57 am to 8:02 am: Statement by me last night in Florida: "Honestly, I don't think Democrats want to make a deal. They talk about DACA, but they don't want to help...We are ready willing and able to make a deal but they don't want to. They don't want security at the border, they don't want …

…to stop drugs, they want to take money away from our military which we cannot do." My standard is very simple, AMERICA FIRST & MAKE AMERICA GREAT AGAIN!

January 16, 2018

9:07 am: The Democrats want to shut down the Government over Amnesty for all and Border Security. The biggest loser will be our rapidly rebuilding Military, at a time we need it more than ever. We need a merit based system of immigration, and we need it now! No more dangerous Lottery.

January 18, 2018

8:49 am: A government shutdown will be devastating to our military... something the Dems care very little about!

January 19, 2018

7:04 am: Government Funding Bill past last night in the House of Representatives. Now Democrats are needed if it is to pass in the Senate—but they want illegal immigration and weak borders. Shutdown coming? We need more Republican victories in 2018!

9:28 pm: Not looking good for our great Military or Safety & Security on the very dangerous Southern Border. Dems want a Shutdown in order to help diminish the great success of the Tax Cuts, and what they are doing for our booming economy.

January 20, 2018

9:27 am: Democrats are holding our Military hostage over their desire to have unchecked illegal immigration. Can't let that happen!

January 22, 2018

8:07 am: The Democrats are turning down services and security for citizens in favor of services and security for non-citizens. Not good!

8:15 am: Democrats have shut down our government in the interests of their far left base. They don't want to do it but are powerless!

10:13 am: End the Democrats Obstruction!

11:30 pm: Big win for Republicans as Democrats cave on Shutdown. Now I want a big win for everyone, including Republicans, Democrats and DACA, but especially for our Great Military and Border Security. Should be able to get there. See you at the negotiating table!

January 26, 2018

12:16 pm: DACA has been made increasingly difficult by the fact that Cryin' Chuck Schumer took such a beating over the shutdown that he is unable to act on immigration!

February 1, 2018

10:32 am: The Democrats just aren't calling about DACA. Nancy Pelosi and Chuck Schumer have to get moving fast, or they'll disappoint you again. We have a great chance to make a deal or, blame the Dems! March 5th is coming up fast.

February 5, 2018

7:11 am: The Democrats are pushing for Universal HealthCare while thousands of people are marching in the UK because their U system is going broke and not working. Dems want to greatly raise taxes for really bad and non-personal medical care. No thanks!

7:39 am: Little Adam Schiff, who is desperate to run for higher office, is one of the biggest liars and leakers in Washington, right up there with Comey, Warner, Brennan and Clapper! Adam leaves closed committee hearings to illegally leak confidential information. Must be stopped!

9:36 am: Any deal on DACA that does not include STRONG border security and the desperately needed WALL is a total waste of time. March 5th is rapidly approaching and the Dems seem not to care about DACA. Make a deal!

February 8, 2018

10:22 pm: Wow!—Senator Mark Warner got caught having extensive contact with a lobbyist for a Russian oligarch. Warner did not want a "paper trail" on a "private" meeting (in London) he requested with Steele of fraudulent Dossier fame. All tied into Crooked Hillary.

February 10, 2018

9:20 am: The Democrats sent a very political and long response memo which they knew, because of sources and methods (and more), would have to be heavily redacted, whereupon they would blame the White House for lack of transparency. Told them to re-do and send back in proper form!

February 24, 2018

3:16 pm: Democrat judges have totally redrawn election lines in the great State of Pennsylvania. @FoxNews. This is very unfair to Republicans and to our country as a whole. Must be appealed to the United States Supreme Court ASAP!

4:18 pm: Dems are no longer talking DACA! "Out of sight, out of mind," they say. DACA beneficiaries should not be happy. Nancy Pelosi truly doesn't care about them. Republicans stand ready to make a deal!

6:16 pm: The Democrat memo response on government surveillance abuses is a total political and legal BUST. Just confirms all of the terrible things that were done. SO ILLEGAL!

6:30 pm: Dem Memo: FBI did not disclose who the clients were—the Clinton Campaign and the DNC. Wow!

March 6, 2018

8:00 am: Total inaction on DACA by Dems. Where are you? A deal can be made!

March 11, 2018

9:49 am: The Democrats continue to Obstruct the confirmation of hundreds of good and talented people who are needed to run our government…A record in U.S. history. State Department, Ambassadors and many others are being slow walked. Senate must approve NOW!

March 14, 2018

8:02 am: Hundreds of good people, including very important Ambassadors and Judges, are being blocked and/or slow walked by the Democrats in the Senate. Many important positions in Government are unfilled because of this obstruction. Worst in U.S. history!

March 21, 2018

10:04 pm: Democrats refused to take care of DACA. Would have been so easy, but they just didn't care. I had to fight for Military and start of Wall.

March 22, 2018

5:19 am: Crazy Joe Biden is trying to act like a tough guy. Actually, he is weak, both mentally and physically, and yet he threatens me, for the second time, with physical assault. He doesn't know me, but he would go down fast and hard, crying all the way. Don't threaten people Jo

April 9, 2018

2:17 pm: The Democrats are not doing what's right for our country. I will not rest until we have secured our borders and restored the rule of law!

April 20, 2018

5:34 pm: Just heard the Campaign was sued by the Obstructionist Democrats. This can be good news in that we will now counter for the DNC Server that they refused to give to the FBI, the Wendy Wasserman Schultz Servers and Documents held by the Pakistani mystery man and Clinton Emails.

April 21, 2018

1:52 pm: So funny, the Democrats have sued the Republicans for Winning. Now he R's counter and force them to turn over a treasure trove of material, including Servers and Emails!

April 28, 2018

2:11 pm: Secret Service has just informed me that Senator Jon Tester's statements on Admiral Jackson are not true. There were no such findings. A horrible thing that we in D.C. must live with, just like phony Russian Collusion. Tester should lose race in Montana. Very dishonest and sick!

May 4, 2018

4:58 pm: Democrats and liberals in Congress want to disarm law-abiding Americans at the same time they are releasing dangerous criminal aliens and savage gang members onto our streets. Politicians who put criminal aliens before American Citizens should be voted out of office!

May 20, 2018

8:37 am: What ever happened to the Server, at the center of so much Corruption, that the Democratic National Committee REFUSED to hand over to the hard charging (except in the case of Democrats) FBI? They broke into homes & offices early in the morning, but were afraid to take the Server?

9:04 am: and why hasn't the Podesta brother been charged and arrested, like others, after being forced to close down his very large and successful firm? Is it because he is a VERY well connected Democrat working in the Swamp of Washington, D.C.?

May 25, 2018

7:04 am: Democrats are so obviously rooting against us in our negotiations with North Korea. Just like they are coming to the defense of MS 13 thugs, saying that they are individuals & must be nurtured, or asking to end your big Tax Cuts & raise your taxes instead. Dems have lost touch!

6:07 pm to 6:13 pm: Senator Schumer and Obama Administration let phone company ZTE flourish with no security checks. I closed it down then let it reopen with high level security guarantees, change of management and board, must purchase U.S. parts and pay a $1.3 Billion fine. Dems do nothing...

...but complain and obstruct. They made only bad deals (Iran) and their so-called Trade Deals are the laughing stock of the world!

May 26, 2018

2:41 pm: This whole Russia Probe is Rigged. Just an excuse as to why the Dems and Crooked Hillary lost the Election and States that haven't been lost in decades. 13 Angry Democrats, and all Dems if you include the people who worked for Obama for 8 years. #SPYGATE & CONFLICTS OF INTEREST!

May 28, 2018

4:22 pm: A Democratic lawmaker just introduced a bill to Repeal the GOP Tax Cuts (no chance). This is too good to be true for Republicans... Remember, the Nancy Pelosi Dems are also weak on Crime, the Border and want to be gentle and kind to MS-13 gang members...not good!

May 29, 2018

5:07 am: Democrats mistakenly tweet 2014 pictures from Obama's term showing children from the Border in steel cages. They thought it was recent pictures in order to make us look bad, but backfires. Dems must agree to Wall and new Border Protection for good of country... Bipartisan Bill!

June 5, 2018

3:07 pm: Imagine how much wasteful spending we'd save if we didn't have Chuck and Nancy standing in our way! For years, Democrats in

Congress have depleted our military and busted our budgets on need-less spending, and to what end? No more.

June 7, 2018

8:07 am: When and where will all of the many conflicts of interest be listed by the 13 Angry Democrats (plus) working on the Witch Hunt Hoax. There has never been a group of people on a case so biased or conflicted. It is all a Democrat Excuse for LOSING the Election. Where is the server?

June 12, 2018

3:12 pm: Mark Sanford has been very unhelpful to me in my campaign to MAGA. He is MIA and nothing but trouble. He is better off in Argentina. I fully endorse Katie Arrington for Congress in SC, a state I love. She is tough on crime and will continue our fight to lower taxes. VOTE K

June 13, 2018

3:11 pm: Senator Claire McCaskill of the GREAT State of Missouri flew around in a luxurious private jet during her RV tour of the state. RV's are not for her. People are really upset, so phony! Josh Hawley should win big, and has my full endorsement.

June 14, 2018

10:09 am: The sleazy New York Democrats, and their now disgraced (and run out of town) A.G. Eric Schneiderman, are doing everything they can to sue me on a foundation that took in $18,800,000 and gave out to charity more money than it took in, $19,200,000. I won't settle this case!…

…Schneiderman, who ran the Clinton campaign in New York, never had the guts to bring this ridiculous case, which lingered in their office for almost 2 years. Now he resigned his office in disgrace, and his disciples brought it when we would not settle.

June 16, 2018

8:03 am: Democrats can fix their forced family breakup at the Border by working with Republicans on new legislation, for a change! This is why we need more Republicans elected in November. Democrats are good at only three things, High Taxes, High Crime and Obstruction. Sad!

June 17, 2018

6:52 am: Chuck Schumer said "the Summit was what the Texans call all cattle and no hat." Thank you Chuck, but are you sure you got that right? No more nuclear testing or rockets flying all over the place, blew up launch sites. Hostages already back, hero remains coming home & much more!

June 18, 2018

7:46 am: Why don't the Democrats give us the votes to fix the world's worst immigration laws? Where is the outcry for the killings and crime being caused by gangs and thugs, including MS-13, coming into our country illegally?

June 21, 2018

9:38 am: Democrats want open Borders, where anyone can come into our Country, and stay. This is Nancy Pelosi's dream. It won't happen!

June 23, 2018

12:05 pm: It's very sad that Nancy Pelosi and her sidekick, Cryin' Chuck Schumer, want to protect illegal immigrants far more than the citizens of our country. The United States cannot stand for this. We wants safety and security at our borders!

June 24, 2018

8:12 am: Democrats, fix the laws. Don't RESIST. We are doing a far better job than Bush and Obama, but we need strength and security at the Border! Cannot accept all of the people trying to break into our Country. Strong Borders, No Crime!

June 25, 2018

12:11 pm: Congresswoman Maxine Waters, an extraordinarily low IQ person, has become, together with Nancy Pelosi, the Face of the Democrat Party. She has just called for harm to supporters, of which there are many, of the Make America Great Again movement. Be careful what you wish for Max!

6:22 pm: Why is Senator Mark Warner (D-VA), perhaps in a near drunken state, claiming he has information that only he and Bob Mueller, the leader of the 13 Angry Democrats on a Witch Hunt, knows? Isn't this highly illegal. Is it being investigated?

June 26, 2018

7:36 am: The face of the Democrats is now Maxine Waters who, together with Nancy Pelosi, have established a fine leadership team. They should always stay together and lead the Democrats, who want Open Borders and Unlimited Crime, well into the future...and pick Crooked Hillary for Pres.

June 27, 2018

6:18 am: Congratulations to Maxine Waters, whose crazy rants have made her, together with Nancy Pelosi, the unhinged FACE of the Democrat Party. Together, they will Make America Weak Again! But have no fear, America is now stronger than ever before, and I'm not going anywhere!

10:24 pm: In recent days we have heard shameless attacks on our courageous law enforcement officers. Extremist Democrat politicians have called for the complete elimination of ICE. Leftwing Activists are trying to block ICE officers from doing their jobs and publicly posting their...

...home addresses—putting these selfless public servants in harm's way. These radical protesters want ANARCHY—but the only response they will find from our government is LAW AND ORDER!

July 1, 2018

7:11 am: The Liberal Left, also known as the Democrats, want to get rid of ICE, who do a fantastic job, and want Open Borders. Crime would be rampant and uncontrollable! Make America Great Again

July 3, 2018

5:16 am: Crazy Maxine Waters, said by some to be one of the most corrupt people in politics, is rapidly becoming, together with Nancy Pelosi, the FACE of the Democrat Party. Her ranting and raving, even referring to herself as a wounded animal, will make people flee the Democrats!

July 5, 2018

7:44 am: A vote for Democrats in November is a vote to let MS-13 run wild in our communities, to let drugs pour into our cities, and to take jobs and benefits away from hardworking Americans. Democrats want anarchy, amnesty and chaos—Republicans want LAW, ORDER and JUSTICE!

July 6, 2018

11:57 am: Just won lawsuit filed by the DNC and a bunch of Democrat crazies trying to claim the Trump Campaign (and others), colluded with Russia. They haven't figured out that this was an excuse for them losing the election!

July 18, 2018

4:30 pm: The two biggest opponents of ICE in America today are the Democratic Party and MS-13!

August 6, 2018

12:43 pm: Governor Jerry Brown must allow the Free Flow of the vast amounts of water coming from the North and foolishly being diverted into the Pacific Ocean. Can be used for fires, farming and everything else. Think of California with plenty of Water—Nice! Fast Federal govt. approvals.

August 10, 2018

4:30 pm: Democrats, please do not distance yourselves from Nancy Pelosi. She is a wonderful person whose ideas & policies may be bad, but who should definitely be given a 4th chance. She is trying very hard & has every right to take down the Democrat Party if she has veered too far left!

August 15, 2018

9:57 am: Happy Birthday to the leader of the Democrat Party, Maxine Waters!

8:53 pm: "WE'RE NOT GONG TO MAKE AMERICA GREAT AGAIN, IT WAS NEVER THAT GREAT." Can you believe this is the Governor of the Highest Taxed State in the U.S., Andrew Cuomo, having a total meltdown!

August 16, 2018

7:56 pm: How can "Senator" Richard Blumenthal, who went around for twenty years as a Connecticut politician bragging that he was a great Marine war hero in Vietnam (then got caught and sobbingly admitted he was neither a Marine nor ever in Vietnam), pass judgement on anyone? Loser!

August 17, 2018

6:44 am: How does a politician, Cuomo, known for pushing people and businesses out of his state, not to mention having the highest taxes in the U.S., survive making the statement, WE'RE NOT GOING

TO MAKE AMERICA GREAT AGAIN, IT WAS NEVER THAT GREAT? Which section of the sentence is worse?

9:10 am: Wow! Big pushback on Governor Andrew Cuomo of New York for his really dumb statement about America's lack of greatness. I have already MADE America Great Again, just look at the markets, jobs, military-setting records, and we will do even better. Andrew "choked" badly, mistake!

9:17 am: When a politician admits that "We're not going to make America great again," there doesn't seem to be much reason to ever vote for him. This could be a career threatening statement by Andrew Cuomo, with many wanting him to resign-he will get higher ratings than his brother Chris!

2:25 pm: Which is worse, Hightax Andrew Cuomo's statement, "WE'RE NOT GOING TO MAKE AMERICA GREAT AGAIN, IT WAS NEVER THAT GREAT" or Hillary Clinton's "DEPLORABLES" statement…

August 21, 2018

5:38 am: A Blue Wave means Crime and Open Borders. A Red Wave means Safety and Strength!

9:15 am: Bill DeBlasio, the high taxing Mayor of NYC, just stole my campaign slogan: PROMISES MADE PROMISES KEPT! That's not at all nice. No imagination! @foxandfriends

September 3, 2018

1:39 pm: …The Democrats, none of whom voted for Jeff Sessions, must love him now. Same thing with Lyin' James Comey. The Dems all hated him, wanted him out, thought he was disgusting—UNTIL I FIRED HIM! Immediately he became a wonderful man, a saint like figure in fact. Really sick!

1:55 pm: I see that John Kerry, the father of the now terminated Iran deal, is thinking of running for President. I should only be so lucky—although the field that is currently assembling looks really good—FOR ME!

September 8, 2018

8:47 pm: The Dems have tried every trick in the playbook-call me everything under the sun. But if I'm all of those terrible things, how come I beat them so badly, 306-223? Maybe they're just not very good! The fact is they are going CRAZY only because they know they can't beat me in 2020!

September 10, 2018

6:10 am: If the Democrats had won the Election in 2016, GDP, which was about 1% and going down, would have been minus 4% instead of up 4.2%. I opened up our beautiful economic engine with Regulation and Tax Cuts. Our system was choking and would have been made worse. Still plenty to do!

4:18 pm: Chuck Schumer is holding up 320 appointments (Ambassadors, Executives, etc.) of great people who have left jobs and given up so much in order to come into Government. Schumer and the Democrats continue to OBSTRUCT

September 11, 2018

8:55 pm: Crazy Maxine Waters: "After we impeach Trump, we'll go after Mike Pence. We'll get him." @FoxNews Where are the Democrats coming from? The best Economy in the history of our country would totally collapse if they ever took control!

September 13, 2018

7:49 am: …This was done by the Democrats in order to make me look as bad as possible when I was successfully raising Billions of Dollars to help rebuild Puerto Rico. If a person died for any reason, like old age, just add them onto the list. Bad politics. I love Puerto Rico!

September 16, 2018

5:18 pm: Best economic numbers in decades. If the Democrats take control, kiss your newfound wealth goodbye!

September 21, 2018

10:25 am: Senator Feinstein and the Democrats held the letter for months, only to release it with a bang after the hearings were OVER—done very purposefully to Obstruct & Resist & Delay. Let her testify, or not, and TAKE THE VOTE!

September 24, 2018

9:37 pm: The Democrats are working hard to destroy a wonderful man, and a man who has the potential to be one of our greatest Supreme Court Justices ever, with an array of False Acquisitions the likes of which have never been seen before!

September 29, 2018

3:33 pm: Senator Richard Blumenthal must talk about his fraudulent service in Vietnam, where for 12 years he told the people of Connecticut, as their Attorney General, that he was a great Marine War Hero. Talked about his many battles of near death, but was never in Vietnam. Total Phony!

October 15, 2018

6:46 am: "The only way to shut down the Democrats new Mob Rule strategy is to stop them cold at the Ballot Box. The fight for America's future is never over!" Ben Shapiro

October 16, 2018

7:06 am: Pocahontas (the bad version), sometimes referred to as Elizabeth Warren, is getting slammed. She took a bogus DNA test and it showed that she may be 1/1024, far less than the average American.

Now Cherokee Nation denies her, "DNA test is useless." Even they don't want her. Phony!

7:16 am: Now that her claims of being of Indian heritage have turned out to be a scam and a lie, Elizabeth Warren should apologize for perpetrating this fraud against the American Public. Harvard called her "a person of color" (amazing con), and would not have taken her otherwise!

9:36 pm: Elizabeth Warren is being hammered, even by the Left. Her false claim of Indian heritage is only selling to VERY LOW I.Q. individuals!

October 17, 2018

6:52 am: Watched the debate last night & Beto O'Rourke, who wants higher taxes and far more regulations, is not in the same league with Ted Cruz & what the great people of Texas stand for & want. Ted is strong on Crime, Border & 2nd A, loves our Military, Vets, Low Taxes. Beto is a Flake!

9:03 pm: Ever since his vicious and totally false statements about Admiral Ron Jackson, the highly respected White House Doctor for Obama, Bush & me, Senator John Tester looks to be in big trouble in the Great State of Montana! He behaved worse than the Democrat Mob did with Justice K!

October 18, 2018

7:11 pm: The only thing keeping Tester alive is he has millions and millions of dollars from outside liberals and leftists, who couldn't care less about our Country!

October 19, 2018

12:43 pm: Beto O'Rourke is a total lightweight compared to Ted Cruz, and he comes nowhere near representing the values and desires of the people of the Great State of Texas. He will never be allowed to turn Texas into Venezuela!

October 31, 2018

9:17 am: …Harry Reid was right in 1993, before he and the Democrats went insane and started with the Open Borders (which brings massive Crime) "stuff." Don't forget the nasty term Anchor Babies. I will keep our Country safe. This case will be settled by the United States Supreme Court!

November 3, 2018

5:45 am: Congresswoman Maxine Waters was called the most Corrupt Member of Congress! @FoxNews If Dems win, she would be put in charge of our Country's finances. The beginning of the end!

3:38 pm: If Chuck Schumer and Nancy Pelosi gain the majority, they will try to raise your taxes, restore job-killing regulations, shut down your coal mines and timber mills, take away your healthcare, impose socialism, and ERASE your borders. VOTE for @MattForMontana and @GregForMontana!

4:05 pm: Rumor has it that Senator Joe Donnelly of Indiana is paying for Facebook ads for his so-called opponent on the libertarian ticket. Donnelly is trying to steal the election? Isn't that what Russia did!

November 7, 2018

8:04 am: If the Democrats think they are going to waste Taxpayer Money investigating us at the House level, then we will likewise be forced to consider investigating them for all of the leaks of Classified Information, and much else, at the Senate level. Two can play that game!

8:31 am: In all fairness, Nancy Pelosi deserves to be chosen Speaker of the House by the Democrats. If they give her a hard time, perhaps we will add some Republican votes. She has earned this great honor!

November 9, 2018

11:52 am: As soon as Democrats sent their best Election stealing lawyer, Marc Elias, to Broward County they miraculously started finding Democrat votes. Don't worry, Florida—I am sending much better lawyers to expose the FRAUD!

1:14 pm: Mayor Gillum conceded on Election Day and now Broward County has put him "back into play." Bill Nelson conceded Election—now he's back in play!? This is an embarrassment to our Country and to Democracy!

November 10, 2018

2:09 pm: Trying to STEAL two big elections in Florida! We are watching closely!

November 13, 2018

11:32 am: When will Bill Nelson concede in Florida? The characters running Broward and Palm Beach voting will not be able to "find" enough votes, too much spotlight on them now!

November 15, 2018

9:59 am: The only "Collusion" is that of the Democrats with Russia and many others. Why didn't the FBI take the Server from the DNC? They still don't have it. Check out how biased Facebook, Google and Twitter are in favor of the Democrats. That's the real Collusion!

November 18, 2018

1:01 pm: So funny to see little Adam Schitt (D-CA) talking about the fact that Acting Attorney General Matt Whitaker was not approved by the Senate, but not mentioning the fact that Bob Mueller (who is highly conflicted) was not approved by the Senate!

November 23, 2018

7:57 am: Really good Criminal Justice Reform has a true shot at major bipartisan support. @senatemajldr Mitch McConnell and @senchuckschumer have a real chance to do something so badly needed in our country. Already past, with big vote, in House. Would be a major victory for ALL!

December 10, 2018

6:46 am: "Democrats can't find a Smocking Gun tying the Trump campaign to Russia after James Comey's testimony. No Smocking Gun... No Collusion." @FoxNews That's because there was NO COLLUSION. So now the Dems go to a simple private transaction, wrongly call it a campaign contribution,...

December 12, 2018

7:50 am: The Democrats and President Obama gave Iran 150 Billion Dollars and got nothing, but they can't give 5 Billion Dollars for National Security and a Wall?

December 17, 2018

8:08 am: Anytime you hear a Democrat saying that you can have good Boarder Security without a Wall, write them off as just another politician following the party line. Time for us to save billions of dollars a year and have, at the same time, far greater safety and control!

December 18, 2018

8:13 pm: The Democrats, are saying loud and clear that they do not want to build a Concrete Wall—but we are not building a Concrete Wall, we are building artistically designed steel slats, so that you can easily see through it...

December 20, 2018

7:28 am: The Democrats, who know Steel Slats (Wall) are necessary for Border Security, are putting politics over Country. What they are just beginning to realize is that I will not sign any of their legislation, including infrastructure, unless it has perfect Border Security. U.S.A. WINS!

December 21, 2018

6:58 am: The Democrats are trying to belittle the concept of a Wall, calling it old fashioned. The fact is there is nothing else's that will work, and that has been true for thousands of years. It's like the wheel, there is nothing better. I know tech better than anyone, & technology...

7:24 am: The Democrats, whose votes we need in the Senate, will probably vote against Border Security and the Wall even though they know it is DESPERATELY NEEDED. If the Dems vote no, there will be a shutdown that will last for a very long time. People don't want Open Borders and Crime!

7:31 am: Shutdown today if Democrats do not vote for Border Security!

10:07 am: The Democrats now own the shutdown!

December 24, 2018

9:31 am: Virtually every Democrat we are dealing with today strongly supported a Border Wall or Fence. It was only when I made it an important part of my campaign, because people and drugs were pouring into our Country unchecked, that they turned against it. Desperately needed!

December 27, 2018

7:06 am: Have the Democrats finally realized that we desperately need Border Security and a Wall on the Southern Border. Need to stop Drugs, Human Trafficking,Gang Members & Criminals from coming into our Country. Do the Dems realize that most of the people not getting paid are Democrats?

December 29, 2018

10:52 am: I am in the White House waiting for the Democrats to come on over and make a deal on Border Security. From what I hear, they are spending so much time on Presidential Harassment that they have little time left for things like stopping crime and our military!

December 31, 2018

10:33 am: I'm in the Oval Office. Democrats, come back from vacation now and give us the votes necessary for Border Security, including the Wall. You voted yes in 2006 and 3013. One more yes, but with me in office, I'll get it built, and Fast!

10:39 am: It's incredible how Democrats can all use their ridiculous sound bite and say that a Wall doesn't work. It does, and properly built, almost 100%! They say it's old technology—but so is the wheel. They now say it is immoral—but it is far more immoral for people to be dying!

3:02 pm: Heads of countries are calling wanting to know why Senator Schumer is not approving their otherwise approved Ambassadors!? Likewise in Government lawyers and others are being delayed at a record pace! 360 great and hardworking people are waiting for approval from...

...Senator Schumer, more than a year longer than any other Administration in history. These are people who have been approved by committees and all others, yet Schumer continues to hold them back from serving their Country! Very Unfair!

7:51 pm to 8:05 pm: The Democrats will probably submit a Bill, being cute as always, which gives everything away but gives NOTHING to Border Security, namely the Wall. You see, without the Wall there can be no Border Security—the Tech "stuff" is just, by comparison, meaningless bells & whistles...

...Remember this. Throughout the ages some things NEVER get better and NEVER change. You have Walls and you have Wheels. It was ALWAYS that way and it will ALWAYS be that way! Please explain to the Democrats that there can NEVER be a replacement for a good old fashioned WALL!

Democrats—2019 News Quotes

Remarks in meeting with conservative leaders on his immigration proposal, January 23, 2019.
Source: https://www.whitehouse.gov/briefings-statements/
remarks-president-trump-meeting-conservative-leaders-immigration-proposal/

"But I would say this: That the State of the Union speech has been cancelled by [Speaker of the House] Nancy Pelosi because she doesn't want to hear the truth. She doesn't want the American public to hear what's going on. And she's afraid of the truth. And the super-left Democrats, the radical Democrats—What's going on in that party is shocking. I know many people that were Democrats and they're switching over right now, and they're switching over quickly. So I hope they know what they're doing for their party. So far, they haven't. If you know, I won the Senate, meaning we won the Senate altogether, but we get no credit for that. They don't talk about that. They talk about the House.

"I didn't have any chance to—Other than a couple of people, like from Kentucky, where I went and campaigned for Andy Barr and for some others, they ended up winning their races. But I couldn't campaign too much. Too many people. But we did a great job with the Senate, and people don't want to talk about it.

"I will say that the American people want to hear the truth. They have to hear the truth. And the truth is all about—And said, I think and I hope, well—We were planning on doing a really very important speech in front of the House and the Senate, the Supreme Court, and everybody else that's there. It's called the State of the Union. It's in the Constitution. We're supposed to be doing it.

"And now, Nancy Pelosi, or Nancy, as I call her, she doesn't want to hear the truth, and she doesn't want to hear—More importantly, the American people hear the truth. So we just found out that she's cancelled it, and I think that's a great blotch on the incredible country that we all love. It's a great, great, horrible mark. I don't believe it's ever

44

happened before, and it's always good to be part of history. But this is a very negative part of history. This is where people are afraid to open up and say what's going on. So it's a very, very negative part of history."

Response to a question from Maggie Haberman of *The New York Times*, January 31, 2019.
Source: https://www.nytimes.com/2019/02/01/us/politics/trump-interview-transcripts.html

"Democrats, I mean the Democrats, I'm watching what's going on. They've really drifted far left. They may even be too left for you folks, you know. I'm not even sure. But they've gone pretty far out there. And, uh—[Peter Baker of *The New York Times* interrupts.]"

Response to a question from Peter Baker of *The New York Times*, January 31, 2019.
Source: https://www.nytimes.com/2019/02/01/us/politics/trump-interview-transcripts.html

"I do think Elizabeth Warren's been hurt very badly with the Pocahontas trap. I think she's been hurt badly. I may be wrong, but I think that was a big part of her credibility and now all of a sudden, it's gone. And I may be wrong about that but, you know, I don't see it. Some—You know, a lot of the folks have not decided to run yet. They might not run."

Response to a question from Griff Jenkins of FOX News, April 6, 2019.
Source: https://www.foxnews.com/politics/trump-declares-the-country-full-in-fox-news-interview-says-american-can-no-longer-accept-illegal-immigrants

"There's never been so many people coming up and that's because they're gaming the system and the system is changed for the worse because of what happened with Democrats and what they've done in terms of Congress."

Response to a question from an unidentified reporter before Marine One departure, September 9, 2019.
Source: https://www.whitehouse.gov/briefings-statements/remarks-president-trump-marine-one-departure-63/

"Well, you're always concerned that it's temporary. But we now have much better legal protection. And we'd have total protection if the

Democrats would get rid of the loopholes which are there. They could do it in, as I say, 15 minutes if they would get rid of the loopholes and fix asylum. But they don't want to do that. They don't want to do it.

"The Democrats want open borders. It means crime. It means drugs. It means human trafficking. And that's what they want. And if they want to run on that, they can run on it.

"But our people, a lot of the people in this country and I would say a very large percentage of people, they don't want to have crossings illegal. They don't want to have open borders. They want to have a strong border.

"And I've always said: without a border, we don't have a country. And without a country, I'll tell you what: we wouldn't be without that border being strong; we are securing the border like it hasn't been before. And when the wall is built—And it's moving rapidly right now. It's moving very rapidly. The lawsuit wins, the legal wins. We've won a lot.

"And we've won a lot in the courts over the last year. You know, if you look at the beginning, where we were losing, we will have about 180 judges approved over the next three or four weeks: 180.

"When I came in, [former U.S.] President [Barack] Obama gave us a beautiful gift. He gave us 138 judges that he wasn't able to get in or didn't pick anybody, or couldn't get them approved. One hundred and thirty-eight. I took that. And now, when you add the other that came through attrition and other things that have happened, we'll have about 180 judges approved very, very quickly."

Response to a question from an unidentified reporter before Marine One departure, September 9, 2019.
Source: https://www.whitehouse.gov/briefings-statements/
remarks-president-trump-marine-one-departure-63/

"Well, we're dealing with Democrats. We're dealing with Republicans. We're talking about a lot of different things having to do with, as you call it, gun control. But we are talking about a lot of different things. But at the same time, we have to protect our Second Amendment very strongly, and we will always do that."

Response to a question from an unidentified reporter before Marine One departure, September 9, 2019.
Source: https://www.whitehouse.gov/briefings-statements/
remarks-president-trump-marine-one-departure-63/

"Well, one of the things is that I disagree with the Republican system. When you're the chairman of a committee—We've lost chairmen because they can't go from being a chairman, back to being a regular congressman or woman. When you're the chairman of a committee, the Democrats, you can stay there forever, like Deny [sic] Hoyer and others. He's a good man, by the way. But like a lot of them, they're there forever. As a Republican, you get six years.

"What happens after they're finished, they leave. And I understand that. And, frankly, there is good to be said about both and there's bad to be said about both, to use the famous expression. But let me just tell you, I agree—One of the only things I agree with the Democrats on: I really think it's better to have a longer term."

Remarks at the signing of an executive order protecting and improving Medicare for senior citizens, Ocala, Florida, October 3, 2019.
Source: https://www.whitehouse.gov/briefings-statements/remarks-president-trump-signing-
executive-order-protecting-improving-medicare-nations-seniors-ocala-fl/

"Our economy is booming. We're doing fantastically well. I think it gets a little bit hurt by politics. But our country is so strong and our economy is so powerful that even politics, and even when you have the, the 'Do-Nothings.' I call them the—Really, the 'Do-Nothing Dems.' They can't even affect it very much."

Remarks at the signing of an executive order protecting and improving Medicare for senior citizens, Ocala, Florida, October 3, 2019.
Source: https://www.whitehouse.gov/briefings-statements/remarks-president-trump-signing-
executive-order-protecting-improving-medicare-nations-seniors-ocala-fl/

"As we gather this afternoon, Medicare is under threat like never before. You know that. You have people that are running for office who— If it ever happened, you will not be very happy here.

"Almost every major Democrat in Washington has backed a massive government healthcare takeover that would totally obliterate Medicare. These Democrat policy proposals may go by different names, they have all of these wonderful names like—[Audience member interrupts.]"

Remarks at the signing of an executive order protecting and improving Medicare for senior citizens, Ocala, Florida, October 3, 2019.

Source: https://www.whitehouse.gov/briefings-statements/remarks-president-trump-signing-executive-order-protecting-improving-medicare-nations-seniors-ocala-fl/

"But they may go by different names, whether it's 'single payer' or the so-called "public option," but they're all based on the totally same, terrible idea. They [the Democrats] want to raid Medicare to fund a thing called socialism. Any socialists in the room? I don't think so. Not too many. Anybody? [Audience boos.]

"No? No? Not too many in The Villages. You don't—You're not big on socialism down here, right? These geniuses, these real estate geniuses that know we're not, not too good.

"Every one of these plans involves rationing care, restricting access, denying coverage, slashing quality, and massively raising taxes. They want to raise your taxes.

"They also want to have open borders, so the people can just come in and do whatever they want to do."

Remarks at the signing of an executive order protecting and improving Medicare for senior citizens, Ocala, Florida, October 3, 2019.

Source: https://www.whitehouse.gov/briefings-statements/remarks-president-trump-signing-executive-order-protecting-improving-medicare-nations-seniors-ocala-fl/

"Congressional Democrats' extreme agenda would destroy our booming economy very quickly. One of the most disturbing proposals from left-wing politicians involves draining your healthcare to finance the open borders that we just discussed. That's how they want to finance it. Leading Democrats have pledged to give free healthcare to illegal immigrants. They put foreign citizens who break our laws and endanger our country—they put them way ahead of American citizens like you who obey our laws.

"I will never allow these politicians to steal your healthcare and give it away to illegal aliens. And now, in New York, I hear they passed a new regulation that, if you use the word, 'illegal immigrant'—Did I hear correctly? They want to charge you a fine of $250,000. In other words, sell your home in The Villages because you happened to say, 'We don't like illegal immigrants pouring into our country illegally.' We want people to come into our country legally, through a process. And we're all in favor of that."

Remarks at the signing of an executive order protecting and improving Medicare for senior citizens, Ocala, Florida, October 3, 2019.
Source: https://www.whitehouse.gov/briefings-statements/remarks-president-trump-signing-executive-order-protecting-improving-medicare-nations-seniors-ocala-fl/

"In the last administration, Democrats slashed Medicare by $800 billion dollars to pay for Obamacare. Not too good, Obamacare."

Remarks at the signing of an executive order protecting and improving Medicare for senior citizens, Ocala, Florida, October 3, 2019.
Source: https://www.whitehouse.gov/briefings-statements/remarks-president-trump-signing-executive-order-protecting-improving-medicare-nations-seniors-ocala-fl/

"Now one of their new proposals, backed by more than 130 Democrat members of Congress, would cost, listen to this number, $32 trillion dollars. And that's on the low side: $32 trillion, with a 'T.' We're beyond the 'B's,' the billions. And reduce Americans' household income by $17,000 per year. Is there anybody in this room that doesn't mind losing $17,000 a year? No? In order to get lousy healthcare.

"Though they use many labels, all of the Democrat plans would devastate our healthcare system. The fake moderates on the left are telling the same lies they did under the last administration. But the last administration, frankly, was moderate compared to the maniacs that you're hearing from today. These are maniacs."

Remarks at the signing of an executive order protecting and improving Medicare for senior citizens, Ocala, Florida, October 3, 2019.

Source: https://www.whitehouse.gov/briefings-statements/remarks-president-trump-signing-executive-order-protecting-improving-medicare-nations-seniors-ocala-fl/

"Democrat lawmakers are not trying to build up the country; they only want to wreck and destroy all of the things that we've built up over the last three and a half years, four years, five years—Prior to us getting in here. You look at the stock market numbers from the time of the election, from that November 9th date, go a date later. Wasn't November 8—Was that one of the great times? Huh? [Audience applauds.] 2016.

"But go a day later, and you look at the numbers in the stock market up way over 50%. The 401(k)s are doing unbelievably well. One of these people gets in—Your 401(k)s are going to hell, the stock market is going to hell. Frankly, I think, and I hate to say it, the country is going to go to hell.

"They're consumed by rage and radicalism and insatiable lust for power. Well, how about Justice [Brett] Kavanaugh? They talk about a woman, they talk about a woman, about horrible things that he never even thought about. Horrible, horrible things. And the following day, they want to impeach him. And then, the following day, she said, 'No, I don't remember anything. I don't remember that.' And they say, 'We don't care. We want to impeach him anyway.' Now, what they're trying to do is turn his vote liberal. But he's a much tougher guy than that. I hope. He's a much tougher guy."

Remarks at the signing of an executive order protecting and improving Medicare for senior citizens, Ocala, Florida, October 3, 2019.

Source: https://www.whitehouse.gov/briefings-statements/remarks-president-trump-signing-executive-order-protecting-improving-medicare-nations-seniors-ocala-fl/

"Democrat healthcare proposals would put everyone into a single, socialist, government-run program that would end private insurance for over 180 million Americans. I'm sort of smiling to myself as I, as I go through these numbers. And I'm dealing with people that I know. I mean, I know the people in this room. Those are the people. I grew up with you. When we were young, I grew up with you. And now we're sort of still young at heart, at least.

"And that I'm even talking about socialism is like—It's just—It's sort of a weird feeling to be talking to you about 'you don't want to be so-cialist.' And you're probably saying, 'Why is he wasting his time?'

"But there's a movement on. And it's not so easy to be beat them when they get up in a debate and they say, 'We're going to cut your college tuition to nothing. We're going kno—Knock off $1.6 trillion. We're going to do all these other things. Everything is free, except for your taxes.' Your taxes are going to go up at a level that nobody has even seen before and that won't be nearly enough to pay for it.

"But I'll not let any of this bad stuff happen. It's very important that we win this race. You know, when we won last time, I said, 'That's the most important election in our country's history.' Because we were ready to go over the edge.

"And now our country is doing great. But, you know, it's like a plant; it's like a tree. It has to grab—Those roots have to grab hold. We still need more time. We've done so much, but we need a little more time. That thing has to grow and it's got to get in there and then nobody is going to be able to take it down no matter what happens later on. So important.

"In America, we believe in freedom and liberty, not government domi-nation and government control. Today, standing in solidarity with our nation's seniors, I declare once again that America will never be a socialist country—It will never be."

Remarks at the signing of an executive order protecting and improving Medicare for senior citizens, Ocala, Florida, October 3, 2019.
Source: https://www.whitehouse.gov/briefings-statements/remarks-president-trump-signing-executive-order-protecting-improving-medicare-nations-seniors-ocala-fl/

"The Democrat plans for socialized medicine will not just put doctors and hospitals out of business, they'll also deny your treatment and everything that you need. Government-run healthcare systems always end up imposing rationing. You see what happens.

"You look at Venezuela; take a look at that. Fifteen years ago, it's one of the wealthiest countries. Now they don't have food. They don't have water. The hospitals are a disaster. No electricity. No anything.

It's very sad. And we're helping the people as much as we can. But we're watching that whole situation; beyond this, we're watching it very, very carefully. We're watching it very carefully. And Cuba, we're watching Cuba very carefully. Very, very carefully.

"But as an example, under the United Kingdom's single-payer system, patients wait 117 days to receive, as an example, a knee replacement. One hundred and seventeen days.

"In Canada, wait times for orthopedic surgery are over 270 days. But currently in the United States, wait times for these surgeries are, we've speeded it up a lot, are typically less than two weeks."

Remarks at the signing of an executive order protecting and improving Medicare for senior citizens, Ocala, Florida, October 3, 2019.
Source: https://www.whitehouse.gov/briefings-statements/remarks-president-trump-signing-executive-order-protecting-improving-medicare-nations-seniors-ocala-fl/

"Like you, all of us today understand the truth. Socialism is not about improving the health of American people; it's about wielding power over the American people, taking things away from the American people."

Remarks at a rally in Minneapolis, Minnesota, October 10, 2019.
Source: https://www.twincities.com/2019/10/10/trump-attacks-joe-biden-ilhan-omar-and-jacob-frey-at-minneapolis-rally/

"How the hell did that ever happen? She [Rep. Ilhan Omar] is a disgrace, and she is one of the reasons I'm going to win and the Republican Party is going to win Minnesota."

Response to a question from an unidentified reporter before Marine One Departure, November 8, 2019.
Source: https://www.whitehouse.gov/briefings-statements/remarks-president-trump-marine-one-departure-76/

"Well, they're making it up. First of all, this whole thing is a phony deal. It's a phony setup. When you look at the lawyer that got it started— The whistleblower lawyer, he got it started. It's a phony deal. These

Democrats are corrupt. [Speaker of the House] Nancy Pelosi is a corrupt politician.

"Shifty Schiff[6] is a double corrupt politician. He took my words on the phone call—And they were so good. He totally changed them. He went before Congress. He made his speech before Congress. And in the speech, John, he said things that were horrible. It bore no relationship to the call. And then, later on, he was embarrassed.

"Let me tell you something: Schiff is a corrupt politician, and our people know it. And they know it too, by the way."

Remarks during a Cabinet meeting, November 19, 2019.
Source: https://www.whitehouse.gov/briefings-statements/
remarks-president-trump-cabinet-meeting-16/

"The woman [Speaker of the House Nancy Pelosi] is grossly incompetent. All she wants to do is focus on impeachment, which is just a little pipe dream she's got. And she can keep playing that game.

"And I've been told—And who knows if this is so, but I think it's so; I have pretty good authority on it—That's she's using USMCA, because she doesn't have the impeach—impeachment votes. So, she's using USMCA to get the impeachment vote. And it doesn't matter, because right now you have a kangaroo court headed by little Shifty Schiff[7], where we don't have lawyers, we don't have witnesses, we don't have anything."

Remarks at a campaign rally in Sunrise, Florida, November 26, 2019.
Source: https://www.c-span.org/video/?466539-1/
president-trump-holds-rally-sunrise-florida&start=4731

"Nancy [Pelosi] is on track to go down as the single worst and least productive Speaker of the House in the history of our country.

---

6   This is President Trump's self-admitted nickname for Congressman Adam Schiff, D-California.

7   This is President Trump's self-admitted nickname for Congressman Adam Schiff, D-California.

Before my election our leaders used the great American middle class as a piggy bank to fund their delusional global projects. It's all over the globe. I'm President of the United States. I'm not President of the world."

Response to an unidentified woman's question at the NATO Summit, December 3, 2019.

Source: https://www.newsweek.com/
donald-trump-adam-schiff-deranged-human-being-maniac-nato-summit-1475436

"From which? I learn nothing from [Congressman] Adam Schiff. I think he's a maniac. I think Adam Schiff is a deranged human being. I think he grew up with a complex, for lots of reasons that are obvious. I think he's a very sick man, and he lies.

"Adam Schiff made up my conversation with the President of Ukraine. And one of the reasons that people keep talking about it is that's what they saw. We have a perfectly beautiful three-to-four page transcription, and then in the other case, a two-page transcription of the conversation. But a lot of people didn't read that.

"How many people call you—A friend of mine called up—A top person in New York called up, great friend of mine, very successful—'Gee, I didn't like what was said.'

"I said, 'Oh, where did you see it? Did you read it?'

"'No, I didn't read it. I heard Adam Schiff give it.'"

"I said, 'Well, that's not what was said.'

"And I sent him a copy of what was said.

"He said, 'This is like—This is great. This isn't what he [Schiff] said.'

"This guy [Schiff] is sick. He made up the conversation. He lied. If he didn't do that in the halls of Congress, he'd be thrown into jail. He did it in the halls of Congress, and he's given immunity. This is a sick person. He's a liar.

"And by the way, [Speaker of the House] Nancy Pelosi knew he [Schiff] was lying, and she went on a show, [George] Stephanopoulos, and she said he told the truth.

"So, she was lying, too.

"These people are deranged."

Democrats—2019 Tweets

January 1, 2019

7:43 pm: For FAR TOO LONG Senate Democrats have been Obstructing more than 350 Nominations. These great Americans left their jobs to serve our Country, but can't because Dems are blocking them, some for two years-historic record. Passed committees, but Schumer putting them on hold. Bad!

January 4, 2019

8:06 am: As I have stated many times, if the Democrats take over the House or Senate, there will be disruption to the Financial Markets. We won the Senate, they won the House. Things will settle down. They only want to impeach me because they know they can't win in 2020, too much success!

January 5, 2019

7:57 am: The Democrats could solve the Shutdown problem in a very short period of time. All they have to do is approve REAL Border Security (including a Wall), something which everyone, other than drug dealers, human traffickers and criminals, want very badly! This would be so easy to do!

9:48 am: I don't care that most of the workers not getting paid are Democrats, I want to stop the Shutdown as soon as we are in agreement on Strong Border Security! I am in the White House ready to go, where are the Dems?

10:54 am: The Democrats want Billions of Dollars for Foreign Aid, but they don't want to spend a small fraction of that number on properly securing our Border.

January 12, 2019

9:47 am: Democrats could solve the Shutdown in 15 minutes! Call your Dem Senator or Congresswoman/man. Tell them to get it done! Humanitarian Crisis.

January 13, 2019

9:58 am: Democrats are saying that DACA is not worth it and don't want to include in talks. Many Hispanics will be coming over to the Republican side, watch!

9:52 pm: If Elizabeth Warren, often referred to by me as Pocahontas, did this commercial from Bighorn or Wounded Knee instead of her kitchen, with her husband dressed in full Indian garb, it would have been a smash! https://t.co/D5KWr8EPan

10:03 pm: Best line in the Elizabeth Warren beer catastrophe is, to her husband, "Thank you for being here. I'm glad you're here" It's their house, he's supposed to be there!

January 14, 2019

7:23 am: I've been waiting all weekend. Democrats must get to work now. Border must be secured!

7:26 am: Nancy and Cryin' Chuck can end the Shutdown in 15 minutes. At this point it has become their, and the Democrats, fault!

January 15, 2019

8:25 am: Why is Nancy Pelosi getting paid when people who are working are not?

January 16, 2019

7:49 am: It is becoming more and more obvious that the Radical Democrats are a Party of open borders and crime. They want nothing to do with the major Humanitarian Crisis on our Southern Border. #2020!

January 17, 2019

9:04 am: The Left has become totally unhinged. They no longer care what is Right for our Countrty!

10:04 am: So funny to watch Schumer groveling. He called for the firing of bad cop James Comey many times—UNTIL I FIRED HIM!

January 18, 2019

9:00 am: Why would Nancy Pelosi leave the Country with other Democrats on a seven day excursion when 800,000 great people are not getting paid. Also, could somebody please explain to Nancy & her "big donors" in wine country that people working on farms (grapes) will have easy access in!

January 20, 2019

8:11 am: Nancy Pelosi and some of the Democrats turned down my offer yesterday before I even got up to speak. They don't see crime & drugs, they only see 2020—which they are not going to win. Best economy! They should do the right thing for the Country & allow people to go back to work.

8:23 am: No, Amnesty is not a part of my offer. It is a 3 year extension of DACA. Amnesty will be used only on a much bigger deal, whether on immigration or something else. Likewise there will be no big push to remove the 11,000,000 plus people who are here illegally-but be careful Nancy!

8:35 am: Nancy Pelosi has behaved so irrationally & has gone so far to the left that she has now officially become a Radical Democrat. She is so petrified of the "lefties" in her party that she has lost control…And by the way, clean up the streets in San Francisco, they are disgusting!

8:51 am: Nancy, I am still thinking about the State of the Union speech, there are so many options—including doing it as per your written offer (made during the Shutdown, security is no problem), and my written acceptance. While a contract is a contract, I'll get back to you soon!

January 21, 2019

5:08 pm: If Nancy Pelosi thinks that Walls are "immoral," why isn't she requesting that we take down all of the existing Walls between the U.S. and Mexico, even the new ones just built in San Diego at their very strong urging. Let millions of unchecked "strangers" just flow into the U.S.

January 23, 2019

11:12 pm: As the Shutdown was going on, Nancy Pelosi asked me to give the State of the Union Address. I agreed. She then changed her mind because of the Shutdown, suggesting a later date. This is her prerogative—I will do the Address when the Shutdown is over. I am not looking for an…

11:18 pm: …alternative venue for the SOTU Address because there is no venue that can compete with the history, tradition and importance of the House Chamber. I look forward to giving a "great" State of the Union Address in the near future!

January 24, 2019

11:16 am: Nancy just said she "just doesn't understand why?" Very simply, without a Wall it all doesn't work. Our Country has a chance to greatly reduce Crime, Human Trafficking, Gangs and Drugs. Should have been done for decades. We will not Cave!

January 28, 2019

8:41 am: Howard Schultz doesn't have the "guts" to run for President! Watched him on @60Minutes last night and I agree with him that he is not the "smartest person." Besides, America already has that! I only hope that Starbucks is still paying me their rent in Trump Tower!

9:46 pm: How does Da Nang Dick (Blumenthal) serve on the Senate Judiciary Committee when he defrauded the American people about his so called War Hero status in Vietnam, only to later admit, with tears pouring down his face, that he was never in Vietnam. An embarrassment to our Country!

January 31, 2019

8:36 am: Democrats are becoming the Party of late term abortion, high taxes, Open Borders and Crime!

10:08 am: Schumer and the Democrats are big fans of being weak and passive with Iran. They have no clue as to the danger they would be inflicting on our Country. Iran is in financial chaos now because of the sanctions and Iran Deal termination. Dems put us in a bad place—but now good!

February 2, 2019

7:39 pm: Democrat Governor Ralph Northam of Virginia just stated, "I believe that I am not either of the people in that photo." This was 24 hours after apologizing for appearing in the picture and after making the most horrible statement on "super" late term abortion. Unforgivable!

February 5, 2019

10:29 am: I see Schumer is already criticizing my State of the Union speech, even though he hasn't seen it yet. He's just upset that he didn't win the Senate, after spending a fortune, like he thought he would. Too bad we weren't given more credit for the Senate win by the media!

February 7, 2019

6:18 am: So now Congressman Adam Schiff announces, after having found zero Russian Collusion, that he is going to be looking at every aspect of my life, both financial and personal, even though there is no reason to be doing so. Never happened before! Unlimited Presidential Harassment…

6:26 am: …The Dems and their committees are going "nuts." The Republicans never did this to President Obama, there would be no time left to run government. I hear other committee heads will do the same thing. Even stealing people who work at White House! A continuation of Witch Hunt!

7:35 am: Democrats at the top are killing the Great State of Virginia. If the three failing pols were Republicans, far stronger action would be taken. Virginia will come back HOME Republican) in 2020!

February 8, 2019

8:41 am: Now we find out that Adam Schiff was spending time together in Aspen with Glenn Simpson of GPS Fusion, who wrote the fake and discredited Dossier, even though Simpson was testifying before Schiff. John Solomon of @thehill

February 9, 2019

9:30 am: The Democrats in Congress yesterday were vicious and totally showed their cards for everyone to see. When the Republicans had the Majority they never acted with such hatred and scorn! The Dems are trying to win an election in 2020 that they know they cannot legitimately win!

5:54 pm: Today Elizabeth Warren, sometimes referred to by me as Pocahontas, joined the race for President. Will she run as our first Native American presidential candidate, or has she decided that after

32 years, this is not playing so well anymore? See you on the campaign TRAIL, Liz!

6:21 pm: I think it is very important for the Democrats to press forward with their Green New Deal. It would be great for the so-called "Carbon Footprint" to permanently eliminate all Planes, Cars, Cows, Oil, Gas & the Military—even if no other country would do the same. Brilliant!

February 10, 2019

9:53 am: African Americans are very angry at the double standard on full display in Virginia!

11:17 am: I don't think the Dems on the Border Committee are being allowed by their leaders to make a deal. They are offering very little money for the desperately needed Border Wall & now, out of the blue, want a cap on convicted violent felons to be held in detention!

4:54 pm: The Border Committee Democrats are behaving, all of a sudden, irrationally. Not only are they unwilling to give dollars for the obviously needed Wall (they overrode recommendations of Border Patrol experts), but they don't even want to take muderers into custody! What's going on?

February 19, 2019

7:30 am: Had the opposition party (no, not the Media) won the election, the Stock Market would be down at least 10,000 points by now. We are heading up, up, up!

February 20, 2019

7:07 am: Crazy Bernie has just entered the race. I wish him well!

February 25, 2019

7:52 am: Former Senator Harry Reid (he got thrown out) is working hard to put a good spin on his failed career. He led through lies and deception, only to be replaced by another beauty, Cryin' Chuck Schumer. Some things just never change!

8:50 pm: Senate Democrats just voted against legislation to prevent the killing of newborn infant children. The Democrat position on abortion is now so extreme that they don't mind executing babies AFTER birth...

...This will be remembered as one of the most shocking votes in the history of Congress. If there is one thing we should all agree on, it's protecting the lives of innocent babies.

February 26, 2019

9:36 pm: The Democrats should stop talking about what I should do with North Korea and ask themselves instead why they didn't do "it" during eight years of the Obama Administration?

February 27, 2019

2:58 am: I have now spent more time in Vietnam than Da Nang Dick Blumenthal, the third rate Senator from Connecticut (how is Connecticut doing?). His war stories of his heroism in Vietnam were a total fraud—he was never even there. We talked about it today with Vietnamese leaders!

March 3, 2019

8:24 pm: Schumer & the Democrats are hurting our Country. Senate Republicans must take BOLD ACTION!

March 4, 2019

11:33 pm: Representative Ilhan Omar is again under fire for her terrible comments concerning Israel. Jewish groups have just sent a petition to Speaker Pelosi asking her to remove Omar from Foreign Relations Committee. A dark day for Israel!

March 5, 2019

9:11 am: The greatest overreach in the history of our Country. The Dems are obstructing justice and will not get anything done. A big, fat, fishing expedition desperately in search of a crime, when in fact the real crime is what the Dems are doing, and have done!

11:53 pm: Weirdo Tom Steyer doesn't have the "guts" or money to run for President. He's all talk!

March 6, 2019

7:05 pm: Democrats just blocked @FoxNews from holding a debate. Good, then I think I'll do the same thing with the Fake News Networks and the Radical Left Democrats in the General Election debates!

March 12, 2019

5:17 pm: New York State and its Governor, Andrew Cuomo, are now proud members of the group of PRESIDENTIAL HARASSERS. No wonder people are fleeing the State in record numbers. The Witch Hunt continues!

11:27 pm: All part of the Witch Hunt Hoax. Started by little Eric Schneiderman & Cuomo. So many leaving New York!

March 14, 2019

6:54 am: The Democrats are "Border Deniers." They refuse to see or acknowledge the Death, Crime, Drugs and Human Trafficking at our Southern Border!

March 15, 2019

7:03 am: The 'Jexodus' movement encourages Jewish people to leave the Democrat Party. Total disrespect! Republicans are waiting with open arms. Remember Jerusalem (U.S. Embassy) and the horrible Iran Nuclear Deal! @OANN @foxandfriends

March 17, 2019

6:16 pm: What the Democrats have done in trying to steal a Presidential Election, first at the "ballot box" and then, after that failed, with the "Insurance Policy," is the biggest Scandal in the history of our Country!

March 18, 2019

8:14 am: Joe Biden got tongue tied over the weekend when he was unable to properly deliver a very simple line about his decision to run for President. Get used to it, another low I.Q. individual!

March 19, 2019

11:04 pm: The Democrats are getting very "strange." They now want to change the voting age to 16, abolish the Electoral College, and Increase significantly the number of Supreme Court Justices. Actually, you've got to win it at the Ballot Box!

March 28, 2019

5:43 am: Congressman Adam Schiff, who spent two years knowingly and unlawfully lying and leaking, should be forced to resign from Congress!

March 29. 2019

5:31 pm to 6:15 pm: Robert Mueller was a Hero to the Radical Left Democrats, until he ruled that there was No Collusion with Russia (so ridiculous to even say!). After more than two years since the "insurance policy" statement was made by a dirty cop, I got the answers I wanted, the Truth...

...The problem is, no matter what the Radical Left Democrats get, no matter what we give them, it will never be enough. Just watch, they will Harass & Complain & Resist (the theme of their movement). So maybe we should just take our victory and say NO, we've got a Country to run!

March 30, 2019

3:31 pm: It would be so easy to fix our weak and very stupid Democrat inspired immigration laws. In less than one hour, and then a vote, the problem would be solved. But the Dems don't care about the crime, they don't want any victory for Trump and the Republicans, even if good for USA!

April 1, 2019

7:13 am: Democrats, working with Republicans in Congress, can fix the Asylum and other loopholes quickly. We have a major National Emergency at our Border. GET IT DONE NOW!

8:03 am: Can you believe that the Radical Left Democrats want to do our new and very important Census Report without the all important Citizenship Question. Report would be meaningless and a waste of the $Billions (ridiculous) that it costs to put together!

9:50 pm to 10:38 pm: The Democrats today killed a Bill that would have provided great relief to Farmers and yet more money to Puerto Rico despite the fact that Puerto Rico has already been scheduled to receive more hurricane relief funding than any "place" in history. The people of Puerto Rico...

...are GREAT, but the politicians are incompetent or corrupt. Puerto Rico got far more money than Texas & Florida combined, yet their government can't do anything right, the place is a mess—nothing works. FEMA & the Military worked emergency miracles, but politicians like...

...the crazed and incompetent Mayor of San Juan have done such a poor job of bringing the Island back to health. 91 Billion Dollars to Puerto Rico, and now the Dems want to give them more, taking dollars away from our Farmers and so many others. Disgraceful!

April 2, 2019

6:58 am: In 1998, Rep. Jerry Nadler strongly opposed the release of the Starr Report on Bill Clinton. No information whatsoever would or could be legally released. But with the NO COLLUSION Mueller Report, which the Dems hate, he wants it all. NOTHING WILL EVER SATISFY THEM! @foxandfriends

7:46 am: Robert Mueller was a God-like figure to the Democrats, until he ruled No Collusion in the long awaited $30,000,000 Mueller Report. Now the Dems don't even acknowledge his name, have become totally unhinged, and would like to go through the whole process again. It won't happen!

7:54 am: There is no amount of testimony or document production that can satisfy Jerry Nadler or Shifty Adam Schiff. It is now time to focus exclusively on properly running our great Country!

April 4, 2019

7:46 am: There is nothing we can ever give to the Democrats that will make them happy. This is the highest level of Presidential Harassment in the history of our Country!

12:53 pm: WELCOME BACK JOE! https://t.co/b2NbBSX3sx

April 9, 2019

7:16 am to 7:33 am: Congressman Jerry Nadler fought me for years on a very large development I built on the West Side of Manhattan. He wanted a Rail Yard built underneath the development or even better, to stop the job. He didn't get either & the development became VERY successful. Nevertheless,...

...I got along very well with Jerry during the zoning and building process. Then I changed course (slightly), became President, and now I am dealing with Congressman Nadler again. Some things never end, but hopefully it will all go well for everyone. Only time will tell!

April 10, 2019

9:33 pm: I think what the Democrats are doing with the Border is TREASONOUS. Their Open Border mindset is putting our Country at risk. Will not let this happen!

April 11, 2019

6:14 pm: House Democrats want to negotiate a $2 TRILLION spending increase but can't even pass their own plan. We can't afford it anyway, and it's not happening!

April 12, 2019

9:19 am: Even the Democrats now say that our Southern Border is a Crisis and a National Emergency. Hopefully, we will not be getting any more BAD (outrageous) court decisions!

11:38 am: Due to the fact that Democrats are unwilling to change our very dangerous immigration laws, we are indeed, as reported, giving strong considerations to placing Illegal Immigrants in Sanctuary Cities only...

The Radical Left always seems to have an Open Borders, Open Arms policy—so this should make them very happy!

10:51 pm: In New York State, Democrats blocked a Bill expanding College Tuition for Gold Star families after approving aid for illegal immigrants. No wonder so many people are leaving N.Y. Very Sad!

April 15, 2019

8:30 am: Before Nancy, who has lost all control of Congress and is getting nothing done, decides to defend her leader, Rep. Omar, she should look at the anti-Semitic, anti-Israel and ungrateful U.S. HATE statements Omar has made. She is out of control, except for her control of Nancy!

April 16, 2019

8:24 pm: I believe it will be Crazy Bernie Sanders vs. Sleepy Joe Biden as the two finalists to run against maybe the best Economy in the history of our Country (and MANY other great things)! I look forward to facing whoever it may be. May God Rest Their Soul!

April 21, 2019

6:40 am: Do you believe this? The New York Times Op-Ed: MEDIA AND DEMOCRATS OWE TRUMP AN APOLOGY. Well, they got that one right!

April 23, 2019

5:18 am: The Radical Left Democrats, together with their leaders in the Fake News Media, have gone totally insane! I guess that means that the Republican agenda is working. Stay tuned for more!

April 25, 2019

7:22 am: Welcome to the race Sleepy Joe. I only hope you have the intelligence, long in doubt, to wage a successful primary campaign. It will be nasty—you will be dealing with people who truly have some very sick & demented ideas. But if you make it, I will see you at the Starting Gate!

April 27, 2019

10:10 pm: The Democratic National Committee, sometimes referred to as the DNC, is again working its magic in its quest to destroy Crazy Bernie Sanders…

for the more traditional, but not very bright, Sleepy Joe Biden. Here we go again Bernie, but this time please show a little more anger and indignation when you get screwed!

April 29, 2019

7:18 am: The NRA is under siege by Cuomo and the New York State A.G., who are illegally using the State's legal apparatus to take down and destroy this very important organization, & others. It must get its act together quickly, stop the internal fighting, & get back to GREATNESS—FAST!

8:23 am: ...People are fleeing New York State because of high taxes and yes, even oppression of sorts. They didn't even put up a fight against SALT—could have won. So much litigation. The NRA should leave and fight from the outside of this very difficult to deal with (unfair) State!

9:51 am: Sleepy Joe Biden is having his first rally in the Great State of Pennsylvania. He obviously doesn't know that Pennsylvania is having one of the best economic years in its history, with lowest unemployment EVER, a now thriving Steel Industry (that was dead) & great future!...

9:55 am: The Dues Sucking firefighters leadership will always support Democrats, even though the membership wants me. Some things never change!

8:23 pm: If the Democrats don't give us the votes to change our weak, ineffective and dangerous Immigration Laws, we must fight hard for these votes in the 2020 Election!

May 2, 2019

10:45 pm: OK, so after two years of hard work and each party trying their best to make the other party look as bad as possible, it's time to get back to business. The Mueller Report strongly stated that there was No Collusion with Russia (of course) and, in fact, they were rebuffed...

...at every turn in attempts to gain access. But now Republicans and Democrats must come together for the good of the American people. No more costly & time consuming investigations. Lets do Immigration (Border), Infrastructure, much lower drug prices & much more—and do it now!

May 5, 2019

1:03 pm: After spending more than $35,000,000 over a two year period, interviewing 500 people, using 18 Trump Hating Angry Democrats & 49 FBI Agents—all culminating in a more than 400 page

Report showing NO COLLUSION—why would the Democrats in Congress now need Robert Mueller…

…to testify. Are they looking for a redo because they hated seeing the strong NO COLLUSION conclusion? There was no crime, except on the other side (incredibly not covered in the Report), and NO OB-STRUCTION. Bob Mueller should not testify. No redos for the Dems!

May 6, 2019

8:30 am: Scott Walker is 100% correct when he says that the Republicans must WAKE UP to the Democrats State by State power grab. They play very dirty, actually, like never before. Don't allow them to get away with what they are doing!

8:48 am: Puerto Rico has been given more money by Congress for Hurricane Disaster Relief, 91 Billion Dollars, than any State in the history of the U.S. As an example, Florida got $12 Billion & Texas $39 Billion for their monster hurricanes. Now the Democrats are saying NO Relief to…

…Alabama, Iowa, Nebraska, Georgia, South Carolina, North Carolina and others unless much more money is given to Puerto Rico. The Dems don't want farmers to get any help. Puerto Rico should be very happy and the Dems should stop blocking much needed Disaster Relief!

May 10, 2019

8:20 am: Looks to me like it's going to be SleepyCreepy Joe over Crazy Bernie. Everyone else is fading fast!

May 12, 2019

4:35 pm: The Democrats new and pathetically untrue sound bite is that we are in a "Constitutional Crisis." They and their partner, the Fake News Media, are all told to say this as loud and as often as possible. They are a sad JOKE! We may have the strongest Economy in our history, best.

...employment numbers ever, low taxes & regulations, a rebuilt military & V.A., many great new judges, & so much more. But we have had a giant SCAM perpetrated upon our nation, a Witch Hunt, a Treasonous Hoax. That is the Constitutional Crisis & hopefully guilty people will pay!

6:19 pm: The "Constitutional Crisis" is the Democrats refusing to work. Let them start by fixing the mess that their Immigration Laws have caused at the Southern Border.

May 13, 2019

9:09 am: Democrat Rep. Tlaib is being slammed for her horrible and highly insensitive statement on the Holocaust. She obviously has tremendous hatred of Israel and the Jewish people. Can you imagine what would happen if I ever said what she said, and says?

May 16, 2019

7:33 am: The Dems are getting another beauty to join their group. Bill de Blasio of NYC, considered the worst mayor in the U.S., will supposedly be making an announcement for president today. He is a JOKE, but if you like high taxes & crime, he's your man. NYC HATES HIM!

5:11 pm: .@BilldeBlasio is the worst Mayor in the history of New York City—he won't last long!

May 17, 2019

5:36 am: The Democrats now realize that there is a National Emergency at the Border and that, if we work together, it can be immediately fixed. We need Democrat votes and all will be well!

5:33 pm: Courts & Dems in Congress, neither of which have a clue, are trying to FORCE migrants into our Country! OUR COUNTRY IS FULL, OUR DETENTION CENTERS, HOSPITALS & SCHOOLS ARE PACKED. Crazy!

May 20, 2019

7:13 am: Why are the Democrats not looking into all of the crimes committed by Crooked Hillary and the phony Russia Investigation? They would get back their credibility. Jerry Nadler, Schiff, would have a whole new future open to them. Perhaps they could even run for President!

9:08 am: Looks like Bernie Sanders is history. Sleepy Joe Biden is pulling ahead and think about it, I'm only here because of Sleepy Joe and the man who took him off the 1% trash heap, President O! China wants Sleepy Joe BADLY!

May 21, 2019

7:32 pm: After spending 40 Million Dollars, reviewing 1.4 million pages of documents, & interviewing 500 people with the total support of the White House, the Mueller Report was a BIG DISAPPOINT-MENT to the Democrats, so they want a DO OVER. It doesn't work that way-so bad for our Country!

7:51 pm: The Democrats are on a fishing expedition, wanting to interview the same people, and see the same things, as we just went through for two years with Robert Mueller and the 18 Angry Dems. Never happened to a president before. Never even happened to President Obama!

8:02 pm: John Brennan on the Mueller probe, "I don't know if I received bad information, but I THINK I SUSPECTED THAT THERE WAS MORE THAN THERE ACTUALLY WAS." Wow, he admits he was wrong! Congress should go back to work on drug prices etc.

May 22, 2019

4:55 am: Everything the Democrats are asking me for is based on an illegally started investigation that failed for them, especially when the Mueller Report came back with a NO COLLUSION finding. Now they say Impeach President Trump, even though he did nothin wrong, while they "fish!"

4:58 am: After two years of an expensive and comprehensive Witch Hunt, the Democrats don't like the result and they want a DO OVER. In other words, the Witch Hunt continues!

5:02 am: The Democrats are getting ZERO work done in Congress. All they are focused on is trying to prove the Mueller Report wrong, the Witch Hunt!

12:01 pm: So sad that Nancy Pelosi and Chuck Schumer will never be able to see or understand the great promise of our Country. They can continue the Witch Hunt which has already cost $40M and been a tremendous waste of time and energy for everyone in America, or get back to work...

But they really want a do-over! You can't investigate and legislate simultaneously—it just doesn't work that way. You can't go down two tracks at the same time. Let Chuck, Nancy, Jerry, Adam and all of the rest finish playing their games...

...In the meantime, my Administration is achieving things that have never been done before, including unleashing perhaps the Greatest Economy in our Country's history...

12:02 pm: ...Democrat leadership is tearing the United States apart, but I will continue to set records for the American People—and Nancy, thank you so much for your prayers, I know you truly mean it!

9:28 pm: In a letter to her House colleagues, Nancy Pelosi said: "President Trump had a temper tantrum for us all to see." This is not true. I was purposely very polite and calm, much as I was minutes later with the press in the Rose Garden. Can be easily proven. It is all such a lie!

9:31 pm: Zero is getting done with the Democrats in charge of the House. All they want to do is put the Mueller Report behind them and start all over again. No Do-Overs!

9:54 pm: Democrats don't want to fix the loopholes at the Border. They don't want to do anything. Open Borders and crime!

May 23, 2019

6:56 am: The Democrats are getting nothing done in Congress. All of their effort is about a Re-Do of the Mueller Report, which didn't turn out the way they wanted. It is not possible for them to investigate and legislate at the same time. Their heart is not into Infrastructure, lower...

...drug prices, pre-existing conditions and our great Vets. All they are geared up to do, six committees, is squander time, day after day, trying to find anything which will be bad for me. A pure fishing expedition like this never happened before, & it should never happen again!

6:58 am: The Democrats have become known as THE DO NOTHING PARTY!

9:13 am: I was extremely calm yesterday with my meeting with Pelosi and Schumer, knowing that they would say I was raging, which they always do, along with their partner, the Fake News Media. Well, so many stories about the meeting use the Rage narrative anyway—Fake & Corrupt Press!

May 24, 2019

7:34 am: I don't know why the Radical Left Democrats want Bob Mueller to testify when he just issued a 40 Million Dollar Report that states, loud & clear & for all to hear, No Collusion and No Obstruction (how do you Obstruct a NO crime?) Dems are just looking for trouble and a Do-Over!

May 25, 2019

2:20 am: Democrat Senator Mark Warner is acting and talking like he is in total control of the Senate Intelligence Committee. Their is nothing bipartisan about him. He should not be allowed to take "command" of that Committee. Too important! Remember when he spoke to the Russian jokester?

May 27, 2019

4:16 pm: …Super Predator was the term associated with the 1994 Crime Bill that Sleepy Joe Biden was so heavily involved in passing. That was a dark period in American History, but has Sleepy Joe apologized? No!

5:35 pm: Anyone associated with the 1994 Crime Bill will not have a chance of being elected. In particular, African Americans will not be able to vote for you. I, on the other hand, was responsible for Criminal Justice Reform, which had tremendous support, & helped fix the bad 1994 Bill!

4:58 pm: I was actually sticking up for Sleepy Joe Biden while on foreign soil. Kim Jong Un called him a "low IQ idiot," and many other things, whereas I related the quote of Chairman Kim as a much softer "low IQ individual." Who could possibly be upset with that?

June 2, 2019

6:43 pm: Democrats can't impeach a Republican President for crimes committed by Democrats. The facts are "pouring" in. The Greatest Witch Hunt in American History! Congress, go back to work and help us at the Border, with Drug Prices and on Infrastructure.

June 4, 2019

1:09 pm: Just had a big victory in Federal Court over the Democrats in the House on the desperately needed Border Wall. A big step in the right direction. Wall is under construction!

7:04 pm: Can you imagine Cryin' Chuck Schumer saying out loud, for all to hear, that I am bluffing with respect to putting Tariffs on Mexico. What a Creep. He would rather have our Country fail with drugs & Immigration than give Republicans a win. But he gave Mexico bad advice, no bluff!

June 5, 2019

12:55 am: Plagiarism charge against Sleepy Joe Biden on his ridiculous Climate Change Plan is a big problem, but the Corrupt Media will save him. His other problem is that he is drawing flies, not people, to his Rallies. Nobody is showing up, I mean nobody. You can't win without people!

June 7, 2019

11:57 am: Nervous Nancy Pelosi is a disgrace to herself and her family for having made such a disgusting statement, especially since I was with foreign leaders overseas. There is no evidence for such a thing to have been said. Nervous Nancy & Dems are getting Zero work done in Congress...

and have no intention of doing anything other than going on a fishing expedition to see if they can find anything on me—both illegal & unprecedented in U.S. history. There was no Collusion—Investigate the Investigators! Go to work on Drug Price Reductions & Infrastructure!

June 9, 2019

5:50 pm: ...No Obstruction. The Dems were devastated—after all this time and money spent ($40,000,000), the Mueller Report was a disaster for them. But they want a Redo, or Do Over. They are even bringing in @CNN sleazebag attorney John Dean. Sorry, no Do Overs—Go back to work!

June 13, 2019

5:51 am: Unrelated to Russia, Russia, Russia (although the Radical Left doesn't use the name Russia anymore since the issuance of the Mueller Report), House Committee now plays the seldom used "Contempt" card on our great A.G. & Sec. of Commerce—this time on the Census. Dems play a...

...can to embarrass the Trump Administration (and Republicans), attack the Trump Administration. This is campaigning by the Dems."

Attorney David Bruno. So true! In the meantime they are getting NO work done on Drug Pricing, Infrastructure & many other things.

8:37 am: When Senator @MarkWarnerVA spoke at length, and in great detail, about extremely negative information on me, with a talented entertainer purporting to be a Russian Operative, did he immediately call the FBI? NO, in fact he didn't even tell the Senate Intelligence Committee of...

...which he is a member. When @RepAdamSchiff took calls from another person, also very successfully purporting to be a Russian Operative, did he call the FBI, or even think to call the FBI? NO! The fact is that the phony Witch Hunt is a giant scam where Democrats,...

...and other really bad people, SPIED ON MY CAMPAIGN! They even had an "insurance policy" just in case Crooked Hillary Clinton and the Democrats lost their race for the Presidency! This is the biggest & worst political scandal in the history of the United States of America. Sad!

June 18, 2019

8:58 pm: On no issue are Democrats more extreme—and more depraved—than when it comes to Border Security. The Democrat Agenda of open borders is morally reprehensible. It is the great betrayal of the American Middle Class and our Country as a whole! #Trump2020

9:04 pm: In the ultimate act of moral cowardice, not one Democrat Candidate for president—not a single one—has stood up to defend the incredible men and women of ICE and Border Patrol. They don't have the character, the virtue, or the spine! #Trump2020

June 19, 2019

9:20 am: DEMOCRAT CONGRESSIONAL HEARINGS ARE #RIGGED!

2:48 pm: So sad that the Democrats are putting wonderful Hope Hicks through hell, for 3 years now, after total exoneration by Robert Mueller & the Mueller Report. They were unhappy with result so they want a Do Over. Very unfair & costly to her. Will it ever end? Why aren't they...

...asking Hillary Clinton why she deleted and acid washed her Emails AFTER getting a subpoena from Congress? Anybody else would be in jail for that, yet the Dems refuse to even bring it up. Rigged House Committee

June 26, 2019

6:13 am: Democrats want Open Borders, which equals violent crime, drugs and human trafficking. They also want very high taxes, like 90%. Republicans want what's good for America—the exact opposite!

3:24 pm: The Democrats would save many lives if they would change our broken and very DANGEROUS Immigration Laws. It can be done instantly!

8:35 pm: BORING!

June 27, 2019

8:37 pm: All Democrats just raised their hands for giving millions of illegal aliens unlimited healthcare. How about taking care of American Citizens first!? That's the end of that race!

July 6, 2019

7:45 am: Joe Biden is a reclamation project. Some things are just not salvageable. China and other countries that ripped us off for years are begging for him. He deserted our military, our law enforcement and our healthcare. Added more debt than all other Presidents combined. Won't win!

8:03 am: Sleepy Joe Biden just admitted he worked with segregationists and separately, has already been very plain about the fact that he will be substantially raising everyone's taxes if he becomes president. Ridiculously, all Democrats want to substantially raise taxes!

July 9, 2019

8:36 pm: More and more the Radical Left is using Commerce to hurt their "Enemy." They put out the name of a store, brand or company, and ask their so-called followers not to do business there. They don't care who gets hurt, but also don't understand that two can play that game!

July 15, 2019

5:54 am: When will the Radical Left Congresswomen apologize to our Country, the people of Israel and even to the Office of the President, for the foul language they have used, and the terrible things they have said. So many people are angry at them & their horrible & disgusting actions!

6:42 am: If Democrats want to unite around the foul language & racist hatred spewed from the mouths and actions of these very unpopular & unrepresentative Congresswomen, it will be interesting to see how it plays out. I can tell you that they have made Israel feel abandoned by the U.S.

4:08 pm: We will never be a Socialist or Communist Country. IF YOU ARE NOT HAPPY HERE, YOU CAN LEAVE! It is your choice, and your choice alone. This is about love for America. Certain people HATE our Country...

...They are anti-Israel, pro Al-Qaeda, and comment on the 9/11 attack, "some people did something." Radical Left Democrats want Open Borders, which means drugs, crime, human trafficking, and much more...

...Detention facilities are not Concentration Camps! America has never been stronger than it is now—rebuilt Military, highest Stock Market EVER, lowest unemployment and more people working than ever before. Keep America Great!

4:26 pm: The Dems were trying to distance themselves from the four "progressives," but now they are forced to embrace them. That means they are endorsing Socialism, hate of Israel and the USA! Not good for the Democrats!

July 16, 2019

6:20 am: The Democrat Congresswomen have been spewing some of the most vile, hateful, and disgusting things ever said by a politician in the House or Senate, & yet they get a free pass and a big embrace from the Democrat Party. Horrible anti-Israel, anti-USA, pro-terrorist & public...

...shouting of the F...word, among many other terrible things, and the petrified Dems run for the hills. Why isn't the House voting to rebuke the filthy and hate laced things they have said? Because they are the Radical Left, and the Democrats are afraid to take them on. Sad!

7:17 am: Our Country is Free, Beautiful and Very Successful. If you hate our Country, or if you are not happy here, you can leave!

8:59 am: Those Tweets were NOT Racist. I don't have a Racist bone in my body! The so-called vote to be taken is a Democrat con game. Republicans should not show "weakness" and fall into their trap. This should be a vote on the filthy language, statements and lies told by the Democrat...

...Congresswomen, who I truly believe, based on their actions, hate our Country. Get a list of the HORRIBLE things they have said. Omar is polling at 8%, Cortez at 21%. Nancy Pelosi tried to push them away, but now they are forever wedded to the Democrat Party. See you in 2020!

July 17, 2019

6:18 am: "In America, if you hate our Country, you are free to leave. The simple fact of the matter is, the four Congresswomen think that America is wicked in its origins, they think that America is even more wicked now, that we are all racist and evil. They're entitled to their...

...opinion, they're Americans. Now I'm entitled to my opinion, & I just think they're left wing cranks. They're the reason there are directions on a shampoo bottle, & we should ignore them. The "squad" has moved the Democrat Party substantially LEFT, and...

...they are destroying the Democrat Party. I'm appalled that so many of our Presidential candidates are falling all over themselves to try to agree with the four horsewomen of the apocalypse. I'm entitled to say that they're Wack Jobs." Louisiana Senator John Kennedy

5:24 pm: The United States House of Representatives has just overwhelmingly voted to kill the Resolution on Impeachment, 332-95-1. This is perhaps the most ridiculous and time consuming project I have ever had to work on. Impeachment of your President, who has led the...

...Greatest Economic BOOM in the history of our Country, the best job numbers, biggest tax reduction, rebuilt military and much more, is now OVER. This should never be allowed to happen to another President of the United States again!

July 19, 2019

7:16 am: It is amazing how the Fake News Media became "crazed" over the chant "send he back" by a packed Arena (a record) crowd in the Great State of North Carolina, but is totally calm & accepting of the most vile and disgusting statements made by the three Radical Left Congresswomen...

...Mainstream Media, which has lost all credibility, has either officially or unofficially become a part of the Radical Left Democrat Party. It is a sick partnership, so pathetic to watch! They even covered a tiny staged crowd as they greeted Foul Mouthed Omar in Minnesota, a...

...State which I will win in #2020 because they can't stand her and her hatred of our Country, and they appreciate all that I have done for them (opening up mining and MUCH more) which has led to the best employment & economic year in Minnesota's long and beautiful history!

July 21, 2019

7:07 am: I don't believe the four Congresswomen are capable of loving our Country. They should apologize to America (and Israel) for the horrible (hateful) things they have said. They are destroying the

81

Democrat Party, but are weak & insecure people who can never destroy our great Nation!

July 22, 2019

9:48 am: The "Squad" is a very Racist group of troublemakers who are young, inexperienced, and not very smart. They are pulling the once great Democrat Party far left, and were against humanitarian aid at the Border...And are now against ICE and Homeland Security. So bad for our Country!

4:44 pm: I am pleased to announce that a deal has been struck with Senate Majority Leader Mitch McConnell, Senate Minority Leader Chuck Schumer, Speaker of the House Nancy Pelosi, and House Minority Leader Kevin McCarthy—on a two-year Budget and Debt Ceiling, with no poison pills...

...This was a real compromise in order to give another big victory to our Great Military and Vets!

July 24, 2019

5:50 am: So Democrats and others can illegally fabricate a crime, try pinning it on a very innocent President, and when he fights back against this illegal and treasonous attack on our Country, they call It Obstruction? Wrong! Why didn't Robert Mueller investigate the investigators?

12:04 pm: I would like to thank the Democrats for holding this morning's hearing. Now, after 3 hours, Robert Mueller has to subject himself to #ShiftySchiff—an Embarrassment to our Country!

4:33 pm: Even Michael Moore agrees that the Dems and Mueller blew it!

5:22 pm: The Democrats lost so BIG today. Their Party is in shambles right now...

July 27, 2019

6:14 am: Rep, Elijah Cummings has been a brutal bully, shouting and screaming at the great men & women of Border Patrol about conditions at the Southern Border, when actually his Baltimore district is FAR WORSE and more dangerous. His district is considered the Worst in the USA…

6:24 am: Why is so much money sent to the Elijah Cummings district when it is considered the worst run and most dangerous anywhere in the United States. No human being would want to live there. Where is all this money going? How much is stolen? Investigate this corrupt mess immediately!

2:55 pm: Consideration is being given to declaring ANTIFA, the gutless Radical Left Wack Jobs who go around hitting (only non-fighters) people over the heads with baseball bats, a major Organization of Terror (along with MS-13 & others). Would make it easier for police to do their job!

4:35 pm: Elijah Cummings spends all of his time trying to hurt innocent people through "Oversight." He does NOTHING for his very poor, very dangerous and very badly run district! Take a look… #BlacksForTrump2020 https://t.co/seNVESZUht

4:55 pm: We gave Nadler and his Trump hating Dems the complete Mueller Report (we didn't have to), and even Mueller himself, but now that both were a total BUST, they say it wasn't good enough. Nothing will ever be good enough for them. Witch Hunt!

5:15 pm: NO COLLUSION, NO OBSTRUCTION, TOTAL EXONERATION. DEMOCRAT WITCH HUNT!

July 28, 2019

6:28 am: Someone please explain to Nancy Pelosi, who was recently called racist by those in her own party, that there is nothing wrong with bringing out the very obvious fact that Congressman Elijah Cummings has done a very poor job for his district and the City of Baltimore. Just take…

…a look, the facts speak far louder than words! The Democrats always play the Race Card, when in fact they have done so little for our Nation's great African American people. Now, lowest unemployment in U.S. history, and only getting better. Elijah Cummings has failed badly!

6:39 am: Speaking of failing badly, has anyone seen what is happening to Nancy Pelosi's district in San Francisco. It is not even recognizeable lately. Something must be done before it is too late. The Dems should stop wasting time on the Witch Hunt Hoax and start focusing on our Country!

1:35 pm: There is nothing racist in stating plainly what most people already know, that Elijah Cummings has done a terrible job for the people of his district, and of Baltimore itself. Dems always play the race card when they are unable to win with facts. Shame!

2:18 pm: If racist Elijah Cummings would focus more of his energy on helping the good people of his district, and Baltimore itself, perhaps progress could be made in fixing the mess that he has helped to create over many years of incompetent leadership. His radical "oversight" is a joke!

July 29, 2019

5:30 am: I have known Al for 25 years. Went to fights with him & Don King, always got along well. He "loved Trump!" He would ask me for favors often. Al is a con man, a troublemaker, always looking for a score. Just doing his thing. Must have intimidated Comcast/NBC. Hates Whites & Cops!

6:04 am: If the Democrats are going to defend the Radical Left "Squad" and King Elijah's Baltimore Fail, it will be a long road to 2020. The good news for the Dems is that they have the Fake News Media in their pocket!

6:26 am: Al Sharpton would always ask me to go to his events. He would say, "it's a personal favor to me." Seldom, but sometimes, I would go. It was fine. He came to my office in T.T. during the presidential campaign to apologize for the way he was talking about me. Just a conman at work!

7:46 am: Crazy Bernie Sanders recently equated the City of Baltimore to a THIRD WORLD COUNTRY! Based on that statement,

I assume that Bernie must now be labeled a Racist, just as a Republican would if he used that term and standard! The fact is, Baltimore can be brought back, maybe…

July 30, 2019

8:55 am: Heading to Jamestown, Virginia. Word is the Democrats will make it as uncomfortable as possible, but that's ok because today is not about them!

11:23 am: Great reception in Jamestown by both REPUBLICANS & DEMOCRATS. Respect for our Country's incredible Heritage. Thank you!

July 31, 2019

4:59 pm: The Radical Left Dems went after me for using the words "drug-infested" concerning Baltimore. Take a look at Elijah C. https://t.co/E08ngbcw3d

6:06 pm: Very low ratings for the Democratic Debate last night— they're desperate for Trump!

11:05 pm: The people on the stage tonight, and last, were not those that will either Make America Great Again or Keep America Great! Our Country now is breaking records in almost every category, from Stock Market to Military to Unemployment. We have prosperity & success like never before.

August 2, 2019

6:58 am: Really bad news! The Baltimore house of Elijah Cummings was robbed. Too bad!

August 6, 2019

10:57 pm: Beto (phony name to indicate Hispanic heritage) O'Rourke, who is embarrassed by my last visit to the Great State of Texas, where I trounced him, and is now even more embarrassed by polling at 1%

in the Democrat Primary, should respect the victims & law enforcement—& be quiet!

August 7, 2019

2:01 pm: Watching Sleepy Joe Biden making a speech. Sooo Boring! The LameStream Media will die in the ratings and clicks with this guy. It will be over for them, not to mention the fact that our Country will do poorly with him. It will be one big crash, but at least China will be happy!

7:23 pm: I don't know who Joaquin Castro is other than the lesser brother of a failed presidential candidate (1%) who makes a fool of himself every time he opens his mouth. Joaquin is not the man that his brother is, but his brother, according to most, is not much. Keep fighting Joaquin!

7:48 pm: The Dems new weapon is actually their old weapon, one which they never cease to use when they are down, or run out of facts, RACISM! They are truly disgusting! They even used it on Nancy Pelosi. I will be putting out a list of all people who have been so (ridiculously) accused!

August 10, 2019

5:44 pm: Joe Biden just said, "We believe in facts, not truth." Does anybody really believe he is mentally fit to be president? We are "playing" in a very big and complicated world. Joe doesn't have a clue!

August 13, 2019

9:04 am: Would Chris Cuomo be given a Red Flag for his recent rant? Filthy language and a total loss of control. He shouldn't be allowed to have any weapon. He's nuts!

August 15, 2019

11:38 am: Representatives Omar and Tlaib are the face of the Democrat Party, and they HATE Israel!

8:57 am: It would show great weakness if Israel allowed Rep. Omar and Rep. Tlaib to visit. They hate Israel & all Jewish people, & there is nothing that can be said or done to change their minds. Minnesota and Michigan will have a hard time putting them back in office. They are a disgrace!

August 16, 2019

5:26 pm: Israel was very respectful & nice to Rep. Rashida Tlaib, allowing her permission to visit her "grandmother." As soon as she was granted permission, she grandstanded & loudly proclaimed she would not visit Israel. Could this possibly have been a setup? Israel acted appropriately!

5:37 pm: Rep. Tlaib wrote a letter to Israeli officials desperately wanting to visit her grandmother. Permission was quickly granted, whereupon Tlaib obnoxiously turned the approval down, a complete setup. The only real winner here is Tlaib's grandmother. She doesn't have to see her now!

5:43 pm: Like it or not, Tlaib and Omar are fast becoming the face of the Democrat Party. Cortez (AOC) is fuming, not happy about this!

August 17, 2019

9:04 am: Major consideration is being given to naming ANTIFA an "ORGANIZATION OF TERROR." Portland is being watched very closely. Hopefully the Mayor will be able to properly do his job!

August 18, 2019

5:03 pm: House Democrats want to take action against Israel because it is fighting back against two (maybe four) people that have said unthinkably bad things about it & the Israeli people. Dems have such disdain for Israel! What happened? AOC Plus 4 is the new face of the Democrat Party!

August 20, 2019

10:22 am: Sorry, I don't buy Rep. Tlaib's tears. I have watched her violence, craziness and, most importantly, WORDS, for far too long. Now tears? She hates Israel and all Jewish people. She is an anti-Semite. She and her 3 friends are the new face of the Democrat Party. Live with it!

August 21, 2019

6:52 am: Rep Tlaib wants to cut off aid to Israel. This is the new face the of Democrat Party? Read the AOC PLUS 3 statements on their hatred of Jews and Israel. Check out Rep. Omar (the great people of Minnesota won't stand for this).

August 27, 2019

9:40 am: No bedbugs at Doral. The Radical Left Democrats, upon hearing that the perfectly located (for the next G-7) Doral National MIAMI was under consideration for the next G-7, spread that false and nasty rumor. Not nice!

September 15, 2019

7:45 am: Now the Radical Left Democrats and their Partner, the LameStream Media, are after Brett Kavanaugh again, talking loudly of their favorite word, impeachment. He is an innocent man who has been treated HORRIBLY. Such lies about him. They want to scare him into turning Liberal!

September 18, 2019

6:55 am: Dummy Beto made it much harder to make a deal. Convinced many that Dems just want to take your guns away. Will continue forward!

7:14 am: Ilhan Omar, a member of AOC Plus 3, will win us the Great State of Minnesota. The new face of the Democrat Party!

September 21, 2019

9:02 am: Now that the Democrats and the Fake News Media have gone "bust" on every other of their Witch Hunt schemes, they are trying to start one just as ridiculous as the others, call it the Ukraine Witch Hunt, while at the same time trying to protect Sleepy Joe Biden. Will fail again!

September 24, 2019

4:08 pm: Such an important day at the United Nations, so much work and so much success, and the Democrats purposely had to ruin and demean it with more breaking news Witch Hunt garbage. So bad for our Country!

4:11 pm: Pelosi, Nadler, Schiff and, of course, Maxine Waters! Can you believe this?

4:14 pm: They never even saw the transcript of the call. A total Witch Hunt!

4:17 pm: PRESIDENTIAL HARASSMENT!

September 25, 2019

8:17 am: Will the Democrats apologize after seeing what was said on the call with the Ukrainian President? They should, a perfect call—got them by surprise!

1:13 pm: Wow! "Ukraine Whistleblower's lead attorney donated to Biden." @FreeBeacon

3:17 pm: I have informed @GOPLeader Kevin McCarthy and all Republicans in the House that I fully support transparency on so-called whistleblower information but also insist on transparency from Joe Biden and his son Hunter, on the millions of dollars that have been quickly and easily...

taken out of Ukraine and China. Additionally, I demand transparency from Democrats that went to Ukraine and attempted to force the new President to do things that they wanted under the form of political threat.

September 26, 2019

7:41 am: THE DEMOCRATS ARE TRYING TO DESTROY THE REPUBLICAN PARTY AND ALL THAT IT STANDS FOR. STICK TOGETHER, PLAY THEIR GAME, AND FIGHT HARD REPUBLICANS. OUR COUNTRY IS AT STAKE!

1:13 pm: Liddle' Adam Schiff, who has worked unsuccessfully for 3 years to hurt the Republican Party and President, has just said that the Whistleblower, even though he or she only had second hand information, "is credible." How can that be with zero info and a known bias. Democrat Scam!

7:29 pm: Rep. Adam Schiff fraudulently read to Congress, with millions of people watching, a version of my conversation with the President of Ukraine that doesn't exist. He was supposedly reading the exact transcribed version of the call, but he completely changed the words to make it…

…sound horrible, and me sound guilty. HE WAS DESPERATE AND HE GOT CAUGHT. Adam Schiff therefore lied to Congress and attempted to defraud the American Public. He has been doing this for two years. I am calling for him to immediately resign from Congress based on this fraud!

September 27, 2019

8:29 am: Rep. Adam Schiff totally made up my conversation with Ukraine President and read it to Congress and Millions. He must resign and be investigated. He has been doing this for two years. He is a sick man!

8:32 am: The Democrats are now to be known as the DO NOTHING PARTY!

September 28, 2019

7:16 am: Can you imagine if these Do Nothing Democrat Savages, people like Nadler, Schiff, AOC Plus 3, and many more, had a

Republican Party who would have done to Obama what the Do Nothings are doing to me. Oh well, maybe next time!

4:14 pm: They are trying to stop ME, because I am fighting for YOU!

September 29, 2019

6:07 pm: These Radical Left, Do Nothing Democrats, are doing great harm to our Country. They are lying & cheating like never before in our Country's history in order to destabilize the United States of America & it's upcoming 2020 Election. They & the Fake News Media are Dangerous & Bad!

October 1, 2019

10:00 am: Why isn't Congressman Adam Schiff being brought up on charges for fraudulently making up a statement and reading it to Congress as if this statement, which was very dishonest and bad for me, was directly made by the President of the United States? This should never be allowed!

October 2, 2019

9:16 am: Congressman Adam Schiff should resign for the Crime of, after reading a transcript of my conversation with the President of Ukraine (it was perfect), fraudulently fabricating a statement of the President of the United States and reading it to Congress, as though mine! He is sick!

9:27 am: #DONOTHINGDEMS

10:39 am: Adam Schiff should only be so lucky to have the brains, honor and strength of Secretary of State Mike Pompeo. For a lowlife like Schiff, who completely fabricated my words and read them to Congress as though they were said by me, to demean a First in Class at West Point, is SAD!

10:48 am: The Do Nothing Democrats should be focused on building up our Country, not wasting everyone's time and energy on

BULLSHIT, which is what they have been doing ever since I got overwhelmingly elected in 2016, 223-306. Get a better candidate this time, you'll need it!

6:41 pm: DEMOCRATS WANT TO STEAL THE ELECTION! #KAG2020

October 3, 2019

6:36 am: Schiff is a lying disaster for our Country. He should resign!

7:09 am: Schiff is a lowlife who should resign (at least!).

8:16 pm: Another big loss for the Do Nothing Dems!

8:27 pm: AOC is a Wack Job!

9:20 pm: Nancy Pelosi today, on @GMA, actually said that Adam Schiffty Schiff didn't fabricate my words in a major speech before Congress. She either had no idea what she was saying, in other words lost it, or she lied. Even Clinton lover @GStephanopoulos strongly called her out. Sue her?

October 4, 2019

5:15 pm: LYIN' SHIFTY SCHIFF!

10:22 pm: "Pelosi Blatantly Lies During @GMA Interview About Schiff's Reading of Ukraine Transcript"

11:11 pm: SHIFTY SCHIFF DUPED BY RUSSIAN PRANKSTERS! https://t.co/CpIL0b5FLW

October 5, 2019

1:33 pm: Not only are the Do Nothing Democrats interfering in the 2020 Election, but they are continuing to interfere in the 2016 Election. They must be stopped!

October 6, 2019

8:25 am: The Democrats are lucky that they don't have any Mitt Romney types. They may be lousy politicians, with really bad policies (Open Borders, Sanctuary Cities etc.), but they stick together!

9:58 am: It is INCREDIBLE to watch and read the Fake News and how they pull out all stops to protect Sleepy Joe Biden and his thrown out of the Military son, Hunter, who was handed $100,000 a month (Plus,Plus) from a Ukrainian based company, even though he had no experience in energy...

...and separately got 1.5 Billion Dollars from China despite no experience and for no apparent reason. There is NO WAY these can be legitimate transactions? As lawyers & others have stated, as President, I have an OBLIGATION to look into possible, or probable, CORRUPTION!

11:42 am: The Democrats are lucky that they don't have any Mitt Romney types. They may be lousy politicians, with really bad policies (Open Borders, Sanctuary Cities etc.), but they stick together!

...And by the way, I would LOVE running against 1% Joe Biden—I just don't think it's going to happen. Sleepy Joe won't get to the starting gate, & based on all of the money he & his family probably "extorted," Joe should hang it up. I wouldn't want him dealing with China & U!

11:56 am: #DONOTHINGDEMOCRATS

5:03 pm: Democrat lawyer is same for both Whistleblowers? All support Obama and Crooked Hillary. Witch Hunt!

9:27 pm: Nancy Pelosi knew of all of the many Shifty Adam Schiff lies and massive frauds perpetrated upon Congress and the American people, in the form of a fraudulent speech knowingly delivered as a ruthless con, and the illegal meetings with a highly partisan "Whistleblower" & lawyer...

...This makes Nervous Nancy every bit as guilty as Liddle' Adam Schiff for High Crimes and Misdemeanors, and even Treason. I guess that

93

means that they, along with all of those that evilly "Colluded" with them, must all be immediately Impeached!

October 7, 2019

9:20 am: The Radical Left Democrats have failed on all fronts, so now they are pushing local New York City and State Democrat prosecutors to go get President Trump. A thing like this has never happened to any President before. Not even close!

11:13 pm: Adam should be Impeached!

October 8, 2019

9:31 am: Someone please tell the Radical Left Mayor of Minneapolis that he can't price out Free Speech. Probably illegal! I stand strongly & proudly with the great Police Officers and Law Enforcement of Minneapolis and the Great State of Minnesota! See you Thursday Night!

11:06 am: Hasn't Adam Schiff been fully discredited by now? Do we have to continue listening to his lies?

October 9, 2019

6:10 am: The Whistleblower's lawyer is a big Democrat. The Whistleblower has ties to one of my DEMOCRAT OPPONENTS. Why does the ICIG allow this scam to continue?

6:14 am: He should be Impeached for Fraud! https://t.co/lu3xKFQaON

9:02 am: Adam Schiff is a disgrace to our Country!

12:55 pm: So pathetic to see Sleepy Joe Biden, who with his son, Hunter, and to the detriment of the American Taxpayer, has ripped off at least two countries for millions of dollars, calling for my impeachment—and I did nothing wrong. Joe's Failing Campaign gave him no other choice!

October 10, 2019

8:12 am: Where is Hunter Biden? He has disappeared while the Fake News protects his Crooked daddy!

8:24 am: Cryin Chuck told his favorite lie when he used his standard sound bite that I "slammed the table & walked out of the room. He had a temper tantrum." Because I knew he would say that, and after Nancy said no to proper Border Security, I politely said bye-bye and left, no slamming!

October 11, 2019

9:58 pm: WHERE'S HUNTER?

October 13, 2019

9:15 am: Where's Hunter? He has totally disappeared! Now looks like he has raided and scammed even more countries! Media is AWOL.

4:22 pm: The Democrats are going to lose a lot of House Seats because of their Fraudulent use of Impeachment. Schiff fabricated phone call, a crime. Democrat Senate Seats will also be put at risk, even some that were supposedly safe. Look at Louisiana last night, North Carolina last week!

October 14, 2019

5:39 am: Adam Schiff now doesn't seem to want the Whistleblower to testify. NO! Must testify to explain why he got my Ukraine conversation sooo wrong, not even close. Did Schiff tell him to do that? We must determine the Whistleblower's identity to determine WHY this was done to the USA.

…Democrat's game was foiled when we caught Schiff fraudulently making up my Ukraine conversation, when I released the exact conversation Transcript, and when Ukrainian President and the Foreign Minister said there was NO PRESSURE, very normal talk! A total Impeachment Scam!

5:54 am: Former Democrat Senator Harry Reid just stated that Donald Trump is very smart, much more popular than people think, is underestimated, and will be hard to beat in the 2020 Election. Thank you Harry, I agree!

11:18 am: Wow! Hunter Biden is being forced to leave a Chinese Company. Now watch the Fake News wrap their greasy and very protective arms around him. Only softball questions of him please!

October 15, 2019

8:40 am: Democrats are allowing no transparency at the Witch Hunt hearings. If Republicans ever did this they would be excoriated by the Fake News. Let the facts come out from the charade of people, most of whom I do not know, they are interviewing for 9 hours each, not selective leaks.

10:14 am: Hunter Biden was really bad on @GMA. Now Sleepy Joe has real problems! Reminds me of Crooked Hillary and her 33,000 deleted Emails, not recoverable!

October 16, 2019

6:10 am: You would think there is NO WAY that any of the Democrat Candidates that we witnessed last night could possibly become President of the United States. Now you see why they have no choice but to push a totally illegal & absurd Impeachment of one of the most successful Presidents!

5:29 pm: Nervous Nancy's unhinged meltdown! https://t.co/RDeUI7sfe7

5:42 pm: The Do Nothing Democrats, Pelosi and Schumer stormed out of the Cabinet Room!

8:14 pm: Hope all House Republicans, and honest House Democrats, will vote to CENSURE Rep. Adam Schiff tomorrow for his brazen and unlawful act of fabricating (making up) a totally phony conversation with the Ukraine President and U.S. President, me. Most have never seen such a thing!

October 17, 2019

7:54 am: My warmest condolences to the family and many friends of Congressman Elijah Cummings. I got to see first hand the strength, passion and wisdom of this highly respected political leader. His work and voice on so many fronts will be very hard, if not impossible, to replace!

10:13 am: Such a disgrace that the Do Nothing Democrats are doing just as their name suggests, Doing Nothing! USMCA anyone?

October 18, 2019

8:28 pm: Corrupt Congressman Adam Schiff is angry that Ambassadors that he thought would be good for his fraudulent Witch Hunt, are turning out to be good for me—some really good! He's got all meetings locked down, no transparency, only his illegal leaks. A very dishonest sleazebag!

9:16 pm: Pelosi and Impeachment—There have already been 3 Votes, and they've all failed miserably. Here's why there may not be a fourth—137 Democrats voted against on the last vote." @JasonChaffetz @seanhannity Many of those voting in favor will be beaten in 2020!

October 21, 2019

7:31 am: Censure (at least) Corrupt Adam Schiff! After what he got caught doing, any pol who does not so vote cannot be honest…are you listening Dems?

October 22, 2019

6:52 am: So some day, if a Democrat becomes President and the Republicans win the House, even by a tiny margin, they can impeach the President, without due process or fairness or any legal rights. All Republicans must remember what they are witnessing here—a lynching. But we will WIN!

October 25, 2019

7:15 am: So Congressman Tim Ryan of Ohio has finally dropped out of the race for President, registering ZERO in the polls & unable to even qualify for the debate stage. See Tim, it's not so easy out there if you don't know what you're doing. He wasn't effective for USA workers, just talk!

4:10 pm: I appreciate the support of Senator @LindseyGraham, @SenateMajLdr Mitch McConnell, and their Great Senate Republican colleagues, on the resolution condemning the Do Nothing Democrats for their Witch Hunt Impeachment inquiry, behind closed doors…

…in the basement of the United States Capitol! They cannot win at the ballot box. Their sham for the past 3 years continues. The good news is that the American People get it, which will be proven once again on November 3, 2020!

6:30 pm: Democrats just announced that they no longer want the Whistleblower to testify. But everything was about the Whistleblower (they no longer want the second Whistleblower either), which they don't want because the account of my call bore NO RELATIONSHIP to the call itself…

…The entire Impeachment Scam was based on my perfect Ukrainian call, and the Whistleblowers account of that call, which turned out to be false (a fraud?). Once I released the actual call, their entire case fell apart. The Democrats must end this Scam now. Witch Hunt!

October 26, 2019

6:23 am: I can't believe that Nancy Pelosi's District in San Francisco is in such horrible shape that the City itself is in violation of many sanitary & environmental orders, causing it to owe the Federal Government billions of dollars—and all she works on is Impeachment…

6:29 am: …We should all work together to clean up these hazardous waste and homeless sites before the whole city rots away. Very bad and dangerous conditions, also severely impacting the Pacific Ocean and water supply. Pelosi must work on this mess and turn her District around!

7:18 am: Badly failing presidential candidate @KamalaHarris will not go to a very wonderful largely African American event today because yesterday I recieved a major award, at the same event, for being able to produce & sign into law major Criminal Justice Reform legislation, which will…

…greatly help the African American community (and all other communities), and which was unable to get done in past administrations despite a tremendous desire for it. This and best unemployment numbers EVER is more than Kamala will EVER be able to do for African Americans!

October 28, 2019

4:22 pm: Can you believe that Shifty Adam Schiff, the biggest leaker in D.C., and a corrupt politician, is upset that we didn't inform him before we raided and killed the #1 terrorist in the WORLD!? Wouldn't be surprised if the Do Nothing Democrats Impeach me over that! DRAIN THE SWAMP!!

10:58 pm: The only crimes in the Impeachment Hoax were committed by Shifty Adam Schiff, when he totally made up my phone conversation with the Ukrainian President and read it to Congress, together with numerous others on Shifty's side. Schiff should be Impeached, and worse!

October 29, 2019

10:14 am: Nervous Nancy Pelosi is doing everything possible to destroy the Republican Party. Our Polls show that it is going to be just the opposite. The Do Nothing Dems will lose many seats in 2020. They have a Death Wish, led by a corrupt politician, Adam Schiff!

October 31, 2019

5:44 pm: While the Do Nothing Democrats FAIL the American People, and continue the Impeachment Scam, my Administration will continue to deliver REAL RESULTS, as seen over the past month, below! https://t.co/dxjHusgiFX

7:48 pm: The home of Nancy Pelosi. I can't believe her voters can be happy with the job she and the Do Nothing Democrats are doing! San Francisco has really gone down hill. So sad! https://t.co/z0Tms6gkDy

9:08 am: Looks like Bernie Sanders is history. Sleepy Joe Biden is pulling ahead and think about it, I'm only here because of Sleepy Joe and the man who took him off the 1% trash heap, President O! China wants Sleepy Joe BADLY!

November 1, 2019

9:08 am: LOUISIANA! Extreme Democrat John Bel Edwards has sided with Nancy Pelosi and Chuck Schumer to support Sanctuary Cities, High Taxes, and Open Borders. He is crushing Louisiana's economy and your Second Amendment rights...

4:11 pm: I love New York, but New York can never be great again under the current leadership of Governor Andrew Cuomo (the brother of Fredo), or Mayor Bill DeBlasio. Cuomo has weaponized the prosecutors to do his dirty work (and to keep him out of jams), a reason some don't want to be...

...in New York, and another reason they are leaving. Taxes and energy costs are way too high, Upstate is being allowed to die as other nearby states frack & drill for Gold (oil) while reducing taxes & creating jobs by the thousands. NYC is getting dirty & unsafe again, as...

...our great police are being disrespected, even with water dumped on them, because a Mayor and Governor just don't "have their backs." New York's Finest must be cherished, respected and loved. Too many prople are leaving our special New York. Great leaders would work...

...with a President and Federal Government that wants our wonerful City and State to flourish and thrive. I Love New York!

4:51 pm: Oh no, Beto just dropped out of race for President despite him saying he was "born for this." I don't think so!

November 2, 2019

4:01 pm: Schiff will change the transcripts just like he fraudulently made up the phone call. He is a corrupt politician!

5:26 pm: Didn't he pick the Whistleblower?

November 3, 2019

9:11 am to 9:12 am: The Governor of California, @GavinNewsom, has done a terrible job of forest management. I told him from the first day we met that he must "clean" his forest floors regardless of what his bosses, the environmentalists, DEMAND of him. Must also do burns and cut fire stoppers...

...Every year, as the fire's rage & California burns, it is the same thing- and then he comes to the Federal Government for $$$ help. No more. Get your act together Governor. You don't see close to the level of burn in other states...But our teams are working well together in...

...putting these massive, and many, fires out. Great firefighters! Also, open up the ridiculously closed water lanes coming down from the North. Don't pour it out into the Pacific Ocean. Should be done immediately. California desperately needs water, and you can have it now!

11:41 am: The Angry Majority!

1:23 pm: The Democrats are Fixers, and they are working overtime to FIX the Impeachment "Process" in order to hurt the Republican Party and me. Nancy Pelosi should instead Fix her broken District and Corrupt Adam should clean up & manage the California forests which are always burning!

7:48 pm: If Shifty Adam Schiff, who is a corrupt politician who fraudulently made up what I said on the "call," is allowed to release transcripts of the Never Trumpers & others that are & were interviewed, he will change the words that were said to suit the Dems purposes. Republicans...

...should give their own transcripts of the interviews to contrast with Schiff's manipulated propaganda. House Republicans must have nothing to do with Shifty's rendition of those interviews. He is a proven liar, leaker & freak who is really the one who should be impeached!

November 5, 2019

9:05 am: So sad to see what is happening in New York where Governor Cuomo & Mayor DeBlasio are letting out 900 Criminals, some hardened & bad, onto the sidewalks of our rapidly declining, because of them, city. The Radical Left Dems are killing our cities. NYPD Commissioner is resigning!

November 7, 2019

9:51 am: "What did Hunter Biden do for the money?" @SenJohnKennedy A very good question. He and Sleepy Joe must testify!

November 9, 2019

1:52 pm: I recommend that Nervous Nancy Pelosi (who backed up Schiff's lie), Shifty Adam Schiff, Sleepy Joe Biden, the Whistleblower (who miraculously disappeared after I released the transcript of the call), the 2nd Whistleblower (who also disappeared), & the I.G., be part of the list!

November 10, 2019

1:58 pm: Corrupt politician Adam Schiff wants people from the White House to testify in his and Pelosi's disgraceful Witch Hunt, yet he will not allow a White House lawyer, nor will he allow ANY of our requested witnesses. This is a first in due process and Congressional history!

November 11, 2019

9:30 am: Shifty Adam Schiff will only release doctored transcripts. We haven't even seen the documents and are restricted from (get this) having a lawyer. Republicans should put out their own transcripts! Schiff must testify as to why he MADE UP a statement from me, and read it to all!

6:18 pm: Schiff is giving Republicans NO WITNESSES, NO LAW-YER & NO DUE PROCESS! It is a totally one sided Witch Hunt. This can't be making the Democrats look good. Such a farce!

6:24 pm: Just like Schiff fabricated my phone call, he will fabricate the transcripts that he is making and releasing!

November 12, 2019

10:41 am: A total Impeachment Scam by the Do Nothing Democrats!

November 15, 2019

8:48 am: The Impeachment Witch Hunt should be over with the statement made last night by the President and Foreign Minister of Ukraine. Nervous Nancy Pelosi, who should be home cleaning up the dangerous & disgusting Slum she is making of her District in San Francisco, where even the...

...filth pouring into the Pacific Ocean is rapidly becoming an environ-mental hazard, is getting NOTHING DONE. She is a Do Nothing Democrat as Speaker, and will hopefully not be in that position very long. Approve USMCA, which has been sitting on her desk for months!

November 17, 2019

9:58 am: Mr. Chairman, Joe Biden may be Sleepy and Very Slow, but he is not a "rabid dog." He is actually somewhat better than that, but I am the only one who can get you where you have to be. You should act quickly, get the deal done. See you soon!

11:56 am: The Do Nothing Dems are now doing even less—and soooo much work to be done!

2:47 pm: Schiff is a Corrupt Politician!

November 18, 2019

8:52 am: Our Crazy, Do Nothing (where's USMCA, infrastructure, lower drug pricing & much more?) Speaker of the House, Nervous

Nancy Pelosi, who is petrified by her Radical Left knowing she will soon be gone (they & Fake News Media are her BOSS), suggested on Sunday's DEFACE THE NATION...

...that I testify about the phony Impeachment Witch Hunt. She also said I could do it in writing. Even though I did nothing wrong, and don't like giving credibility to this No Due Process Hoax, I like the idea & will, in order to get Congress focused again, strongly consider it!

10:41 pm: The Do Nothing Democrats have disgraced our great Country!

November 19, 2019

12:15 am: Nancy Pelosi just stated that "it is dangerous to let the voters decide Trump's fate." @FoxNews In other words, she thinks I'm going to win and doesn't want to take a chance on letting the voters decide. Like Al Green, she wants to change our voting system. Wow, she's CRAZY!

November 20, 2019

8:29 am: Nancy Pelosi will go down as the least productive Speaker of the House in history. She is dominated by AOC Plus 3 and the Radical Left. Mexico and Canada, after waiting for 6 months to be approved, are ready to flee—and who can blame them? Too bad!

November 23, 2019

7:17 am: Adam Schiff will be compelled to testify should the Democrats decide, despite the fact that my presidential conversations were totally appropriate (perfect), to go forward with the Impeachment Hoax. Polls have now turned very strongly against Impeachment!

November 24, 2019

7:30 am: Nancy Pelosi, Adam Schiff, AOC and the rest of the Democrats are not getting important legislation done, hence, the Do

Nothing Democrats. USMCA, National Defense Authorization Act, Gun Safety, Prescription Drug Prices, & Infrastructure are dead in the water because of the Dems!

5:42 pm: Democrats going back to their Districts for Thanksgiving are getting absolutely hammered by their constituents over the phony Impeachment Scam. Republicans will have a great #2020 Election!

November 30, 2019

6:43 pm: Nancy Pelosi won't put it up for a vote. Has delayed it for 6 months. See you in #2020!

December 3, 2019

6:25 pm: Too bad. We will miss you Kamala!

December 5, 2019

11:49 am: Nancy Pelosi just had a nervous fit. She hates that we will soon have 182 great new judges and sooo much more. Stock Market and employment records. She says she "prays for the President." I don't believe her, not even close. Help the homeless in your district Nancy. USMCA?

December 8, 2019

5:52 pm: What he did is illegal. Schiff is a corrupt politician and a criminal!

December 10, 2019

10:07 am: Shifty Schiff, a totally corrupt politician, made up a horrible and fraudulent statement, read it to Congress, and said those words came from me. He got caught, was very embarrassed, yet nothing happened to him for committing this fraud. He'll eventually have to answer for this!

December 12, 2019

10:53 pm: Nancy Pelosi just got duped in an interview to admitting that she has been working on impeaching me for "two and a half years." In other words, she lied. This was the Radical Left, Do Nothing Democrats plan all along, long before the Ukraine phone call. Impeachment Hoax!

December 13, 2019

7:05 am: The Do Nothing Democrats have become the Party of lies and deception! The Republicans are the Party of the American Dream!

December 14, 2019

8:07 am: After watching the disgraceful way that a wonderful man, @ BrettKavanaugh, was treated by the Democrats, and now seeing first hand how these same Radical Left, Do Nothing Dems are treating the whole Impeachment Hoax, I understand why so many Dems are voting Republican!

December 15, 2019

12:26 am: Thank you for your honesty Jeff. All of the Democrats know you are right, but unlike you, they don't have the "guts" to say so!

12:40 am: Wow, that would be big. Always heard Jeff is very smart!

5:11 pm: Because Nancy's teeth were falling out of her mouth, and she didn't have time to think!

5:28 pm: Congressional Do Nothing Democrats are being absolutely decimated in their districts on the subject of the Impeachment Hoax. People that voted for them are literally screaming in their faces. Crazy Nancy is finding defending Shifty Schiff harder than she thought! #2020Election

December 17, 2019

12:44 am: Congressman Jeff Van Drew is very popular in our great and very united Republican Party. It was a tribute to him that he was able to win his heavily Republican district as a Democrat. People like that are not easily replaceable!

December 18, 2019

10:49 am: Will go down in history as worst Speaker. Already thrown out once!

12:44 pm: SUCH ATROCIOUS LIES BY THE RADICAL LEFT, DO NOTHING DEMOCRATS. THIS IS AN ASSAULT ON AMERICA, AND AN ASSAULT ON THE REPUBLICAN PARTY!!!!

December 19, 2019

11:07 am: Pelosi feels her phony impeachment HOAX is so pathetic she is afraid to present it to the Senate, which can set a date and put this whole SCAM into default if they refuse to show up! The Do Nothings are so bad for our Country!

7:16 pm: So after the Democrats gave me no Due Process in the House, no lawyers, no witnesses, no nothing, they now want to tell the Senate how to run their trial. Actually, they have zero proof of anything, they will never even show up. They want out. I want an immediate trial!

8:56 pm: The reason the Democrats don't want to submit the Articles of Impeachment to the Senate is that they don't want corrupt politician Adam Shifty Schiff to testify under oath, nor do they want the Whistleblower, the missing second Whistleblower, the informer, the Bidens, to testify!

December 20, 2019

4:04 pm: The Democrat Party's Witch Hunt and CRAZY EXTREME policies are chasing common sense people out of the Dem Party. That's why Jeff Van Drew (@CongressmanJVD) voted NO on the Impeachment Hoax. Jeff will be joining our growing Republican Party...

4:28 pm: Nancy Pelosi is looking for a Quid Pro Quo with the Senate. Why aren't we Impeaching her?

11:50 pm: The great Democrat disgrace. But we are winning!

December 22, 2019

3:18 pm: Crazy Nancy wants to dictate terms on the Impeachment Hoax to the Republican Majority Senate, but striped away all Due Process, no lawyers or witnesses, on the Democrat Majority House. The Dems just wish it would all end. Their case is dead, their poll numbers are horrendous!

5:14 pm: The Democrats and Crooked Hillary paid for & provided a Fake Dossier, with phony information gotten from foreign sources, pushed it to the corrupt media & Dirty Cops, & have now been caught. They spied on my campaign, then tried to cover it up—Just Like Watergate, but bigger!

December 23, 2019

8:38 am: Pelosi gives us the most unfair trial in the history of the U.S. Congress, and now she is crying for fairness in the Senate, and breaking all rules while doing so. She lost Congress once, she will do it again!

December 26, 2019

7:18 am: The Radical Left, Do Nothing Democrats said they wanted to RUSH everything through to the Senate because "President Trump is a threat to National Security" (they are vicious, will say anything!), but now they don't want to go fast anymore, they want to go very slowly. Liars!

7:59 am: Nancy Pelosi's District in California has rapidly become one of the worst anywhere in the U.S. when it come to the homeless &

crime. It has gotten so bad, so fast—she has lost total control and, along with her equally incompetent governor, Gavin Newsom, it is a very sad sight!

6:53 pm: California leads the nation, by far, in both the number of homeless people, and the percentage increase in the homeless population—two terrible stats. Crazy Nancy should focus on that in her very down district, and helping her incompetent governor with the big homeless problem!

December 27, 2019

3:43 pm: So interesting to see Nancy Pelosi demanding fairness from @senatemajldr McConnell when she presided over the most unfair hearing in the history of the United States Congress!

9:31 pm: Wow Crazy Nancy, what's going on? This is big stuff! https://t.co/hoHSERKgh9

9:57 pm: What kind of an animal is this? https://t.co/oQSExXIxDV

10:54 pm: A true Democrat Party leader! https://t.co/vQZSEG0vpg

11:28 pm: Nancy, this just doesn't seem right! https://t.co/0fmQj79DLX

December 28, 2019

8:33 am: California and New York must do something about their TREMENDOUS Homeless problems. They are setting records! If their Governors can't handle the situation, which they should be able to do very easily, they must call and "politely" ask for help. Would be so easy with competence!

3:45 pm: Crazy Nancy Pelosi should spend more time in her her decaying city and less time on the Impeachment Hoax!

4:14 pm: So sad to see that New York City and State are falling apart. All they want to do is investigate to make me hate them even more than I should. Governor Cuomo has lost control, and lost his mind. Very bad for the homeless and all!

December 29, 2019

9:55 am: Crazy Nancy Pelosi should spend more time in her decaying city and less time on the Impeachment Hoax!

December 31, 2019

6:16 am: The Democrats will do anything to avoid a trial in the Senate in order to protect Sleepy Joe Biden, and expose the millions and millions of dollars that "Where's" Hunter, & possibly Joe, were paid by companies and countries for doing NOTHING. Joe wants no part of this mess!

12:42 pm: Remember when Pelosi was screaming that President Trump is a danger to our nation and we must move quickly. They didn't get one Republican House vote, and lost 3 Dems. They produced no case so now she doesn't want to go to the Senate. She's all lies. Most overrated person I know!

6:19 pm: Get this straightened out, Governor @GavinNewsom

Republicans—2017 News Quotes

Response to a question from David Muir of ABC News, January 26, 2017.
Source: https://www.telegraph.co.uk/news/2017/01/26/
full-transcript-president-donald-trumps-interview-abc-news/

"It's going to be—What my plan is, is that I want to take care of every-body. I'm not going to leave the lower 20% that can't afford insurance. Just so you understand, people talk about Obamacare. And I told the Republicans this, the best thing we could do is nothing for two years, let it explode. And then we'll go in and we'll do a new plan and, and the Democrats will vote for it. Believe me.

"Because this year you'll have 150% increases. Last year in Arizona 116% increase, Minnesota 60 some-odd percent increase. And I told them, except for one problem, I want to get it fixed. The best thing I could do as the leader of this country. But as wanting to get something approved with support of the Democrats, if I didn't do anything for two years, they'd be begging me to do something. But I don't want to do that. So just so you unders—Obamacare is a disaster.

"It's too expensive. It's horrible healthcare. It doesn't cover what you have to cover. It's a disaster. You know it and I know it. And I said to the Republican folks, and they're terrific folks, Mitch [McConnell][8] and Paul Ryan[9], I said, 'Look, if you go fast, and I'm okay in doing

---

8   Mitch McConnell, R-Kentucky, is the Senate Majority Leader.

9   At the time of the interview, Paul Ryan (R-Wisconsin) was the Speaker of the
     U.S. House of Representatives.

it because it's the right thing to do. We want to get good coverage at much less cost.' I said, 'If you go fast, we then own Obamacare. They're going to put it on us. And Obamacare is a disaster waiting to explode. If you sit back and let it explode, it's going to be much easier.' That's the thing to do. But the right thing to do is to get something done now."

Response to a question from Tucker Carlson of FOX News, March 15, 2017.
Source: https://www.youtube.com/watch?v=RYGH6ejacNO

"I think he's [Paul Ryan[10] is] on board with the American people. I do believe that strongly. I think he is on board with my presidency. I think he wants to make it very successful. I like him. We have had our run-ins, as you probably have heard, initially. But I think he is very much on what he wants to do the right thing. That I believe 100%.

"We're going to take care of the people and by the way, we're not going to take care of the people. I am not signing anything. I'm not going to be doing it. Just so you understand. I am an—In a little way, I'm an arbitrator.

"We have the conservatives, we have the moral liberal side of the Republican Party, we have the left, we have the right. Within the Republicans themselves, we have a lot of fighting going on.

"We have no Democrats. Again, no matter what we do, we will never get a Democrat. Maybe we'll get one along the way."

Remarks on healthcare vote in the House of Representatives, May 4, 2017.
Source: https://www.whitehouse.gov/briefings-statements/
remarks-president-trump-healthcare-vote-house-representatives/

"We just have developed a bond. This has really brought the Republican Party together, as much as we've come up with a really incredible healthcare plan. This has brought the Republican Party together. We're going to get this finished, and then we're going—As you know we put our tax plan in, it's a massive tax cut, the biggest tax cut in the

---

10   At the time of the interview, Paul Ryan (R-Wisconsin) was the Speaker of the U.S. House of Representatives.

history of our country. I used to say the biggest since [former U.S. President] Ronald Reagan. Now, it's bigger than that. Also, pure tax reform. So we're going to get that done next."

Remarks on healthcare vote in the House of Representatives, May 4, 2017.
Source: https://www.whitehouse.gov/briefings-statements/
remarks-president-trump-healthcare-vote-house-representatives/

"So, I just want to introduce somebody to say a few words who really has been I think treated very unfairly, but it no longer matters because we won and we're going to finish it off. And we're going to go on with a lot of other things, and we are going to have a tremendous four years and maybe, even more importantly, we're going to have a tremendous eight years. But we're going to start off with just a great first year.

"And, Paul Ryan[11], come up and say a few words. Congratulations on a job well done."

Response to a question from Laura Ingraham of FOX News, November 2, 2017.
Source: https://www.youtube.com/watch?v=yTdDH-o_ICM

"I don't think any Republican would vote for anything having to do with leaving chain migration. Chain migration is a disaster for this country, and it's horrible."

---

11   At the time of President Trump's remarks, Paul Ryan (R-Wisconsin) was the Speaker of the U.S. House of Representatives.

Republicans—2017 Tweets

January 29. 2017

4:45 pm to 4:49 pm: The joint statement of former presidential candidates John McCain & Lindsey Graham is wrong—they are sadly weak on immigration. The two...

...Senators should focus their energies on ISIS, illegal immigration and border security instead of always looking to start World War III.

February 9, 2017

8:26 am to 8:52 am: Sen. McCain should not be talking about the success or failure of a mission to the media. Only emboldens the enemy! He's been losing so...

...long he doesn't know how to win anymore, just look at the mess our country is in—bogged down in conflict all over the place. Our hero...

...Ryan died on a winning mission (according to General Mattis), not a "failure." Time for the U.S. to get smart and start winning again!

February 21, 2017

6:23 pm: The so-called angry crowds in home districts of some Republicans are actually, in numerous cases, planned out by liberal activists. Sad!

February 27, 2017

4:48 pm: GOP now viewed more favorably than Dems, in Trump era (per NBC/WSJ poll)

March 27, 2017

8:41 pm: The Republican House Freedom Caucus was able to snatch defeat from the jaws of victory. After so many bad years they were ready for a win!

April 17, 2017

9:18 pm: With eleven Republican candidates running in Georgia (on Tuesday) for Congress, a runoff will be a win. Vote "R" for lower taxes & safety!

April 18, 2017

5:46 am: Republicans must get out today and VOTE in Georgia 6. Force runoff and easy win! Dem Ossoff will raise your taxes-very bad on crime & 2nd A.

3:38 pm: Just learned that Jon @Ossoff, who is running for Congress in Georgia, doesn't even live in the district. Republicans, get out and vote!

11:09 pm: Despite major outside money, FAKE media support and eleven Republican candidates, BIG "R" win with runoff in Georgia. Glad to be of help!

April 19, 2017

7:43 am: Dems failed in Kansas and are now failing in Georgia. Great job Karen Handel! It is now Hollywood vs. Georgia on June 20th.

May 2, 2017

8:01 am to 8:07 am: The reason for the plan negotiated between the Republicans and Democrats is that we need 60 votes in the Senate which are not there! We...

either elect more Republican Senators in 2018 or change the rules now to 51%. Our country needs a good "shutdown" in September to fix mess!

May 30, 2017

8:59 am: The U.S. Senate should switch to 51 votes, immediately, and get Healthcare and TAX CUTS approved, fast and easy. Dems would do it, no doubt!

May 31, 2017

8:05 am: Hopefully Republican Senators, good people all, can quickly get together and pass a new (repeal & replace) HEALTHCARE bill. Add saved $'s

June 14, 2017

7:48 am: Rep. Steve Scalise of Louisiana, a true friend and patriot, was badly injured but will fully recover. Our thoughts and prayers are with him.

June 30, 2017

5:37 am: If Republican Senators are unable to pass what they are working on now, they should immediately REPEAL, and then REPLACE at a later date!

July 18, 2017

8:15 am: With only a very small majority, the Republicans in the House & Senate need more victories next year since Dems totally obstruct, no votes!

June 20, 2017

5:02 am: KAREN HANDEL FOR CONGRESS. She will fight for lower taxes, great healthcare strong security-a hard worker who will never give up! VOTE TODAY

9:41 pm: Congratulations to Karen Handel on her big win in Georgia 6th. Fantastic job, we are all very proud of you!

10:12 pm: Ralph Norman ran a fantastic race to win in the Great State of South Carolina's 5th District. We are all honored by your success tonight!

10:48 pm: Well, the Special Elections are over and those that want to MAKE AMERICA GREAT AGAIN are 5 and O! All the Fake News, all the money spent = 0

July 23, 2017

3:14 pm: It's very sad that Republicans, even some that were carried over the line on my back, do very little to protect their President.

7:01 pm: If Republicans don't Repeal and Replace the disastrous ObamaCare, the repercussions will be far greater than any of them understand!

July 26, 2017

6:13 am: Senator @lisamurkowski of the Great State of Alaska really let the Republicans, and our country, down yesterday. Too bad!

July 29, 2017

6:20 am: Republican Senate must get rid of 60 vote NOW! It is killing the R Party, allows 8 Dems to control country. 200 Bills sit in Senate. A JOKE!

6:28 am: The very outdated filibuster rule must go. Budget reconciliation is killing R's in Senate. Mitch M, go to 51 Votes NOW and WIN. IT'S TIME!

6:32 am to 6:39 am: Republicans in the Senate will NEVER win if they don't go to a 51 vote majority NOW. They look like fools and are just wasting time...

...8 Dems totally control the U.S. Senate. Many great Republican bills will never pass, like Kate's Law and complete Healthcare. Get smart!

3:36 pm: Unless the Republican Senators are total quitters, Repeal & Replace is not dead! Demand another vote before voting on any other bill!

August 8, 2017

8:16 pm: Senator Luther Strange has done a great job representing the people of the Great State of Alabama. He has my complete and total endorsement!

August 16, 2017

5:18 am: Congratulation to Roy Moore and Luther Strange for being the final two and heading into a September runoff in Alabama. Exciting race

9:51 am: Wow, Senator Luther Strange picked up a lot of additional support since my endorsement. Now in September runoff. Strong on Wall & Crime!

August 17, 2017

5:19 pm to 5:24 pm: Publicity seeking Lindsey Graham falsely stated that I said there is moral equivalency between the KKK, neo-Nazis & white supremacists...

and people like Ms. Heyer. Such a disgusting lie. He just can't forget his election trouncing. The people of South Carolina will remember!

5:56 am: Great to see that Dr. Kelli Ward is running against Flake Jeff Flake, who is WEAK on borders, crime and a non-factor in Senate. He's toxic!

August 24, 2017

8:42 am: The only problem I have with Mitch McConnell is that, after hearing Repeal & Replace for 7 years, he failed! That should NEVER have happened!

August 25, 2017

7:25 am: Strange statement by Bob Corker considering that he is constantly asking me whether or not he should run again in '18. Tennessee not happy!

September 8, 2017

7:57 am: Republicans must start the Tax Reform/Tax Cut legislation ASAP. Don't wait until the end of September. Needed now more than ever. Hurry!

September 16, 2017

5:59 pm: Attorney General Bill Shuette will be a fantastic Governor for the great State of Michigan. I am bringing back your jobs and Bill will help!

September 20, 2017

7:42 pm: The NRA strongly endorses Luther Strange for Senator of Alabama. That means all gun owners should vote for Big Luther. He won't let you down!

September 21, 2017

5:23 pm: Senator Luther Strange has gone up a lot in the polls since I endorsed him a month ago. Now a close runoff. He will be great in D.C.

September 22, 2017

6:30 am: Will be in Alabama tonight. Luther Strange has gained mightily since my endorsement, but will be very close. He loves Alabama, and so do I!

September 26, 2017

5:55 pm: Luther Strange has been shooting up in the Alabama polls since my endorsement. Finish the job—vote today for "Big Luther."

9:17 pm: Congratulations to Roy Moore on his Republican Primary win in Alabama. Luther Strange started way back & ran a good race. Roy, WIN in Dec!

September 27, 2017

5:56 am: Spoke to Roy Moore of Alabama last night for the first time. Sounds like a really great guy who ran a fantastic race. He will help to #MAGA!

October 8, 2017

8:59 am to 9:13 am: Senator Bob Corker "begged" me to endorse him for re-election in Tennessee. I said "NO" and he dropped out (said he could not win without...

...,my endorsement). He also wanted to be Secretary of State, I said " NO THANKS.' He is also largely responsible for the horrendous Iran Deal!

...Hence, I would fully expect Corker to be a negative voice and stand in the way of our great agenda. Didn't have the guts to run!

3:51 pm: Bob Corker gave us the Iran Deal, & that's about it. We need HealthCare, we need Tax Cuts/Reform, we need people that can get the job done!

October 18, 2017

1:20 pm: It was an honor to welcome Republican and Democratic members of the Senate Finance Committee to the @WhiteHouse today. #TaxReform https://t.co/ge4Xic9fId

October 19, 2017

5:54 am: Republicans are going for the big Budget approval today, first step toward massive tax cuts. I think we have the votes, but who knows?

October 24, 2017

7:13 am to 7:20 am: Bob Corker, who helped President O give us the bad Iran Deal & couldn't get elected dog catcher in Tennessee, is now fighting Tax Cuts...

...Corker dropped out of the race in Tennesse when I refused to endorse him, and now is only negative on anything Trump. Look at his record!

8:30 am: Isn't it sad that lightweight Senator Bob Corker, who couldn't get re-elected in the Great State of Tennessee, will now fight Tax Cuts plus!

9:13 am to 9:20 am: Sen. Corker is the incompetent head of the Foreign Relations Committee, & look how poorly the U.S. has done. He doesn't have a clue as...

...the entire World WAS laughing and taking advantage of us. People like liddle' Bob Corker have set the U.S. way back. Now we move forward!

October 25, 2017

6:27 am: The reason Flake and Corker dropped out of the Senate race is very simple, they had zero chance of being elected. Now act so hurt & wounded!

7:33 am: Jeff Flake, with an 18% approval rating in Arizona, said "a lot of my colleagues have spoken out." Really, they just gave me a standing O!

October 26, 2017

9:11 am: Ed Gillespie will be a great Governor of Virginia. His opponent doesn't even show up to meetings/work, and will be VERY weak on crime!

9:30 am: Do not underestimate the UNITY within the Republican Party!

October 26, 2017

10:05 am: Big news—Budget just passed!

November 6, 2017

4:12 pm: The state of Virginia economy, under Democrat rule, has been terrible. If you vote Ed Gillespie tomorrow, it will come roaring back!

November 7, 2017

5:53 am: Ralph Northam will allow crime to be rampant in Virginia. He's weak on crime, weak on our GREAT VETS, Anti-Second Amendment…

…and has been horrible on Virginia economy. Vote @EdWGillespie today!

5:56 am: .@EdWGillespie will totally turn around the high crime and poor economic performance of VA. MS-13 and crime will be gone. Vote today, ASAP!

8:40 pm: Ed Gillespie worked hard but did not embrace me or what I stand for. Don't forget, Republicans won 4 out of 4 House seats, and with the economy doing record numbers, we will continue to win, even bigger than before!

November 19, 2017

6:22 pm: Sen. Jeff Flake(y), who is unelectable in the Great State of Arizona (quit race, anemic polls) was caught (purposely) on "mike" saying bad things about your favorite President. He'll be a NO on tax cuts because his political career anyway is "toast."

November 26, 2017

9:33 am: I endorsed Luther Strange in the Alabama Primary. He shot way up in the polls but it wasn't enough. Can't let Schumer/Pelosi win this race. Liberal Jones would be BAD!

December 12, 2017

9:09 am: The people of Alabama will do the right thing. Doug Jones is Pro-Abortion, weak on Crime, Military and Illegal Immigration, Bad for Gun Owners and Veterans and against the WALL. Jones is a Pelosi/Schumer Puppet. Roy Moore will always vote with us. VOTE ROY MOORE!

December 13, 2017

6:22 am: The reason I originally endorsed Luther Strange (and his numbers went up mightily), is that I said Roy Moore will not be able to win the General Election. I was right! Roy worked hard but the deck was stacked against him!

9:45 am: If last night's election proved anything, it proved that we need to put up GREAT Republican candidates to increase the razor thin margins in both the House and Senate.

December 18, 2017

6:23 am: Remember, Republicans are 5-0 in Congressional Races this year. The media refuses to mention this. I said Gillespie and Moore would lose (for very different reasons), and they did. I also predicted "I" would win. Republicans will do well in 2018, very well! @foxandfriends

Republicans—2018 News Quotes

Remarks before Marine One departure, January 5, 2018.
Source: https://www.whitehouse.gov/briefings-statements/
remarks-president-trump-marine-one-departure-5/

"So again, we're going to Camp David with a lot of the great Republican senators, and we're making America great again."

Response to a question from Bret Baier of FOX News, June 12, 2018.
Source: https://www.youtube.com/watch?v=zogD8bnGJu4

"I think it's a whole different ball game. I think the economy is so good. I think the tax cuts have been incredible, far greater than even I thought they would be. The regulation cuts have been great. I mean I've done more in 500 days than any president has ever done in their first 500 days. There's nobody close, and that's not—That's a lot of people saying that. People that would rather not say it are saying it. And I really think that we are going to do very good. Now, history is against me because history for whatever reason, you win the election and then you lose lots of seats. I think we are going to do very well; I really do. The economy is doing so well. We are doing so well as a nation. I think we are going to surprise people and if you look at the numbers and if you look at the kind of turnouts like Texas, how many people showed up to vote as an example, how many Republicans showed up to vote— People were very surprised."

Remarks at a rally in Tampa, Florida, July 31, 2018.
Source: https://www.tampabay.com/florida-politics/buzz/2018/08/01/
heres-a-full-transcript-of-president-trumps-speech-from-his-tampa-rally/

"If you want safety, if you want borders, if you want to have a country, then you need to go out and vote Republican. And very importantly, you need to go out and vote for Ron DeSantis for governor of Florida."

Remarks at a rally in Tampa, Florida, July 31, 2018.

Source: https://www.tampabay.com/florida-politics/buzz/2018/08/01/
heres-a-full-transcript-of-president-trumps-speech-from-his-tampa-rally/

"Instead of apologizing for America, we're standing up for America. We're standing up for the heroes who protect America and, yes, we are proudly standing up for our great National Anthem.

"With every promise we keep, every record we break, every factory we open, we are restoring American strength and American pride.

"But to continue this incredible moment of this incredible movement. And that's what we have, we have a movement. This may be, in fact it probably is, the greatest movement in the history of our country. Even they will say that.

"Even they will say that.

"But to keep it going, we need to elect more Republicans. We need more votes. And we need to elect Ron DeSantis as your governor. Got to do it.

"And I'm telling you, I know him well, he's a great, great guy. He is going to be an incredible governor; I have no doubt, I have no doubt. I don't do these endorsements easily."

Remarks at a rally in Tampa, Florida, July 31, 2018.

Source: https://www.tampabay.com/florida-politics/buzz/2018/08/01/
heres-a-full-transcript-of-president-trumps-speech-from-his-tampa-rally/

"Get your friends, get your colleagues, get your neighbors, and get out and vote in November. You've got to do it. Because, remember, we're going to win this primary, but don't take any chances. Nice lead, nice lead. Don't take any chances. And then about, give yourself about 10, 15 minutes of happiness, and then go back to work for November.

"Because we have to remember they're putting up—I know some of the candidates, these are people that don't care about stopping crime. These are people that don't care about people pouring into our country when they shouldn't be here.

"They don't care about stopping drugs from poisoning our youth and pouring over the border. They don't care.

"Your future governor cares. And your current governor cares, Rick Scott.

"Loyal citizens like you, incredible people from the great state of Florida helped build this country. And, together, we are taking back our country. We are returning power to where it belongs, the American people.

"This state was settled by pioneers and visionaries who explored the marshes and raised up cities right on the sea. This state was built by red-blooded American patriots who opened the force Naval Air Station at Pensacola and launched the first brave Americans soaring into the heavens. We stand on the shoulders of generations of proud Americans who knew how to work, knew how to fight, and knew how to win. Win.

"And you know, when you elect Ron DeSantis as your governor—Because you see it already, we're winning so much. Some people are getting a little tired of winning, right?

"Well, by then it will be another year and two years and three years, and you'll be insisting, 'Governor DeSantis, please see our President. It's too much winning. We can't, we can't stand it. The people of Florida, we can't stand it.'

"Because under previous administrations, we never won. We got used to never winning. And he's going to come to me, in Washington, in the Oval Office, the beautiful Oval Office, and he's going to say, 'Mr. President, the people of Florida are just downright tired of winning. They can't stand it.

"'It's just too much, Mr. President. The economy is too good. The jobs are too strong. We're doing too well, is there anything you can do?' I'm going to say, 'Ron, I don't care what you say, we're going to keep on winning.'

"We're going to keep on winning. We're going to win so much, and the people of Florida actually love, don't they? They love it.

"Remember what I said right at the beginning, we're respected again. And that man [Ron DeSantis] is respected and always has been.

"We will never give up. We will never give in. We will never, ever back down, and we will never, ever surrender.

"Because we are Americans and our hearts bleed red, white, and blue.

"We are one people. We are one family. And we are one glorious nation under God.

"And together we will make America wealthy again. We will make America strong again. We will make America safe again. And we will make America great again!"

Remarks at White House dinner with evangelical leaders, August 27, 2018.
Source: https://www.whitehouse.gov/briefings-statements/
remarks-president-trump-dinner-evangelical-leaders/

"Also, our hearts and prayers are going to the family of Senator John McCain. There's going to be a lot of activity over the next number of days. And we very much appreciate everything that Senator McCain has done for our country."

Republicans—2018 Tweets

January 20, 2018

6:44 am: For those asking, the Republicans only have 51 votes in the Senate, and they need 60. That is why we need to win more Republicans in 2018 Election! We can then be even tougher on Crime (and Border), and even better to our Military & Veterans!

January 22, 2018

11:30 pm: Big win for Republicans as Democrats cave on Shutdown. Now I want a big win for everyone, including Republicans, Democrats and DACA, but especially for our Great Military and Border Security.

March 28, 2018

4:52 am: THE SECOND AMENDMENT WILL NEVER BE RE-PEALED! As much as Democrats would like to see this happen, and despite the words yesterday of former Supreme Court Justice Stevens, NO WAY. We need more Republicans in 2018 and must ALWAYS hold the Supreme Court!

April 21, 2018

1:52 pm: So funny, the Democrats have sued the Republicans for Winning. Now he R's counter and force them to turn over a treasure trove of material, including Servers and Emails!

May 9, 2018

6:24 am: The Republican Party had a great night. Tremendous voter energy and excitement, and all candidates are those who have a great chance of winning in November. The Economy is sooo strong, and with Nancy Pelosi wanting to end the big Tax Cuts and Raise Taxes, why wouldn't we win?

May 16, 2018

1:40 pm: Lou Barletta will be a great Senator for Pennsylvania but his opponent, Bob Casey, has been a do-nothing Senator who only shows up at election time. He votes along the Nancy Pelosi, Elizabeth Warren lines, loves sanctuary cities, bad and expensive healthcare...

...and voted against the massive Tax Cut Bill. He's also weak on borders and crime. Sadly, our great Military and Vets mean nothing to Bobby Jr. Lou Barletta will win! #MAGA

May 18, 2018

5:00 pm: California finally deserves a great Governor, one who understands borders, crime and lowering taxes. John Cox is the man—he'll be the best Governor you've ever had. I fully endorse John Cox for Governor and look forward to working with him to Make California Great Again!

May 28, 2018

4:22 pm: A Democratic lawmaker just introduced a bill to Repeal the GOP Tax Cuts (no chance). This is too good to be true for Republicans...Remember, the Nancy Pelosi Dems are also weak on Crime, the Border and want to be gentle and kind to MS-13 gang members... not good!

May 31, 2018

8:18 am: Will be giving a Full Pardon to Dinesh D'Souza today. He was treated very unfairly by our government!

June 5, 2018

8:02 am: In High Tax, High Crime California, be sure to get out and vote for Republican John Cox for Governor. He will make a BIG difference!

8:09 am: Get the vote out in California today for Rep. Kevin McCarthy and all of the great GOP candidates for Congress. Keep our country out of the hands of High Tax, High Crime Nancy Pelosi.

8:44 am: Vote for Congressman Devin Nunes, a true American Patriot the likes of which we rarely see in our modern day world...he truly loves our country and deserves everyone's support!

11:02 pm: Mitch McConnell announced he will cancel the Senate's August Recess. Great, maybe the Democrats will finally get something done other than their acceptance of High Crime and High Taxes. We need Border Security!

June 6, 2018

8:16 am: Great night for Republicans! Congratulations to John Cox on a really big number in California. He can win. Even Fake News CNN said the Trump impact was really big, much bigger than they ever thought possible. So much for the big Blue Wave, it may be a big Red Wave. Working hard!

June 12, 2018

3:12 pm: Mark Sanford has been very unhelpful to me in my campaign to MAGA. He is MIA and nothing but trouble. He is better off in Argentina. I fully endorse Katie Arrington for Congress in SC, a state I love. She is tough on crime and will continue our fight to lower taxes. VOTE Katie!

June 14, 2018

7:34 am: The Republican Party is starting to show very big numbers. People are starting to see what is being done. Results are speaking loudly. North Korea and our greatest ever economy are leading the way!

June 20, 2018

3:04 pm: Had a great meeting with the House GOP last night at the Capitol. They applauded and laughed loudly when I mentioned my experience with Mark Sanford. I have never been a fan of his!

June 21, 2018

7:47 am: Henry McMaster has done a great job as Governor of South Carolina. The State is BOOMING, with jobs and new industry setting records. He is tough on Crime and strong on Borders, Health Care, the Mititary and our great Vets. Henry has my full and complete Endorsement! #MAGA

June 22, 2018

5:41 am: Our great Judge Jeanine Pirro is out with a new book, "Liars, Leakers and Liberals, the Case Against the Anti-Trump Conspiracy," which is fantastic. Go get it!

5:54 am: Even if we get 100% Republican votes in the Senate, we need 10 Democrat votes to get a much needed Immigration Bill—& the Dems are Obstructionists who won't give votes for political reasons & because they don't care about Crime coming from Border! So we need to elect more R's!

June 24, 2018

7:08 pm: House Republicans could easily pass a Bill on Strong Border Security but remember, it still has to pass in the Senate, and for that we need 10 Democrat votes, and all they do is RESIST. They want Open Borders and don't care about Crime! Need more Republicans to WIN in November!

June 26, 2018

10:52 pm: Big and conclusive win by Mitt Romney. Congratulations! I look forward to working together—there is so much good to do. A great and loving family will be coming to D.C.

June 30, 2018

2:17 pm: I never pushed the Republicans in the House to vote for the Immigration Bill, either GOODLATTE 1 or 2, because it could never have gotten enough Democrats as long as there is the 60 vote threshold. I released many prior to the vote knowing we need more Republicans to win in Nov.

July 5, 2018

7:44 pm: A vote for Democrats in November is a vote to let MS-13 run wild in our communities, to let drugs pour into our cities, and to take jobs and benefits away from hardworking Americans. Democrats want anarchy, amnesty and chaos—Republicans want LAW, ORDER and JUSTICE!

July 10, 2018

9:49 am: Informing the Republican Senators of my nomination of Judge Brett Kavanaugh. #SCOTUS

July 25, 2018

7:16 pm: Thank you Georgia! They say that my endorsement last week of Brian Kemp, in the Republican Primary for Governor against a very worthy opponent, lifted him from 5 points down to a 70% to 30% victory! Two very good and talented men in a great race, but congratulations to Brian!

July 31, 2018

5:14 am to 5:23 am: The globalist Koch Brothers, who have become a total joke in real Republican circles, are against Strong Borders and Powerful Trade. I never sought their support because I don't need their money or bad ideas. They love my Tax & Regulation Cuts, Judicial picks & more. I made…

…them richer. Their network is highly overrated, I have beaten them at every turn. They want to protect their companies outside the U.S. from being taxed, I'm for America First & the American Worker—a puppet for no one. Two nice guys with bad ideas. Make America Great Again!

5:50 am: Rush Limbaugh is a great guy who truly gets it!

August 2, 2018

5:38 am: Charles Koch of Koch Brothers, who claims to be giving away millions of dollars to politicians even though I know very few who have seen this (?), now makes the ridiculous statement that what President Trump is doing is unfair to "foreign workers." He is correct, AMERICA FIRST!

August 7, 2018

9:59 pm: When I decided to go to Ohio for Troy Balderson, he was down in early voting 64 to 36. That was not good. After my speech on Saturday night, there was a big turn for the better. Now Troy wins a great victory during a very tough time of the year for voting. He will win BIG in Nov.

August 8, 2018

10:14 am: The Republicans have now won 8 out of 9 House Seats, yet if you listen to the Fake News Media you would think we are being clobbered. Why can't they play it straight, so unfair to the Republican Party and in particular, your favorite President!

10:25 am: As long as I campaign and/or support Senate and House candidates (within reason), they will win! I LOVE the people, & they certainly seem to like the job I'm doing. If I find the time, in between China, Iran, the Economy and much more, which I must, we will have a giant Red Wave!

1:51 pm: RED WAVE!

August 15, 2018

7:30 am: Great Republican election results last night. So far we have the team we want. 8 for 9 in Special Elections. Red Wave!

8:07 am: Scott Walker is very special and will have another great win in November. He has done a fantastic job as Governor of Wisconsin and will always have my full support and Endorsement!

August 20, 2018

10:53 pm: I am hearing so many great things about the Republican Party's California Gubernatorial Candidate, John Cox. He is a very successful businessman who is tired of high Taxes & Crime. He will

Make California Great Again & make you proud of your Great State again. Total Endorsement!

September 8, 2018

4:08 pm: So true! "Mr. Trump remains the single most popular figure in the Republican Party, whose fealty has helped buoy candidates in competitive Republican primaries and remains a hot commodity among general election candidates." Nicholas Fandos, @nytimes

September 15, 2018

5:38 pm: When will Republican leadership learn that they are being played like a fiddle by the Democrats on Border Security and Building the Wall? Without Borders, we don't have a country. With Open Borders, which the Democrats want, we have nothing but crime! Finish the Wall!

September 20, 2018

6:43 am: I want to know, where is the money for Border Security and the WALL in this ridiculous Spending Bill, and where will it come from after the Midterms? Dems are obstructing Law Enforcement and Border Security. REPUBLICANS MUST FINALLY GET TOUGH!

September 24, 2018

9:38 pm: REMEMBER THE MIDTERMS!

September 25, 2018

5:41 am: Republican Party Favorability is the highest it has been in 7 years—3 points higher than Democrats! Gallup

October 18, 2018

10:11 pm: Jon Tester says one thing to voters and does the EXACT OPPOSITE in Washington. Tester takes his orders form Pelosi &

Schumer. Tester wants to raise your taxes, take away your 2A, open your borders, and deliver MOB RULE. Retire Tester & Elect America-First Patriot Matt Rosendale!

October 19, 2018

12:43 pm: Jon Tester says one thing to voters and does the EXACT OPPOSITE in Washington. Tester takes his orders form Pelosi & Schumer. Tester wants to raise your taxes, take away your 2A, open your borders, and deliver MOB RULE. Retire Tester & Elect America-First Patriot Matt Rosendale!

October 26, 2018

9:19 am: Republicans are doing so well in early voting, and at the polls, and now this "Bomb" stuff happens and the momentum greatly slows—news not talking politics. Very unfortunate, what is going on. Republicans, go out and vote!

October 31, 2018

10:28 am: Republicans will protect people with pre-existing conditions far better than the Dems!

November 2, 2018

7:49 pm: Republicans believe our Country should be a Sanctuary for law-abiding Americans—not criminal aliens. And Republicans will ALWAYS stand with the HEROES of @ICEgov, @CBP, and Law Enforcement!

November 3, 2018

6:49 am: Indiana Rally, and Coach Bobby Knight, were incredible last night. Packed House in Honor of Mike Braun for Senate. Mike will be a GREAT Senator. Don't forget to VOTE!

November 5, 2018

8:36 am: No matter what she says, Senator Claire McCaskill will always vote against us and the Great State of Missouri! Vote for Josh Hawley—he will be a great Senator!

November 7, 2018

7:07 am: Those that worked with me in this incredible Midterm Election, embracing certain policies and principles, did very well. Those that did not, say goodbye! Yesterday was such a very Big Win, and all under the pressure of a Nasty and Hostile Media!

November 9, 2018

12:10 pm: Jeff Flake(y) doesn't want to protect the Non-Senate confirmed Special Counsel, he wants to protect his future after being unelectable in Arizona for the "crime" of doing a terrible job! A weak and ineffective guy!

12:36 pm: Rick Scott was up by 50,000+ votes on Election Day, now they "found" many votes and he is only up 15,000 votes. "The Broward Effect." How come they never find Republican votes?

November 12, 2018

7:44 am: The Florida Election should be called in favor of Rick Scott and Ron DeSantis in that large numbers of new ballots showed up out of nowhere, and many ballots are missing or forged. An honest vote count is no longer possible-ballots massively infected. Must go with Election Night!

November 28, 2018

11:36 pm: Sebastian Gorka, a very talented man who I got to know well while he was working at the White House, has just written an excellent book, "Why We Fight." Much will be learned from this very good read!

December 1, 2018

6:16 am: President George H.W. Bush led a long, successful and beautiful life. Whenever I was with him I saw his absolute joy for life and true pride in his family. His accomplishments were great from beginning to end. He was a truly wonderful man and will be missed by all!

December 3, 2018

11:37 am: Looking forward to being with the Bush Family to pay my respects to President George H.W. Bush.

December 5, 2018

8:56 am: Looking forward to being with the Bush family. This is not a funeral, this is a day of celebration for a great man who has led a long and distinguished life. He will be missed!

December 6, 2018

7:27 pm: Does the Fake News Media ever mention the fact that Republicans, with the very important help of my campaign Rallies, WON THE UNITED STATES SENATE, 53 to 47? All I hear is that the Open Border Dems won the House. Senate alone approves judges & others. Big Republican Win!

December 11, 2018

5:09 pm: Does the Fake News Media ever mention the fact that Republicans, with the very important help of my campaign Rallies, WON THE UNITED STATES SENATE, 53 to 47? All I hear is that the Open Border Dems won the House. Senate alone approves judges & others. Big Republican Win!

December 20, 2018

2:22 pm: So hard to believe that Lindsey Graham would be against saving soldier lives & billions of $$$. Why are we fighting for our enemy, Syria, by staying & killing ISIS for them, Russia, Iran & other locals? Time to focus on our Country & bring our youth back home where they belong!

December 21, 2018

7:19 am: No matter what happens today in the Senate, Republican House Members should be very proud of themselves. They flew back to Washington from all parts of the World in order to vote for Border Security and the Wall. Not one Democrat voted yes, and we won big. I am very proud of you!

December 23, 2018

10:47 pm: Mitch McConnell just told a group of people, and me, that he has been in the U.S. Senate for 32 years and the last two have been by far the best & most productive of his career. Tax & Regulation Cuts, VA Choice, Farm Bill, Criminal Justice Reform, Judgeships & much more. Great!

2:56 pm to 3:20 pm: Senator Bob Corker just stated that, "I'm so priveledged to serve in the Senate for twelve years, and that's what I told the people of our state that's what I'd do, serve for two terms." But that is Not True—wanted to run but poll numbers TANKED when I wouldn't endorse him...

...Bob Corker was responsible for giving us the horrible Iran Nuclear Deal, which I ended, yet he badmouths me for wanting to bring our young people safely back home. Bob wanted to run and asked for my endorsement. I said NO and the game was over. #MAGA I LOVE TENNESSEE!

Republicans—2019 News Quotes

Remarks in meeting with conservative leaders on his immigration proposal, January 23, 2019.

Source: https://www.whitehouse.gov/briefings-statements/
remarks-president-trump-meeting-conservative-leaders-immigration-proposal/

"I'd like to start today, we're talking about shutdown; we're talking about some conservative values. These are the great conservative leaders of our country, and they have very strong views. And we'll be doing that after the press leaves. But they have very strong views on the shutdown. And it's not that we have a choice. I don't think we have a choice. We have to make our country safe. We have done such an incredible job with such poor tools. We have catch-and-release, where you catch somebody and then you have to release that person into our country.

"We have so many different elements of rule and regulation. It's a very sad thing that's gone on. And this has happened over a long period of time.

"If you take a look at the visa lottery—When there's a lottery, do you think they're putting their best people into those lotteries? It's a lottery. You know what a lottery is. Does anybody think they're putting their best people in?

"You have chain migration, where, as an example, the killer, the man who ran over people on the West Side Highway in New York—Eight people killed, 12 injured. And when you say '12 injured,' nobody knows how badly injured they are. This isn't like they had a headache. This is big, big, and horrible problems. Loss of legs and arms, and worse. And this man brought in many people, many, many people, through chain migration, it's called.

"So these are all Democrat principles that are no good for our country; they're hurting our country. And if we did what we had to do, you would bring crime down in half in our country, because so much of it comes through our southern border.

"Honduras is doing nothing for us. Guatemala is doing nothing for us. El Salvador is doing nothing for us. And we pay them hundreds of millions of dollars a year, but we're going to be stopping pretty soon. In fact, we're looking at it right now. We don't want to do it. Because when caravans form in the middle of a country, the country can very easily stop those caravans from forming, very easily. I actually think they encourage the caravans because they want to get rid of the people from their country, and certain people. A lot of gang members are there. In the last caravan, we had 618 people with criminal records, and some of them very serious records.

"I won't soon forget the man that was interviewed where he wanted some kind of pardon, or whatever, when he came into the country. And the network person said, 'Well, what did you do?' And he said 'murder' or something to that effect. And she goes, 'Whoa, murder.' Well, we have—That's what we have. We have a lot of very dangerous people that want to come into our country. And we're not letting them in.

"We want people to come in based on merit. We want people to come in that can help us successfully run all these companies that are pouring into the United States because of what we've done and because of all of the incentives, Steve, that we've given, and because this is where the action is. Steve Moore is one of the great financial gurus, and he would tell you how well we're doing as a country.

"But we have a lot of people that, really, we need. We have the lowest unemployment rate we've had in much more than 50 years, with African American, with Asian American, with Hispanic American. We have the lowest unemployment rate we've had in the history of our country.

"And that's why, when you look at the Hispanic polls, I'm up 19%. And the reason I'm up 19%—I don't even think it's the unemployment; I think it's the fact that they understand, better than anybody, what's going on at the border.

"And they say that President Trump is the only one that's saying it right, and he's doing what you have to. That's why people were so surprised when they saw the poll that just came out, where I'm up to 50% with the Hispanic and up 19 points in a short period of time. Because they get it better than anybody at the border. They know what's happening at the border and they know it's a big scam.

"And the Democrats don't want to stop people. That means automatically massive amounts of crime. And we're not going to put up with it.

"So [Speaker of the House] Nancy Pelosi, knowing these facts, and knowing it's something that she can't win, that she just went out and said, let's cancel, for the first time in the history of our country, 'Let's cancel the State of the Union Address.' And it's a disgrace. Just so you know, she uses on the basis of the shutdown. But when she asked me to make the address—Formally, in writing; most of you have a copy of the letter—When she asked me to make the address, she did it during the shutdown, well into the shutdown, by a couple of weeks.

"So the shutdown was going on. Now she's blaming the shutdown. So if it was because of the shutdown, why do you ask that the address be made? And she asked that the address be made during a shutdown, and now she's blaming the shutdown.

"She also knew, because she went to our people and she asked, 'Would it be a security problem?' She knew it wasn't a security problem. She blamed security, but she knew it wasn't a security problem, and she knew that loud and clear.

"And she went to the people. She asked. They said, 'We have no problem whatsoever.' I just got back from Iraq. I was very safe in Iraq, and I felt very safe. We had great, great security. If we can handle Iraq, we can handle the middle of Washington in a very, very spectacular building, and a beautiful room that we should be in, and that's where it's been for a very long time.

"So, it's a sad thing for our country. We'll do something in the alternative. We'll be talking to you about that at a later date.

"But I have to say, it's an honor to have these great leaders with us, and we're going to be talking about shutdown. We're going to be talking about other things. And we're going to be talking about, outside of this event that we just discussed, how well our country is doing, because we're setting records in so many different ways. We're setting jobs records.

"Right now, at this very moment, we have more people working in the United States than at any time in the history of our country. Think of that. That's a big, big statement. I just had a meeting on drug pricing and various other things. And prescription drugs, for the first time in history, the history of our country, have gone down in 2018.

"So for last year, just got the numbers, for the first time in the history of our country, prescription drug prices have gone down. They've been like a rocket ship until I got here. And we have more to do. They're going to go down further. But think of that: for the first time—I say it because you guys don't want to report it, but that's a big thing, because drug pricing has been very important to me, as is healthcare.

"First time in the history of our country, in 2018, prescription drug prices have gone down. That's a big number. And you didn't even know that. I don't think anybody at this table knew that. It just came out. So we'll let you know.

"So it's too bad with Nancy Pelosi, what she's done. It's radical Democrats. They've become a radicalized party. They really have. They have become a radicalized party. I actually think they've become a very dangerous party for this country. If you listen to what they're saying, what they're doing, I think they've become a very dangerous, a very, very dangerous party for this country.

"I think that [Senator] Chuck Schumer, sadly, is dominated by the radical left, and he is dominated by Nancy Pelosi. Very strongly dominated. He can't move; he's a puppet. He's a puppet for Nancy Pelosi, if you can believe that. But that's what's become and that's what's happening.

"And we're not going to let it happen to our nation, and we are not going to allow the radical left to control our borders. Because if they do, you will see crime; you will see drugs; you will see human trafficking like you have never seen ever in the history of our country. You will never see anything like what you would see. So we will never let the radical left control our borders."

Response to a question from Maggie Haberman of *The New York Times*, January 31, 2019.
Source: https://www.nytimes.com/2019/02/01/us/politics/trump-interview-transcripts.html

"No. No. I have great support in the party. We have great support. I guess anything is possible. But look, we have among the highest polls, and actually the highest polls, but among the highest polls ever in the history of the Republican Party."

From State of the Union address, February 5, 2019.
Source: https://www.whitehouse.gov/briefings-statements/
president-donald-j-trumps-state-union-address-2/

"On Friday, it was announced that we added another 304,000 jobs last month alone; almost double what was expected. An economic miracle is taking place in the United States, and the only thing that can stop it are foolish wars, politics, or ridiculous partisan investigations.

"If there is going to be peace and legislation, there cannot be war and investigation. It just doesn't work that way!

"We must be united at home to defeat our adversaries abroad.

"This new era of cooperation can start with finally confirming the more than 300 highly qualified nominees who are still stuck in the Senate, some after years of waiting. The Senate has failed to act on these nominations, which is unfair to the nominees and to our country.

"Now is the time for bipartisan action. Believe it or not, we have already proven that it is possible.

"In the last Congress, both parties came together to pass unprecedented legislation to confront the opioid crisis, a sweeping new Farm Bill, historic VA reforms, and after four decades of rejection, we passed VA Accountability so we can finally terminate those who mistreat our wonderful veterans."

From State of the Union address, February 5, 2019.

Source: https://www.whitehouse.gov/briefings-statements/
president-donald-j-trumps-state-union-address-2/

"Both parties should be able to unite for a great rebuilding of America's crumbling infrastructure.

"I know that the Congress is eager to pass an infrastructure bill, and I am eager to work with you on legislation to deliver new and important infrastructure investment, including investments in the cutting edge industries of the future. This is not an option. This is a necessity."

Remarks during a visit to the Lima Army Tank Plant in Ohio, March 20, 2019.

Source: https://www.c-span.org/video/?458966-1/
president-trump-delivers-remarks-lima-army-tank-plant-ohio

"I endorsed him [the late U.S. Senator John McCain] at his request, and I gave him the kind of funeral that he wanted, which, as President, I had to approve. I don't care about this. I didn't get 'Thank you.' That's okay. We sent him on the way. But I wasn't a fan of John McCain.

"So now, what we could say is: now we're all set. I don't think I have to answer that question, but the press keeps, 'What do you think of McCain? What do you think?' Not my kind of guy. But some people like him, and I think that's great."

Response to an unidentified reporter's question at the signing of H.R. 3401, July 1, 2019.

Source: https://www.whitehouse.gov/briefings-statements/
remarks-president-trump-signing-h-r-3401/

"Well, I don't know what they're saying about members of Congress. I know that the Border Patrol is not happy with the Democrats in Congress. I will say the Republicans do want border security. The Democrats want open borders. Open borders means tremendous crime.

"If you look, there was a report that came out where approximately 600 people in the last caravan were serious criminals. I don't want them in our country.

"So, the Border Patrol, they're patriots. They're great people. They love our country. They know what's coming in.

"And you know who knows it better than anybody? Hispanics. Hispanics love what I'm doing because, number one, they don't want to lose their job. They don't want to take a pay cut. And very importantly, most importantly, they don't want to have crime. They understand it.

"The people that understand the border the best are Hispanics. They understand it better than anybody. And they don't want to have to suffer crime. And they don't want to take a pay cut. They don't want to lose their job. That's why my poll numbers went way up with Hispanics because they really understand the border the best of anybody."

Response to a question from an unidentified reporter before Marine One departure, September 9, 2019.
Source: https://www.whitehouse.gov/briefings-statements/
remarks-president-trump-marine-one-departure-63/

"Well, we're dealing with Democrats. We're dealing with Republicans. We're talking about a lot of different things having to do with, as you call it, gun control. But we are talking about a lot of different things. But at the same time, we have to protect our Second Amendment very strongly, and we will always do that."

Response to a question from an unidentified reporter before Marine One departure, September 9, 2019.
Source: https://www.whitehouse.gov/briefings-statements/
remarks-president-trump-marine-one-departure-63/

"Well, one of the things is that I disagree with the Republican system. When you're the chairman of a committee—We've lost chairmen because they can't go from being a chairman, back to being a regular congressman. When you're the chairman of a committee, the Democrats, you can stay there forever, like Deny [sic] Hoyer and others. He's a good man, by the way. But like a lot of them, they're there forever. As a Republican, you get six years.

145

"What happens after they're finished, they leave. And I understand that. And, frankly, there is good to be said about both and there's bad to be said about both, to use the famous expression. But let me just tell you, I agree—One of the only things I agree with the Democrats on: I really think it's better to have a longer term."

Remarks at the signing of an executive order protecting and improving Medicare for senior citizens, Ocala, Florida, October 3, 2019.
Source: https://www.whitehouse.gov/briefings-statements/remarks-president-trump-signing-executive-order-protecting-improving-medicare-nations-seniors-ocala-fl/

"Our economy is booming. We're doing fantastically well. I think it gets a little bit hurt by politics. But our country is so strong and our economy is so powerful that even politics, and even when you have the, the 'Do-Nothings.' I call them the—Really, the 'Do-Nothing Dems.' They can't even affect it very much."

Remarks at the signing of an executive order protecting and improving Medicare for senior citizens, Ocala, Florida, October 3, 2019.
Source: https://www.whitehouse.gov/briefings-statements/remarks-president-trump-signing-executive-order-protecting-improving-medicare-nations-seniors-ocala-fl/

"As we gather this afternoon, Medicare is under threat like never before. Your know that. You have people that are running for office who—If it ever happened, you will not be very happy here.

"Almost every major Democrat in Washington has backed a massive government healthcare takeover that would totally obliterate Medicare. These Democrat policy proposals may go by different names, they have all of these wonderful names like—[Audience member interrupts.]"

Remarks at the signing of an executive order protecting and improving Medicare for senior citizens, Ocala, Florida, October 3, 2019.
Source: https://www.whitehouse.gov/briefings-statements/remarks-president-trump-signing-executive-order-protecting-improving-medicare-nations-seniors-ocala-fl/

"But they may go by different names, whether it's 'single payer' or the so-called "public option," but they're all based on the totally same, terrible idea. They [the Democrats] want to raid Medicare to fund a thing called socialism. Any socialists in the room? I don't think so. Not too many. Anybody? [Audience boos.]

"No? No? Not too many in The Villages. You don't—You're not big on socialism down here, right? These geniuses, these real estate geniuses that know we're not, not too good.

"Every one of these plans involves rationing care, restricting access, denying coverage, slashing quality, and massively raising taxes. They want to raise your taxes.

"They also want to have open borders, so the people can just come in and do whatever they want to do."

Remarks at the signing of an executive order protecting and improving Medicare for senior citizens, Ocala, Florida, October 3, 2019.

Source: https://www.whitehouse.gov/briefings-statements/remarks-president-trump-signing-executive-order-protecting-improving-medicare-nations-seniors-ocala-fl/

"Congressional Democrats' extreme agenda would destroy our booming economy very quickly. One of the most disturbing proposals from left-wing politicians involves draining your healthcare to finance the open borders that we just discussed. That's how they want to finance it. Leading Democrats have pledged to give free healthcare to illegal immigrants. They put foreign citizens who break our laws and endanger our country, they put them way ahead of American citizens like you who obey our laws.

"I will never allow these politicians to steal your healthcare and give it away to illegal aliens. And now, in New York, I hear they passed a new regulation that, if you use the word, 'illegal immigrant'—Did I hear correctly? They want to charge you a fine of $250,000. In other words, sell your home in The Villages because you happened to say, 'We don't like illegal immigrants pouring into our country illegally.' We want people to come into our country legally, through a process. And we're all in favor of that."

147

Remarks at the signing of an executive order protecting and improving Medicare for senior citizens, Ocala, Florida, October 3, 2019.
Source: https://www.whitehouse.gov/briefings-statements/remarks-president-trump-signing-executive-order-protecting-improving-medicare-nations-seniors-ocala-fl/

"Now one of their new proposals, backed by more than 130 Democrat members of Congress, would cost, listen to this number: $32 trillion dollars. And that's on the low side: $32 trillion, with a 'T.' We're beyond the 'Bs,' the billions. And reduce Americans' household income by $17,000 per year. Is there anybody in this room that doesn't mind losing $17,000 a year? No? In order to get lousy healthcare.

"Though they use many labels, all of the Democrat plans would devastate our healthcare system. The fake moderates on the left are telling the same lies they did under the last administration. But the last administration, frankly, was moderate compared to the maniacs that you're hearing from today. These are maniacs."

Remarks at the signing of an executive order protecting and improving Medicare for senior citizens, Ocala, Florida, October 3, 2019.
Source: https://www.whitehouse.gov/briefings-statements/remarks-president-trump-signing-executive-order-protecting-improving-medicare-nations-seniors-ocala-fl/

"Democrat lawmakers are not trying to build up the country; they only want to wreck and destroy all of the things that we've built up over the last three and a half years, four years, five years prior to us getting in here. You look at the stock market numbers from the time of the election, from that November 9th date, go a date later. Wasn't November 8—Was that one of the great times? Huh? [Audience applauds.] 2016.

"But go a day later, and you look at the numbers in the stock market up way over 50%. The 401(k)s are doing unbelievably well. One of these people gets in—Your 401(k)s are going to hell, the stock market is going to hell. Frankly, I think, and I hate to say it, the country is going to go to hell.

"They're consumed by rage and radicalism and insatiable lust for power. Well, how about Justice [Brett] Kavanaugh? They talk about a woman, they talk about a woman, about horrible things that he never even thought about. Horrible, horrible things. And the following day, they want to impeach him. And then, the following day, she said, 'No, I don't remember anything. I don't remember that.' And they say, 'We don't care. We want to impeach him anyway.' Now, what they're trying to do is turn his vote liberal. But he's a much tougher guy than that. I hope. He's a much tougher guy."

Remarks at the signing of an executive order protecting and improving Medicare for senior citizens, Ocala, Florida, October 3, 2019.
Source: https://www.whitehouse.gov/briefings-statements/remarks-president-trump-signing-executive-order-protecting-improving-medicare-nations-seniors-ocala-fl/

"Democrat healthcare proposals would put everyone into a single, socialist, government-run program that would end private insurance for over 180 million Americans. I'm sort of smiling to myself as I, as I go through these numbers. And I'm dealing with people that I know. I mean, I know the people in this room. Those are the people. I grew up with you. When we were young, I grew up with you. And now we're sort of still young at heart, at least.

"And that I'm even talking about socialism is like—It's just, it's sort of a weird feeling to be talking to you about 'you don't want to be socialist.' And you're probably saying, 'Why is he wasting his time?'

"But there's a movement on. And it's not so easy to be beat them when they get up in a debate and they say, 'We're going to cut your college tuition to nothing. We're going kno—knock off $1.6 trillion. We're going to do all these other things. Everything is free, except for your taxes.' Your taxes are going to go up at a level that nobody has even seen before and that won't be nearly enough to pay for it.

"But I'll not let any of this bad stuff happen. It's very important that we win this race. You know, when we won last time, I said, 'That's the most important election in our country's history.' Because we were ready to go over the edge.

"And now our country is doing great. But, you know, it's like a plant; it's like a tree. It has to grab—Those roots have to grab hold. We still need more time. We've done so much, but we need a little more time. That thing has to grow and it's got to get in there and then nobody is going to be able to take it down no matter what happens later on. So important.

"In America, we believe in freedom and liberty, not government domination and government control. Today, standing in solidarity with our nation's seniors, I declare once again that America will never be a socialist country; it will never be."

Remarks at the signing of an executive order protecting and improving Medicare for senior citizens, Ocala, Florida, October 3, 2019.
Source: https://www.whitehouse.gov/briefings-statements/remarks-president-trump-signing-executive-order-protecting-improving-medicare-nations-seniors-ocala-fl/

"Among those who would be hit hardest by the socialist takeover are 24 million seniors on Medicare Advantage: a lot of you. One out of two Hispanic seniors, one out of three African-American seniors is enrolled in Medicare Advantage. This very popular Medicare program, been around for a long time, allows private plans to compete to offer senior citizens the absolute best healthcare. They want to destroy it.

"While many Democrat plans would eliminate Medicare Advantage, my administration is fighting to make it even better and much, much stronger.

"And thanks to our efforts, there are nearly 1,200 more Medicare Advantage plans today than there were just two years ago. Think of that. Premiums have plummeted by 28%; they've gone down. And they're now at the lowest level in over 10 years."

Remarks at the signing of an executive order protecting and improving Medicare for senior citizens, Ocala, Florida, October 3, 2019.
Source: https://www.whitehouse.gov/briefings-statements/remarks-president-trump-signing-executive-order-protecting-improving-medicare-nations-seniors-ocala-fl/

"The Democrat plans for socialized medicine will not just put doctors and hospitals out of business, they'll also deny your treatment and everything that you need. Government-run healthcare systems always end up imposing rationing. You see what happens.

"You look at Venezuela; take a look at that. Fifteen years ago, it's one of the wealthiest countries. Now they don't have food. They don't have water. The hospitals are a disaster. No electricity. No anything. It's very sad. And we're helping the people as much as we can. But we're watching that whole situation—Beyond this, we're watching it very, very carefully. We're watching it very carefully. And Cuba—we're watching Cuba very carefully. Very, very carefully.

"But as an example, under the United Kingdom's single-payer system, patients wait 117 days to receive, as an example, a knee replacement. One hundred and seventeen days.

"In Canada, wait times for orthopedic surgery are over 270 days. But currently in the United States, wait times for these surgeries are, we've speeded it up a lot, are typically less than two weeks."

Remarks at the signing of an executive order protecting and improving Medicare for senior citizens, Ocala, Florida, October 3, 2019.
Source: https://www.whitehouse.gov/briefings-statements/remarks-president-trump-signing-executive-order-protecting-improving-medicare-nations-seniors-ocala-fl/

"Like you, all of us today understand the truth. Socialism is not about improving the health of American people; it's about wielding power over the American people, taking things away from the American people."

Remarks at a rally in Minneapolis, Minnesota, October 10, 2019.
Source: https://www.twincities.com/2019/10/10/
trump-attacks-joe-biden-ilhan-omar-and-jacob-frey-at-minneapolis-rally/

"How the hell did that ever happen? She [Rep. Ilhan Omar] is a disgrace, and she is one of the reasons I'm going to win and the Republican Party is going to win Minnesota."

Remarks at a rally in Lexington, Kentucky, November 4, 2019.
Source: https://www.youtube.com/watch?v=pGjRidJuGnA#action=share

"This place—Look at this. Wow. Hello, up there. This is incredible, with thousands of proud, hardworking, freedom-loving American patriots, which is what you are. What you are. Tomorrow, the people of

151

Kentucky will head to the polls, and you will vote to re-elect your terrific Republican Governor Matt Bevin.

"Republican leadership, the economy is booming, wages are rising, confidence is soaring, Kentucky is thriving like never ever before, and America is stronger than ever before. True. Kentucky's unemployment rate has reached the lowest point in the history of our country. That's not bad.

"And I want to just tell you that you have incredible representatives and the job that Matt Bevin has done as governor. He's had to do some things that you had to do and he's done unbelievably well, and it sets you up to be a rocket ship in the future, you had to do it. So, I just want to thank him for having the courage to do what he had to do, but you have the best numbers you've ever had in the history of the state."

Remarks at a campaign rally in Sunrise, Florida, November 26, 2019.
Source: https://www.c-span.org/video/?466539-1/
president-trump-holds-rally-sunrise-florida&start=4731

"They like to try and demean, always best, well, this and that. Let me tell you, we're winning, you're smarter, you're better looking, you're sharper, and they call themselves elite. But if they're elite, then, we're the super-elite. It's true. It's true. They talk about these people that are elite, that you know, that are running."

Remarks at a campaign rally in Sunrise, Florida, November 26, 2019.
Source: https://www.c-span.org/video/?466539-1/
president-trump-holds-rally-sunrise-florida&start=4731

"The Republican Party is the party of the American worker, the American family, the American dream. And remember this, the Republican Party is the party of Abraham Lincoln, we forget. Abraham Lincoln and I've always heard that the most important thing a President can do is the appointment of judges. I say, maybe the military, because, without the military, we're not so interested in judges, right?"

Remarks at Turning Point USA Student Action Summit in West Palm Beach, Florida, December 22, 2019.

Source: https://www.whitehouse.gov/briefings-statements/
remarks-president-trump-turning-point-usa-student-action-summit-west-palm-beach-fl/

"Well, thank you very much. Thank you everybody. What a group. What a group. What a group. I also want to thank a true American legend, and a beloved national hero, Rush Limbaugh. Thank you, Rush.

"You know, I don't know if you know it or not: he's got like 39 million people listening. He's been—From day one, he's been so incredible. Good times, bad times, he doesn't waver because he's tough as hell. He makes like—They tell me he makes like $50 million a year. And it may be—That may be on the low side. So if anybody wants to be a nice conservative talk show host, it's not a bad living. I will say.

"But I have to say, he's a very unique guy and he's a great man and he's been a great friend. So thank you to Rush. Thank you."

Republicans—2019 Tweets

January 7, 2019

8:38 am: Congressman Adam Smith, the new Chairman of the House Armed Services Committee, just stated, "Yes, there is a provision in law that says a president can declare an emergency. It's been done a number of times." No doubt, but let's get our deal done in Congress!

January 10, 2019

8:34 am: There is GREAT unity with the Republicans in the House and Senate, despite the Fake News Media working in overdrive to make the story look otherwise. The Opposition Party & the Dems know we must have Strong Border Security, but don't want to give "Trump" another one of many wins!

January 23, 2019

7:57 am: BUILD A WALL & CRIME WILL FALL! This is the new theme, for two years until the Wall is finished (under construction now), of the Republican Party. Use it and pray!

February 1, 2019

2:25 pm: Thank you to Senator Rob Portman and Senator Cory Gardner for the early and warm endorsement. We will ALL WIN in 2020 together!

February 2, 2019

8:01 pm: Ed Gillespie, who ran for Governor of the Great State of Virginia against Ralph Northam, must now be thinking Malpractice and Dereliction of Duty with regard to his Opposition Research Staff. If they find that terrible picture before the election, he wins by 20 points!

February 7, 2019

9:05 pm: Highly respected Senator Richard Burr, Chairman of Senate Intelligence, said today that, after an almost two year investigation, he saw no evidence of Russia collusion. "We don't have anything that would suggest there was collusion by the Trump campaign and Russia." Thank you!

February 23, 2019

12:52 pm: There is far more ENERGY on the Right than there is on the Left. That's why we just won the Senate and why we will win big in 2020. The Fake News just doesn't want to report the facts. Border Security is a big factor. The under construction Wall will stop Gangs, Drugs and Crime!

March 14, 2019

5:44 am: A big National Emergency vote today by The United States Senate on Border Security & the Wall (which is already under major construction). I am prepared to veto, if necessary. The Southern Border is a National Security and Humanitarian Nightmare, but it can be easily fixed!

March 15, 2019

7:03 am: The 'Jexodus' movement encourages Jewish people to leave the Democrat Party. Total disrespect! Republicans are waiting with open arms. Remember Jerusalem (U.S. Embassy) and the horrible Iran Nuclear Deal! @OANN @foxandfriends

12:42 pm: I'd like to thank all of the Great Republican Senators who bravely voted for Strong Border Security and the WALL. This will help stop Crime, Human Trafficking, and Drugs entering our Country. Watch, when you get back to your State, they will LOVE you more than ever before!

March 17, 2019

3:58 pm: Those Republican Senators who voted in favor of Strong Border Security (and the Wall) are being uniformly praised as they return to their States. They know there is a National Emergency at the Southern Border, and they had the courage to ACT. Great job!

March 20, 2019

6:51 am: George Conway, often referred to as Mr. Kellyanne Conway by those who know him, is VERY jealous of his wife's success & angry that I, with her help, didn't give him the job he so desperately wanted. I barely know him but just take a look, a stone cold LOSER & husband from hell!

March 26, 2019

4:31 pm: Thank you to the House Republicans for sticking together and the BIG WIN today on the Border. Today's vote simply re-affirms Congressional Democrats are the party of Open Borders, Drugs and Crime!

April 4, 2019

6:49 am: THE REPUBLICAN PARTY IS THE PARTY OF THE AMERICAN DREAM!

April 29, 2019

7:18 am: The NRA is under siege by Cuomo and the New York State A.G., who are illegally using the State's legal apparatus to take down and destroy this very important organization, & others. It must get its act together quickly, stop the internal fighting, & get back to GREATNESS—FAST!

8:23 am: ...People are fleeing New York State because of high taxes and yes, even oppression of sorts. They didn't even put up a fight against SALT—could have won. So much litigation. The NRA should leave and fight from the outside of this very difficult to deal with (unfair) State!

May 2, 2019

10:45 pm: OK, so after two years of hard work and each party trying their best to make the other party look as bad as possible, it's time to get back to business. The Mueller Report strongly stated that there was No Collusion with Russia (of course) and, in fact, they were rebuffed...

... at every turn in attempts to gain access. But now Republicans and Democrats must come together for the good of the American people. No more costly & time consuming investigations. Lets do Immigration (Border), Infrastructure, much lower drug prices & much more—and do it now!

May 6, 2019

8:30 am: Scott Walker is 100% correct when he says that the Republicans must WAKE UP to the Democrats State by State power grab. They play very dirty, actually, like never before. Don't allow them to get away with what they are doing!

May 9, 2019

6:11 pm: House Republicans should not vote for the BAD DEMOCRAT Disaster Supplemental Bill which hurts our States, Farmers & Border Security. Up for vote tomorrow. We want to do much better than this. All sides keep working and send a good BILL for immediate signing!

10:58 pm: Republicans must stick together!

May 23, 2019

7:29 am: Rex Tillerson, a man who is "dumb as a rock" and totally ill prepared and ill equipped to be Secretary of State, made up a story (he got fired) that I was out-prepared by Vladimir Putin at a meeting in Hamburg, Germany. I don't think Putin would agree. Look how the U.S. is doing!

June 15, 2019

7:51 am: All in for Senator Steve Daines as he proposes an Amendment for a strong BAN on burning our American Flag. A no brainer!

June 26, 2019

6:13 am: Democrats want Open Borders, which equals violent crime, drugs and human trafficking. They also want very high taxes, like 90%. Republicans want what's good for America—the exact opposite!

4:47 pm: The Republican Senate just passed bipartisan humanitarian assistance for our Southern Border, 84-8! In addition to aid, Congress must close the catastrophic loopholes that are driving the Crisis.

We must end incentives for Smuggling Children, Trafficking Women, and Selling Drugs.

July 4, 2019

8:05 am: Great news for the Republican Party as one of the dumbest & most disloyal men in Congress is "quitting" the Party. No Collusion, No Obstruction! Knew he couldn't get the nomination to run again in the Great State of Michigan. Already being challenged for his seat. A total loser!

July 9, 2019

7:13 pm: Democrats are coming after our great Kentucky Senator, Mitch McConnell, with someone who compared my election to September 11th...

...Why would Kentucky ever think of giving up the most powerful position in Congress, the Senate Majority Leader, for a freshman Senator with little power in what will hopefully be the minority party. We need Mitch in the Senate to Keep America Great!!

July 11, 2019

10:10 pm: Paul Ryan, the failed V.P. candidate & former Speaker of the House, whose record of achievement was atrocious (except during my first two years as President), ultimately became a long running lame duck failure, leaving his Party in the lurch both as a fundraiser & leader...

...When Mitt chose Paul I told people that's the end of that Presidential run. He quit Congress because he didn't know how to Win. They gave me standing O's in the Great State of Wisconsin, & booed him off the stage. He promised me the Wall, & failed (happening anyway!).

...He had the Majority & blew it away with his poor leadership and bad timing. Never knew how to go after the Dems like they go after us. Couldn't get him out of Congress fast enough!

July 13, 2019

4:19 pm: House Minority Leader Kevin McCarthy is a far superior leader than was Lame Duck Speaker Paul Ryan. Tougher, smarter and a far better fundraiser, Kevin is already closing in on 44 Million Dollars. Paul's final year numbers were, according to Breitbart, "abysmal." People like…

…Paul Ryan almost killed the Republican Party. Weak, ineffective & stupid are not exactly the qualities that Republicans, or the CITIZENS of our Country, were looking for. Right now our spirit is at an all time high, far better than the Radical Left Dems. You'll see next year!

4:21 pm: 94% Approval Rating in the Republican Party, an all time high. Ronald Reagan was 87%. Thank you!

August 1, 2019

9:30 am: Budget Deal is phenomenal for our Great Military, our Vets, and Jobs, Jobs, Jobs! Two year deal gets us past the Election. Go for it Republicans, there is always plenty of time to CUT!

September 1, 2019

7:53 pm: "We hold that legislative prayer is government speech not open to attack via those channels." Third Circuit, Court of Appeals. "Lou, that's why this next Election is so important, the soul of America. They want to take religion out of American lives. Thank God for judges like…

…this (Judge Thomas Ambro, Majotity Opinion), and thank God for a President like Donald J. Trump, who will appoint judges like this. He will soon have appointed 180 new Federal Judges, not even including two great new Supreme Court Justices." @robertjeffress @LouDobbs

September 7, 2019

5:52 am: I want to congratulate @senatemajldr Mitch McConnell and all Republicans. Today I signed the 160th Federal Judge to the Bench.

Within a short period of time we will be at over 200 Federal Judges, including many in the Appellate Courts & two great new U.S. Supreme Court Justices!

September 9, 2019

5:58 am: When the former Governor of the Great State of South Carolina, @MarkSanford, was reported missing, only to then say he was away hiking on the Appalachian Trail, then was found in Argentina with his Flaming Dancer friend, it sounded like his political career was over. It was,

...but then he ran for Congress and won, only to lose his re-elect after I Tweeted my endorsement, on Election Day, for his opponent. But now take heart, he is back, and running for President of the United States. The Three Stooges, all badly failed candidates, will give it a go!

6:08 am: House Republicans should allow Chairs of Committees to remain for longer than 6 years. It forces great people, and real leaders, to leave after serving. The Dems have unlimited terms. While that has its own problems, it is a better way to go. Fewer people, in the end, will leave!

6:29 am: 94% Approval Rating in the Republican Party, a record. Thank you!

September 10, 2019

9:30 pm: Dan Bishop was down 17 points 3 weeks ago. He then asked me for help, we changed his strategy together, and he ran a great race. Big Rally last night. Now it looks like he is going to win. @CNN & @MSNBC are moving their big studio equipment and talent out. Stay tuned!

9:38 pm: BIG NIGHT FOR THE REPUBLICAN PARTY. CONGRATULATIONS TO ALL!

September 11, 2019

12:08 am: Greg Murphy won big, 62% to 37%, in North Carolina 03, & the Fake News barely covered the race. The win was far bigger than anticipated—there was just nothing the Fakers could say to diminish or demean the scope of this victory. So we had TWO BIG VICTORIES tonight, Greg & Dan

September 26, 2019

6:01 pm: No one has done more behind the scenes for STRONG BORDER SECURITY than @SenCapito. Her bill passed Committee today with $5B for the BORDER WALL. West Virginia is a great State and Shelley gets it done. Keep it up!

September 30, 2019

2:45 pm: My great friend, @RepMarkMeadows, has been an EXCELLENT Chairman of the House @FreedomCaucus, which has been a tremendous success. I am looking forward to close collaboration with his successor (starting Tuesday) and Strong Leader, @RepAndyBiggsAZ!

October 3, 2019

12:04 pm: Leader McCarthy, we look forward to you soon becoming Speaker of the House. The Do Nothing Dems don't have a chance!

12:16 pm: 95% Approval Rating in the Republican Party, and record setting fundraising that has taken place over the past two weeks. Thank you!

October 5, 2019

9:06 am: Somebody please wake up Mitt Romney and tell him that my conversation with the Ukrainian President was a congenial and very appropriate one, and my statement on China pertained to corruption, not politics. If Mitt worked this hard on Obama, he could have won. Sadly, he choked!

6:24 pm: Mitt, get off the stage, you've had your turn (twice)!

October 11, 2019

6:55 pm: Just landed in Louisiana! Vote against John Bel Edwards, he has the worst jobs record in the United States. Louisiana will do much better by electing a REPUBLICAN. See everyone soon! @LAGOP

October 15, 2019

10:30 am: Governor @MattBevin has done a wonderful job for the people of Kentucky! He continues to protect your very important Second Amendment. Matt is Strong on Crime and the Border, he Loves our Great Vets and Military. Matt has my Complete and Total Endorsement, and always has!

October 16, 2019

6:25 am: 95% Approval Rating in the Republican Party. Thank you! Just won two Congressional Seats in North Carolina, & a Governors runoff in Louisiana, which Republicans should now win! Because of Impeachment Fraud, we will easily take back the House, add in the Senate, & again win Pres!

6:46 am: Republicans are totally deprived of their rights in this Impeachment Witch Hunt. No lawyers, no questions, no transparency! The good news is that the Radical Left Dems have No Case. It is all based on their Fraud and Fabrication!

8:14 pm: Hope all House Republicans, and honest House Democrats, will vote to CENSURE Rep. Adam Schiff tomorrow for his brazen and unlawful act of fabricating (making up) a totally phony conversation with the Ukraine President and U.S. President, me. Most have never seen such a thing!

October 22, 2019

6:52 am: So some day, if a Democrat becomes President and the Republicans win the House, even by a tiny margin, they can impeach the President, without due process or fairness or any legal rights. All Republicans must remember what they are witnessing here—a lynching. But we will WIN!

6:54 am: Thank you Republicans. 185 out of 185 present voted for "US" last night. Really good!

October 23, 2019

6:36 am: Republicans are going to fight harder than ever to win back the House because of what the Do Nothing Democrats have done to our Country!

12:48 pm: The Never Trumper Republicans, though on respirators with not many left, are in certain ways worse and more dangerous for our Country than the Do Nothing Democrats. Watch out for them, they are human scum!

1:58 pm: Never Trumper Republican John Bellinger, represents Never Trumper Diplomat Bill Taylor (who I don't know), in testimony before Congress! Do Nothing Democrats allow Republicans Zero Representation, Zero due process, and Zero Transparency...

...Does anybody think this is fair? Even though there was no quid pro quo, I'm sure they would like to try. Worse than the Dems!

2:01 pm: It would be really great if the people within the Trump Administration, all well-meaning and good (I hope!), could stop hiring Never Trumpers, who are worse than the Do Nothing Democrats. Nothing good will ever come from them!

October 24, 2019

9:28 am: Thank you to House Republicans for being tough, smart, and understanding in detail the greatest Witch Hunt in American History. It has been going on since long before I even got Elected (the Insurance Policy!). A total Scam!

October 25, 2019

4:10 pm: appreciate the support of Senator @LindseyGraham, @SenateMajLdr Mitch McConnell, and their Great Senate Republican colleagues, on the resolution condemning the Do Nothing Democrats for their Witch Hunt Impeachment inquiry, behind closed doors...

November 1, 2019

9:08 am: LOUISIANA! Extreme Democrat John Bel Edwards has sided with Nancy Pelosi and Chuck Schumer to support Sanctuary Cities, High Taxes, and Open Borders. He is crushing Louisiana's economy and your Second Amendment rights...

...Our Republican candidate @EddieRispone is a successful conservative businessman who will stand with me to create jobs and protect your Second Amendment. GET OUT AND VOTE for Eddie, the next Governor of the GREAT State of Louisiana!

4:40 pm: Republicans have never been more unified than they are right now! The Dems are a mess under the corrupt leadership of Nervous Nancy Pelosi and Shifty Adam Schiff!

November 2, 2019

1:12 pm: Tate Reeves will be a great Governor of Mississippi, and what an electric Rally last night. Vote for Tate on Tuesday!

1:18 pm : Louisiana has a chance to have a really great Governor in @EddieRispone. Auto insurance costs and taxes will be coming way down with Eddie, and your 2nd Amendment will be protected. Current Democrat governor has done a really poor job! VOTE EARLY FOR EDDIE!

3:55 pm: Big Rally in Kentucky on Monday night for a man who has worked really hard & done a GREAT job, Governor @MattBevin. Kentucky is having the best economic year ever under Matt's leadership. He is a fantastic guy who loves our Military, our Vets and our 2nd Amendment. Vote Tuesday!

November 3, 2019

10:01 am: …Matt has been a GREAT Governor. Kentucky (I Love You!), please be sure to vote for Matt Bevin on TUESDAY. Matt will never let you down, and we have to send a strong signal to Nancy Pelosi and the Radical Left Democrats. See you on Monday night, VOTE TUESDAY!!!

3:18 pm: I hope everyone in the Great State of Virginia will get out and VOTE on Tuesday in all of the local and state elections to send a signal to D.C. that you want lower taxes, a strong Military, Border & 2nd Amendment, great healthcare, and must take care of our Vets. VOTE REPUBLICAN

3:23 pm: Virginia has the best Unemployment and Economic numbers in the history of the State. If the Democrats get in, those numbers will go rapidly in the other direction. On Tuesday, Vote Republican!

November 4, 2019

12:01 am: Great Republican Geary Higgins has my complete and to-tal Endorsement for Virginia Senate, 13th District. He is strong on Crime, the Border, our Military, Cutting Taxes, and protecting your 2nd Amendment. Dem John Bell will take your guns & raise your taxes. Vote for Geary Higgins

12:15 am: Louisiana, get out and Vote Early for @EddieRispone as your next Governor. Lower Taxes and car insurance. Will protect your 2nd Amendment. John Bel Edwards is always fighting our MAGA Agenda. Wants to raise your taxes and car insurance to the sky. Vote for Republican Eddie R!

9:51 am: Big Rally in Kentucky TONIGHT for a man who has worked really hard & done a GREAT job, Gov @MattBevin. Kentucky is hav-ing the best economic year ever under Matt's leadership. He is a fan-tastic guy who loves our Military, our Vets and our 2A. Vote Tuesday!

8:55 pm: THANK YOU Lexington, Kentucky! Get out tomorrow and VOTE for Governor @MattBevin and the entire Republican ticket. America is thriving like never before—and the BEST IS YET TO COME!

November 5, 2019

7:47 am: Fantastic being in the Great State of Kentucky last night. Vote for Matt Bevin NOW! @MattBevin One of Best Governors in U.S. He will never let you down!

12:19 pm: KENTUCKY! Get out today and VOTE for @MattBevin and the entire Republican ticket! MISSISSIPPI! Get out today and VOTE for @TateReeves and the entire Republican ticket! #VoteOn-Nov5 #ElectionDay Find your polling location below!

1:58 pm: Thank you so much CLUB 45. You are truly Great Americans. See you in Florida!

3:42 pm: KENTUCKY! #KYGov Get out today and VOTE for @MattBevin and the entire Republican ticket! MISSISSIPPI! #MSGov Get out today and VOTE for @TateReeves and the entire Republican ticket! Polls are open for a few more hours, find your location below!

8:02 pm: 95% Approval Rating in the Republican Party. Thank you!

9:38 pm: Great going Daniel, proud of you! https://t.co/0dUY5HoATN

11:37 pm: #ElectionNight Won 5 out of 6 elections in Kentucky, including 5 great candidates that I spoke for and introduced last night. @MattBevin picked up at least 15 points in last days, but perhaps not enough (Fake News will blame Trump!). Winning in Mississippi Governor race!

11:51 pm: Congratulations to @tatereeves on winning Governor of the Great State of Mississippi. Our big Rally on Friday night moved the numbers from a tie to a big WIN. Great reaction under pressure Tate!

11:56 pm: A lot of winning in Kentucky. Check out the numbers.

November 6, 2019

12:18 am: Great going Tate!

7:51 am: Based on the Kentucky results, Mitch McConnell @senatemajldr will win BIG in Kentucky next year!

6:56 pm: A great evening last night in Kentucky and Mississippi for the Republican Party with 13 BIG WINS, including a Governorship in Mississippi. Congratulations to everyone!

10:36 pm: LOUISIANA! Early voting is underway until Saturday, it's time to get out and VOTE to REPLACE Radical Liberal Democrat John Bel Edwards with a great new REPUBLICAN Governor, @EddieRispone!

November 14, 2019

10:53 pm: This Saturday, the eyes of history are looking at the people of Louisiana. If you want to defend your values, your jobs, and your freedom, then you need to REPLACE Radical Liberal John Bel Edwards with a true Louisiana Patriot: @EddieRispone! #GeauxVote

November 15, 2019

9:33 pm: Big day in LOUISIANA tomorrow! Get out and VOTE to replace Radical Liberal Democrat John Bel Edwards with a great new REPUBLICAN Governor, @EddieRispone! #GeauxVote #LAgov

November 16, 2019

8:08 am: Good morning Louisiana! Polls are open at 7AM. Get out and VOTE for @EddieRispone to be your next Gov! He will get your taxes and auto insurance (highest in Country!) way down. Loves our Military & Vets. Will protect your 2A. Find your polling place below:

8:51 am: LOUISIANA, VOTE @EddieRispone TODAY! He will be a great governor!

6:22 pm: Louisiana, 3 hours left, get out and Vote for @EddieRispone for Governor. Lower taxes and much more

November 17, 2019

7:59 am: I agree Katrina, Pam Bondi is a great womem!

November 18, 2019

7:29 am: Never has the Republican Party been so united as it is now. 95% A.R. This is a great fraud being played out against the American people by the Fake News Media & their partner, the Do Nothing Democrats. The rules are rigged by Pelosi & Schiff, but we are winning, and we will win!

November 22, 2019

1:53 pm: Thank you to @senatemajldr Mitch McConnell and @GOPLeader Kevin McCarthy for their Great Leadership! There has never been so much unity and spirit in the Republican Party, as there is right now!

November 23, 2019

12:02 pm: Daniel Cameron, who just won the A.G. race in the Great Commonwealth of Kentucky, is a young and very talented political star. You will be hearing much from Cameron in the yesrs to come!

November 24, 2019

5:01 pm: The Impeachment Scam is driving Republican Poll Numbers UP, UP, UP! Thank you Shifty.

November 27, 2019

5:11 pm: 95% Approval Rating in the Republican Party. Thank you!

December 2, 2019

11:47 am: Thank you to Great Republican @SenJohnKennedy for the job he did in representing both the Republican Party and myself against Sleepy Eyes Chuck Todd on Meet the Depressed!

12:56 pm: The Republican Party has NEVER been so united! This Impeachment Scam is just a continuation of the 3 year Witch Hunt, but it is only bringing us even closer together!

1:12 pm: Great job by @RepDougCollins of Georgia over the weekend in representing the Republican Party, and myself, against the Impeachment Hoax!

December 6, 2019

6:42 pm: Congressman @LanceGooden has done a wonderful job for the people of Texas while supporting our #MAGA Agenda. He continues to protect your very important #2A. Lance is Strong on Crime and the Border, he Loves our Great Vets and Military. Lance has my Complete & Total Endorsement!

7:06 pm: GREAT WORK yesterday by the Senate to support our Historically Black Colleges and Universities! Thank you @BetsyDeVosED, @SenAlexander, and @SenatorTimScott for your leadership...

...This Bill HELPS students get the student aid they need to go to college! STOP the headaches, and STOP the PAPERWORK barriers to HIGHER EDUCATION! Congrats to Lamar!

December 11, 2019

6:45 pm: Great Rally in Pennsylvania last night. Congressman Lloyd Smucker (PA-11) was there and I informed him that he has my complete and total Endorsement for the upcoming 2020 Election. Lloyd has done a great job. I am with him all the way! #MAGA

December 13, 2019

7:05 am: The Do Nothing Democrats have become the Party of lies and deception! The Republicans are the Party of the American Dream!

7:07 pm: The Republican Party is more united now than at any time in its history—by far!

December 17, 2019

4:14 pm: Congresswoman Kay @GrangerCampaign has worked hard for Texas and been a strong supporter of our #MAGA Agenda. She's strong on #2A and Securing our Border and is 100% pro-life. Kay has my Complete and Total Endorsement!

4:17 pm: Congressman @MarkwayneMullin is a big time #MAGA supporter! Markwayne has fought hard for Oklahoma Veterans and Military, he loves our Farmers and he's Strong on Border Security. I give Markwayne my Complete and Total Endorsement!

4:19 pm: Congressman @Denver4VA Riggleman is a true CONSER-VATIVE leader who has done a great job for Virginia and will support our #MAGA Agenda. He defends our right to bear arms, protect our Borders & help small businesses. Denver has my Total Endorsement!

4:20 pm: .@Buddy_Carter is a BUSINESSMAN first. He takes care of our Vets and Troops and is leading the fight to SLASH drug prices! Buddy's 100% pro-Wall & 100% pro-jobs. He will KEEP AMERICA GREAT and has my total, Strong Endorsement!

4:44 pm: Senator Dan Sullivan is doing a great job for the people of Alaska while supporting our #MAGA Agenda. He fights hard every-day to support our Veterans and the Military. Dan is Strong on the #2A and is 100% pro-jobs. I give Dan Sullivan my Complete and Total Endorsement!

December 18, 2019

8:27 am: Sean is a great patriot and will do a fantastic job. Has my total and complete endorsement!

8:33 am: Sean P is a much stronger candidate!

December 19, 2019

7:31 am: 100% Republican Vote. That's what people are talking about. The Republicans are united like never before!

10:33 am: Our great Congressman Gohmert is a TRUE patriot fighting back against people that must hate our Country!

December 20, 2019

3:59 pm: Congressman @ScottRTipton is a great supporter of the #MAGA Agenda! He fights for your #2A rights and the Border Wall. Scott is working hard for Colorado and has my Complete and Total Endorsement!

4:04 pm: The Democrat Party's Witch Hunt and CRAZY EXTREME policies are chasing common sense people out of the Dem Party. That's why Jeff Van Drew (@CongressmanJVD) voted NO on the Impeachment Hoax. Jeff will be joining our growing Republican Party...

...and has my FULL Endorsement. This is a BIG win for our GOP and a BIG win for South Jersey. South Jersey is TRUMP COUNTRY, so I know ALL NJ Republicans will join me in supporting Jeff Van Drew. The Dems are already coming after him, so help Jeff win.

4:07 pm: ...and has my FULL Endorsement. This is a BIG win for our GOP and a BIG win for South Jersey. South Jersey is TRUMP COUNTRY, so I know ALL NJ Republicans will join me in supporting Jeff Van Drew. The Dems are already coming after him, so help Jeff win.

...Kevin is strong on Securing the Border, #USMCA, protecting our #2A, and Loves our Vets and Military. Kevin is a true friend, and has my Complete and Total Endorsement!

10:40 pm: Proud of @JimInhofe's tenacious Oklahoma spirit that got the NDAA done. Maybe the best yet because it takes care of troops & establishes SPACE FORCE, which is 1st new branch since 1947 (Air Force). Another huge win for Jim's legacy. To many more! @SASCMajority

10:43 pm: BIG thank you to Mac Thornberry (@MacTXPress) for a GREAT Defense Deal! Mac has been a champion for our Military and Vets his whole career, and now he can add Space Force to his accomplishments. Look forward to another great defense bill next year, Mac! @HASCRepublicans

December 27, 2019

11:07 pm: Congresswoman Lesko, a great American!

Healthcare/Obamacare—2017 News Quotes

Response to a question from David Muir of ABC News, January 26, 2017.
Source: https://www.telegraph.co.uk/news/2017/01/26/
full-transcript-president-donald-trumps-interview-abc-news/

"So, I wanna make sure that nobody's dying on the streets when I'm President. Nobody's gonna be dying on the streets. We will unleash something that's gonna be terrific. And remember this, before Obamacare you had a lot of people that were very, very happy with their healthcare.

"And now those people in many cases don't even have healthcare. They don't even have anything that's acceptable to them. Remember this, keep your doctor, keep your plan, 100%. Remember the $5 billion website? Remember the website fiasco. I mean, you do admit that I think, right? The website fiasco.

"Obamacare is a disaster. We are going to come up with a new plan ideally not an amended plan. Because right now if you look at the pages, they're this high. We're gonna come up with a new plan that's going to be better healthcare for more people at a lesser cost."

Response to a question from David Muir of ABC News, January 26, 2017.
Source: https://www.telegraph.co.uk/news/2017/01/26/
full-transcript-president-donald-trumps-interview-abc-news/

"So, nobody ever deducts all the people that have already lost their health insurance that liked it. You had millions of people that liked their health insurance and their healthcare and their doctor and where they went. You had millions of people that now aren't insured anymore."

Response to a question from Bill O'Reilly of FOX News, February 7, 2017.
Source: https://www.foxnews.com/transcript/
bill-oreillys-exclusive-interview-with-president-trump

"Well, in the process, and maybe it will take until sometime into next year, but we are certainly going to be in the process. Very complicated. Obamacare is a disaster. You have to remember, Obamacare doesn't work. You look at Arizona, 160% increase. You look at Minnesota, all of these places, it's going through the roof."

Response to a question from Bill O'Reilly of FOX News, February 7, 2017.
Source: https://www.foxnews.com/transcript/
bill-oreillys-exclusive-interview-with-president-trump

"We're going to be putting it in very soon. I think that yes, I would like to say by the end of the year. At least the rudiments, but we should have something within a year into the following year. And by the way, we will have something that is good. Less expensive and really great healthcare."

Response to a question from Tucker Carlson of FOX News, March 15, 2017.
Source: https://www.youtube.com/watch?v=RYGH6ejacNO

"And one of the reasons I want to get the healthcare taken care of and it has to come statutorily and for other reasons, various complex reasons. Having to do with politics and also Congress. It has to come first. It really has to come first. But one of the reasons I want to get it finished, ideally soon, is because I want to start on the taxes.

"People are paying too high; companies are paying too high. It is affecting our jobs. It is affecting a lot of things.

"Now, with that being said, the country is doing right now really well. The level of optimism is up highest it's been in 15 years. You see the kind of numbers coming out, it's amazing. The enthusiasm. I saw it this morning on *FOX & Friends*, I watched, I liked that group of three people. But they had a man who is saying Trump is the greatest president ever and there will never be one like him.

"Now, the thing is, I've only been there for like 50 days. But he was very enthusiastic. But he was talking. He is a manufacturer. And I have taken off regulations by the thousands."

Response to a question from Tucker Carlson of FOX News, March 15, 2017.
Source: https://www.youtube.com/watch?v=RYGH6ejacNO

"There is tremendous waste in this country. There is tremendous, you know, the bidding procedures in the country.

"I'll give you an example, medicine. I met with a man that I really like. Elijah Cummings, Congressman. And he was in my office. And so passionate about prescription drugs and drugs. The fact that they are so expensive in this country and so expensive for people.

"And I'm going to work and put in this bill or shortly thereafter a new bill, bidding for drugs and prescription drugs. If you go to Europe, they buy them for a fraction, from the same company. They buy them for a fraction of what they pay in the United States. Because we have a middleman system.

"And we have a lot of bad systems, but basically we do not have a good bidding system.

"And we are going to get drug prices so far lower than they are now. Your head will spin."

Response to a question from Tucker Carlson of FOX News, March 15, 2017.
Source: https://www.youtube.com/watch?v=RYGH6ejacNO

"Phase 2, which is really not a phase. That's where our secretary, who is a terrific guy by the way, Tom Price is going to sign away. He's going to sign his heart away. And he is going to get rid of those horrible things that have been signed over the years.

"And then Phase 3, a lot of the goodies are added in and we're going to add now in medicine. We think we're going to be able to do that. Or I'm going to have a separate bill for the bidding of medicine.

"We're going to bring the cost of medicine way down. Prescription drugs and drugs."

Response to a question from John Dickerson of CBS News, April 30, 2017.
Source: https://www.cbsnews.com/news/face-the-nation-transcript-april-30-2017-president-trump/

"Pre-existing conditions are in the bill. And I just watched another network than yours, and they were saying, pre-existing is not covered. Pre-existing conditions are in the bill. And I mandate it. I said, 'Has to be.' So, we have, we're going to have lower premiums. And before you start there, let me just tell you something. Obamacare is dead. Obamacare, right now, all the insurance companies are fleeing. Places like Tennessee have already lost half of their state with the insurance companies. They're all going. Obamacare, John [Dickerson of CBS News], is dead, OK, because we're being, we're being compared to Obamacare. Just so, Obamacare doesn't work."

Response to a question from John Dickerson of CBS News, April 30, 2017.
Source: https://www.cbsnews.com/news/face-the-nation-transcript-april-30-2017-president-trump/

"With Obamacare... [Dickerson interrupts; Trump continues.] ...the premiums are too high. The deductibles are through the roof, so you never get to use it. But, more importantly, it's dead."

Response to a question from John Dickerson of CBS News, April 30, 2017.
Source: https://www.cbsnews.com/news/face-the-nation-transcript-april-30-2017-president-trump/

"This bill is much different than it was a little while ago, OK? This bill has evolved. And we didn't have a failure on the bill. You know, it was reported like a failure. Now, the one thing I wouldn't have done again is put a timeline. That's why, on the second iteration, I didn't put a timeline. But we have now pre-existing conditions in the bill. We have, we've set up a pool for the pre-existing conditions, so that the premiums can be allowed to fall. We're taking across all of the borders or the lines, so that insurance companies can compete... [Dickerson interrupts; Trump continues.] ...nationwide."

Response to a question from John Dickerson of CBS News, April 30, 2017.
Source: https://www.cbsnews.com/news/face-the-nation-transcript-april-30-2017-president-trump/

"There will be such competition. Right now, there's no competition. There will be such competition by insurance companies, so that they can get healthcare and the people taking care of healthcare. The other thing we're going to have is groups. Groups of people can negotiate. What's going to happen is, the competition is going to drive down the premiums, in my opinion, much, much more than people understand."

Response to a question from John Dickerson of CBS News, April 30, 2017.
Source: https://www.cbsnews.com/news/face-the-nation-transcript-april-30-2017-president-trump/

"But we're going to, most importantly, we're going to drive down premiums. We're going to drive down deductibles, because, right now, deductibles are so high, you never, unless you're going to die a long, hard death, you never can get to use your healthcare... [Dickerson interrupts; Trump continues.] ...because the deductibles are so high."

From proclamation of May 2017 as National Mental Health Awareness Month, May 7, 2017.
Source: https://www.whitehouse.gov/presidential-actions/
president-donald-j-trump-proclaims-may-2017-national-mental-health-awareness-month/

"National Mental Health Awareness Month is a time to recognize the millions of American families affected by mental illness and to redouble our efforts to ensure that those who are suffering get the care and treatment they need. Nearly 10 million Americans suffer from a serious mental illness, such as schizophrenia, bipolar disorder, or major depression. Unfortunately, approximately 60% of adults and 50% of adolescents with mental illness do not get the treatment or other services they need. As a result, instead of receiving ongoing expert psychiatric care, these individuals often find themselves in emergency rooms, prisons, or living on the streets.

"This month, and for the course of my administration, I am committed to working with the Department of Health and Human Services, States, and communities throughout the country to find a better answer for the millions of Americans who need mental health services and their families. We must further empower States, law enforcement, first responders, doctors, and families to help those with the most severe mental illnesses; to ensure that people with mental illness have access to evidence-based treatment and services; and to fight the stigma associated with mental illness, which can prevent people from seeking care. We must also resolve to enhance our understanding of mental illness and its relationship to other complex societal challenges, including homelessness, substance abuse, and suicide; and we reaffirm our commitment to improving prevention, diagnosis, and treatment through innovative medical strategies.

"Addressing substance abuse, addiction, and overdose is often critical to improving mental health outcomes. An estimated 8.1 million adults in America suffering with a mental illness also struggle with substance abuse. Many of those who struggled with both were among the 52,000 people in our country who died from a drug overdose in 2015. Approximately 44,000 Americans took their own lives in the past year, a preventable tragedy that frequently correlates with mental illness and substance abuse.

"No American should suffer in silence and solitude. During Mental Health Awareness Month, I encourage all Americans to seek to better understand mental illness and to look for opportunities to help those with mental health issues. We must support those in need and remain committed to hope and healing. Through compassion and committed action, we will enrich the spirit of the American people and improve the well-being of our nation.

"Now, therefore, I, Donald J. Trump, President of the United States of America, by virtue of the authority vested in me by the Constitution and the laws of the United States, do hereby proclaim May 2017 as National Mental Health Awareness Month. I call upon all Americans to support citizens suffering from mental illness, raise awareness of mental health conditions through appropriate programs and activities, and commit our nation to innovative prevention, diagnosis, and treatment."

Response to a question from Maggie Haberman of *The New York Times*, July 19, 2017.
Source: https://www.nytimes.com/2017/07/19/us/politics/trump-interview-transcript.html

"So pre-existing conditions are a tough deal. Because you are basically saying from the moment the insurance, you're 21 years old, you start working and you're paying $12 a year for insurance, and by the time you're 70, you get a nice plan. Here's something where you walk up and say, 'I want my insurance.' It's a very tough deal, but it is something that we're doing a good job of."

Healthcare/Obamacare—2017 Tweets

February 14, 2017

5:50 pm: Obamacare continues to fail. Humana to pull out in 2018. Will repeal, replace & save healthcare for ALL Americans.

February 15, 2017

4:34 pm: Aetna CEO: Obamacare in 'Death Spiral' #RepealAndReplace

February 27, 2017

12:06 pm: Great meeting with CEOs of leading U.S. health insurance companies who provide great healthcare to the American people.

March 7, 2017

7:13 am: Our wonderful new Healthcare Bill is now out for review and negotiation. ObamaCare is a complete and total disaster—is imploding fast!

8:46 am: I am working on a new system where there will be competition in the Drug Industry. Pricing for the American people will come way down!

March 9. 2017

12:01 pm: Despite what you hear in the press, healthcare is coming along great. We are talking to many groups and it will end in a beautiful picture!

March 11, 2017

9:30 am: We are making great progress with healthcare. ObamaCare is imploding and will only get worse. Republicans coming together to get job done!

March 23, 2017

11:07 am: We are taking action to #RepealANDReplace #Obamacare! Contact your Rep & tell them you support #AHCA. #PassTheBill...

March 24, 2017

7:14 am: After seven horrible years of ObamaCare (skyrocketing premiums & deductibles, bad healthcare), this is finally your chance for a great plan!

March 25, 2017

9:37 am: ObamaCare will explode and we will all get together and piece together a great healthcare plan for THE PEOPLE. Do not worry!

April 1, 2017

10:59 am to 11:06 am: The failing @nytimes finally gets it—"In places where no insurance company offers plans, there will be no way for ObamaCare customers to...

...use subsidies to buy health plans." In other words, Ocare is dead. Good things will happen, however, either with Republicans or Dems.

April 2, 2017

7:56 am: Anybody (especially Fake News media) who thinks that Repeal & Replace of ObamaCare is dead does not know the love and strength in R Party!

April 23, 2017

9:20 am: ObamaCare is in serious trouble. The Dems need big money to keep it going—otherwise it dies far sooner than anyone would have thought.

April 24, 2017

12:18 pm: If our healthcare plan is approved, you will see real healthcare and premiums will start tumbling down. ObamaCare is in a death spiral!

April 28, 2017

7:28 am to 7:32 am: You can't compare anything to ObamaCare because ObamaCare is dead. Dems want billions to go to Insurance Companies to bail out donors...New

...healthcare plan is on its way. Will have much lower premiums & deductibles while at the same time taking care of pre-existing conditions!

May 4, 2017

7:28 am: Death spiral! 'Aetna will exit Obamacare markets in VA in 2018, citing expected losses on INDV plans this year'
https://t.co/5YnzDitF8r

12:43 pm: I am watching the Democrats trying to defend the "you can keep you doctor, you can keep your plan & premiums will go down" ObamaCare lie."

12:56 pm: Insurance companies are fleeing ObamaCare—it is dead. Our healthcare plan will lower premiums & deductibles—and be great healthcare!

9:55 pm: It was a GREAT day for the United States of America! This is a great plan that is a repeal & replace of ObamaCare. Make no mistake about it.

May 5, 2017

2:13 pm: Of course the Australians have better healthcare than we do—everybody does. ObamaCare is dead! But our healthcare will soon be great.

May 7, 2017

7:49 am: Republican Senators will not let the American people down! ObamaCare premiums and deductibles are way up—it was a lie and it is dead!

May 28, 2017

6:57 pm: I suggest that we add more dollars to Healthcare and make it the best anywhere. ObamaCare is dead—the Republicans will do much better!

June 13, 2017

8:56 am: 2 million more people just dropped out of ObamaCare. It is in a death spiral. Obstructionist Democrats gave up, have no answer = resist!

July 10, 2017

5:47 am: I cannot imagine that Congress would dare to leave Washington without a beautiful new HealthCare bill fully approved and ready to go!

July 14, 2017

5:35 am: After all of these years of suffering thru ObamaCare, Republican Senators must come through as they have promised!

July 15, 2017

12:56 pm: Next week the Senate is going to vote on legislation to save Americans from the ObamaCare DISASTER. #WeeklyAddress https://t.co/xjVDkgo1NK

July 18, 2017

6:56 am: We were let down by all of the Democrats and a few Republicans. Most Republicans were loyal, terrific & worked really hard. We will return!

6:58 am: As I have always said, let ObamaCare fail and then come together and do a great healthcare plan. Stay tuned!

July 19, 2017

7:30 am: I will be having lunch at the White House today with Republican Senators concerning healthcare. They MUST keep their promise to America!

4:33 pm: Any senator who votes against starting debate is telling America that you are fine w/ the #OCareNightmare! Remarks: https://t.co/DI7e78hr6N

July 25, 2017

5:27 am: Big day for HealthCare. After 7 years of talking, we will soon see whether or not Republicans are willing to step up to the plate!

5:38 am: ObamaCare is torturing the American People. The Democrats have fooled the people long enough. Repeal or Repeal & Replace! I have pen in hand

5:44 am: So great that John McCain is coming back to vote. Brave—American hero! Thank you John.

10:20 am: The American people have waited long enough. There has been enough talk and no action for seven years. Now is the time for action!

2:24 pm: .@SenJohnMcCain-Thank you for coming to D.C. for such a vital vote. Congrats to all Rep. We can now deliver grt healthcare to all Americans!

July 28, 2017

1:25 am: 3 Republicans and 48 Democrats let the American people down. As I said from the beginning, let ObamaCare implode, then deal. Watch!

8:46 am to 9:00 am: If Republicans are going to pass great future legislation in the Senate, they must immediately go to a 51 vote majority, not senseless 60...

...Even though parts of healthcare could pass at 51, some really good things need 60. So many great future bills & budgets need 60 votes...

August 10, 2017

5:54 am: Can you believe that Mitch McConnell, who has screamed Repeal & Replace for 7 years, couldn't get it done. Must Repeal & Replace ObamaCare!

September 14, 2017

2:31 pm to 2:32 pm: Bernie Sanders is pushing hard for a single payer healthcare plan—a curse on the U.S. & its people...

...I told Republicans to approve healthcare fast or this would happen. But don't worry, I will veto because I love our country & its people.

September 20, 2017

6:07 pm: I would not sign Graham-Cassidy if it did not include coverage of pre-existing conditions. It does! A great Bill. Repeal & Replace.

September 23, 2017

5:42 am: John McCain never had any intention of voting for this Bill, which his Governor loves. He campaigned on Repeal & Replace. Let Arizona down!

5:50 am: Arizona had a 116% increase in ObamaCare premiums last year, with deductibles very high. Chuck Schumer sold John McCain a bill of goods. Sad

5:59 am: Large Block Grants to States is a good thing to do. Better control & management. Great for Arizona. McCain let his best friend L.G. down!

6:04 am: I know Rand Paul and I think he may find a way to get there for the good of the Party!

6:13 am: Alaska had a 200% plus increase in premiums under ObamaCare, worst in the country. Deductibles high, people angry! Lisa M comes through.

September 24, 2017

5:21 pm: Alaska, Arizona, Maine and Kentucky are big winners in the Healthcare proposal. 7 years of Repeal & Replace and some Senators not there.

September 25, 2017

8:24 pm: A few of the many clips of John McCain talking about Repealing & Replacing O'Care. My oh my has he changed-complete turn from years of talk! https://t.co/t9cXG2Io86

September 27, 2017

6:32 am: With one Yes vote in hospital & very positive signs from Alaska and two others (McCain is out), we have the HCare Vote, but not for Friday!

6:36 am: We will have the votes for Healthcare but not for the reconciliation deadline of Friday, after which we need 60. Get rid of Filibuster Rule!

October 7, 2017

7:17 am: I called Chuck Schumer yesterday to see if the Dems want to do a great HealthCare Bill. ObamaCare is badly broken, big premiums. Who knows!

October 10, 2017

5:30 am: Since Congress can't get its act together on HealthCare, I will be using the power of the pen to give great HealthCare to many people—FAST

October 12, 2017

12:06 pm: The time has come to take action to IMPROVE access, INCREASE choices, and LOWER COSTS for HEALTHCARE! →https://t.co/mz5fdveTVh https://t.co/dDZLsKuNSe

October 13, 2017

4:36 am: The Democrats ObamaCare is imploding. Massive subsidy payments to their pet insurance companies has stopped. Dems should call me to fix!

6:14 am: ObamaCare is a broken mess. Piece by piece we will now begin the process of giving America the great HealthCare it deserves!

8:10 pm: Money pouring into Insurance Companies profits, under the guise of ObamaCare, is over. They have made a fortune. Dems must get smart & deal!

8:17 pm: ObamaCare is causing such grief and tragedy for so many. It is being dismantled but in the meantime, premiums & deductibles are way up!

October 14, 2017

6:18 am: Health Insurance stocks, which have gone through the roof during the ObamaCare years, plunged yesterday after I ended their Dems windfall!

6:27 am: Very proud of my Executive Order which will allow greatly expanded access and far lower costs for HealthCare. Millions of people benefit!

October 18, 2017

8:41 am: I am supportive of Lamar as a person & also of the process, but I can never support bailing out ins co's who have made a fortune w/ O'Care.

November 23, 2017

6:18 pm: ObamaCare premiums are going up, up, up, just as I have been predicting for two years. ObamaCare is OWNED by the Democrats, and it is a disaster. But do not worry. Even though the Dems want to Obstruct, we will Repeal & Replace right after Tax Cuts!

December 22, 2017

5:11 pm: Remember, the most hated part of ObamaCare is the Individual Mandate, which is being terminated under our just signed Tax Cut Bill.

Healthcare/Obamacare—2018 News Quotes

Remarks at a rally in Tampa, Florida, July 31, 2018.
Source: https://www.tampabay.com/florida-politics/buzz/2018/08/01/
heres-a-full-transcript-of-president-trumps-speech-from-his-tampa-rally/

"We repealed the core of Obamacare. The individual mandate is gone. You know, the individual mandate. That's a beauty. Only the past administration could have come up with this. That's where you pay a lot of money for the privilege of not paying in order to have poor healthcare. Other than that, it's a wonderful thing.

"So, you pay all this money for the privilege of not having to pay and the healthcare is no good to start off with. And we're doing great on healthcare. We're allowing Americans to buy better healthcare for less money through association health plans, including across state lines, bidding, you're getting tremendous competition."

Remarks at the Congressional Ball, December 15, 2018.
Source: https://www.whitehouse.gov/briefings-statements/
remarks-president-trump-congressional-ball/

"I believe we're going to get really good healthcare. Exciting things happened over the last 24 hours. And if everybody is smart, because we have a lot of Democrats here tonight, and I'm very happy about that. People don't realize it; I have a lot of friends who are Democrats. And we have Democrats here. And if the Republicans and the Democrats get together, we are going to end up with incredible healthcare, which is the way it should have been from day one. And it's going to happen. It now has a chance to happen."

Healthcare/Obamacare—2018 Tweets

February 5, 2018

7:11 am: The Democrats are pushing for Universal HealthCare while thousands of people are marching in the UK because their U system is going broke and not working. Dems want to greatly raise taxes for really bad and non-personal medical care. No thanks!

May 11, 2018

2:30 pm: Today, my Administration is launching the most sweeping action in history to lower the price of prescription drugs for the American People. We will have tougher negotiation, more competition, and much lower prices at the pharmacy counter!

May 30, 2018

12:09 pm: Today I am proud to keep another promise to the American people as I sign the #RightToTry Legislation into law.

12:11 pm: With the #RightToTry Law I signed today, patients with life threatening illnesses will finally have access to experimental treatments that could improve or even cure their conditions. These are experimental treatments and products that have shown great promise...

June 4, 2018

7:18 am: ...We had Repeal & Replace done (and the saving to our country of one trillion dollars) except for one person, but it is getting done anyway. Individual Mandate is gone and great, less expensive plans will be announced this month. Drug prices coming down & Right to Try!

July 9, 2018

12:08 pm: Pfizer & others should be ashamed that they have raised drug prices for no reason. They are merely taking advantage of the poor & others unable to defend themselves, while at the same time giving bargain basement prices to other countries in Europe & elsewhere. We will respond!

July 10, 2018

5:37 pm: Just talked with Pfizer CEO and @SecAzar on our drug pricing blueprint. Pfizer is rolling back price hikes, so American patients don't pay more. We applaud Pfizer for this decision and hope other companies do the same. Great news for the American people!

July 19, 2018

5:23 am: Thank you to Novartis for not increasing your prices on prescription drugs. Likewise to Pfizer. We are making a big push to actually reduce the prices, maybe substantially, on prescription drugs.

August 24, 2018

7:40 pm: Great to see the Senate working on solutions to end the secrecy around ridiculously high drug prices, something I called for in my drug pricing Blueprint. Will now work with the House to help American patients! #AmericanPatientsFirst

September 17, 2018

1:10 pm: Americans deserve to know the lowest drug price at their pharmacy, but "gag clauses" prevent your pharmacist from telling you! I support legislation that will remove gag clauses and urge the Senate to act. #AmericanPatientsFirst

October 15, 2018

6:51 pm: Open enrollment starts today on lower-priced Medicare Advantage plans so loved by our great seniors. Crazy Bernie and his band of Congressional Dems will outlaw these plans. Disaster!

October 18, 2018

2:43 pm: All Republicans support people with pre-existing conditions, and if they don't, they will after I speak to them. I am in total support. Also, Democrats will destroy your Medicare, and I will keep it healthy and well!

October 24, 2018

7:45 am: Republicans will totally protect people with Pre-Existing Conditions, Democrats will not! Vote Republican.

December 14, 2018

9:07 pm: As I predicted all along, Obamacare has been struck down as an UNCONSTITUTIONAL disaster! Now Congress must pass a STRONG law that provides GREAT healthcare and protects pre-existing conditions. Mitch and Nancy, get it done!

9:16 pm: Wow, but not surprisingly, ObamaCare was just ruled UNCONSTITUTIONAL by a highly respected judge in Texas. Great news for America!

December 17, 2018

8:02 am: The DEDUCTIBLE which comes with ObamaCare is so high that it is practically not even useable! Hurts families badly. We have a chance, working with the Democrats, to deliver great HealthCare! A confirming Supreme Court Decision will lead to GREAT HealthCare results for Americans!

Healthcare/Obamacare—2019 News Quotes

Response to a question from Maggie Haberman of *The New York Times*, January 31, 2019.
Source: https://www.nytimes.com/2019/02/01/us/politics/trump-interview-transcripts.html

"No, because it's a very big job and there is a lot to do. And I would say that I would really start focusing—You know, we've done a lot on healthcare, and people haven't given us too much credit. We have a lot of the different plans, the cooperative plans and other plans. Healthcare was terminated, and if the Obamacare were repealed and replaced, except for John McCain[12], it would have been, you know, he campaigned against it for six years, and then when he had the chance, he went thumbs down at two o'clock in the morning.

"Um, but, I believe it's going to be terminated, whether it be through the Texas case, which is going through the court system as a victory right now, because of, you know, the various elements of that case, you would think it would have to be terminated. But a deal will be made for good healthcare in this country. That's one of the things I'll be doing."

From State of the Union address, February 5, 2019.
Source: https://www.whitehouse.gov/briefings-statements/
president-donald-j-trumps-state-union-address-2/

"The next major priority for me, and for all of us, should be to lower the cost of healthcare and prescription drugs, and to protect patients with pre-existing conditions.

"Already, as a result of my administration's efforts, in 2018 drug prices experienced their single largest decline in 46 years.

"But we must do more. It is unacceptable that Americans pay vastly more than people in other countries for the exact same drugs, often

---

12   Senator John McCain (R-Arizona) served from 1987 until his death in August 2018.

made in the exact same place. This is wrong, unfair, and together we can stop it.

"I am asking the Congress to pass legislation that finally takes on the problem of global freeloading and delivers fairness and price transparency for American patients. We should also require drug companies, insurance companies, and hospitals to disclose real prices to foster competition and bring costs down.

"No force in history has done more to advance the human condition than American freedom. In recent years we have made remarkable progress in the fight against HIV and AIDS. Scientific breakthroughs have brought a once-distant dream within reach. My budget will ask Democrats and Republicans to make the needed commitment to eliminate the HIV epidemic in the United States within 10 years. Together, we will defeat AIDS in America.

"Tonight, I am also asking you to join me in another fight that all Americans can get behind: the fight against childhood cancer."

From State of the Union address, February 5, 2019.
Source: https://www.whitehouse.gov/briefings-statements/
president-donald-j-trumps-state-union-address-2/

"Many childhood cancers have not seen new therapies in decades. My budget will ask the Congress for $500 million over the next 10 years to fund this critical life-saving research."

From State of the Union address, February 5, 2019.
Source: https://www.whitehouse.gov/briefings-statements/
president-donald-j-trumps-state-union-address-2/

"To defend the dignity of every person, I am asking the Congress to pass legislation to prohibit the late-term abortion of children who can feel pain in the mother's womb.

"Let us work together to build a culture that cherishes innocent life. And let us reaffirm a fundamental truth: all children, born and unborn, are made in the holy image of God."

Remarks during a visit to the Lima Army Tank Plant in Ohio, March 20, 2019.
Source: https://www.c-span.org/video/?458966-1/
president-trump-delivers-remarks-lima-army-tank-plant-ohio

"John McCain[13] campaigned for years to repeal and replace Obamacare—For years, in Arizona. A great state. I love the people of Arizona. But he campaigned, for years, for 'repeal and replace.' So did Rob and so did a lot of senators.

"When he [McCain] finally had the chance to do it, he voted against 'repeal and replace.' He voted against, at two o'clock in the morning. Remember 'thumbs down?' We said, 'What the hell happened?' He said, two hours before, he was voting to repeal and replace. And then he went thumbs down, badly hurting the Republican Party, badly hurting our nation, and hurting many sick people who desperately wanted good, affordable healthcare. We would've had it.

"This would've saved our country over a trillion dollars in entitlements, and we would have ended up making a great healthcare plan, frankly, with the Democrats because they would have had no choice."

Remarks at the signing of an executive order protecting and improving Medicare for senior citizens, Ocala, Florida, October 3, 2019.
Source: https://www.whitehouse.gov/briefings-statements/remarks-president-trump-signing-executive-order-protecting-improving-medicare-nations-seniors-ocala-fl/

"So in my campaign for President, I made you a sacred pledge that I would strengthen, protect, and defend Medicare for all of our senior citizens. And you see it's under siege, but it's not going to happen.

"Today, I will sign a very historic executive order that does exactly that: we are making your Medicare even better, and we are not letting anyone—It will never be taken away from you. We're not letting anyone get close.

"You see these people on the other side? These people are crazy, by the way. They're totally crazy. But they want to take it away and give you lousy healthcare. It's pretty incredible. You want to keep your doctors,

13   Senator John McCain (R-Arizona) served from 1987 until his death in August 2018.

right? Remember, with Obama—[former U.S.] President [Barack] Obama, right? He said, 'You can keep your doctor. You can keep your plan.' That didn't work out too well for the people."

Remarks at the signing of an executive order protecting and improving Medicare for senior citizens, Ocala, Florida, October 3, 2019.
Source: https://www.whitehouse.gov/briefings-statements/remarks-president-trump-signing-executive-order-protecting-improving-medicare-nations-seniors-ocala-fl/

"As long as I'm President, no one will lay a hand on your Medicare benefits. And that's what we're here to do today.

"This order is the latest step in my administration's drive to ensure the world's best healthcare for all Americans. Together, we're creating a healthcare system that protects vulnerable patients, makes healthcare more affordable, gives you more choice and control, and delivers the high-quality care Americans deserve. And that's what we're doing; we're strengthening our healthcare system to a level that nobody thought would be possible."

Remarks at the signing of an executive order protecting and improving Medicare for senior citizens, Ocala, Florida, October 3, 2019.
Source: https://www.whitehouse.gov/briefings-statements/remarks-president-trump-signing-executive-order-protecting-improving-medicare-nations-seniors-ocala-fl/

"In the last administration, Democrats slashed Medicare by $800 billion dollars to pay for Obamacare. Not too good, Obamacare."

Remarks at the signing of an executive order protecting and improving Medicare for senior citizens, Ocala, Florida, October 3, 2019.
Source: https://www.whitehouse.gov/briefings-statements/remarks-president-trump-signing-executive-order-protecting-improving-medicare-nations-seniors-ocala-fl/

"In a few moments, I will sign an executive order to strengthen Medicare for seniors, and very substantially. I'll provide Medicare Advantage plans with new tools and options, and it will help Medicare beneficiaries gain faster access to the very latest and greatest medical devices and therapies.

"My order also pursues reductions in the unnecessary regulations that you don't need, you don't want to see, that never come into effect and that cost a lot of money, enabling doctors and nurses to spend less time on paperwork and more time with their patients that they love.

"To further protect seniors, we are taking action to stop fraud and to stop abuse. It's tremendous amounts of money saved with that. And we'll be able to put that money right back into what we want to have it to take care of you.

"I'm directing [Health and Human Services] Secretary [Alex] Azar to crack down on criminals, cheaters, and dishonest providers who rob Medicare of the funds you have and the money that you've paid into the system all of your lives. Charles said it. Charles said, 'You know, I paid for it.' He said he paid for it. And now they want to say, 'Let's give it to everybody else.' And it's going to be gone in a very short number of years. But you did pay for it. You both paid for it.

"Today's action is the only really great action that we can take. It's the only choice we have because this is going to be something that's better than any place anywhere in the world. It's the latest of many important steps that we're taking to dramatically improve healthcare for the American people.

"Our vision for the future of health in America has four crucial parts. And we will protect vulnerable patients, number one. We will protect those patients that are so terribly vulnerable. We will deliver the affordability that you need. Prices coming down. As I said, prescription drug prices—First time in over 50 years, Alex, that drug prices have come down for the year. Your average prescription drug price—First time in 50 years, over 50 years.

"And we're going to get them a lot lower. And I think Ron [DeSantis, governor of Florida] is going to have some big surprises. We'll be announcing that pretty soon. Some—For really, really big reductions. People are already—They're not even going to know what happened. So that's what we want.

"And we're going to give you options and control that you want. And we will provide the quality you deserve.

"First, we're protecting vulnerable Americans. We have made a clear promise to America's patients: We will always protect patients with pre-existing conditions. The Republicans will always protect pre-existing conditions. To stop families from being blindsided by outrageous medical bills—And this is something that is one of the most exciting things to me; I have challenged Congress to send a bill to my desk that stops the horrendous practice of surprise medical billing. So many of you, you go in and you have something, and then you get a bill and you say, 'How is it possible?' And we're going to end that practice. That practice is not a fair practice.

"And we're also confronting the opioid and drug addiction epidemic that is plaguing too many American communities. And thanks to our efforts—And we've worked so hard on it; the First Lady worked so hard. Kellyanne Conway; where's Kellyanne? Where's Kellyanne? Where is she? Kellyanne, thank you.

"Last year, drug overdose deaths declined for the first time in nearly three decades. Early data shows that drug overdose deaths dropped 10% last year in the state of Florida. Now, think of that. That's—You know, we'd like to better. It's a very, very tough situation. And one of the things we're doing with the 'pain pills'—We can call them—We're trying to find, and we're really working hard and we're funding a lot of research to find pain pills that aren't addictive. You go into to a hospital with a broken arm, and you come out and you're drug addict. And we're trying to find, and we're getting closer—I think we're getting very close, actually, to finding painkillers that aren't addictive. And we'll have that in the not-too-distant future."

Remarks at the signing of an executive order protecting and improving Medicare for senior citizens, Ocala, Florida, October 3, 2019.

Source: https://www.whitehouse.gov/briefings-statements/remarks-president-trump-signing-executive-order-protecting-improving-medicare-nations-seniors-ocala-fl/

"The second part of our healthcare agenda is to promote the affordability of America's needs. Thanks to our focus on lower drug prices, the FDA approved more low-cost generic drugs in my first two years than ever before in the history of our country. Think of that. Think of that.

"And every time I'd see the folks over at FDA, I'd say, 'Come on, fellas. Let's go. Faster. Faster.' You know, don't forget, when somebody was dying and we had a drug that looked like it was really good but it wasn't going be approved for like four more years. It used to be 12 years and we brought it way down. I mean, it's too long. But we brought it way, way down. But a person is dying and they said, 'No, sir, we can't give that because it may harm the person.' I said, 'Wait a minute, you don't understand. A person is terminally ill, they've got four weeks to live, and you don't want to give them a drug because you think it's going to harm them? I guarantee you I can get them to sign a document.'

"Now we got that approved: Right to Try. And, by the way, miracles are happening. Right? Miracles. Miracles are happening.

"Hopefully, it never happens to anybody in this room. But, frankly, people would go to Asia, they'd go to Europe, they'd go all over the world seeking a cure, if they had money. If they didn't have money, they'd go home and they'd die. But now they don't have to do that.

"And it wasn't easy because the drug companies didn't want it because they didn't want to have terminally ill because it looks bad on the percentage record, right? The insurance companies didn't want it because there are a lot of reasons. You know what the reasons are. Our government didn't want it because they didn't want to be sued by a patient that died that would've died anyway. So I said, 'Here's what we do, folks: We sign an agreement. And the agreement holds everybody non-liable.'

"We took the drug companies and we created a separate list, so they're not on that list—Because it is, right? It's a problem. And we took a separate list. So now we have a totally separate list, confidential list, but they don't get hurt by somebody that was so sick that this person may not make it. And I got everybody to sign it and we were done. It was pretty amazing. And then we got it approved in Congress because of these five great congressmen back there, including Ron [DeSantis, governor of Florida], who at the time was in Congress. Right? With Greg and everybody, we got it done and we got the Senate to approve it. And I signed it. And I was really happy. Right to Try. Hopefully you never need it.

"We also ended the terrible gag clauses that prevented pharmacists from telling you about cheaper options at the pharmacy counter. Do you believe it? I thought this was—I thought they were kidding me the first time. Don't forget, I've only been doing this for three years, okay? So, you know.

"These guys have been doing it a long time. But they're not allowed to talk to you about pricing. I said, 'Wait. You've got to be kidding.' And they weren't. But I got rid of that. Now they can talk about pricing. You can go out and price. You can go to different places. They have to be open and transparent. That was a big deal. That was a big deal.

"And all of these things, you know, they sound so simple; they're tough to get. They've been that way for many years for a reason. You have very powerful lobbyists. You have drug companies, frankly, that don't want that. Why would they want that, where you can negotiate price? Why would they want a thing like that?

"My administration is also working to require drug companies to disclose prices in their television advertisements. And we're almost getting to a point where we're going to be able to get that. So you're going to know what you're paying up front. They can't triple-hit you.

"Essentially, we're holding Big Pharma accountable. And that's okay; they do just fine.

"Earlier this year, we announced another groundbreaking action seniors have wanted for decades. We will soon allow the safe and legal importation of prescription drugs from other countries, including the country of Canada, where, believe it or not, they pay much less money for the exact same drug. Stand up, Ron [DeSantis, governor of Florida]. Boy, he wants this so badly.

"No, I mean, you go to some countries and the price is like 50, 60 percent lower—Even more than that, I guess, Ron, in some cases. And it's 50, 60 percent lower: the exact same pill, from the exact same factory, from the exact same company. And I say, 'Why is it that in Europe, certain places, in particular, it's 25% of what we pay back here?' I said, 'It must be a different manufacturer.' 'No, sir, it's the same one.' 'Must be made in a different factory.' 'No, sir, it's the same one.' Everything is identical; they pay 25%. We pick up all of the research and development. We pick up everything like a bunch of, excuse me, schmucks. Schmucks. Right?

"Not anymore, folks, because in a little while—In a little while, your governor is going to be able to go out and negotiate until his heart is content. And he's going to go to Canada. I know he's gone there already and he's looking at their pricing, and he's going to some of the European countries and others, and he's going to get his drug price down to a level that you can't believe. It's going to be a great thing. And we'll see what happens. It's going to be very interesting.

"And I have a feeling when that happens, the drug companies are just going to say, 'We can't have this.' And they're going to drop their price, I think.

"Now, they're very smart. They may go the other way, and if they do, don't blame me, okay? But I'm pretty sure you're going to do fantastically, Ron. You feel good about it? Huh? You better do good; otherwise, you're making us both look bad. You hear that, Casey?

"American patients must no longer be forced to subsidize lower drug prices in other countries through higher prices in America. That's what we were doing. We were paying a much higher price. My administration will never stop fighting for lower costs for American patients and American seniors.

"The third part of our healthcare vision is to provide the choice and control Americans want. We eliminated Obamacare's horrible, horrible, very expensive and very unfair, unpopular individual mandate. A total disaster. That was a big penalty. That was a big thing. Where you paid a lot of money for the privilege of not having to pay a lot of money for the privilege of having no healthcare. You paid not to have healthcare. It was a penalty. And how it ever held up in Supreme Court, I don't know, but it did. But we just got rid of it. We just did it the old-fashioned way: we got rid of it.

"We vastly expanded affordable insurance options, including association health plans, short-term plans, and health reimbursement arrangements—which are incredible. And many of these options are up to 60% less expensive than 'O-bomb-a-care.' Nobody got that. Nobody got that. That's okay. 'O-bomb-a-care.' I didn't say 'Obamacare.' I said 'O-bomb-a-care.' President 'O-bomb-a-care.' He [former U.S. President Barack Obama] can have it.

"But we've done a great job in running it. We almost had it done. We unfortunately had one vote, middle of the night, just when thumbs down. That wasn't good. After years and years of campaigning— 'Repeal and replace,' right? But we've done a great job because we get rid of the individual mandate. And we're running it better. It's still no good, because it's too expensive. The premium is way too high and all of the elements of it. It's just not good. But we're coming up with an incredible plan that if the Republicans take back the House, keep the Senate, keep the presidency, we're going to have a fantastic plan. Right?

"Following my administration's recommendation, Florida has taken an important step to lower cost and increase choice by repealing a misguided Certificate of Need law, used by hospitals to block competition. We encourage other states to follow Florida's example. They've done a great job right here.

"And I also signed, just recently, a revolutionary executive order requiring price and quality transparency. And the man who's really the leader in the world of this—It's transparency. You can pick your doctor; you can look at their records; you can see how well they did. You can go and negotiate. A man—What really sold me on it—The man who's the best in the world at it, who we used, and we gave you the max plan. Did we give that? The max plan, right? That's the maximum plan. We gave it to you. And he said something that I loved. He said, 'Sir, this is more important and will go down as more important than any healthcare that you'll ever come up with.' And I said, 'I like the sound of that.' Now, who knows if it's true, but I guess, from what I'm hearing, they've done it in certain limited areas and it's phenomenal.

"And it's really transparency. And you'll be able to negotiate all over the place. And you'll be able to pick everything you want, from the hospital to the doctor. And it's going to save you a tremendous amount of money. And there are those that say it's more important than even healthcare at a high, at a high level.

"And fourth, my administration is fighting to ensure the high-quality care that Americans deserve. Americans have to get the highest quality. So we have the highest quality that Americans deserve.

"On behalf of 5 million Americans living with Alzheimer's disease, I signed into law a $1 billion increase in funding for critical Alzheimer's research. And we've made a lot of progress.

"And just one other thing I will tell you, because it even surprised me—But we've funded it now, and, within 10 years, our country will be AIDS-free. Can you believe that? AIDS-free. Tremendous progress has been made.

"And when we were talking about that, I said, 'I don't understand. How does this...' It's like somewhat of a secret, but it's incredible—The tremendous progress that we've made over the last few years on AIDS and AIDS research. And we should be essentially AIDS-free. Do you agree with that, Mr. Secretary?

"In my State of the Union, I announced a plan to invest—She liked it—$500 million dollars in new treatments, and cures, and all of the things that we have to go through with our incredible children, in some cases, for childhood cancers. It's a tremendous problem.

"And to bring new hope to the nearly 100,000 Americans currently awaiting a kidney operation, I signed an executive order that will significantly increase the supply of kidneys available for transplant. It's such a big deal. It's so big. You have no idea.

"And we worked hard on that. And, you know, what a lot of people don't know—A lot of it is just the work. The people die fairly quickly because it's not—They could go on forever. But it's, it's unbelievable amounts of work, going in all the time for step-by-step—What you have to do.

"And so, with kidney transplants, we're making tremendous progress. And we funded a lot of money toward it. And I think it's going to be a tremendous thing for people that are just literally suffering with something they can really do very well with.

"We're delivering better, fairer, and more affordable healthcare for all Americans, especially our cherished senior citizens. And we will stop at nothing to deliver better healthcare for you and for your family. I will never let you down. You have been incredible to me and I will never ever forget you. I will never let you down. I promise that. Thank you. Thank you very much.

"We're lowering the cost of prescription drugs, taking on the pharmaceutical companies. And you think that's easy? It's not easy. It's not easy. They come at you from all different sides. I wouldn't be surprised if the hoax didn't come a little bit from some of the people that we're taking on. They're very powerful. They spend a lot of money. Spend, I think, more money than any other group in the world actually, in terms of lobbying and lobbying abilities.

"And I wouldn't be surprised if some of the nonsense that we all have to go through, but that I go through—Wouldn't be surprised if it was from these, some of these industries like pharmaceuticals that we take on because I want—I don't care. I did great. I've had a great life. I want to get drug prices down. I don't care about the companies; I want to get drug prices down.

"I want to continue to give them the incentive to come out with new and better answers, but got to get drug prices down. And they've made a fortune over the last 40 years. They've made so much money. And they've got the system wired. Because everything you do, their stock goes up. I said, 'What the hell is going on? Their stock just went up.' They said, 'Sir, it's going to be wonderful.' I said, 'It's not going to be wonderful.' Let their stock go down a little bit. But their stock goes up. And what we've done is incredible.

"And, by the way, you have some incredible companies. The answers that they—We—We want to keep them strong and powerful and wealthy, and we want them to con—Really continue to do that research. But we got to get those prices down. They're far too high, especially when you compare them to other countries.

"And we want to ensure access to the doctors of your choice. And every day, we are going to—As I said, we are going to defend Medicare like Medicare has never been defended again. And it's never needed the defense. It's always been incredible. It's something that worked and they want to destroy it.

"In my administration, we know that Medicare is personal. Great healthcare is about more time with the ones you love, more days with your grandkids, and more freedom to enjoy the most rewarding years of your life—Or what should be, by far, the most rewarding years of your life. You've worked hard. You've worked so hard. And you paid for it. And you've got to enjoy it. It's about getting better when you're sick, it's improving your well-being, and it's getting the treatment you need, right when you need it.

"That's why, in everything we do, we are defending the principles that made America the envy of the world and the American way of life the greatest in our history. And our country has never been greater than it's been right now. Our military is the strongest it's ever built—We rebuilt our entire military.

"And even medical research is at a new level. It's at a level that we've never had it before.

"We stand for freedom. We stand for choice. We stand for justice, and fairness, and accountability. We stand for loyalty to our citizens, love for our country, allegiance to our flag, and long and healthy lives for our great seniors.

"And with your help, we are going to continue building the best, most advanced, most cutting-edge healthcare system anywhere in the world. We are going to expand our growing economy to make retirement easier, and better, and far more secure. We're going to defend American lives, American values, American families, and America's glorious destiny. There is no country like our country. We see and read things, but there is no country like our country. Right?

"With every ounce of strength and every bit of soul, we are going to protect Medicare for you, for everyone at The Villages, and for every senior across this magnificent land.

"You are going to be protected in many ways, but you are going to be protected."

Statement from the President, December 18, 2019.

Source: https://www.whitehouse.gov/briefings-statements/statement-by-the-president-31/

"Today's decision in *Texas v. Azar* is a win for all Americans and confirms what I have said all along: that the individual mandate, by far the worst element of Obamacare, is unconstitutional.

"This decision will not alter the current healthcare system. My administration continues to work to provide access to high-quality healthcare at a price you can afford, while strongly protecting those with preexisting conditions. The radical healthcare changes being proposed by the far left would strip Americans of their current coverage. I will not let this happen. Providing affordable, high-quality healthcare will always be my priority. They are trying to take away your healthcare, and I am trying to give the American people the best healthcare in the world."

Healthcare/Obamacare—2019 Tweets

January 5, 2019

3:49 pm: Drug makers and companies are not living up to their commitments on pricing. Not being fair to the consumer, or to our Country!

March 15, 2019

2:43 pm: I look forward to VETOING the just passed Democrat inspired Resolution which would OPEN BORDERS while increasing Crime, Drugs, and Trafficking in our Country. I thank all of the Strong Republicans who voted to support Border Security and our desperately needed WALL!

April 1, 2019

9:13 pm: Everybody agrees that ObamaCare doesn't work. Premiums & deductibles are far too high—Really bad HealthCare! Even the Dems want to replace it, but with Medicare for all, which would cause 180 million Americans to lose their beloved private health insurance. The Republicans...

9:23 pm: ...are developing a really great HealthCare Plan with far lower premiums (cost) & deductibles than ObamaCare. In other words it will be far less expensive & much more usable than ObamaCare. Vote will be taken right after the Election when Republicans hold the Senate & win...

9:37 pm: ...back the House. It will be truly great HealthCare that will work for America. Also, Republicans will always support Pre-Existing Conditions. The Republican Party will be known as the Party of Great HealtCare. Meantime, the USA is doing better than ever & is respected again!

April 3, 2019

8:26 am: I was never planning a vote prior to the 2020 Election on the wonderful HealthCare package that some very talented people are now developing for me & the Republican Party. It will be on full display during the Election as a much better & less expensive alternative to ObamaCare...

8:37 am: ...This will be a great campaign issue. I never asked Mitch McConnell for a vote before the Election as has been incorrectly reported (as usual) in the @nytimes, but only after the Election when we take back the House etc. Republicans will always support pre-existing conditions!

May 8, 2019

4:01 pm: Big announcement today: Drug companies have to come clean about their prices in TV ads. Historic transparency for American patients is here. If drug companies are ashamed of those prices—lower them!

5:34 pm: Great news today: My Administration just secured a historic donation of HIV prevention drugs from Gilead to help expand access to PrEP for the uninsured and those at risk. Will help us achieve our goal of ending the HIV epidemic in America!

June 14, 2019

2:14 pm: Announcing great, expanded HRAs—big win for small employers and workers. This is a fantastic plan! My Administration has worked very hard on creating more affordable health coverage.

June 27, 2019

8:37 pm: All Democrats just raised their hands for giving millions of illegal aliens unlimited healthcare. How about taking care of American Citizens first!? That's the end of that race!

July 7, 2019

8:13 am: Last year was the first in 51 years where prescription drug prices actually went down, but things have been, and are being, put in place that will drive them down substantially. If Dems would work with us in a bipartisan fashion, we would get big results very fast!

July 31, 2019

10:10 am: Lowering drug prices for many Americans—including our great seniors! At my direction, @HHSGov @SecAzar just released a Safe Importation Action Plan. Our Governors will be very happy too! @GovRonDeSantis @GovofCO

September 19, 2019

4:42 pm: Because of my Administration, drug prices are down for the first time in almost 50 years—but the American people need Congress to help. I like Sen. Grassley's drug pricing bill very much, and it's great to see Speaker Pelosi's bill today. Let's get it done in a bipartisan way!

October 2, 2019

10:31 am: Nancy Pelosi just said that she is interested in lowering prescription drug prices & working on the desperately needed USMCA. She is incapable of working on either. It is just camouflage for trying to win an election through impeachment. The Do Nothing Democrats are stuck in mud!

October 3, 2019

5:49 pm: Today at The Villages in Florida, it was my great honor to sign an Executive Order on protecting and improving Medicare for our Nation's Seniors. Today's action is only the latest of many important steps we are taking to dramatically improve healthcare for the American People!

October 4, 2019

4:57 pm: Under my Administration, Medicare Advantage premiums next year will be their lowest in the last 13 years. We are providing GREAT healthcare to our Seniors. We cannot let the radical socialists take that away through Medicare for All!

November 11, 2019

9:00 am: Will be meeting with representatives of the Vaping industry, together with medical professionals and individual state representatives, to come up with an acceptable solution to the Vaping and E-cigarette dilemma. Children's health & safety, together with jobs, will be a focus!

November 22, 2019

2:04 pm: .@SecAzar and I will soon release a plan to let Florida and other States import prescription drugs that are MUCH CHEAPER than what we have now! Hard-working Americans don't deserve to pay such high prices for the drugs they need. We are fighting DAILY to make sure this HAPPENS...

.@SecAzar and I will soon release a plan to let Florida and other States import prescription drugs that are MUCH CHEAPER than what we have now! Hard-working Americans don't deserve to pay such high prices for the drugs they need. We are fighting DAILY to make sure this HAPPENS...

...Pelosi and her Do Nothing Democrats drug pricing bill doesn't do the trick. FEWER cures! FEWER treatments! Time for the Democrats to get serious about bipartisan solutions to lowering prescription drug prices for families...

...House Republicans are showing real LEADERSHIP and prepared to enact bipartisan solutions for drug prices. Do Nothing Democrats are playing partisan politics with YOUR drug prices! We are READY to work together if they actually want to get something done!

December 1, 2019

1:31 pm: On World AIDS Day, The First Lady and I express our support for those living with HIV/AIDS and mourn the lives lost. We reaffirm our commitment to end the HIV/AIDS epidemic...

...in America, community by community where we will eradicate AIDS in 10 years, program already started. American leadership has proven that together we can save lives.

December 31, 2019

5:24 pm: I am far better on HealthCare than the Democrats!

Obama/Hillary—2017 News Quotes

Response to a question from David Muir of ABC News, January 26, 2017.
Source: https://www.telegraph.co.uk/news/2017/01/26/
full-transcript-president-donald-trumps-interview-abc-news/

"Now, you have to understand I, I focused on those four or five states that I had to win. Maybe she [Hillary Clinton] didn't. She should've gone to Michigan. She thought she had it in the bag. She should've gone to Wisconsin, she thought she had it because you're talking about 38 years of, you know, Democrat wins. But they didn't. I went to Michigan. I went to Wisconsin. I went to Pennsylvania all the time. I went to all of the states that are, Florida and North Carolina. That's all I focused on."

Response to a question from David Muir of ABC News, January 26, 2017.
Source: https://www.telegraph.co.uk/news/2017/01/26/
full-transcript-president-donald-trumps-interview-abc-news/

"One of the greatest victories ever. But, again, I ran for the Electoral College. I didn't run for the popular vote. What I'm saying is if there are these problems that many people agree with me that there might be. Look, [former U.S. President] Barack Obama, if you look back eight years ago when he first ran, he was running for office in Chicago, for we needed Chicago vote.

"And he was laughing at the system because he knew all of those votes were going to him. You look at Philadelphia, you look at what's going on in Philadelphia. But take a look at the tape of Barack Obama who wrote me, by the way, a very beautiful letter in the drawer of the desk.

Very beautiful. And I appreciate it. But look at what he said, it's on tape. Look at what he said about voting in Chicago eight years ago. It's not changed. It hasn't changed, believe me. Chicago. Look what's going on in Chicago. It's only gotten worse.

"But he [Obama] was smiling and laughing about the vote in Chicago. Now, once he became President he didn't do that. All of a sudden it became this is the foundation of our country. So, here's the point, you have a lot of stuff going on possibly. I say probably. But possibly. We're going to get to the bottom of it."

Response to a question from David Muir of ABC News, January 26, 2017.
Source: https://www.telegraph.co.uk/news/2017/01/26/
full-transcript-president-donald-trumps-interview-abc-news/

"Here's what I can assure you, we are going to have a better plan, much better healthcare, much better service treatment, a plan where you can have access to the doctor that you want and the plan that you want. We're going to have a much better healthcare plan at much less money.

"And remember Obamacare is ready to explode. And you [David Muir of ABC News] interviewed me a couple of years ago. I said, "17— Right now, this year. '17 is going to be a disaster. I'm very good at this stuff. '17 is going to be a disaster cost-wise for Obamacare. It's going to explode in '17.'

"And why not? [former U.S. President Barack] Obama's a smart guy. So, let it all come do because that's what's happening. It's all coming do in '17. We're going to have an explosion. And to do it right, sit back, let it explode and let the Democrats come begging us to help them because it's on them. But I don't want to do that. I wanna give great healthcare at a much lower cost."

Response to a question from David Muir of ABC News, January 26, 2017.
Source :https://www.telegraph.co.uk/news/2017/01/26/
full-transcript-president-donald-trumps-interview-abc-news/

"You know, when you say no one, I think no one. Ideally, in the real world, you're talking about millions of people. Will no one. And then, you know, knowing ABC, you'll have this one person on television saying how they were hurt. Okay. We want no one. We want the answer to be no one.

"But I will say millions of people will be happy. Right now, you have millions and millions and millions of people that are unhappy. It's too expensive and it's no good. And the Governor of Minnesota [Mark Dayton] who unfortunately had a very, very sad incident yesterday 'cause he's a very nice guy, but a couple of months ago, he said that the Affordable Care Act is no longer affordable.

"He's a staunch Democrat. Very strong Democrat. He said it's no longer affordable. He made that statement. And Bill Clinton on the campaign trail, and he probably had a bad night that night when he went home, but he said, 'Obamacare is crazy. It's crazy.' And you know what, they were both right."

Response to a question from Tucker Carlson of FOX News, March 15, 2017.
Source: https://www.youtube.com/watch?v=RYGH6ejacN0

"Because I don't want to do anything that is going to violate any strength of an agency. You know, we have enough problems.

"And by the way, with the CIA, I just want people to know, the CIA was hacked and a lot of things were taken. That was during the Obama years. That was not during us. That was during the Obama situation.

"Mike Pompeo is there now doing a fantastic job.

"But we will be submitting certain things and I will be perhaps speaking about this next week but it is right now before the committee and I think I want to leave it there. I have a lot of confidence—[Carlson interrupts.]"

Response to a question from Peter Baker of *The New York Times*, July 19, 2017.
Source: https://www.nytimes.com/2017/07/19/us/politics/trump-interview-transcript.html

"It's a tough—You know, healthcare. Look, Hillary Clinton worked eight years in the White House with her husband as President and having majorities and couldn't get it done. Smart people, tough people—Couldn't get it done. [Former U.S. President Barack] Obama worked so hard. They had 60 in the Senate. They had big majorities and had the White House. I mean, ended up giving away the state of Nebraska. They owned the state of Nebraska. Right. Gave it away. Their best senator did one of the greatest deals in the history of politics. What happened to him?

"But I think we are going to do OK. I think we are going to see—I mean, one of my ideas was repeal. But I certainly rather would get repeal and replace, because the next last thing I want to do is start working tomorrow morning on replace. And it is time. It is tough. It's a very narrow path, winding this way. You think you have it, and then you lose four on the other side because you gave. It is a brutal process. And it was for Democrats, in all fairness.

"I mean, you think of Hillary Clinton, and you look, she went eight years—Very capable—Went eight years as the First Lady, and could not get healthcare. So, this is not an easy crack. The one thing I'll say about myself, so, Obama was in there for eight years and got Obamacare. Hillary Clinton was in there eight years and they never got Hillarycare, whatever they called it at the time. I am not in here six months, and they'll say, 'Trump hasn't fulfilled his agenda.' I say to myself, 'Wait a minute, I'm only here a very short period of time compared to Obama. How long did it take to get Obamacare?'"

Response to a question from Michael S. Schmidt of *The New York Times*, July 19, 2017.

Source: https://www.nytimes.com/2017/07/19/us/politics/trump-interview-transcript.html

"You know, he [former U.S. President Barack Obama] can talk tough all he wants. In the meantime, he talked tough to North Korea. And he didn't, actually. He didn't talk tough to North Korea. You know, we have a big problem with North Korea. Big. Big, big. You look at all of the things; you look at the line in the sand. The red line in the sand in Syria. He [Obama] didn't do the shot. I did the shot. Had he [Obama] done that shot, he wouldn't have had—had he done something dramatic, because if you remember, they [Syria] had a tremendous gas attack after he [Obama] made that statement. Much bigger than the one they [Syria] had with me."

Obama/Hillary—2017 Tweets

February 1, 2017

10:55 pm: Do you believe it? The Obama Administration agreed to take thousands of illegal immigrants from Australia. Why? I will study this dumb deal!

February 15, 2017

7:42 am: Crimea was TAKEN by Russia during the Obama Administration. Was Obama too soft on Russia?

February 16, 2017

6:44 pm: 'Trump signs bill undoing Obama coal mining rule' https://t.co/yMfT5r5RGh

March 4, 2017

6:42 am: Just out: The same Russian Ambassador that met Jeff Sessions visited the Obama White House 22 times, and 4 times last year alone.

6:49 am: Is it legal for a sitting President to be "wire tapping" a race for president prior to an election? Turned down by court earlier. A NEW LOW!

7:02 am: How low has President Obama gone to tapp my phones during the very sacred election process. This is Nixon/Watergate. Bad (or sick) guy!

March 7, 2017

7:04 am: 122 vicious prisoners, released by the Obama Administration from Gitmo, have returned to the battlefield. Just another terrible decision!

8:13 am: For eight years Russia "ran over" President Obama, got stronger and stronger, picked-off Crimea and added missiles. Weak! @ foxandfriends

March 27, 2017

8:26 am to 8:35 am: Why isn't the House Intelligence Committee looking into the Bill & Hillary deal that allowed big Uranium to go to Russia, Russian speech…

…money to Bill, the Hillary Russian "reset," praise of Russia by Hillary, or Podesta Russian Company. Trump Russia story is a hoax. #MAGA

April 3, 2017

6:16 am: Was the brother of John Podesta paid big money to get the sanctions on Russia lifted? Did Hillary know?

6:21 am: Did Hillary Clinton ever apologize for receiving the answers to the debate? Just asking!

April 18, 2017

4:39 am: The weak illegal immigration policies of the Obama Admin. allowed bad MS 13 gangs to form in cities across U.S. We are removing them fast!

May 4, 2017

5:40 am to 5:49 am: Susan Rice, the former National Security Advisor to President Obama, is refusing to testify before a Senate Subcommittee next week on...

...allegations of unmasking Trump transition officials. Not good!

May 7, 2017

5:58 pm: Rexnord of Indiana made a deal during the Obama Administration to move to Mexico. Fired their employees. Tax product big that's sold in U.S.

May 8, 2017

7:14 am: Ask Sally Yates, under oath, if she knows how classified information got into the newspapers soon after she explained it to W.H. Council.

May 18, 2017

6:39 am: With all of the illegal acts that took place in the Clinton campaign & Obama Administration, there was never a special councel appointed!

May 31, 2017

7:40 pm: Crooked Hillary Clinton now blames everybody but herself, refuses to say she was a terrible candidate. Hits Facebook & even Dems & DNC.

June 1, 2017

6:05 am: The big story is the "unmasking and surveillance" of people that took place during the Obama Administration.

June 15, 2017

2:15 pm: Why is that Hillary Clintons family and Dems dealings with Russia are not looked at, but my non-dealings are?

2:56 pm: Crooked H destroyed phones w/ hammer, 'bleached' emails, & had husband meet w/AG days before she was cleared—& they talk about obstruction?

June 23, 2017

7:43 pm: Just out: The Obama Administration knew far in advance of November 8th about election meddling by Russia. Did nothing about it. WHY?

June 24, 2017

3:28 pm: Since the Obama Administration was told way before the 2016 Election that the Russians were meddling, why no action? Focus on them, not T!

3:44 pm: Obama Administration official said they "choked" when it came to acting on Russian meddling of election. They didn't want to hurt Hillary?

June 25, 2017

7:00 am: Hillary Clinton colluded with the Democratic Party in order to beat Crazy Bernie Sanders. Is she allowed to so collude? Unfair to Bernie!

June 26, 2017

7:37 am to 7:50 am: The reason that President Obama did NOTHING about Russia after being notified by the CIA of meddling is that he expected Clinton would win…

…and did not want to "rock the boat." He didn't "choke," he colluded or obstructed, and it did the Dems and Crooked Hillary no good.

July 10, 2017

6:47 am: If Chelsea Clinton were asked to hold the seat for her mother, as her mother gave our country away, the Fake News would say CHELSEA FOR PRES!

July 16, 2017

5:35 am: HillaryClinton can illegally get the questions to the Debate & delete 33,000 emails but my son Don is being scorned by the Fake News Media?

July 22, 2017

6:44 am: So many people are asking why isn't the A.G. or Special Council looking at the many Hillary Clinton or Comey crimes. 33,000 e-mails deleted?

6:47 am: ...What about all of the Clinton ties to Russia, including Podesta Company, Uranium deal, Russian Reset, big dollar speeches etc.

September 13, 2017

9:47 pm: Crooked Hillary Clinton blames everybody (and every thing) but herself for her election loss. She lost the debates and lost her direction!

9:52 pm: The "deplorables" came back to haunt Hillary.They expressed their feelings loud and clear. She spent big money but, in the end, had no game!

October 16, 2017

8:12 am: I was recently asked if Crooked Hillary Clinton is going to run in 2020? My answer was, "I hope so!"

October 19, 2017

6:17 am: Uranium deal to Russia, with Clinton help and Obama Administration knowledge, is the biggest story that Fake Media doesn't want to follow!

October 29, 2017

8:53 am to 9:17 am: Never seen such Republican ANGER & UNITY as I have concerning the lack of investigation on Clinton made Fake Dossier (now $12,000,000?),...

...the Uranium to Russia deal, the 33,000 plus deleted Emails, the Comey fix and so much more. Instead they look at phony Trump/Russia,...

"collusion," which doesn't exist. The Dems are using this terrible (and bad for our country) Witch Hunt for evil politics, but the R's.

.are now fighting back like never before. There is so much GUILT by Democrats/Clinton, and now the facts are pouring out. DO SOMETHING!

November 18, 2017

8:31 am: Crooked Hillary Clinton is the worst (and biggest) loser of all time. She just can't stop, which is so good for the Republican Party. Hillary, get on with your life and give it another try in three years!

November 28, 2017

9:45 pm: Charles McCullough, the respected fmr Intel Comm Inspector General, said public was misled on Crooked Hillary Emails. "Emails endangered National Security." Why aren't our deep State authorities looking at this? Rigged & corrupt? @TuckerCarlson @seanhannity

November 29, 2017

9:00 pm: "Had the information (Crooked Hillary's emails) been released there would have been harm to National Security..." Charles McCullough Fmr Intel Comm Inspector General https://t.co/b0tLW5TVhX

December 2, 2017

9:06 pm: So General Flynn lies to the FBI and his life is destroyed, while Crooked Hillary Clinton, on that now famous FBI holiday "interrogation" with no swearing in and no recording, lies many times... and nothing happens to her? Rigged system, or just a double standard?

9:13 pm: Many people in our Country are asking what the "Justice" Department is going to do about the fact that totally Crooked Hillary, AFTER receiving a subpoena from the United States Congress, deleted and "acid washed" 33,000 Emails? No justice! [

December 3, 2017

8:36 am: Report: "ANTI-TRUMP FBI AGENT LED CLINTON EMAIL PROBE" Now it all starts to make sense!

Obama/Hillary—2018 News Quote

Response to a question from Chris Wallace of FOX News, November 18, 2018.
Source: https://www.youtube.com/watch?v=rMgJnnG-Nql

"And I won against [former U.S.] President [Barack] Obama and Oprah Winfrey and Michelle Obama in a great state called Georgia for the governor."

Obama/Hillary—2018 Tweets

January 1, 2018

7:48 am: Crooked Hillary Clinton's top aid, Huma Abedin, has been accused of disregarding basic security protocols. She put Classified Passwords into the hands of foreign agents. Remember sailors pictures on submarine? Jail! Deep State Justice Dept must finally act? Also on Comey & others

January 7, 2018

10:23 pm to 10:24 pm: "His is turning out to be an enormously consequential presidency. So much so that, despite my own frustration over his missteps, there has never been a day when I wished Hillary Clinton were president. Not one. Indeed, as Trump's accomplishments accumulate, the mere thought of...

...Clinton in the WH, doubling down on Barack Obama's failed policies, washes away any doubts that America made the right choice. This was truly a change election—and the changes Trump is bringing are far-reaching & necessary." Thank you Michael Goodwin! https://t.co/4fHNcx2Ydg

January 11, 2018

11:57 pm: Reason I canceled my trip to London is that I am not a big fan of the Obama Administration having sold perhaps the best located and finest embassy in London for "peanuts," only to build a new one in an off location for 1.2 billion dollars. Bad deal. Wanted me to cut ribbon-NO!

February 2, 2018

6:49 am: "You had Hillary Clinton and the Democratic Party try to hide the fact that they gave money to GPS Fusion to create a

Dossier which was used by their allies in the Obama Administration to convince a Court misleadingly, by all accounts, to spy on the Trump Team." Tom Fitton, JW

February 8, 2018

10:22 pm: Wow!—Senator Mark Warner got caught having extensive contact with a lobbyist for a Russian oligarch. Warner did not want a "paper trail" on a "private" meeting (in London) he requested with Steele of fraudulent Dossier fame. All tied into Crooked Hillary.

February 18, 2017

7:02 am: Never gotten over the fact that Obama was able to send $1.7 Billion Dollars in CASH to Iran and nobody in Congress, the FBI or Justice called for an investigation!

7:22 am: Finally, Liddle' Adam Schiff, the leakin' monster of no control, is now blaming the Obama Administration for Russian meddling in the 2016 Election. He is finally right about something. Obama was President, knew of the threat, and did nothing. Thank you Adam

February 19, 2018

2:55 pm: Obama was President up to, and beyond, the 2016 Election. So why didn't he do something about Russian meddling?

February 20, 2018

8:38 am: I have been much tougher on Russia than Obama, just look at the facts. Total Fake News!

February 21, 2018

9:03 am: Question: If all of the Russian meddling took place during the Obama Administration, right up to January 20th, why aren't they the subject of the investigation? Why didn't Obama do something about the meddling? Why aren't Dem crimes under investigation? Ask Jeff Session!

March 5, 2018

8:22 am: Why did the Obama Administration start an investigation into the Trump Campaign (with zero proof of wrongdoing) long before the Election in November? Wanted to discredit so Crooked H would win. Unprecedented. Bigger than Watergate! Plus, Obama did NOTHING about Russian meddling.

March 6, 2018

8:46 am: Federal Judge in Maryland has just ruled that "President Trump has the right to end DACA." President Obama had 8 years to fix this problem, and didn't. I am waiting for the Dems, they are running for the hills!

March 17, 2018

7:12 pm: The Mueller probe should never have been started in that there was no collusion and there was no crime. It was based on fraudulent activities and a Fake Dossier paid for by Crooked Hillary and the DNC, and improperly used in FISA COURT for surveillance of my campaign. WITCH HUNT

March 23, 2018

3:50 pm: Obama Administration legalized bump stocks. BAD IDEA. As I promised, today the Department of Justice will issue the rule banning BUMP STOCKS with a mandated comment period. We will BAN all devices that turn legal weapons into illegal machine guns.

April 8, 2018

8:12 am: If President Obama had crossed his stated Red Line In The Sand, the Syrian disaster would have ended long ago! Animal Assad would have been history!

May 17, 2018

6:56 am: Wow, word seems to be coming out that the Obama FBI "SPIED ON THE TRUMP CAMPAIGN WITH AN IMBEDDED INFORMANT." Andrew McCarthy says, "There's probably no doubt that they had at least one confidential informant in the campaign." If so, this is bigger than Watergate!

May 20, 2018

8:11 am to 8:19 am: …At what point does this soon to be $20,000,000 Witch Hunt, composed of 13 Angry and Heavily Conflicted Democrats and two people who have worked for Obama for 8 years, STOP! They have found no Collussion with Russia, No Obstruction, but they aren't looking at the corruption…

…in the Hillary Clinton Campaign where she deleted 33,000 Emails, got $145,000,000 while Secretary of State, paid McCabes wife $700,000 (and got off the FBI hook along with Terry M) and so much more. Republicans and real Americans should start getting tough on this Scam.

May 21, 2018

7:51 am: The Wall Street Journal asks, "WHERE IN THE WORLD WAS BARACK OBAMA?" A very good question!

May 22, 2018

8:13 pm: If the person placed very early into my campaign wasn't a SPY put there by the previous Administration for political purposes, how come such a seemingly massive amount of money was paid for services rendered—many times higher than normal…

…Follow the money! The spy was there early in the campaign and yet never reported Collusion with Russia, because there was no Collusion. He was only there to spy for political reasons and to help Crooked Hillary win—just like they did to Bernie Sanders, who got duped!

May 25, 2018

5:45 pm: Funny to watch the Democrats criticize Trade Deals being negotiated by me when they don't even know what the deals are and when for 8 years the Obama Administration did NOTHING on trade except let other countries rip off the United States. Lost almost $800 Billion/year under "O"

May 27, 2018

3:32 pm: Why didn't President Obama do something about the so-called Russian Meddling when he was told about it by the FBI before the Election? Because he thought Crooked Hillary was going to win, and he didn't want to upset the apple cart! He was in charge, not me, and did nothing

May 29, 2018

6:09 am: Why aren't the 13 Angry and heavily conflicted Democrats investigating the totally Crooked Campaign of totally Crooked Hillary Clinton. It's a Rigged Witch Hunt, that's why! Ask them if they enjoyed her after election celebration!

June 3, 2018

12:25 pm: Mark Penn "Why are there people from the Clinton Foundation on the Mueller Staff? Why is there an Independent Councel? To go after people and their families for unrelated offenses…Constitution was set up to prevent this…Stormtrooper tactics almost." A disgrace

June 5, 2018

5:38 am: What is taking so long with the Inspector General's Report on Crooked Hillary and Slippery James Comey. Numerous delays. Hope Report is not being changed and made weaker! There are so many horrible things to tell, the public has the right to know. Transparency

June 7, 2018

10:15 am: The Obama Administration is now accused of trying to give Iran secret access to the financial system of the United States. This is totally illegal. Perhaps we could get the 13 Angry Democrats to divert some of their energy to this "matter" (as Comey would call it). Investigate

June 18, 2018

9:57 am: If President Obama (who got nowhere with North Korea and would have had to go to war with many millions of people being killed) had gotten along with North Korea and made the initial steps toward a deal that I have, the Fake News would have named him a national hero

July 3, 2018

7:03 am: Just out that the Obama Administration granted citizenship, during the terrible Iran Deal negotiation, to 2,500 Iranians—including to government officials. How big (and bad) is that?

July 14, 2018

4:53 am: The stories you heard about the 12 Russians yesterday took place during the Obama Administration, not the Trump Administrations. Why didn't they do something about it, especially when it was reported that President Obama was informed by the FBI in September, before the Election?

1:17 pm: These Russian individuals did their work during the Obama years. Why didn't Obama do something about it? Because he thought Crooked Hillary Clinton would win, that's why. Had nothing to do with the Trump Administration, but Fake News doesn't want to report the truth, as usual

July 16, 2018

12:37 am: President Obama thought that Crooked Hillary was going to win the election, so when he was informed by the FBI about

Russian Meddling, he said it couldn't happen, was no big deal, & did NOTHING about it. When I won it became a big deal and the Rigged Witch Hunt headed by Strzok!

July 22, 2018

5:23 pm: So President Obama knew about Russia before the Election. Why didn't he do something about it? Why didn't he tell our campaign? Because it is all a big hoax, that's why, and he thought Crooked Hillary was going to win!!

July 23, 2018

5:30 am: So we now find out that it was indeed the unverified and Fake Dirty Dossier, that was paid for by Crooked Hillary Clinton and the DNC, that was knowingly & falsely submitted to FISA and which was responsible for starting the totally conflicted and discredited Mueller Witch Hunt!

August 6, 2018

9:13 am to 9:25 am: "Collusion with Russia was very real. Hillary Clinton and her team 100% colluded with the Russians, and so did Adam Schiff who is on tape trying to collude with what he thought was Russians to obtain compromising material on DJT. We also know that Hillary Clinton paid through…

…a law firm, eventually Kremlin connected sources, to gather info on Donald Trump. Collusion is very real with Russia, but only with Hillary and the Democrats, and we should demand a full investigation." Dan Bongino on @foxandfriends Looking forward to the new IG Report!

August 14, 2018

7:06 am: "They were all in on it, clear Hillary Clinton and FRAME Donald Trump for things he didn't do." Gregg Jarrett on @foxandfriends If we had a real Attorney General, this Witch Hunt would never have been started! Looking at the wrong people.

August 17, 2018

2:25 pm: Which is worse, Hightax Andrew Cuomo's statement, "WE'RE NOT GOING TO MAKE AMERICA GREAT AGAIN, IT WAS NEVER THAT GREAT" or Hillary Clinton's "DEPLOR-ABLES" statement…

August 22, 2018

8:37 am: Michael Cohen plead guilty to two counts of campaign finance violations that are not a crime. President Obama had a big campaign finance violation and it was easily settled!

7:56 pm: The only thing that I have done wrong is to win an election that was expected to be won by Crooked Hillary Clinton and the Democrats. The problem is, they forgot to campaign in numerous states!

August 25, 2018

8:11 am: "The FBI only looked at 3000 of 675,000 Crooked Hillary Clinton Emails." They purposely didn't look at the disasters. This news is just out. @FoxNews

8:14 am: "The FBI looked at less than 1%" of Crooked's Emails!

August 28, 2018

8:16 pm: Report just out: "China hacked Hillary Clinton's private Email Server." Are they sure it wasn't Russia (just kidding!)? What are the odds that the FBI and DOJ are right on top of this? Actually, a very big story. Much classified information!

August 29, 2018

7:12 am: "The Obama people did something that's never been done… They spied on a rival presidential campaign. Would it be OK if Trump did it next? I am losing faith that our system is on the level. I'm beginning to think it is rotten & corrupt. Scary stuff Obama did." @TuckerCarlson

7:18 am: "Hillary Clinton and the DNC paid for information from the Russian government to use against her government—there's no doubt about that!" @TuckerCarlson

September 1, 2018

7:46 pm to 7:53 pm: "There's no fairness here, if you're a Democrat or a friend of Hillary you get immunity or off scott free. If you're connected to Donald Trump, you get people like Robert Mueller & Andrew Weissman, and his team of partisans, coming after you with a vengeance and abusing their…

…positions of power. That's part of the story of the Russia Hoax. Christopher Steele is on the payroll of Hillary Clinton & the FBI, & when they fired him for lying, they continued to use him. Violation of FBI regulations. Kept trying to verify the unverifiable." @GreggJarrett

September 9, 2018

8:10 am: "Barrack Obama talked a lot about hope, but Donald Trump delivered the American Dream. All the economic indicators, what's happening overseas, Donald Trump has proven to be far more successful than Barrack Obama. President Trump is delivering the American Dream." Jason Chaffetz

September 10, 2018

9:42 am: "President Trump would need a magic wand to get to 4% GDP," stated President Obama. I guess I have a magic wand, 4.2%, and we will do MUCH better than this! We have just begun.

November 25, 2018

3:39 pm: Clinton Foundation donations drop 42%—which shows that they illegally played the power game. They monetized their political influence through the Foundation. "During her tenure the State Department was put in the service of the Clinton Foundation." Andrew McCarthy

December 16, 2018

11:25 am: The Democrats policy of Child Seperation on the Border during the Obama Administration was far worse than the way we handle it now. Remember the 2014 picture of children in cages—the Obama years. However, if you don't separate, FAR more people will come. Smugglers use the kids!

December 30, 2018

4:59 pm: President and Mrs. Obama built/has a ten foot Wall around their D.C. mansion/compound. I agree, totally necessary for their safety and security. The U.S. needs the same thing, slightly larger version!

Obama/Hillary—2019 News Quotes

Response to a question from Maggie Haberman of *The New York Times*, January 31, 2019.
Source: https://www.nytimes.com/2019/02/01/us/politics/trump-interview-transcripts.html

"I don't—You know, I'd like to see him [Joe Biden[14]] run. I'd like to see him run.

"Because you pit him, and you take what happened to [former U.S. President Barack] Obama. When you look at my numbers, and you look how we've done for the economy, we had a news conference before, where we had a lot of workers behind us, manufacturers and workers from manufacturing plants, and it was really impressive to see what they've done. And they said, 'Two years ago, we were dead,' and now they're thriving."

---

14   Joe Biden was Vice President in the Obama Administration.

Response to a question from Peter Baker of *The New York Times*, January 31, 2019.

Source: https://www.nytimes.com/2019/02/01/us/politics/trump-interview-transcripts.html

"I have nothing. All I did was be a good candidate. Russia didn't help me. Russia did not help me. There was no collusion. There was none of that. I was a good candidate. I did a good job. I won't say whether she was a good candidate or not. I mean, the primary collusion was Hillary Clinton. If you take a look, Peter [Baker of *The New York Times*]. I mean, look at that phony dossier. Some of that money, they say, went to Russia. [Tony] Podesta was involved with Russia. You look at the kind of relationships they had. They had real relationships with Russia. I had a potential, a deal that frankly wasn't even a deal. It was literally—I viewed it as an option. But maybe it was called a letter of intent. Something like that."

Remarks at Conservative Political Action Conference (CPAC), March 3, 2019.

Source: https://www.nbcnews.com/politics/donald-trump/
trump-lets-loose-cpac-longest-speech-his-presidency-n978556

"I've learned with the fake news, if you tell a joke, if you are sarcastic, if you're having fun with the audience, if you are on live television with millions of people and 25,000 people in an arena, and if you say something like 'Russia, please, if you can, get us Hillary Clinton's emails! Please, Russia, please! Please get us the emails! Please!'"

Response to a question from Catherine Herridge of FOX News, May 2, 2019.

Source: https://www.foxnews.com/politics/transcript-fox-news-interview-with-president-trump

"Well I think we've done a lot of sanctioning of Russia. I brought up the pipeline, I'm helping Ukraine far more than [former U.S.] President [Barack] Obama did. We're doing a lot of sanctions on Russia, I've signed a lot of sanctions on Russia."

Response to a question from Catherine Herridge of FOX News, May 2, 2019.

Source: https://www.foxnews.com/politics/transcript-fox-news-interview-with-president-trump

"Well he [former U.S. President Barack Obama] could have done something, I mean he could have called out to [Russian President Vladmir] Putin and he could have said let's look at this very closely. He [Obama] did absolutely nothing, because he thought that Crooked Hillary was going to win the election and she didn't even come close.

"So it's just one of those things, you know? And it had nothing to do, by the way, with Russia because everybody said it didn't affect the vote, you've heard that many times it didn't affect the vote. But I don't want Russia or anybody else playing around with our elections."

Response to a POLITICO reporter's[15] question, May 10, 2019.

Source: https://www.politico.com/story/2019/05/10/trump-interview-transcript-1317598

"So, you know, it's all based on high crimes and misdemeanors. And if you look at the Mueller report, there was no collusion. There was no conspiracy. And there was no obstruction. He [Special Counsel Robert Mueller] said that in the first half of the sentence, and then said he couldn't prove it. But there was no obstruction. And then the attorney general, based on the facts, and the deputy attorney general, Rod Rosenstein, they ruled there was no obstruction. So you have no crime. And impeachment's based on crime. And, specifically it's based on high crimes and misdemeanors. Not 'plus' or whatever. It's 'and' misdemeanors. Not separately, but together. So you need both.

"And, you know, look, I know it would be a very, very impossible thing. Plus, you know if you haven't had—In fact, the crimes were actually committed, but they were committed by the Democrats. They were committed by the DNC, the Clinton campaign, Hillary Clinton. Those were the crimes. They weren't committed by us."

---

15 POLITICO reporters Andrew Restuccia, Eliana Johnson, and Daniel Lippman conducted the telephone interview with President Trump, but the transcript does not indicate which reporter asked which question.

Remarks at a rally in Minneapolis, Minnesota, October 10, 2019.
Source: https://www.twincities.com/2019/10/10/
trump-attacks-joe-biden-ilhan-omar-and-jacob-frey-at-minneapolis-rally/

"He [Joe Biden] was never a good Vice President because he only understood how to kiss [then-U.S. President] Barack Obama's ass."

Remarks at Turning Point USA Student Action Summit in West Palm Beach, Florida, December 22, 2019.
Source: https://www.whitehouse.gov/briefings-statements/
remarks-president-trump-turning-point-usa-student-action-summit-west-palm-beach-fl/

"Did you see the other day? Crooked Hillary came out. Did you see the other day? She said that Jill Stein—Jill Stein, from the Greeny Party—she said Jill Stein was a Russian agent. Now, I don't know, Jill Stein. I'm sure she's a fine woman. But I know she's not a Russian agent.

"Then she said Tulsi Gabbard[16] is a weapon of Russia. And they lost also credibility, because we know that Tulsi Gabbard—And I give her respect. She didn't vote the other day. I give her a lot of respect because she knew it was wrong. She took a pass. But I don't know her. But I know one thing: She is not an agent of Russia."

Obama/Hillary—2019 Tweets

January 22, 2019

8:15 am: FBI top lawyer confirms "unusual steps." They relied on the Clinton Campaign's Fake & Unverified "Dossier," which is illegal. "That has corrupted them. That has enabled them to gather evidence

---

16 Congresswoman Tulsi Gabbard (D-Hawaii) is also a 2020 presidential candidate as of the time of this manuscript's preparation.

by UNCONSTITUTIONAL MEANS, and that's what they did to the President." Judge Napolitano

10:53 am: Former FBI top lawyer James Baker just admitted involvement in FISA Warrant and further admitted there were IRREGULARITIES in the way the Russia probe was handled. They relied heavily on the unverified Trump "Dossier" paid for by the DNC & Clinton Campaign, & funded through a...

11:06 am: ...big Crooked Hillary law firm, represented by her lawyer Michael Sussmann (do you believe this?) who worked Baker hard & gave him Oppo Research for "a Russia probe." This meeting, now exposed, is the subject of Senate inquiries and much more. An Unconstitutional Hoax. @FoxNews

January 26, 2019

8:42 am: If Roger Stone was indicted for lying to Congress, what about the lying done by Comey, Brennan, Clapper, Lisa Page & lover, Baker and soooo many others? What about Hillary to FBI and her 33,000 deleted Emails? What about Lisa & Peter's deleted texts & Wiener's laptop? Much more!

8:39 pm to 8:49 pm: CBS reports that in the Roger Stone indictment, data was "released during the 2016 Election to damage Hillary Clinton." Oh really! What about the Fake and Unverified "Dossier," a total phony conjob, that was paid for by Crooked Hillary to damage me and the Trump Campaign? What...

...about all of the one sided Fake Media coverage (collusion with Crooked H?) that I had to endure during my very successful presidential campaign. What about the now revealed bias by Facebook and many others. Roger Stone didn't even work for me anywhere near the Election!

January 30, 2019

6:40 am: ...Time will tell what will happen with North Korea, but at the end of the previous administration, relationship was horrendous and very bad things were about to happen. Now a whole different story. I look forward to seeing Kim Jong Un shortly. Progress being made-big difference!

February 1, 2019

8:23 am: I inherited a total mess in Syria and Afghanistan, the "Endless Wars" of unlimited spending and death. During my campaign I said, very strongly, that these wars must finally end. We spend $50 Billion a year in Afghanistan and have hit them so hard that we are now talking peace.

February 9, 2019

9:36 am: We have a great economy DESPITE the Obama Administration and all of its job killing Regulations and Roadblocks. If that thinking prevailed in the 2016 Election, the U.S. would be in a Depression right now! We were heading down, and don't let the Democrats sound bites fool you!

February 10, 2019

1:39 pm: …The fact is, when I took over as President, our Country was a mess. Depleted Military, Endless Wars, a potential War with North Korea, V.A., High Taxes & too many Regulations, Border, Immigration & HealthCare problems, & much more. I had no choice but to work very long hours!

February 11, 2019

7:43 am: No president ever worked harder than me (cleaning up the mess I inherited)!

February 14, 2019

9:39 am: Disgraced FBI Acting Director Andrew McCabe pretends to be a "poor little Angel" when in fact he was a big part of the Crooked Hillary Scandal & the Russia Hoax—a puppet for Leakin' James

Comey. I.G. report on McCabe was devastating. Part of "insurance policy" in case I won...

9:55 am: ...Many of the top FBI brass were fired, forced to leave, or left. McCabe's wife received BIG DOLLARS from Clinton people for her campaign—he gave Hillary a pass. McCabe is a disgrace to the FBI and a disgrace to our Country. MAKE AMERICA GREAT AGAIN!

February 19, 2019

11:05 am: I never said anything bad about Andrew McCabe's wife other than she (they) should not have taken large amounts of campaign money from a Crooked Hillary source when Clinton was under investigation by the FBI. I never called his wife a loser to him (another McCabe made up lie)!

February 24, 2019

11:51 am: The only Collusion with the Russians was with Crooked Hillary Clinton and the Democratic National Committee...And, where's the Server that the DNC refused to give to the FBI? Where are the new Texts between Agent Lisa Page and her Agent lover, Peter S? We want them now!

March 5, 2019

8:14 am: Now that they realize the only Collusion with Russia was done by Crooked Hillary Clinton & the Democrats, Nadler, Schiff and the Dem heads of the Committees have gone stone cold CRAZY. 81 letter sent to innocent people to harass them. They won't get ANYTHING done for our Country!

5:18 pm: "(Crooked) Hillary Clinton confirms she will not run in 2020, rules out a third bid for White House." Aw-shucks, does that mean I won't get to run against her again? She will be sorely missed!

March 13, 2019

7:21 am: The just revealed FBI Agent Lisa Page transcripts make the Obama Justice Department look exactly like it was, a broken and corrupt machine. Hopefully, justice will finally be served. Much more to come!

9:14 am: Comey testified (under oath) that it was a "unanimous" decision on Crooked Hillary. Lisa Page transcripts show he LIED.

March 17, 2019

7:13 am: Report: Christopher Steele backed up his Democrat & Crooked Hillary paid for Fake & Unverified Dossier with information he got from "send in watchers" of low ratings CNN. This is the info that got us the Witch Hunt!

March 25, 2019

8:54 pm: WSJ: Obama Admin Must Account for 'Abuse of Surveillance Powers' https://t.co/mIE0vOFZae via @BreitbartNews

April 12, 2019

8:37 am: President Obama's top White House lawyer, Gregory B. Craig, was indicted yesterday on very serious charges. This is a really big story, but the Fake News New York Times didn't even put it on page one, rather page 16. @washingtonpost not much better, "tiny" page one. Corrupt News!

April 17, 2019

6:34 am: Wow! FBI made 11 payments to Fake Dossier's discredited author, Trump hater Christopher Steele. @OANN @JudicialWatch The Witch Hunt has been a total fraud on your President and the American people! It was brought to you by Dirty Cops, Crooked Hillary and the DNC.

April 29. 2019

9:42 am: The Media (Fake News) is pushing Sleepy Joe hard. Funny, I'm only here because of Biden & Obama. They didn't do the job and now you have Trump, who is getting it done—big time!

May 1, 2019

7:28 am: Why didn't President Obama do something about Russia in September (before November Election) when told by the FBI? He did NOTHING, and had no intention of doing anything!

May 17, 2019

7:16 am: Will Jerry Nadler ever look into the fact that Crooked Hillary deleted and acid washed 33,000 emails AFTER getting a most powerful demand notice for them from Congress?

June 11, 2019

11:28 pm: "Someone should call Obama up. The Obama Administration spied on a rival presidential campaign using Federal Agencies. I mean, that seems like a headline to me?" @TuckerCarlson It will all start coming out, and the Witch Hunt will end. Presidential Harassment!

June 19, 2019

9:18 am: The Dems are very unhappy with the Mueller Report, so after almost 3 years, they want a Redo, or Do Over. This is extreme Presidential Harassment. They gave Crooked Hillary's people complete Immunity, yet now they bring back Hope Hicks. Why aren't the Dems looking at the...

...33,000 Emails that Hillary and her lawyer deleted and acid washed AFTER GETTING A SUBPOENA FROM CONGRESS? That is real Obstruction that the Dems want no part of because their hearings are RIGGED and a disgrace to our Country!

2:48 pm: So sad that the Democrats are putting wonderful Hope Hicks through hell, for 3 years now, after total exoneration by Robert Mueller & the Mueller Report. They were unhappy with result so they want a Do Over. Very unfair & costly to her. Will it ever end? Why aren't they...

...asking Hillary Clinton why she deleted and acid washed her Emails AFTER getting a subpoena from Congress? Anybody else would be in jail for that, yet the Dems refuse to even bring it up. Rigged House Committee

July 9, 2019

8:44 pm: So now the Obama appointed judge on the Census case (Are you a Citizen of the United States?) won't let the Justice Department use the lawyers that it wants to use. Could this be a first?

July 10, 2019

9:14 am: Iran has long been secretly "enriching," in total violation of the terrible 150 Billion Dollar deal made by John Kerry and the Obama Administration. Remember, that deal was to expire in a short number of years. Sanctions will soon be increased, substantially!

July 15, 2019

4:43 pm: The Obama Administration built the Cages, not the Trump Administration! DEMOCRATS MUST GIVE US THE VOTES TO CHANGE BAD IMMIGRATION LAWS.

July 24, 2019

6:43 am: So why didn't the highly conflicted Robert Mueller investigate how and why Crooked Hillary Clinton deleted and acid washed 33,000 Emails immediately AFTER getting a SUBPOENA from the United States Congress? She must have GREAT lawyers!

July 27, 2019

10:49 pm: The real Collusion, the Conspiracy, the Crime, was between the Clinton Campaign, the DNC, Fusion GPS, Christopher Steele... (and many others including Comey, McCabe, Lisa Page and her lover, Ohr and his wonderful wife, and on and on!). @replouiegohmert

July 31, 2019

8:46 pm: The cages for kids were built by the Obama Administration in 2014. He had the policy of child separation. I ended it even as I realized that more families would then come to the Border! @CNN

August 15, 2019

7:26 am: Go out and get Andrew McCarthy's new book, "Ball of Collusion." "Supervision became the investigator, and when they pushed the envelope, there was nobody there to tell them NO. It goes right to the President (Obama). Plenty of information that Obama was informed & knew exactly...

...what they were doing. There's plenty of indication, we don't have to speculate." @SteveDoocy "Holy cow, got to read this book." @ainsleyearhardt "WOW!" @foxandfriends A very serious situation. Can never be allowed to happen again! DRAIN THE SWAMP

August 25, 2019

11:35 am: So @donnabrazile gives Crooked Hillary the Questions, and now she's on @FoxNews!

September 26, 2019

6:20 pm: Obama loving (wrote Obama book) Peter Baker of the Failing New York Times, married to an even bigger Trump Hater than himself, should not even be allowed to write about me. Every story is a made up disaster with sources and leakers that don't even exist. I had a simple and very...

October 5, 2019

2:25 pm: So Crooked Hillary Clinton can delete and acid wash 33,000 emails AFTER getting a Subpoena from the United States Congress, but I can't make one totally appropriate telephone call to the President of Ukraine? Witch Hunt!

October 8, 2019

9:06 am: I think that Crooked Hillary Clinton should enter the race to try and steal it away from Uber Left Elizabeth Warren. Only one condition. The Crooked one must explain all of her high crimes and misdemeanors including how & why she deleted 33,000 Emails AFTER getting "C" Subpoena!

October 9, 2019

9:10 am: Crooked Hillary should try it again!

11:22 am: So why is someone a good or great President if they needed to Spy on someone else's Campaign in order to win (that didn't work out so well), and if they were unable to fill 142 important Federal Judgeships (a record by far), handing them all to me to choose. Will have 182 soon!

October 16, 2019

7:58 pm: "What has happened here with the Anthony Wiener laptop, the Server, all of the Emails between Huma Abedin and Hillary Clinton, the deleted Clinton Emails—what is going on?" @LouDobbs Joe D & Victoria T!

11:29 pm: "About 500,000 human beings were killed in Syria while Barack Obama was president & leading for a "political settlement" to that civil war. Media has been more outraged in the last 72 hours over our Syria policy than they were at any point during 7 years of slaughter." BuckSexton

October 18, 2019

9:59 pm: Susan Rice, who was a disaster to President Obama as National Security Advisor, is now telling us her opinion on what to do in Syria. Remember RED LINE IN THE SAND? That was Obama. Millions killed! No thanks Susan, you were a disaster.

October 19, 2019

2:47 pm: Crooked Hillary Clinton just called the respected environmentalist and Green Party candidate, Jill Stein, a "Russian Asset." They need a Green Party more than ever after looking at the Democrats disastrous environmental program!

9:41 pm: So now Crooked Hillary is at it again! She is calling Congresswoman Tulsi Gabbard "a Russian favorite," and Jill Stein "a Russian asset." As you may have heard, I was called a big Russia lover also (actually, I do like Russian people. I like all people!). Hillary's gone Crazy!

Own Presidency/Administration—2017 News Quotes

Response to a question from David Muir of ABC News, January 26, 2017.
Source: https://www.telegraph.co.uk/news/2017/01/26/
full-transcript-president-donald-trumps-interview-abc-news/

"I didn't want to talk about the inauguration speech. But I think I did a very good job and people really liked it. You saw the poll. Just came out this morning. You bring it up. I didn't bring it up."

Response to a question from David Muir of ABC News, January 26, 2017.
Source: https://www.telegraph.co.uk/news/2017/01/26/
full-transcript-president-donald-trumps-interview-abc-news/

"Well, you keep bringing it up. I had a massive amount of people here. They were showing pictures that were very unflattering, as unflattering from certain angles that were taken early and lots of other things. I'll show you a picture later if you'd like of a massive crowd.

"In terms of a total audience including television and everything else that you have, we had supposedly the biggest crowd in history. The audience watching the show. And I think you would even agree to that. They say I had the biggest crowd in the history of inaugural speeches. I'm honored by that. But I didn't bring it up. You just brought it up."

243

Response to a question from David Muir of ABC News, January 26, 2017.

Source: https://www.telegraph.co.uk/news/2017/01/26/
full-transcript-president-donald-trumps-interview-abc-news/

"Part of my whole victory was that the men and women of this country who have been forgotten will never be forgotten again. Part of that is when they try and demean me unfairly 'cause we had a massive crowd of people. We had a crowd. I looked over that sea of people and I said to myself, 'Wow.'

"And I've seen crowds before. Big, big crowds. That was some crowd. When I looked at the numbers that happened to come in from all of the various sources, we had the biggest audience in the history of inaugural speeches. I said the men and women that I was talking to who came out and voted will never be forgotten again. Therefore, I won't allow you or other people like you to demean that crowd and to demean the people that came to Washington D.C. from faraway places because they like me. But more importantly they like what I'm saying."

Response to a question from David Muir of ABC News, January 26, 2017.

Source: https://www.telegraph.co.uk/news/2017/01/26/
full-transcript-president-donald-trumps-interview-abc-news/

"Well, don't let it get your attention too much because we'll see what happens. I mean, we're gonna see what happens. You know, I told you and I told everybody else that wants to talk when it comes to the military I don't wanna discuss things.

"I wanna let, I wanna let the action take place before the talk takes place. I watched in Mosul when a number of months ago generals and politicians would get up and say, 'We're going into Mosul in four months.' Then they'd say, 'We're going in in three months, two months, one month. We're going in next week.'

"Okay, and I kept saying to myself, 'Gee, why do they have to keep talking about going in?' All right, so now they go in and it is tough because they're giving the enemy all this time to prepare. I don't wanna do a lot of talking on the military. I wanna talk after it's finished, not before it starts."

Response to a question from Bill O'Reilly of FOX News, February 7, 2017.
Source: https://www.foxnews.com/transcript/
bill-oreillys-exclusive-interview-with-president-trump

"Well, I respect a lot of people. But that doesn't mean I am going to get along with him [Vladimir Putin, President of Russia]. He's a leader of his country. I say it's better to get along with Russia than not. Will I get along with them? I have no idea."

At the Signing of an Executive Order to Reorganize the Executive Branch, March 13, 2017.
Source: https://www.whitehouse.gov/presidential-actions/
remarks-president-signing-executive-order-reorganize-executive-branch/

"Today we're beginning the process of a long-overdue reorganization of our federal departments and agencies."

At the Signing of an Executive Order to Reorganize the Executive Branch, March 13, 2017.
Source: https://www.whitehouse.gov/presidential-actions/
remarks-president-signing-executive-order-reorganize-executive-branch/

"We've assembled one of the greatest Cabinets in history, and I believe that so strongly. And we want to empower them to make their agencies as lean and effective as possible, and they know how to do it."

At the Signing of an Executive Order to Reorganize the Executive Branch, March 13, 2017.
Source: https://www.whitehouse.gov/presidential-actions/
remarks-president-signing-executive-order-reorganize-executive-branch/

"This order requires a thorough examination of every executive department and agency to see where money is being wasted, how services can be improved, and whether programs are truly serving American citizens."

At the Signing of an Executive Order to Reorganize the Executive Branch, March 13, 2017.

Source: https://www.whitehouse.gov/presidential-actions/
remarks-president-signing-executive-order-reorganize-executive-branch/

"The Director of Office of Management and Budget will oversee the evaluation working with experts inside and outside of the federal government, as well as seeking input from the American people themselves.

"Based on this input, we will develop a detailed plan to make the federal government work better; reorganizing, consolidating, and eliminating where necessary. In other words, making the federal government more efficient and very, very cost productive.

"So, we're going to do something I think very, very special. They never have been done to the extent that we're going to be able to do it. And you're already seeing results.

"We will then work with Congress to implement these recommendations on behalf of the American people.

"So, with that, I want to thank everybody very much, and I want to wish the Cabinet good luck. I think we have some of the finest people ever assembled for a Cabinet. We're going to do a great job for the American people."

Response to a question from Tucker Carlson of FOX News, March 15, 2017.

Source: https://www.youtube.com/watch?v=RYGH6ejacNO

"I do. I do. But I, I think that frankly we have a lot right now.

"And I think if you watched, watched the Bret Baier and what he was saying, and what he was talking about, and how he mentioned the word wiretapped, you would feel very confident that you could mention the name. He mentioned it.

"And other people have mentioned it, but if you take a look at some of the things written about wiretapping and eavesdropping. And don't forget, when I say wiretapped, those words were in quotes, that really covers because wiretapping is pretty old-fashioned stuff but that really covers surveillance and many other things. And nobody ever talks about the fact that it was in quotes but that's a very important thing.

"But wiretap covers a lot of different things. I think you're gonna find some very interesting items coming to the forefront over the next two weeks."

Video clip shown on CBS News, April 30, 2017.
Source: https://www.cbsnews.com/news/face-the-nation-transcript-april-30-2017-president-trump/

"I love doing it. I'm, you know, thoroughly enjoying it. It's always a challenge, like life itself is a challenge. But it's something that I really love and I think I've done a very good job at it."

Video clip shown on CBS News, April 30, 2017.
Source: https://www.cbsnews.com/news/face-the-nation-transcript-april-30-2017-president-trump/

"I am signing away. I have signed 29 new bills, a record not surpassed since the Truman administration."

Response to a question from John Dickerson of CBS News, April 30, 2017.
Source: https://www.cbsnews.com/news/face-the-nation-transcript-april-30-2017-president-trump/

"Well, it's a tough job. But I've had a lot of tough jobs. I've had things that were tougher, although I'll let you know that better at the end of eight years, perhaps eight years, hopefully eight years. But I'll let you know later on. I think we've done very well with foreign policy. I think we've done very, very well with relationships with other leaders. I think we're doing great on trade deals. It's set. And I think we're doing well. I mean, our country is being outtraded at every single point. We're losing tremendous amounts of money on trade. And I think, actually, I've been very consistent. You know, it's very funny when the fake media goes out, you know, which we call the mainstream media, which, sometimes, I must say, is you. But when— [Dickerson interrupts.]"

Response to a question from Maggie Haberman of *The New York Times*, July 19, 2017.
Source: https://www.nytimes.com/2017/07/19/us/politics/trump-interview-transcript.html

"This healthcare is a tough deal. I said it from the beginning. Number one, you know, a lot of the papers were saying—Actually, these guys couldn't believe it, how much I know about it. I know a lot about healthcare."

Response to a question from Michael S. Schmidt of *The New York Times*, July 19, 2017.
Source: https://www.nytimes.com/2017/07/19/us/politics/trump-interview-transcript.html

"I've given the farmers back their farms. I've given the builders back their land to build houses and to build other things."

Response to a question from Michael S. Schmidt of *The New York Times*, July 19, 2017.
Source: https://www.nytimes.com/2017/07/19/us/politics/trump-interview-transcript.html

"The energy stuff is going really well. We're going to be an exporter— We already are an exporter of energy. We're doing well. I mean, the banks, you look at rules and regulations, you look at Dodd-Frank, Dodd-Frank is going to be, you know, modified, and again, I want rules and regulations. But you don't want to choke, right? People can't get loans to buy a pizza parlor, to buy a—You know, I saw out on the trail—People say, 'Mr. Trump, we've dealt with banks, my own bank, and they can't loan me anymore.' I've never had a bad day with a bank. You know?"

Own Presidency/Administration—2017 Tweets

January 20, 2017

7:31 am: It all begins today! I will see you at 11:00 A.M. for the swearing-in. THE MOVEMENT CONTINUES—THE WORK BEGINS!

12:51 pm to 12:55 pm: Today we are not merely transferring power from one Administration to another, or from one party to another—but we are transferring…

power from Washington, D.C. and giving it back to you, the American People. #InaugurationDay

What truly matters is not which party controls our government, but whether our government is controlled by the people.

January 20th 2017, will be remembered as the day the people became the rulers of this nation again.

The forgotten men and women of our country will be forgotten no longer. From this moment on, it's going to be #AmericaFirst🇺🇸

We will bring back our jobs. We will bring back our borders. We will bring back our wealth—and we will bring back our dreams!

We will follow two simple rules: BUY AMERICAN & HIRE AMERICAN! #InaugurationDay #MAGA🇺🇸

January 22, 2017

9:23 am: Peaceful protests are a hallmark of our democracy. Even if I don't always agree, I recognize the rights of people to express their views.

January 24, 2017

12:49 pm: Signing orders to move forward with the construction of the Keystone XL and Dakota Access pipelines in the Oval Office.

January 25, 2017

7:10 am to 7:13 am: I will be asking for a major investigation into VOT-ER FRAUD, including those registered to vote in two states, those who are illegal and...

even, those registered to vote who are dead (and many for a long time). Depending on results, we will strengthen up voting procedures!

February 2, 2017

6:18 am: Congratulations to Rex Tillerson on being sworn in as our new Secretary of State. He will be a star!

February 7, 2017

7:04 am: I don't know Putin, have no deals in Russia, and the haters are going crazy—yet Obama can make a deal with Iran, #1in terror, no problem!

February 8, 2017

8:05 pm: Congratulations to our new Attorney General, @SenatorSessions! https://t.co/e0buP1K83z

February 12, 2017

6:34 am: The crackdown on illegal criminals is merely the keeping of my campaign promise. Gang members, drug dealers & others are being removed!

February 14, 2017

9:28 am: The real story here is why are there so many illegal leaks coming out of Washington? Will these leaks be happening as I deal on N.Korea etc?

February 20, 2017

4:00 pm: Just named General H.R. McMaster National Security Advisor.

March 29, 2017

7:21 am: If the people of our great country could only see how viciously and inaccurately my administration is covered by certain media!

March 31, 2017

6:04 am: Mike Flynn should ask for immunity in that this is a witch hunt (excuse for big election loss), by media & Dems, of historic proportion!

April 12, 2017

6:10 pm: One by one we are keeping our promises—on the border, on energy, on jobs, on regulations. Big changes are happening!

7:32 pm: Jobs are returning, illegal immigration is plummeting, law, order and justice are being restored. We are truly making America great again!

April 13, 2017

8:16 am: Things will work out fine between the U.S.A. and Russia. At the right time everyone will come to their senses & there will be lasting peace!

April 17, 2017

5:38 pm: TRUMP APPROVAL HITS 50%

April 21. 2017

5:50 am: No matter how much I accomplish during the ridiculous standard of the first 100 days, & it has been a lot (including S.C.), media will kill!

7:43 pm: 'Presidential Executive Order on Identifying and Reducing Tax Regulatory Burdens' Executive Order:... https://t.co/dpE6hDzlAt

April 22, 2017

4:49 pm: I am committed to keeping our air and water clean but always remember that economic growth enhances environmental protection. Jobs matter!

April 27, 2017

9:37 am: I promise to rebuild our military and secure our border. Democrats want to shut down the government. Politics!

5:43 pm: Today, I signed an Executive Order on Improving Accountability and Whistleblower Protection at the @DeptVetAffairs.

May 5, 2017

8:02 am: Rather than causing a big disruption in N.Y.C., I will be working out of my home in Bedminster, N.J. this weekend. Also saves country money!

May 11, 2017

2:34 pm: 'Presidential Executive Order on Strengthening the Cybersecurity of Federal Networks and Critical Infrastructure'... https://t.co/kQDBvXPekk

4:54 pm: Yesterday, on the same day—I had meetings with Russian Foreign Minister Sergei Lavrov and the FM of Ukraine, Pavlo Klimkin. #LetsMakePeace!

May 12, 2017

6:59 am to 7:07 am: As a very active President with lots of things happening, it is not possible for my surrogates to stand at podium with perfect accuracy!...

...Maybe the best thing to do would be to cancel all future "press briefings" and hand out written responses for the sake of accuracy???

May 16, 2017

6:03 am to 6:13 am: As President I wanted to share with Russia (at an openly scheduled W.H. meeting) which I have the absolute right to do, facts pertaining...

May 18, 2017

6:39 am: This is the single greatest witch hunt of a politician in American history!

May 31, 2017

8:08 am: I will be announcing my decision on the Paris Accord over the next few days. MAKE AMERICA GREAT AGAIN!

3:04 pm: We traveled the world to strengthen long-standing alliances, and to form new partnerships. See more at:... https://t.co/FT4kyPoAl0

June 1, 2017

5:50 pm: My job as President is to do everything within my power to give America a level playing field. #AmericaFirst

June 17, 2017

9:08 am: Thoughts and prayers with the sailors of USS Fitzgerald and their families. Thank you to our Japanese allies for their assistance.

June 18, 2018

5:38 am to 5:46 am: The MAKE AMERICA GREAT AGAIN agenda is doing very well despite the distraction of the Witch Hunt. Many new jobs, high business enthusiasm,...

...massive regulation cuts, 36 new legislative bills signed, great new S.C.Justice, and Infrastructure, Healthcare and Tax Cuts in works!

June 19, 2017

3:15 pm: My heartfelt thoughts and prayers are with the 7 @USNavy sailors of the #USSFitzgerald and their families.
→... https://t.co/L3u5c8Iymh

June 29, 2017

4:13 pm: "Mattis Says Trump's Warning Stopped Chemical Weapons Attack In Syria" https://t.co/XL9LLNKh8i

4:37 pm: Good news, House just passed #KatesLaw. Hopefully Senate will follow.

5:28 pm: Good news out of the House with the passing of 'No Sanctuary for Criminals Act.' Hopefully Senate will follow.

6:09 pm: When it comes to the future of America's energy needs, we will FIND IT, we will DREAM IT, and we will BUILD IT....

June 30, 2017

5:43 pm: America will THINK BIG once again. We will inspire millions of children to carry on the proud tradition of American space leadership!

July 1, 2017

8:07 am: Numerous states are refusing to give information to the very distinguished VOTER FRAUD PANEL. What are they trying to hide?

July 7, 2017

2:42 am: I look forward to all meetings today with world leaders, including my meeting with Vladimir Putin. Much to discuss. #G20Summit #USA

July 14, 2017

8:34 pm: Honored to serve as Commander-in-Chief to the courageous men and women of our U.S. Armed Forces. A grateful nation thanks you!

July 15, 2017

3:29 pm: Just got to the #USWomensOpen in Bedminster, New Jersey. People are really happy with record high stock market—up over 17% since election!

July 16, 2017

9:10 am: The ABC/Washington Post Poll, even though almost 40% is not bad at this time, was just about the most inaccurate poll around election time!

July 21, 2017

8:46 pm: Sean Spicer is a wonderful person who took tremendous abuse from the Fake News Media—but his future is bright!

July 22, 2017

5:52 am: This morning I will be going to the Commissioning Ceremony for the largest aircraft carrier in the world, The Gerald R. Ford. Norfolk, Va.

6:35 am: While all agree the U. S. President has the complete power to pardon, why think of that when only crime so far is LEAKS against us.FAKE NEWS

5:57 pm: American steel & American hands have constructed a 100,000 ton message to the world: American MIGHT IS SECOND TO NONE! #USSGeraldRFord #USA

July 23, 2017

3:09 pm: As the phony Russian Witch Hunt continues, two groups are laughing at this excuse for a lost election taking hold, Democrats and Russians!

July 26, 2017

7:55 am to 8:08 am: After consultation with my Generals and military experts, please be advised that the United States Government will not accept or allow...

...Transgender individuals to serve in any capacity in the U.S. Military. Our military must be focused on decisive and overwhelming...

.victory and cannot be burdened with the tremendous medical costs and disruption that transgender in the military would entail. Thank you

July 26, 2017

12:21 pm: IN AMERICA WE DON'T WORSHIP GOVERN-MENT—WE WORSHIP GOD!

July 27, 2017

5:49 pm: It was my great HONOR to present our nation's highest award for a public safety officer—THE MEDAL OF VALOR to FIVE AMERICAN HEROES!

July 28, 2017

3:49 pm to 3:54 pm: I am pleased to inform you that I have just named General/Secretary John F Kelly as White House Chief of Staff. He is a Great American...

...and a Great Leader. John has also done a spectacular job at Homeland Security. He has been a true star of my Administration

4:00 pm: I would like to thank Reince Priebus for his service and dedication to his country. We accomplished a lot together and I am proud of him!

August 8, 2017

1:10 pm: After 200 days, rarely has any Administration achieved what we have achieved…not even close! Don't believe the Fake News Suppression Polls!

August 9, 2017

6:56 am to 7:03 am: My first order as President was to renovate and modernize our nuclear arsenal. It is now far stronger and more powerful than ever before…

…Hopefully we will never have to use this power, but there will never be a time that we are not the most powerful nation in the world!

August 10, 2017

6:51 pm: "Trump approval rebounds to 45%, surges among Hispanics, union homes, men" https://t.co/vvJMDv9Gjl

August 16, 2017

12:14 pm: Rather than putting pressure on the businesspeople of the Manufacturing Council & Strategy & Policy Forum, I am ending both. Thank you all!

August 17, 2017

8:07 am to 8:21 am: Sad to see the history and culture of our great country being ripped apart with the removal of our beautiful statues and monuments. You…

…can't change history, but you can learn from it. Robert E Lee, Stonewall Jackson—who's next, Washington, Jefferson? So foolish! Also…

the beauty that is being taken out of our cities, towns and parks will be greatly missed and never able to be comparably replaced!

August 25, 2017

5:40 am: General John Kelly is doing a fantastic job as Chief of Staff. There is tremendous spirit and talent in the W.H. Don't believe the Fake News

5:44 am: Few, if any, Administrations have done more in just 7 months than the Trump A. Bills passed, regulations killed, border, military, ISIS, SC!

9:00 pm: I am pleased to inform you that I have just granted a full Pardon to 85 year old American patriot Sheriff Joe Arpaio. He kept Arizona safe!

August 26, 2017

8:15 am: I will also be going to a wonderful state, Missouri, that I won by a lot in '16. Dem C.M. is opposed to big tax cuts. Republican will win S!

September 1, 2017

7:35 am to 7:47 am: General John Kelly is doing a great job as Chief of Staff. I could not be happier or more impressed—and this Administration continues to...

get things done at a record clip. Many big decisions to be made over the coming days and weeks. AMERICA FIRST!

September 5, 2017

7:36 am: I am allowing Japan & South Korea to buy a substantially increased amount of highly sophisticated military equipment from the United States.

September 7, 2017

8:33 pm: We will confront ANY challenge, no matter how strong the winds or high the water. I'm proud to stand with Presidents for #OneAmericaAppeal.

September 8, 2017

7:56 pm: Churches in Texas should be entitled to reimbursement from FEMA Relief Funds for helping victims of Hurricane Harvey (just like others).

September 18, 2017

11:18 pm: We call for the full restoration of democracy and political freedoms in Venezuela, and we want it to happen very, very soon!

September 19, 2017

5:04 pm: It was a great honor to have spoken before the countries of the world at the United Nations. #USAatUNGA

September 18, 2017

6:32 pm: Such an honor to have my good friend, Israel PM @Netanyahu, join us w/ his delegation in NYC this afternoon. #UNGA

September 20, 2017

5:14 am: Big meetings today at the United Nations. So many interesting leaders. America First will MAKE AMERICA GREAT AGAIN!

September 21, 2017

10:17 am: It was wonderful to have President Petro Poroshenko of Ukraine with us in New York City today. #UNGA

11:06 am: It was a great privilege to meet with President Moon of South Korea. Stay tuned! #UNGA

September 25, 2017

5:28 pm: General John Kelly totally agrees w/ my stance on NFL players and the fact that they should not be disrespecting our FLAG or GREAT COUNTRY!

5:29 pm: Tremendous backlash against the NFL and its players for disrespect of our Country. #StandForOurAnthem

October 8, 2017

6:37 pm: Nobody could have done what I've done for #PuertoRico with so little appreciation. So much work!

October 13, 2017

11:30 am: I have no greater privilege than to serve as your Commander-in-Chief. HAPPY BIRTHDAY to the incredible men and women @USNavy! #242NavyBday

12:07 pm: In America, we don't worship government—we worship God. #ValuesVotersSummit

October 21, 2017

7:35 am: Subject to the receipt of further information, I will be allowing, as President, the long blocked and classified JFK FILES to be opened.

6:57 pm to 7:09 pm: I agree getting Tax Cuts approved is important (we will also get HealthCare), but perhaps no Administration has done more in its first...

...9 months than this Administration. Over 50 Legislation approvals, massive regulation cuts, energy freedom, pipelines, border security...

...2nd Amendment, Strong Military, ISIS, historic VA improvement, Supreme Court Justice, Record Stock Market, lowest unemployment in 17 yrs!

October 25, 2017

2:56 pm: The long anticipated release of the #JFKFiles will take place tomorrow. So interesting!

October 27, 2017

4:17 pm: People are anxiously awaiting my decision as to who the next head of the Fed will be…

October 28, 2017

4:09 pm to 4:10 pm: After strict consultation with General Kelly, the CIA and other Agencies, I will be releasing ALL #JFKFiles other than the names and…

…addresses of any mentioned person who is still living. I am doing this for reasons of full disclosure, transparency and…

…in order to put any and all conspiracy theories to rest.

November 2, 2017

5:35 pm: Today, it was my pleasure and great honor to announce my nomination of Jerome Powell to be the next Chairman of the @ FederalReserve.

November 7, 2017

10:09 pm: The U.S., under my administration, is completely rebuilding its military, and they're spending hundreds of billions of dollars to the newest and finest military equipment anywhere in the world, being built right now. I want peace through strength!

November 11, 2017

7:18 pm: When will all the haters and fools out there realize that having a good relationship with Russia is a good thing, not a bad thing.

There always playing politics—bad for our country. I want to solve North Korea, Syria, Ukraine, terrorism, and Russia can greatly help!

November 15, 2017

10:11 am: Do you think the three UCLA Basketball Players will say thank you President Trump? They were headed for 10 years in jail!

11:35 am to 11:39 am: The failing @nytimes hates the fact that I have developed a great relationship with World leaders like Xi Jinping, President of China…

…They should realize that these relationships are a good thing, not a bad thing. The U.S. is being respected again. Watch Trade!

November 16, 2017

6:30 am to 6:34 am: To the three UCLA basketball players I say: You're welcome, go out and give a big Thank You to President Xi Jinping of China who made…

.your release possible and, HAVE A GREAT LIFE! Be careful, there are many pitfalls on the long and winding road of life!

November 17, 2017

7:47 pm: Put big game trophy decision on hold until such time as I review all conservation facts. Under study for years. Will update soon with Secretary Zinke. Thank you!

November 19, 2017

6:57 pm: Big-game trophy decision will be announced next week but will be very hard pressed to change my mind that this horror show in any way helps conservation of Elephants or any other animal.

November 22, 2017

4:32 pm: I have long given the order to help Argentina with the Search and Rescue mission of their missing submarine. 45 people aboard and not much time left. May God be with them and the people of Argentina!

November 25, 2017

4:48 pm: The Consumer Financial Protection Bureau, or CFPB, has been a total disaster as run by the previous Administrations pick. Financial Institutions have been devastated and unable to properly serve the public. We will bring it back to life!

November 28, 2017

10:28 pm: Just won the lawsuit on leadership of Consumer Financial Protection Bureau, CFPB. A big win for the Consumer!

December 2, 2017

12:14 pm: I had to fire General Flynn because he lied to the Vice President and the FBI. He has pled guilty to those lies. It is a shame because his actions during the transition were lawful. There was nothing to hide!

December 3, 2017

6:15 am: I never asked Comey to stop investigating Flynn. Just more Fake News covering another Comey lie!

December 8, 2017

10:18 am: Fines and penalties against Wells Fargo Bank for their bad acts against their customers and others will not be dropped, as has incorrectly been reported, but will be pursued and, if anything, substantially increased. I will cut Regs but make penalties severe when caught cheating!

December 9, 2017

1:19 pm: It was my great honor to celebrate the opening of two extraordinary museums-the Mississippi State History Museum & the Mississippi Civil Rights Museum. We pay solemn tribute to our heroes of the past & dedicate ourselves to building a future of freedom, equality, justice & peace.

December 13, 2017

6:58 pm: Thank you Omarosa for your service! I wish you continued success.

December 14, 2017

3:13 pm: Today, we gathered in the Roosevelt Room for one single reason: to CUT THE RED TAPE! For many decades, an ever-growing maze of regs, rules, and restrictions has cost our country trillions of dollars, millions of jobs, countless American factories, & devastated entire industries.

3:27 pm: When Americans are free to thrive, innovate, & prosper, there is no challenge too great, no task too large, & no goal beyond our reach. We are a nation of explorers, pioneers, innovators & inventors. We are nation of people who work hard, dream big, & who never, ever give up…

3:35 pm: In 1960, there were approximately 20,000 pages in the Code of Federal Regulations. Today there are over 185,000 pages, as seen in the Roosevelt Room. Today, we CUT THE RED TAPE! It is time to SET FREE OUR DREAMS and MAKE AMERICA GREAT AGAIN!

December 18, 2017

1:41 pm: The train accident that just occurred in DuPont, WA shows more than ever why our soon to be submitted infrastructure plan must be approved quickly. Seven trillion dollars spent in the Middle East while our roads, bridges, tunnels, railways (and more) crumble! Not for long!

December 22, 2017

10:04 am: With all my Administration has done on Legislative Approvals (broke Harry Truman's Record), Regulation Cutting, Judicial Appointments, Building Military, VA, TAX CUTS & REFORM, Record Economy/Stock Market and so much more, I am sure great credit will be given by mainstream news?

December 31, 2017

8:26 am: If the Dems (Crooked Hillary) got elected, your stocks would be down 50% from values on Election Day. Now they have a great future—and just beginning!

5:18 pm: As our Country rapidly grows stronger and smarter, I want to wish all of my friends, supporters, enemies, haters, and even the very dishonest Fake News Media, a Happy and Healthy New Year. 2018 will be a great year for America!

6:43 pm: HAPPY NEW YEAR! We are MAKING AMERICA GREAT AGAIN, and much faster than anyone thought possible!

Own Presidency/Administration—2018 News Quotes

Reply to a question from an unidentified reporter before a dinner with then-House Majority Leader Kevin McCarthy at the Trump International Golf Club in Palm Beach, Florida, January 14, 2018.
Source: https://www.whitehouse.gov/briefings-statements/
remarks-president-trump-dinner-house-majority-leader-kevin-mccarthy-palm-beach-fl/

"I'm not a racist."

Remarks before a bilateral meeting with Prime Minister Benjamin Netanyahu of Israel. The meeting was held in Davos, Switzerland on January 25, 2018.

Source: https://www.whitehouse.gov/briefings-statements/
remarks-president-trump-prime-minister-netanyahu-israel-bilateral-meeting-davos-switzerland/

"Israel has always supported the United States. So, what I did with Jerusalem was my honor. And hopefully, we can do something with peace. I would love to see it.

"You know, if you look back at the various peace proposals, and they are endless, and I spoke to some of the people involved, and I said, 'Did you ever talk about the vast amounts of funds, money that we give to the Palestinians?' We give, you know, hundreds of millions of dollars. And they said, 'We never talk.' Well, we do talk about it.

"And when they disrespected us a week ago by not allowing our great Vice President to see them, and we give them hundreds of millions of dollars in aid and support, tremendous numbers; numbers that nobody understands. That money is on the table, and that money is not going to them unless they sit down and negotiate peace. Because I can tell you that Israel does want to make peace. And they're going to have to want to make peace too, or we're going to have nothing to do with it any longer.

"This was never brought up by other negotiators, but it's brought up by me. So, I will say that the hardest subject they had to talk about was Jerusalem. We took Jerusalem off the table, so we don't have to talk about it anymore. They never got past Jerusalem. We took it off the table. We don't have to talk about it anymore. You won one point, and you'll give up some points later on in the negotiation, if it ever takes place. I don't know that it ever will take place.

"But they have to respect the process also, and they have to respect the fact that the U.S. has given tremendous support to them over the years, in terms of monetary support and other support.

"So, we'll see what happens with the peace process, but respect has to be shown to the U.S. or we're just not going any further."

Response to an unidentified reporter's question before a bilateral meeting with Prime Minister Benjamin Netanyahu of Israel. The meeting was held in Davos, Switzerland on January 25, 2018.
Source: https://www.whitehouse.gov/briefings-statements/
remarks-president-trump-prime-minister-netanyahu-israel-bilateral-meeting-davos-switzerland/

"Yes, we have a proposal for peace. It's a great proposal for the Palestinians. I think it's a very good proposal for Israel. It covers a lot of the things that were, over the years, discussed and agreed on. But the fact is, and I think you know this better than anybody, there were never any deals that came close, because Jerusalem—You could never get past Jerusalem.

"So, when people said, 'Oh, I set it back.' I didn't set it back; I helped it. Because by taking it off the table, that was the toughest issue. And Israel will pay for that. Look, Israel—Something is going to happen. They'll do something that's going to be a very good thing. But they want to make peace, and I hope the Palestinians want to make peace. And if they do, everybody is going to be very happy in the end."

Response to an unidentified reporter's question before a bilateral meeting with Prime Minister Benjamin Netanyahu of Israel. The meeting was held in Davos, Switzerland on January 25, 2018.
Source: https://www.whitehouse.gov/briefings-statements/
remarks-president-trump-prime-minister-netanyahu-israel-bilateral-meeting-davos-switzerland/

"You know what, it's many years of killing people. It's many years of killing each other. They [The Palestinians] have to be tired and disgusted of it. So, let's see what happens. I think, eventually, very sound minds—I hope sound minds are going to prevail. And it would be a great achievement of mine. I've said it from day one, if we could make peace between Israel and the Palestinians—If we do that, I would consider that one of our truly great achievements.

"But the money is on the table. The money was never on the table. I'll tell you up front, we give them tremendous amounts, hundreds of millions of dollars a year. That money is on the table. Because why should we do that, as a country, if they're doing nothing for us? And what we want to do for them is help them. We want to create peace and save lives. And we'll see what happens. We'll see what happens. But the money is on the table."

Response to an unidentified reporter's question at remarks before a bilateral meeting with Prime Minister Leo Varadkar of Ireland, March 15, 2018.
Source: https://www.whitehouse.gov/briefings-statements/ remarks-president-trump-prime-minister-varadkar-ireland-bilateral-meeting/

"I mean, they wrote a story about staff changes today that was very false. We had made a wonderful change. I think Mike Pompeo is going to be an incredible Secretary of State. We have some wonderful ideas.

"I've gotten to know a lot of people over the last year. You know, I've been in Washington for a little bit more than a year, whereas some people have been here for 30, 40 years. I've gotten to know great people.

"So, there will always be change, but very little. It was a very false story. It was very, a very exaggerated, a very exaggerated and false story. But there will always be change, and I think you want to see change.

"And I want to also see different ideas. Larry Kudlow just came in a little while ago, and I think Larry is going to be outstanding as economic adviser, so we look forward to it. But we'll talk to you about it later."

Response to a question from Steve Doocy of FOX News, April 26, 2018.
Source: https://www.bbc.com/news/world-us-canada-43913798

"I would give myself an A-plus. Nobody has done what I've been able to do, and I did it despite the fact that I have a phony cloud over my head that doesn't exist."

Response to a question from Steve Doocy of FOX News, April 26, 2018.
Source: https://www.bbc.com/news/world-us-canada-43913798

"Because of the fact that they have this witch hunt going on with people in the Justice Department that shouldn't be there, they have a witch hunt against the President of the United States going on, I've taken the position, and I don't have to take this position, and maybe I'll change, that I will not be involved with the Justice Department."

Response to His Majesty King Abdullah II bin Al-Hussein of the Hashemite Kingdom of Jordan before their bilateral meeting, June 25, 2018.
Source: https://www.whitehouse.gov/briefings-statements/remarks-president-trump-majesty-king-abdullah-ii-bin-al-hussein-hashemite-kingdom-jordan-bilateral-meeting/

"Remember, he [His Majesty King Abdullah II bin Al-Hussein of the Hashemite Kingdom of Jordan] used the word 'humility' with respect to me, so I am very happy with that word. That's probably the nicest compliment I've been given in a long time."

Remarks at a rally in Tampa, Florida, July 31, 2018.
Source: https://www.tampabay.com/florida-politics/buzz/2018/08/01/heres-a-full-transcript-of-president-trumps-speech-from-his-tampa-rally/

"Thank you. And, you know, we have a big thing happening because you know this, look at all those hats. White ones, red ones, they all have the same thing, Make America Great.

"Well, make America great again. Only to be replaced by Keep America Great in about, I don't know, I guess we could do it now, but let's wait another year. We could do it right now, frankly. We're doing fantastically well."

Remarks at a rally in Tampa, Florida, July 31, 2018.
Source: https://www.tampabay.com/florida-politics/buzz/2018/08/01/heres-a-full-transcript-of-president-trumps-speech-from-his-tampa-rally/

"I mean, these people, [the press] how they have gotten us wrong. And you know what they were asking, Election Day, 'Where did all these people come from? Where did they come from?'

"In Tennessee, that was an early state. They came in and they were pouring in with the early vote. And the fake news was saying, 'Where are these people coming from?'

269

"You know where they came from? They came from the heart. They came from people that were never happy with anybody until we came along. That's where they came from.

"That's where they came from.

"But one of the pundits said that, 'He's made a lot of promises. And you won't believe it, but he's actually kept far more promises than he made.' Did you ever hear that one? So. Of course they'll probably be throwing him out of broadcasting tomorrow."

Remarks at a rally in Tampa, Florida, July 31, 2018.

Source: https://www.tampabay.com/florida-politics/buzz/2018/08/01/
heres-a-full-transcript-of-president-trumps-speech-from-his-tampa-rally/

"The lobbyists and special interests fighting against my administration, many of them are globalist. They care what happens in other countries. I care what's happening in the USA.

"They're the geniuses who came up with our terrible trade deals one after another, how about NAFTA, remember when they signed NAFTA?

"Remember they signed NAFTA, and everybody just moved their companies down to Mexico, and these people were saying, 'Isn't that a wonderful thing?' No, it's not a wonderful thing and those companies are now moving back.

"These are the people who lost trillions of dollars overseas and who gave us our horrible immigration laws. These laws are the worst. I am for America first and the American worker. We want to be a puppet for no one any longer. We're not going to be a puppet any longer.

"My only special interest is you, the citizens of the United States. I've had a great career. I've got a lot of fun, even in Florida, I've had a great career, I've had a lot of fun. I've done great. I've done really well, beyond anything I could've ever expected. And then I ran for President with no experience and I won. Isn't that—But you actually won."

Remarks at White House dinner with evangelical leaders, August 27, 2018.

Source: https://www.whitehouse.gov/briefings-statements/
remarks-president-trump-dinner-evangelical-leaders/

"We're here this evening to celebrate America's heritage of faith, family, and freedom. As you know, in recent years, the government tried to undermine religious freedom. But the attacks on communities of faith are over. We've ended it. We've ended it. Unlike some before us, we are protecting your religious liberty.

"In the last 18 months alone, we have stopped the Johnson Amendment from interfering with your First Amendment rights. A big deal. It's a big deal.

"We've taken action to defend the religious conscience of doctors, nurses, teachers, students, preachers, faith groups, and religious employers.

"We sent the entire executive branch guidance on protecting religious liberty. Big deal. Brought the Faith and Opportunity Initiative to the White House.

"Reinstated the Mexico City Policy we first put into place. And if you know, if you study it, and most of you know about this, first under President Ronald Reagan, not since then—The Mexico City Policy.

"We proposed regulations to prevent Title 10 taxpayer funding from subsidizing abortion. I was the first President to stand in the Rose Garden to address the March for Life. First one.

"My administration has strongly spoken out against religious persecution around the world, including the persecution of Christians. All over the world, what's going on. And for that, we've become not only a strong voice but a very, very powerful force. We're stopping a lot of bad things from happening."

Response to a question from Lesley Stahl of *60 Minutes*, October 15, 2018.

Source: https://www.theguardian.com/us-news/2018/oct/15/
donald-trumps-60-minutes-interview-eight-takeaways

"I think he's [then-U.S. Secretary of Defense Gen. James N. Mattis is] sort of a Democrat, if you want to know the truth. But General Mattis is a good guy. We get along very well. He may leave. I mean, at some point, everybody leaves. Everybody. People leave. That's Washington."

Response to a question from the Associated Press[17], published October 17, 2018[18].

Source: https://www.cnbc.com/2018/10/17/read-the-transcript-of-aps-interview-with-president-trump.html

"They have to do whatever they do, and I'll do whatever I do. But I've had the most successful two years. I would say, without question, first two years of office, I've had the most successful two years in the history of this country as a President. And we're not even close, actually, if you think about it. It's not until January 20, so we're not even really close to two years. And, would get me the list? Would you get me the list, please?"

Response to a question from the Associated Press[19], published October 17, 2018[20].

Source: https://www.cnbc.com/2018/10/17/read-the-transcript-of-aps-interview-with-president-trump.html

"Nobody has done what I've done, and nobody has come close in the first two years of office. And that's despite the fighting, the Democrats' obstruction."

---

17 AP White House reporters Catherine Lucey, Zeke Miller, and Jonathan Lemire conducted this interview. However, the transcript does not indicate which reporter asked President Trump which question.

18 The interview was conducted by the AP before the midterm elections of October 16, 2018. However, it was published by CNBC on October 17, 2018.

19 AP White House reporters Catherine Lucey, Zeke Miller, and Jonathan Lemire conducted this interview. However, the transcript does not indicate which reporter asked President Trump which question.

20 The interview was conducted by the AP before the midterm elections of October 16, 2018. However, it was published by CNBC on October 17, 2018.

Response to a question from the Associated Press[21], published October 17, 2018[22].

Source: https://www.cnbc.com/2018/10/17/read-the-transcript-of-aps-interview-with-president-trump.html

"I mean, you go point after point, each point is a major event, but you just take a look. Confirmed more circuit court judges than any other new administration. Soon it will be than any administration in history. Who is the one, who's the one President that percentage-wise has done better than me? There's only one. George Washington—100%. Nobody has gotten that yet."

Response to a question from Chris Wallace of FOX News, November 18, 2018.

Source: https://www.youtube.com/watch?v=rMgJnnG-Nql

"We've made, I think, some great decisions for the people of this country. And I do, you know, I put America first and other countries should put themselves first. It's not like we should put—And everybody else should be second to us, no. Other countries are proud of their countries and their leadership put their countries first. But we were putting our country in many cases last. We were more worried about the world than we were worried about the United States; that's not going to happen with me."

Response to a question from Chris Wallace of FOX News, November 18, 2018.

Source: https://www.youtube.com/watch?v=rMgJnnG-Nql

"I think that if I was very different, I wouldn't have gotten what we had to get. We got the biggest tax cuts in history, we got ANWR approved, we have—We got rid of the individual mandate, which was the most unpopular thing you can imagine—

---

21 AP White House reporters Catherine Lucey, Zeke Miller, and Jonathan Lemire conducted this interview. However, the transcript does not indicate which reporter asked President Trump which question.

22 The interview was conducted by the AP before the midterm elections of October 16, 2018. However, it was published by CNBC on October 17, 2018.

"Healthcare, I got rid of it; everybody said it would be impossible to get rid of it. And many, many—

"You know, the regulations. I think if I was a more modified, more moderate, in that sense, I don't think I would have done half of the things that I was able to get completed.

"With that being said, other than you have to have a certain ability to fight back and, as you know, people have—You know, they take strong stands on me both ways, you know, love and hate. I'd like to see it a little bit, maybe, more right down the middle. But tone is something that is important to me. But a lot of times you can't practice tone because you have people coming at you so hard that if you don't fight back in a somewhat vigorous way you're not going to win. And we have to win. This country has to win. We have a lot of victories coming and I think if I, if I go too low key we're not going to have those victories."

Response to a question from Chris Wallace of FOX News, November 18, 2018.
Source: https://www.youtube.com/watch?v=rMgJnnG-Nql

"I have. I feel very comfortable. It took me a little while. You know, it's sort of incredible. You say you're the President of the United States, and I say, 'Wow!' And it takes a little while to get over that."

Response to a question from Chris Wallace of FOX News, November 18, 2018.
Source: https://www.youtube.com/watch?v=rMgJnnG-Nql

"And I will tell you I'm extremely upbeat, the White House is running like a well-oiled machine, it's doing really well, I have great people. I will make some changes but not very many. I'm very happy with my cabinet, other than, you know a couple of exceptions and even there I'm not unhappy. And I will tell you that it's so wrong, the reporting about me is so wrong. I'm loving what I'm doing, I did well in France, I did have a problem where I wasn't able to go to a cemetery because the Secret Service would not let me do it."

Own Presidency/Administration—2018 Tweets

January 5, 2018

10:34 am: The Mercer Family recently dumped the leaker known as Sloppy Steve Bannon. Smart!

January 6, 2018

7:19 am: Now that Russian collusion, after one year of intense study, has proven to be a total hoax on the American public, the Democrats and their lapdogs, the Fake News Mainstream Media, are taking out the old Ronald Reagan playbook and screaming mental stability and intelligence...

7:27 am to 7:30 am: ...Actually, throughout my life, my two greatest assets have been mental stability and being, like, reallysmart. Crooked Hillary Clinton also played these cards very hard and, as everyone knows, went down in flames. I went from VERY successful business-man, to top T.V. Star...

...to President of the United States (on my first try). I think that would qualify as not smart, but genius...and a very stable genius at that!

January 17, 2018

8:11 pm: ISIS is in retreat, our economy is booming, investments and jobs are pouring back into the country, and so much more! Together there is nothing we can't overcome—even a very biased media. We ARE Making America Great Again!

January 20, 2018

5:31 pm: Unprecedented success for our Country, in so many ways, since the Election. Record Stock Market, Strong on

Military, Crime, Borders, & ISIS, Judicial Strength & Numbers, Lowest Unemployment for Women & ALL, Massive Tax Cuts, end of Individual Mandate—and so much more. Big 2018!

7:47 pm: The Trump Administration has terminated more UNNECESSARY Regulation, in just twelve months, than any other Administration has terminated during their full term in office, no matter what the length. The good

news is, THERE IS MUCH MORE TO COME!

January 23, 2018

9:16 am: Thank you to General John Kelly, who is doing a fantastic job, and all of the Staff and others in the White House, for a job well done. Long hours and Fake reporting makes your job more difficult, but it is always great to WIN, and few have won more than us!

February 9, 2018

8:39 am: Just signed Bill. Our Military will now be stronger than ever before. We love and need our Military and gave them everything—and more. First time this has happened in a long time. Also means JOBS, JOBS, JOBS!

February 13, 2018

5:43 am: Our infrastructure plan has been put forward and has received great reviews by everyone except, of course, the Democrats. After many years we have taken care of our Military, now we have to fix our roads, bridges, tunnels, airports and more. Bipartisan, make deal Dems?

February 22, 2018

8:13 am: I will be strongly pushing Comprehensive Background Checks with an emphasis on Mental Health. Raise age to 21 and end sale of Bump Stocks! Congress is in a mood to finally do something on this issue—I hope!

March 12, 2018

7:49 pm: THE HOUSE INTELLIGENCE COMMITTEE HAS, AFTER A 14 MONTH LONG IN-DEPTH INVESTIGATION, FOUND NO EVIDENCE OF COLLUSION OR COORDINATION BETWEEN THE TRUMP CAMPAIGN AND RUSSIA TO INFLUENCE THE 2016 PRESIDENTIAL ELECTION.

March 13, 2018

7:44 am: Mike Pompeo, Director of the CIA, will become our new Secretary of State. He will do a fantastic job! Thank you to Rex Tillerson for his service! Gina Haspel will become the new Director of the CIA, and the first woman so chosen. Congratulations to all!

March 14, 2018

6:11 am: Larry Kudlow will be my Chief Economic Advisor as Director of the National Economic Council. Our Country will have many years of Great Economic & Financial Success, with low taxes, unparalleled innovation, fair trade and an ever expanding labor force leading the way! #MAGA

March 18, 2018

7:35 am: Why does the Mueller team have 13 hardened Democrats, some big Crooked Hillary supporters, and Zero Republicans? Another Dem recently added...does anyone think this is fair? And yet, there is NO COLLUSION!

March 21, 2018

1:56 pm to 2:05 pm: I called President Putin of Russia to congratulate him on his election victory (in past, Obama called him also). The Fake News Media is crazed because they wanted me to excoriate him. They are wrong! Getting along with Russia (and others) is a good thing, not a bad thing...

...They can help solve problems with North Korea, Syria, Ukraine, ISIS, Iran and even the coming Arms Race. Bush tried to get along, but didn't have the "smarts." Obama and Clinton tried, but didn't have the energy or chemistry (remember RESET). PEACE THROUGH STRENGTH!

March 22, 2018

5:26 pm: I am pleased to announce that, effective 4/9/18, @AmbJohn-Bolton will be my new National Security Advisor. I am very thankful for the service of General H.R. McMaster who has done an outstanding job & will always remain my friend. There will be an official contact handover on 4/9.

March 28, 2018

4:31 pm: I am pleased to announce that I intend to nominate highly respected Admiral Ronny L. Jackson, MD, as the new Secretary of Veterans Affairs...

...In the interim, Hon. Robert Wilkie of DOD will serve as Acting Secretary. I am thankful for Dr. David Shulkin's service to our country and to our GREAT VETERANS!

March 29, 2018

3:06 pm: Washington spent trillions building up foreign countries while allowing OUR OWN infrastructure to fall into a state of total disrepair. No more! It's time to REBUILD, and we will do it with American WORKERS, American GRIT, and American PRIDE!

April 11, 2018

6:37 am: Our relationship with Russia is worse now than it has ever been, and that includes the Cold War. There is no reason for this. Russia needs us to help with their economy, something that would be very easy to do, and we need all nations to work together. Stop the arms race?

8:00 am: Much of the bad blood with Russia is caused by the Fake & Corrupt Russia Investigation, headed up by the all Democrat loyalists, or people that worked for Obama. Mueller is most conflicted of all (except Rosenstein who signed FISA & Comey letter). No Collusion, so they go crazy!

April 15, 2018

7:32 am: I never asked Comey for Personal Loyalty. I hardly even knew this guy. Just another of his many lies. His "memos" are self serving and FAKE!

8:07 am: Slippery James Comey, a man who always ends up badly and out of whack (he is not smart!), will go down as the WORST FBI Director in history, by far!

April 17, 2018

9:49 pm: While Japan and South Korea would like us to go back into TPP, I don't like the deal for the United States. Too many contingencies and no way to get out if it doesn't work. Bilateral deals are far more efficient, profitable and better for OUR workers. Look how bad WTO is to U.S.

April 25, 2018

9:11 am: Looking forward to my meeting with Tim Cook of Apple. We will be talking about many things, including how the U.S. has been treated unfairly for many years, by many countries, on trade.

April 27, 2018

9:14 am: Just Out: House Intelligence Committee Report released. "No evidence" that the Trump Campaign "colluded, coordinated or conspired with Russia." Clinton Campaign paid for Opposition Research obtained from Russia—Wow! A total Witch Hunt! MUST END NOW!

April 30, 2018

6:02 pm: The White House is running very smoothly despite phony Witch Hunts etc. There is great Energy and unending Stamina, both necessary to get things done. We are accomplishing the unthinkable and setting positive records while doing so! Fake News is going "bonkers!"

May 7, 2018

6:04 am: My highly respected nominee for CIA Director, Gina Haspel, has come under fire because she was too tough on Terrorists. Think of that, in these very dangerous times, we have the most qualified person, a woman, who Democrats want OUT because she is too tough on terror. Win Gina!

6:39 am: The 13 Angry Democrats in charge of the Russian Witch Hunt are starting to find out that there is a Court System in place that actually protects people from injustice...and just wait 'till the Courts get to see your unrevealed Conflicts of Interest!

May 17, 2018

8:52 am: Despite the disgusting, illegal and unwarranted Witch Hunt, we have had the most successful first 17 month Administration in U.S. history—by far! Sorry to the Fake News Media and "Haters," but that's the way it is!

May 20, 2018

8:11 am: ...At what point does this soon to be $20,000,000 Witch Hunt, composed of 13 Angry and Heavily Conflicted Democrats and two people who have worked for Obama for 8 years, STOP! They have found no Collussion with Russia, No Obstruction, but they aren't looking at the corruption...

8:29 am: Now that the Witch Hunt has given up on Russia and is looking at the rest of the World, they should easily be able to take it into the Mid-Term Elections where they can put some hurt on the Republican Party. Don't worry about Dems FISA Abuse, missing Emails or Fraudulent Dossier!

May 21, 2018

7:40 pm: For the first time since Roe v. Wade, America has a Pro-Life President, a Pro-Life Vice President, a Pro-Life House of Representatives and 25 Pro-Life Republican State Capitals!

May 23, 2018

6:58 am: Big legislation will be signed by me shortly. After many years, RIGHT TO TRY and big changes to DODD FRANK.

May 26, 2018

8:22 am: Good news about the release of the American hostage from Venezuela. Should be landing in D.C. this evening and be in the White House, with his family, at about 7:00 P.M. The great people of Utah will be very happy!

2:56 pm: When will the 13 Angry Democrats (& those who worked for President O), reveal their disqualifying Conflicts of Interest? It's been a long time now! Will they be indelibly written into the Report along with the fact that the only Collusion is with the Dems, Justice, FBI & Russia?

May 30, 2018

12:09 pm: Today I am proud to keep another promise to the American people as I sign the #RightToTry Legislation into law.

10:21 pm: "The recusal of Jeff Sessions was an unforced betrayal of the President of the United States." JOE DIGENOVA, former U.S. Attorney.

May 31, 2018

8:18 am: Will be giving a Full Pardon to Dinesh D'Souza today. He was treated very unfairly by our government!

June 1, 2018

6:05 am: A.P. has just reported that the Russian Hoax Investigation has now cost our government over $17 million, and going up fast. No Collusion, except by the Democrats!

June 3, 2018

8:25 am to 8:34 am: As only one of two people left who could become President, why wouldn't the FBI or Department of "Justice" have told me that they were secretly investigating Paul Manafort (on charges that were 10 years old and had been previously dropped) during my campaign? Should have told me!

...Paul Manafort came into the campaign very late and was with us for a short period of time (he represented Ronald Reagan, Bob Dole & many others over the years), but we should have been told that Comey and the boys were doing a number on him, and he wouldn't have been hired!

June 4, 2018

7:35 am: As has been stated by numerous legal scholars, I have the absolute right to PARDON myself, but why would I do that when I have done nothing wrong? In the meantime, the never ending Witch Hunt, led by 13 very Angry and Conflicted Democrats (& others) continues into the mid-terms!

9:01 am: The appointment of the Special Counsel is totally UNCON-STITUTIONAL! Despite that, we play the game because I, unlike the Democrats, have done nothing wrong!

9:55 pm: The Philadelphia Eagles Football Team was invited to the White House. Unfortunately, only a small number of players decided to come, and we canceled the event. Staying in the Locker Room for the playing of our National Anthem is as disrespectful to our country as kneeling. Sorry!

June 5, 2018

6:21 am: We have had many Championship teams recently at the White House including the Chicago Cubs, Houston Astros, Pittsburgh Penguins, New England Patriots, Alabama and Clemson National Champions, and many others. National Anthem & more great music today at 3:00 P.M.

6:31 am: The Russian Witch Hunt Hoax continues, all because Jeff Sessions didn't tell me he was going to recuse himself...I would have quickly picked someone else. So much time and money wasted, so many lives ruined...and Sessions knew better than most that there was No Collusion!

3:06 pm: The HISTORIC Rescissions Package we've proposed would cut $15,000,000,000 in Wasteful Spending! We are getting our government back on track.

June 6, 2018

6:57 pm: Isn't it Ironic? Getting ready to go to the G-7 in Canada to fight for our country on Trade (we have the worst trade deals ever made), then off to Singapore to meet with North Korea & the Nuclear Problem...But back home we still have the 13 Angry Democrats pushing the Witch Hunt!

8:05 am: Alan Dershowitz, Harvard Law Professor: "It all proves that we never needed a Special Counsel...All of this could have been done by the Justice Dept. Don't need a multi-million dollar group of people with a target on someone's back. Not the way Justice should operate." So true!

June 7, 2018

10:10 am: When will people start saying, "thank you, Mr. President, for firing James Comey?"

2:51 pm: Today, I am greatly honored to welcome my good friend, PM Abe of Japan to the @WhiteHouse. Over the past 16 months the

Prime Minister and I have worked closely together to address common challenges, of which there are many...

2:55 pm: PM Abe and I are also working to improve the trading relationship between the U.S. and Japan, something we have to do. The U.S. seeks a bilateral deal with Japan that is based on the principle of fairness and reciprocity. We're working hard to reduce our trade imbalance...

June 12, 2018

3:53 pm: Robert De Niro, a very Low IQ individual, has received to many shots to the head by real boxers in movies. I watched him last night and truly believe he may be "punch-drunk." I guess he doesn't...

...realize the economy is the best it's ever been with employment being at an all time high, and many companies pouring back into our country. Wake up Punchy!

June 15, 2018

12:41 pm: Wow, what a tough sentence for Paul Manafort, who has represented Ronald Reagan, Bob Dole and many other top political people and campaigns. Didn't know Manafort was the head of the Mob. What about Comey and Crooked Hillary and all of the others? Very unfair!

5:03 pm: I have a great relationship with Angela Merkel of Germany, but the Fake News Media only shows the bad photos (implying anger) of negotiating an agreement—where I am asking for things that no other American President would ask for!

June 20, 2018

3:39 pm: Don't worry, the Republicans, and your President, will fix it! https://t.co/xsbuPzXbHj

June 25, 2018

6:41 am: The Red Hen Restaurant should focus more on cleaning its filthy canopies, doors and windows (badly needs a paint job) rather than refusing to serve a fine person like Sarah Huckabee Sanders. I always had a rule, if a restaurant is dirty on the outside, it is dirty on the inside!

June 28, 2018

7:43 am to 7:56 am: When is Bob Mueller going to list his Conflicts of Interest? Why has it taken so long? Will they be listed at the top of his $22,000,000 Report...And what about the 13 Angry Democrats, will they list their conflicts with Crooked H? How many people will be sent to jail and...

persecuted on old and/or totally unrelated charges (there was no collusion and there was no obstruction of the no collusion)...And what is going on in the FBI & DOJ with Crooked Hillary, the DNC and all of the lies? A disgraceful situation!

July 1, 2018

2:39 pm: A big week, especially with our numerous victories in the Supreme Court. Heading back to the White House now. Focus will be on the selection of a new Supreme Court Justice. Exciting times for our country. Economy may be stronger than it has ever been!

July 3, 2018

4:19 pm: After having written many best selling books, and somewhat priding myself on my ability to write, it should be noted that the Fake News constantly likes to pour over my tweets looking for a mistake. I capitalize certain words only for emphasis, not b/c they should be capitalized!

July 5, 2018

2:37 pm: I have accepted the resignation of Scott Pruitt as the Administrator of the Environmental Protection Agency. Within the Agency Scott has done an outstanding job, and I will always be thankful to him for this. The Senate confirmed Deputy at EPA, Andrew Wheeler, will…

…on Monday assume duties as the acting Administrator of the EPA. I have no doubt that Andy will continue on with our great and lasting EPA agenda. We have made tremendous progress and the future of the EPA is very bright!

July 15, 2018

11:18 am: Heading to Helsinki, Finland—looking forward to meeting with President Putin tomorrow. Unfortunately, no matter how well I do at the Summit, if I was given the great city of Moscow as retribution for all of the sins and evils committed by Russia…

…over the years, I would return to criticism that it wasn't good enough—that I should have gotten Saint Petersburg in addition! Much of our news media is indeed the enemy of the people and all the Dems…

…know how to do is resist and obstruct! This is why there is such hatred and dissension in our country—but at some point, it will heal!

July 16, 2018

1:05 am: Our relationship with Russia has NEVER been worse thanks to many years of U.S. foolishness and stupidity and now, the Rigged Witch Hunt!

3:29 pm: I would rather take a political risk in pursuit of peace, than to risk peace in pursuit of politics. #HELSINKI2018

3:34 pm: A productive dialogue is not only good for the United States and good for Russia, but it is good for the world. #HELSINKI2018

July 17, 2018

7:24 pm: The meeting between President Putin and myself was a great success, except in the Fake News Media!

July 18, 2018

4:53 am: So many people at the higher ends of intelligence loved my press conference performance in Helsinki. Putin and I discussed many important subjects at our earlier meeting. We got along well which truly bothered many haters who wanted to see a boxing match. Big results will come!

July 18, 2018

6:27 am: Some people HATE the fact that I got along well with President Putin of Russia. They would rather go to war than see this. It's called Trump Derangement Syndrome!

July 19, 2018

8:24 am to 8:30 am: The Summit with Russia was a great success, except with the real enemy of the people, the Fake News Media. I look forward to our second meeting so that we can start implementing some of the many things discussed, including stopping terrorism, security for Israel, nuclear…

…proliferation, cyber attacks, trade, Ukraine, Middle East peace, North Korea and more. There are many answers, some easy and some hard, to these problems…but they can ALL be solved!

July 24, 2018

10:50 am: I'm very concerned that Russia will be fighting very hard to have an impact on the upcoming Election. Based on the fact that no President has been tougher on Russia than me, they will be pushing very hard for the Democrats. They definitely don't want Trump!

July 25, 2018

6:08 am: When you have people snipping at your heels during a negotiation, it will only take longer to make a deal, and the deal will never be as good as it could have been with unity. Negotiations are going really well, be cool. The end result will be worth it!

July 26, 2018

10:22 am: The United States will impose large sanctions on Turkey for their long time detainment of Pastor Andrew Brunson, a great Christian, family man and wonderful human being. He is suffering greatly. This innocent man of faith should be released immediately!

July 27, 2018

6:26 am to 6:56 am: Arrived back in Washington last night from a very emotional reopening of a major U.S. Steel plant in Granite City, Illinois, only to be greeted with the ridiculous news that the highly conflicted Robert Mueller and his gang of 13 Angry Democrats obviously cannot find Collusion...

...,the only Collusion with Russia was with the Democrats, so now they are looking at my Tweets (along with 53 million other people)—the rigged Witch Hunt continues! How stupid and unfair to our Country...And so the Fake News doesn't waste my time with dumb questions, NO,...

...I did NOT know of the meeting with my son, Don jr. Sounds to me like someone is trying to make up stories in order to get himself out of an unrelated jam (Taxi cabs maybe?). He even retained Bill and Crooked Hillary's lawyer. Gee, I wonder if they helped him make the choice!

July 29, 2018

8:13 am: I would be willing to "shut down" government if the Democrats do not give us the votes for Border Security, which includes the

Wall! Must get rid of Lottery, Catch & Release etc. and finally go to system of Immigration based on MERIT! We need great people coming into our Country!

3:20 pm: ...Also, why is Mueller only appointing Angry Dems, some of whom have worked for Crooked Hillary, others, including himself, have worked for Obama...And why isn't Mueller looking at all of the criminal activity & real Russian Collusion on the Democrats side-Podesta, Dossier?

July 30, 2018

7:56 pm: A highly respected Federal judge today stated that the "Trump Administration gets great credit" for reuniting illegal families. Thank you, and please look at the previous administrations record—not good!

July 31, 2018

6:58 am: Collusion is not a crime, but that doesn't matter because there was No Collusion (except by Crooked Hillary and the Democrats)!

7:03 am: I am looking into 3-D Plastic Guns being sold to the public. Already spoke to NRA, doesn't seem to make much sense!

August 1, 2018

10:35 am: Looking back on history, who was treated worse, Alfonse Capone, legendary mob boss, killer and "Public Enemy Number One," or Paul Manafort, political operative & Reagan/Dole darling, now serving solitary confinement—although convicted of nothing? Where is the Russian Collusion?

August 3, 2018

3:31 pm: "Pastor praises Trump as 'pro-black' at prison reform event" https://t.co/xFKflarebx

August 5, 2018

3:01 pm: Presidential Approval numbers are very good—strong economy, military and just about everything else. Better numbers than Obama at this point, by far. We are winning on just about every front and for that reason there will not be a Blue Wave, but there might be a Red Wave!

August 10, 2018

7:47 am: I have just authorized a doubling of Tariffs on Steel and Aluminum with respect to Turkey as their currency, the Turkish Lira, slides rapidly downward against our very strong Dollar! Aluminum will now be 20% and Steel 50%. Our relations with Turkey are not good at this time!

August 13, 2018

8:27 am to 8:50 am: Wacky Omarosa, who got fired 3 times on the Apprentice, now got fired for the last time. She never made it, never will. She begged me for a job, tears in her eyes, I said Ok. People in the White House hated her. She was vicious, but not smart. I would rarely see her but heard…

. …really bad things. Nasty to people & would constantly miss meetings & work. When Gen. Kelly came on board he told me she was a loser & nothing but problems. I told him to try working it out, if possible, because she only said GREAT things about me—until she got fired!

9:21 am: … While I know it's "not presidential" to take on a lowlife like Omarosa, and while I would rather not be doing so, this is a modern day form of communication and I know the Fake News Media will be working overtime to make even Wacky Omarosa look legitimate as possible. Sorry

5:36 pm: It was my great honor to sign our new Defense Bill into law and to pay tribute to the greatest soldiers in the history of the world: THE U.S. ARMY. The National Defense Authorization Act is the most significant investment in our Military and our warfighters in modern history!

August 14, 2018

6:31 am: When you give a crazed, crying lowlife a break, and give her a job at the White House, I guess it just didn't work out. Good work by General Kelly for quickly firing that dog!

August 16, 2018

1:55 pm: Thank you for the kind words Omarosa!
https://t.co/PMmNG6iIsi

6:30 pm: Turkey has taken advantage of the United States for many years. They are now holding our wonderful Christian Pastor, who I must now ask to represent our Country as a great patriot hostage. We will pay nothing for the release of an innocent man, but we are cutting back on Turkey!

August 17, 2018

6:57 am to 7:10 am: The local politicians who run Washington, D.C. (poorly) know a windfall when they see it. When asked to give us a price for holding a great celebratory military parade, they wanted a number so ridiculously high that I cancelled it. Never let someone hold you up! I will instead...

...attend the big parade already scheduled at Andrews Air Force Base on a different date, & go to the Paris parade, celebrating the end of the War, on November 11th. Maybe we will do something next year in D.C. when the cost comes WAY DOWN. Now we can buy some more jet fighters!

August 18, 2018

6:46 am: All of the fools that are so focused on looking only at Russia should start also looking in another direction, China. But in the end, if we are smart, tough and well prepared, we will get along with everyone!

5:04 pm: I allowed White House Counsel Don McGahn, and all other requested members of the White House Staff, to fully cooperate with the Special Councel. In addition we readily gave over one million pages of documents. Most transparent in history. No Collusion, No Obstruction. Witch Hunt!

August 22, 2018

9:28 pm: I have asked Secretary of State @SecPompeo to closely study the South Africa land and farm seizures and expropriations and the large scale killing of farmers. "South African Government is now seizing land from white farmers." @TuckerCarlson @FoxNews

August 23, 2018

2:21 pm: I have authorized an emergency disaster declaration to provide Hawaii the necessary support ahead of #HurricaneLane. Our teams are closely coordinating with the state and local authorities. You are in our thoughts!

August 25, 2018

7:36 am: Jeff Sessions said he wouldn't allow politics to influence him only because he doesn't understand what is happening underneath his command position. Highly conflicted Bob Mueller and his gang of 17 Angry Dems are having a field day as real corruption goes untouched. No Collusion!

7:44 pm: My deepest sympathies and respect go out to the family of Senator John McCain. Our hearts and prayers are with you!

August 28, 2018

8:21 pm: Add the 2026 World Cup to our long list of accomplishments!

August 29, 2018

9:30 am: White House Counsel Don McGahn will be leaving his position in the fall, shortly after the confirmation (hopefully) of Judge Brett Kavanaugh to the United States Supreme Court. I have worked with Don for a long time and truly appreciate his service!

August 30, 2018

8:17 am: The Rigged Russia Witch Hunt did not come into play, even a little bit, with respect to my decision on Don McGahn!

September 5, 2018

8:20 am: Almost everyone agrees that my Administration has done more in less than two years than any other Administration in the history of our Country. I'm tough as hell on people & if I weren't, nothing would get done. Also, I question everybody & everything-which is why I got elected!

5:15 pm: TREASON?

10:22 pm: I'm draining the Swamp, and the Swamp is trying to fight back. Don't worry, we will win!

September 7, 2018

6:32 am: The Woodward book is a scam. I don't talk the way I am quoted. If I did I would not have been elected President. These quotes were made up. The author uses every trick in the book to demean and belittle. I wish the people could see the real facts—and our country is doing GREAT!

September 10, 2018

6:35 am: The White House is a "smooth running machine." We are making some of the biggest and most important deals in our country's history—with many more to come! The Dems are going crazy!

September 13, 2018

7:37 am: 3000 people did not die in the two hurricanes that hit Puerto Rico. When I left the Island, AFTER the storm had hit, they had anywhere from 6 to 18 deaths. As time went by it did not go up by much. Then, a long time later, they started to report really large numbers, like 3000…

September 14, 2018

9:05 pm to 9:23 pm: "When Trump visited the island territory last October, OFFICIALS told him in a briefing 16 PEOPLE had died from Maria." The Washington Post. This was long AFTER the hurricane took place. Over many months it went to 64 PEOPLE. Then, like magic, "3000 PEOPLE KILLED." They hired…

…GWU Research to tell them how many people had died in Puerto Rico (how would they not know this?). This method was never done with previous hurricanes because other jurisdictions know how many people were killed. FIFTY TIMES LAST ORIGINAL NUMBER—NO WAY

September 15, 2018

5:08 pm: While my (our) poll numbers are good, with the Economy being the best ever, if it weren't for the Rigged Russian Witch Hunt, they would be 25 points higher! Highly conflicted Bob Mueller & the 17 Angry Democrats are using this Phony issue to hurt us in the Midterms. No Collusion!

September 18, 2018

1:21 pm: Today, I took action to strengthen our Nation's defenses against biological threats. For the first time in history, the Federal Government has a National Biodefense Strategy to address the FULL RANGE of biological threats!

September 21, 2018

7:56 am: Judge Brett Kavanaugh is a fine man, with an impeccable reputation, who is under assault by radical left wing politicians who don't want to know the answers, they just want to destroy and delay. Facts don't matter. I go through this with them every single day in D.C.

September 24, 2018

9:17 am: "Remarks by President Trump at 'Global Call to Action on the World Drug Problem' Event" #UNGA →https://t.co/kvUZegWdlH http s://t.co/BGdrQeZuId

3:44 pm: US-Korea Free Trade Agreement Signing Ceremony! https://t.co/yLFkAZgagG

September 25, 2018

8:14 am: Will be speaking at the United Nations this morning. Our country is much stronger and much richer than it was when I took office less than two years ago. We are also MUCH safer!

October 2, 2018

9:18 pm: Today, my Administration provided HISTORIC levels of funding to improve school safety through STOP School Violence grants—a top priority for @sandyhook. I am committed to keeping our children SAFE in their schools!

October 5, 2018

8:03 am: The very rude elevator screamers are paid professionals only looking to make Senators look bad. Don't fall for it! Also, look at all of the professionally made identical signs. Paid for by Soros and others. These are not signs made in the basement from love! #Troublemakers

October 6, 2018

3:15 pm: I applaud and congratulate the U.S. Senate for confirming our GREAT NOMINEE, Judge Brett Kavanaugh, to the United States Supreme Court. Later today, I will sign his Commission of Appointment, and he will be officially sworn in. Very exciting!

October 17, 2018

6:30 am: "Trump could be the most honest president in modern history. When you look at the real barometer of presidential truthfulness, which is promise keeping, he is probably the most honest president in American history. He's done exactly what he said he would do." Marc Thiessen, WPost

October 29, 2018

7:28 am: Had a very good conversation with the newly elected President of Brazil, Jair Bolsonaro, who won his race by a substantial margin. We agreed that Brazil and the United States will work closely together on Trade, Military and everything else! Excellent call, wished him congrats!

November 7, 2018

7:07 am: Those that worked with me in this incredible Midterm Election, embracing certain policies and principles, did very well. Those that did not, say goodbye! Yesterday was such a very Big Win, and all under the pressure of a Nasty and Hostile Media!

2:44 pm: We are pleased to announce that Matthew G. Whitaker, Chief of Staff to Attorney General Jeff Sessions at the Department of Justice, will become our new Acting Attorney General of the United States. He will serve our Country well...

...We thank Attorney General Jeff Sessions for his service, and wish him well! A permanent replacement will be nominated at a later date.

November 9, 2018

10:52 pm: Matthew G. Whitaker is a highly respected former U.S. Attorney from Iowa. He was chosen by Jeff Sessions to be his Chief of Staff. I did not know Mr. Whitaker. Likewise, as Chief, I did not know Mr. Whitaker except primarily as he traveled with A.G. Sessions. No social contact.

November 10, 2018

3:08 am: There is no reason for these massive, deadly and costly forest fires in California except that forest management is so poor. Billions of dollars are given each year, with so many lives lost, all because of gross mismanagement of the forests. Remedy now, or no more Fed payments!

2:06 pm: Had very productive meetings and calls for our Country today. Meeting tonight with World Leaders!

November 12, 2018

8:19 pm: I just approved an expedited request for a Major Disaster Declaration for the State of California. Wanted to respond quickly in order to alleviate some of the incredible suffering going on. I am with you all the way. God Bless all of the victims and families affected.

November 14, 2018

2:58 pm: Just spoke to Governor Jerry Brown to let him know that we are with him, and the people of California, all the way!

5:10 pm: I am grateful to be here today w/ Members of the House & Senate who have poured their time, heart and energy into the crucial issue of Prison Reform. Working together w/ my Admin over the last two years, these members have reached a bipartisan agreement...

6:26 pm: Our pledge to hire American includes those leaving prison and looking for a very fresh start—new job, and new life. The legislation I am supporting today contains many sig-

nificant reforms. Read more here: https://t.co/BwQ3qd9Fyk
https://t.co/6DUY9KNTpR

November 17, 2018

11:42 am: ... The New York Times did a phony story, as usual, about
my relationship with @VP Mike Pence. They made up sources and
refused to ask me, the only one that would know, for a quote...

I can't imagine any President having a better or closer relationship
with their Vice President then the two of us. Just more FAKE NEWS,
the Enemy of the People!

November 29, 2018

11:34 am: Based on the fact that the ships and sailors have not been
returned to Ukraine from Russia, I have decided it would be best for
all parties concerned to cancel my previously scheduled meeting...

...in Argentina with President Vladimir Putin. I look forward to a
meaningful Summit again as soon as this situation is resolved!

December 6, 2018

10:17 am: Without the phony Russia Witch Hunt, and with all that
we have accomplished in the last almost two years (Tax & Regulation
Cuts, Judge's, Military, Vets, etc.) my approval rating would be at 75%
rather than the 50% just reported by Rasmussen. It's called Presidential Harassment!

December 7, 2018

8:39 am: It has been incorrectly reported that Rudy Giuliani and others will not be doing a counter to the Mueller Report. That is Fake
News. Already 87 pages done, but obviously cannot complete until we
see the final Witch Hunt Report.

11:16 am: I am pleased to announce that Heather Nauert, Spokeswoman
for the United States Department of State, will be nominated to serve

as United Nations Ambassador. I want to congratulate Heather, and thank Ambassador Nikki Haley for her great service to our Country!

11:18 am: I am pleased to announce that I will be nominating The Honorable William P. Barr for the position of Attorney General of the United States. As the former AG for George H.W. Bush...

...and one of the most highly respected lawyers and legal minds in the Country, he will be a great addition to our team. I look forward to having him join our very successful Administration!

3:02 pm: Mike Pompeo is doing a great job, I am very proud of him. His predecessor, Rex Tillerson, didn't have the mental capacity needed. He was dumb as a rock and I couldn't get rid of him fast enough. He was lazy as hell. Now it is a whole new ballgame, great spirit at State!

December 8, 2018

9:19 am: I am pleased to announce my nomination of four-star General Mark Milley, Chief of Staff of the United States Army—as the Chairman of the Joint Chiefs of Staff, replacing General Joe Dunford, who will be retiring...

I am thankful to both of these incredible men for their service to our Country! Date of transition to be determined.

December 9, 2018

5:43 pm: The Trump Administration has accomplished more than any other U.S. Administration in its first two (not even) years of existence, & we are having a great time doing it! All of this despite the Fake News Media, which has gone totally out of its mind-truly the Enemy of the People!

December 14, 2018

5:18 pm: I am pleased to announce that Mick Mulvaney, Director of the Office of Management & Budget, will be named Acting White House Chief of Staff, replacing General John Kelly, who has served our Country with distinction. Mick has done an outstanding job while in the Administration…

…I look forward to working with him in this new capacity as we continue to MAKE AMERICA GREAT AGAIN! John will be staying until the end of the year. He is a GREAT PATRIOT and I want to personally thank him for his service!

7:31 pm: For the record, there were MANY people who wanted to be the White House Chief of Staff. Mick M will do a GREAT job!

December 15, 2018

9:14 am: Secretary of the Interior @RyanZinke will be leaving the Administration at the end of the year after having served for a period of almost two years. Ryan has accomplished much during his tenure and I want to thank him for his service to our Nation…

December 18, 2018

6:41 am: Good luck today in court to General Michael Flynn. Will be interesting to see what he has to say, despite tremendous pressure being put on him, about Russian Collusion in our great and, obviously, highly successful political campaign. There was no Collusion!

9:07 pm: America is the greatest Country in the world and my job is to fight for ALL citizens, even those who have made mistakes. Congratulations to the Senate on the bi-partisan passing of a historic Criminal Justice Reform Bill…

December 21, 2018

9:41 am: There has never been a president who has been tougher (but fair) on China or Russia—Never, just look at the facts. The Fake News tries so hard to paint the opposite picture.

December 22, 2018

3:28 pm: I will not be going to Florida because of the Shutdown—Staying in the White House! #MAGA

December 23, 2018

11:46 am: I am pleased to announce that our very talented Deputy Secretary of Defense, Patrick Shanahan, will assume the title of Acting Secretary of Defense starting January 1, 2019. Patrick has a long list of accomplishments while serving as Deputy, & previously Boeing. He will be great!

11:59 am: I just had a long and productive call with President @RT_Erdogan of Turkey. We discussed ISIS, our mutual involvement in Syria, & the slow & highly coordinated pullout of U.S. troops from the area. After many years they are coming home. We also discussed heavily expanded Trade.

December 24, 2018

9:41 am: To those few Senators who think I don't like or appreciate being allied with other countries, they are wrong, I DO. What I don't like, however, is when many of these same countries take advantage of their friendship with the United States, both in Military Protection and Trade.

11:55 am: I never "lashed out" at the Acting Attorney General of the U.S., a man for whom I have great respect. This is a made up story, one of many, by the Fake News Media!

December 30, 2018

11:56 am: Great work by my Administration over the holidays to save Coast Guard pay during this #SchumerShutdown. No thanks to the Democrats who left town and are not concerned about the safety and security of Americans!

December 31, 2018

9:38 am: Great work by my Administration over the holidays to save Coast Guard pay during this #SchumerShutdown. No thanks to the Democrats who left town and are not concerned about the safety and security of Americans!

Own Presidency/Administration—2019 News Quotes

Response to a question from Maggie Haberman of *The New York Times*, January 31, 2019.
Source: https://www.nytimes.com/2019/02/01/us/politics/trump-interview-transcripts.html

"Past presidents, yeah. I think for the most part, yeah, past presidents. I really believe, when I say that we've accomplished—When you look at that list, whether it's the biggest regulation cuts in history, that's one of the reasons the economy is doing well. Before the taxes, actually. But the tax cuts, but so many other things when you look at that and you go down the list: Veterans Choice, VA Choice. They've been trying—As long as you've been writing, they've been trying to get VA Choice. And now I'm going to do Phase 2 on VA Choice, which is, you know, the next step. But the first step was just a massive step. Nobody thought it could be done."

Response to a question from Maggie Haberman of *The New York Times*, January 31, 2019.
Source: https://www.nytimes.com/2019/02/01/us/politics/trump-interview-transcripts.html

"I think what we'll be focusing on will be national security, very much. So we've very largely—We're in the process of rebuilding the military. Which was truly depleted."

Response to a question from Maggie Haberman of *The New York Times*, January 31, 2019.
Source: https://www.nytimes.com/2019/02/01/us/politics/trump-interview-transcripts.html

"You know, we've had polls as high as 93%. Which is the highest there is. Reagan was 86."

302

Response to a question from Maggie Haberman of *The New York Times*, January 31, 2019.

Source: https://www.nytimes.com/2019/02/01/us/politics/trump-interview-transcripts.html

"Now I do tell the story about driving down Pennsylvania Avenue, you know. Because I'd been in Washington probably 17 times in my life. And on the 18th time, I was President of the United States. And you know, Washington wasn't really my place. And I didn't know people. I didn't know a lot of people. And I got—I put some people in that I wasn't happy with and I put some people in that I was very happy with.

"But we've gotten it very—You know, as I've—Now I know a lot of people."

Response to a question from Maggie Haberman of *The New York Times*, January 31, 2019.

Source: https://www.nytimes.com/2019/02/01/us/politics/trump-interview-transcripts.html

"So I wasn't happy with [former U.S. Secretary of Defense General James] Mattis. I told Mattis to give me a letter. He didn't just give me that letter. I told him. And you could have seen that on *60 Minutes*. I did *60 Minutes* and Lesley Stahl asked me a question: 'What do you think of General Mattis?'"

Response to a question from Maggie Haberman of *The New York Times*, January 31, 2019.

Source: https://www.nytimes.com/2019/02/01/us/politics/trump-interview-transcripts.html

"And I said, 'Let me be generous.' But I just—I didn't like the job he [former U.S. Secretary of Defense General James Mattis] was doing. I wasn't happy with it. I wasn't happy with the—I got him more money than the military has ever seen before. And I wasn't happy with the job that he was doing at all. And I said it's time.

"That's why in the letter he wrote, 'You have to have your own choice.' The reason he said that was because I said, 'You're just not my choice.'"

Response to a question from Maggie Haberman of *The New York Times*, January 31, 2019.
Source: https://www.nytimes.com/2019/02/01/us/politics/trump-interview-transcripts.html

"Well, I'm not saying I'm doing anything in terms of the military option in Venezuela. But I can say very pointedly we're not taking that off the table."

Response to a question from Maggie Haberman of *The New York Times*, January 31, 2019.
Source: https://www.nytimes.com/2019/02/01/us/politics/trump-interview-transcripts.html

"We're involved in wars that are 6,000 miles away. We're involved in wars where it's just absolutely insane what we're doing, and the money we're spending, where in Afghanistan, we're spending $50 billion. That's more than most countries spend for everything."

Response to a question from Maggie Haberman of *The New York Times*, January 31, 2019.
Source: https://www.nytimes.com/2019/02/01/us/politics/trump-interview-transcripts.html

"There are terrible things happening in Venezuela."

Response to a question from Peter Baker of *The New York Times*, January 31, 2019.
Source: https://www.nytimes.com/2019/02/01/us/politics/trump-interview-transcripts.html

"I have access to things, Peter [Baker of *The New York Times*], that are absolutely terrible, what's going on in Venezuela."

Response to a question from Peter Baker of *The New York Times*, January 31, 2019.
Source: https://www.nytimes.com/2019/02/01/us/politics/trump-interview-transcripts.html

"I'm just saying this: Terrible things are going on. Terrible things are going on in Venezuela. And I look at that, and I see what's happening. Now in Saudi Arabia, a lot of improvement has been made in Saudi Arabia. But you look at Iran, and they kill many, many people in Iran. You have the access and we have the access also. And Saudi Arabia also has a lot to do with economic development. They're a country that pays us a tremendous amount of money, creates a tremendous amount of jobs. And Saudi Arabia, I'm not making excuses for anybody. I think that was a terrible event. It was a terrible tragedy. It was a terrible crime."

Response to a question from Maggie Haberman of *The New York Times*, January 31, 2019.
Source: https://www.nytimes.com/2019/02/01/us/politics/trump-interview-transcripts.html

"You look at Iran, not so far away from Saudi Arabia, and take a look at what they're doing there. So you know, that's just the way I feel. Venezuela is very much in flux. We've been hearing about it for probably 14 years now, between the two of them. And some terrible things are happening in Venezuela. So if I can do something to help people. It's really helping humanity, if we can do something to help people, I'd like to do that."

Response to a question from Maggie Haberman of *The New York Times*, January 31, 2019.
Source: https://www.nytimes.com/2019/02/01/us/politics/trump-interview-transcripts.html

"You see what's happening. There's been turmoil between the Justice Department, the FBI. You look at all of the statements made. You look at all of the firings, not firings by me, by the way. But you look at all of the people that have left and been fired and terminated and all of the terrible statements being made. And it is a terrible thing that's gone on there."

Response to a question from Maggie Haberman of *The New York Times*, January 31, 2019.
Source: https://www.nytimes.com/2019/02/01/us/politics/trump-interview-transcripts.html

"You have a lot of people that are in from other administrations that frankly you keep because you're not allowed to do anything but keep them, OK? And so they'll do reports. And by the way, you're going to have people that are from my administration in years from now that would be very critical of perhaps another President where they disagree with something.

"But as you know, you have many, many people in this administration and every other administration that wasn't put there by me, and they have to stay there. It's a job for life."

Response to a question from Margaret Brennan of CBS News, February 3, 2019.
Source: https://www.cbsnews.com/news/transcript-president-trump-on-face-the-nation-february-3-2019/

"So we have a great cabinet. I have great people. I think now we have a really great cabinet. I think Bill Barr will be a fantastic attorney general, and I think that we have—Mike Pompeo's been doing a fantastic job. We have—[Brennan interrupts.]"

Response to a question from Margaret Brennan of CBS News, February 3, 2019.
Source: https://www.cbsnews.com/news/transcript-president-trump-on-face-the-nation-february-3-2019/

"Well, look the Russia thing is a hoax. I have been tougher on Russia than any President, maybe ever. But than any President."

From State of the Union address, February 5, 2019.
Source: https://www.whitehouse.gov/briefings-statements/president-donald-j-trumps-state-union-address-2/

"We meet tonight at a moment of unlimited potential. As we begin a new Congress, I stand here ready to work with you to achieve historic breakthroughs for all Americans.

"Millions of our fellow citizens are watching us now, gathered in this great chamber, hoping that we will govern not as two parties but as one nation.

"The agenda I will lay out this evening is not a Republican agenda or a Democrat agenda. It is the agenda of the American people.

"Many of us campaigned on the same core promises: to defend American jobs and demand fair trade for American workers; to rebuild and revitalize our Nation's infrastructure; to reduce the price of healthcare and prescription drugs; to create an immigration system that is safe, lawful, modern and secure; and to pursue a foreign policy that puts America's interests first.

"There is a new opportunity in American politics, if only we have the courage to seize it. Victory is not winning for our party. Victory is winning for our country.

From State of the Union address, February 5, 2019.
Source: https://www.whitehouse.gov/briefings-statements/
president-donald-j-trumps-state-union-address-2/

"In the 20th century, America saved freedom, transformed science, and redefined the middle class standard of living for the entire world to see. Now, we must step boldly and bravely into the next chapter of this great American adventure, and we must create a new standard of living for the 21st century. An amazing quality of life for all of our citizens is within our reach.

"We can make our communities safer, our families stronger, our culture richer, our faith deeper, and our middle class bigger and more prosperous than ever before.

"But we must reject the politics of revenge, resistance, and retribution, and embrace the boundless potential of cooperation, compromise, and the common good.

"Together, we can break decades of political stalemate. We can bridge old divisions, heal old wounds, build new coalitions, forge new solutions, and unlock the extraordinary promise of America's future. The decision is ours to make.

"We must choose between greatness or gridlock, results or resistance, vision or vengeance, incredible progress or pointless destruction.

"Tonight, I ask you to choose greatness.

"Over the last two years, my administration has moved with urgency and historic speed to confront problems neglected by leaders of both parties over many decades."

Response to an unidentified reporter's question before Marine One departure, March 20, 2019.

Source: https://www.whitehouse.gov/briefings-statements/
remarks-president-trump-marine-one-departure-34/

"I'm going to Ohio right now. They were going to close the plant; it's where they make the tanks. It was going to be closed, and I stopped them from closing it. And now it's thriving and doing great. And the people of Ohio, they like Trump because I've done a great job in Ohio. And I've done a great job all over the country. That's what the people want to hear."

Remarks during a visit to the Lima Army Tank Plant in Ohio, March 20, 2019.

Source: https://www.c-span.org/video/?458966-1/
president-trump-delivers-remarks-lima-army-tank-plant-ohio

"We took over a mess. We took over a mess with North Korea. We took over a mess in the Middle East. We took over. A lot of bad things were happening and the economy was not doing well. It was heading in the wrong direction. You remember that. It was going to go bad, and then we opened up with the regulation cuts and all of the other things we've done, including the big tax cut. But it made a big difference. Made a big difference. And we'll show you some numbers in a little while."

Response to a question from Catherine Herridge of FOX News, May 2, 2019.

Source: https://www.foxnews.com/politics/transcript-fox-news-interview-with-president-trump

"But again, nobody has been tougher on Russia than Donald Trump."

Response to a question from Catherine Herridge of FOX News, May 2, 2019.

Source: https://www.foxnews.com/politics/transcript-fox-news-interview-with-president-trump

"I would say it's done. We both knew this. Nobody has ever done what I've done. I've given total transparency. It's never happened before like this."

Response to a POLITICO reporter's[23] question, May 10, 2019.
Source: https://www.politico.com/story/2019/05/10/trump-interview-transcript-1317598

"So I must say, you know you mentioned the word [impeachment], I haven't heard that word in a while. Because since the report came out, it said no collusion, no obstruction, no conspiracy. And that was the end. I haven't heard the word mentioned, really, essentially, since the Mueller report came out. And it's not like it's not like they were friends of mine."

Response to an unidentified reporter's question at the signing of H.R. 3401, July 1, 2019.
Source: https://www.whitehouse.gov/briefings-statements/
remarks-president-trump-signing-h-r-3401/

"We're going to have a great Fourth of July in Washington, D.C. It'll be like no other. It'll be special. And I hope a lot of people come, and it's going to be about this country and it's a salute to America.

"And I'm going to be here, and I'm going to say a few words. And we're going to have planes going overhead: the best fighter jets in the world and other planes too. And we're going to have some tanks stationed outside.

"You've got to be pretty careful with the tanks because the roads have a tendency not to like to carry heavy tanks, so we have to put them in certain areas. But we have the brand new Sherman tanks and we have the brand new Abram tanks. And we have some incredible equipment, military equipment on display—Brand new. And we're very proud of it.

"You know, we're making a lot of new tanks right now. We're building a lot of new tanks in Lima, Ohio; our great tank factory that people wanted to close down until I got elected. And I stopped it from being closed down, and now it's a very productive facility. And they do—Nobody—It's the greatest tank in the world, the Abrams."

---

23   POLITICO reporters Andrew Restuccia, Eliana Johnson, and Daniel Lippman conducted the telephone interview with President Trump, but the transcript does not indicate which reporter asked which question.

Response to an unidentified reporter's question at the signing of H.R. 3401, July 1, 2019.

Source: https://www.whitehouse.gov/briefings-statements/
remarks-president-trump-signing-h-r-3401/

"I think so. I think so. I think I've reached most Americans. Most Americans want no crime. Most Americans want a strong military. They want good education. They want good healthcare. If you look at pre-existing conditions, the Republicans are going to save pre-existing conditions. The Democrats won't be able to do it. What the Democrats' plan is going to destroy the country and it's going to be horrible healthcare. Horrible healthcare.

"And everybody's taxes are going to go to 95%. And, by the way, that's not enough. But the taxes—If they ever did what they want to do, your taxes go to 95% and that isn't nearly enough."

Remarks at the signing of an executive order protecting and improving Medicare for senior citizens, Ocala, Florida, October 3, 2019.

Source: https://www.whitehouse.gov/briefings-statements/remarks-president-trump-signing-executive-order-protecting-improving-medicare-nations-seniors-ocala-fl/

"And nobody has done more in two and a half years, their first two and a half years, than what we've done. Whether it's Right to Try, whether it's tax cuts—No matter what it is, nobody has done we've done. Not even close."

Remarks at the signing of an executive order protecting and improving Medicare for senior citizens, Ocala, Florida, October 3, 2019.

Source: https://www.whitehouse.gov/briefings-statements/remarks-president-trump-signing-executive-order-protecting-improving-medicare-nations-seniors-ocala-fl/

"A nation must put its own citizens first. My administration is standing up for American seniors. And we'll always protect the Medicare benefits you earned and paid for."

Remarks at Turning Point USA Student Action Summit in West Palm Beach, Florida, December 22, 2019.

Source: https://www.whitehouse.gov/briefings-statements/
remarks-president-trump-turning-point-usa-student-action-summit-west-palm-beach-fl/

"So I'm a loyalist. I don't take things and just throw it to the side. But the truth is, our country is doing better than ever before. We're so respected again. Leaders come in from other countries—prime ministers, presidents, kings, queens, dictators, in some cases—They just don't know they're dictators or our people don't either, but they come in and they say, 'Congratulations. What you've done is amazing.' They're talking about all of us. And you know what? It is."

Remarks at Turning Point USA Student Action Summit in West Palm Beach, Florida, December 22, 2019.

Source: https://www.whitehouse.gov/briefings-statements/
remarks-president-trump-turning-point-usa-student-action-summit-west-palm-beach-fl/

"You know, it's a funny thing: They never talk about my speaking ability, and yet I've never had an empty seat. I'm trying to figure it out. It's true. [Audience applauds.] No, it's true. I don't know how you figure that out. We've never had—From the time we came down."

Remarks at Turning Point USA Student Action Summit in West Palm Beach, Florida, December 22, 2019.

Source: https://www.whitehouse.gov/briefings-statements/
remarks-president-trump-turning-point-usa-student-action-summit-west-palm-beach-fl/

"But despite crooked leadership at the top of the FBI—They were crooked. There were dirty cops at the top. FBI: great people. But at the top of the FBI, you had dirty cops. Deep state sabotage. Eighteen angry Democrat prosecutors. These were all put in there to destroy us. Think of what we did. You heard Rush [Limbaugh]. Think of what we did. Think of what we've—Where we've come, how vicious it was. They had 13 angry Democrats that were smart, vicious, evil—And it built up to 18. They had 49 FBI agents, thousands of subpoenas, hundreds of people, and they found nothing. There's nobody in this room that could have gone through that and found nothing. I really mean that, too. It's incredible. They found nothing. How clean am I? No, think of that.

"But endless congressional investigations—But think of it. Hundreds of people, interviewing everybody that I—And they found nothing. The Mueller report came out; it was a total dud. After two and a half years, they have a baseless impeachment, millions of pages of fake-news propaganda, because the news was totally on their side. It's a Democrat—It's part of the Democrat Party. It's a wing; the media is a wing of the Democrat Party.

"And all of the Washington powers—They were all arrayed against us. They're losing. We're winning. And we're succeeding in our mission to make America great again."

Remarks at Turning Point USA Student Action Summit in West Palm Beach, Florida, December 22, 2019.

Source: https://www.whitehouse.gov/briefings-statements/
remarks-president-trump-turning-point-usa-student-action-summit-west-palm-beach-fl/

"They didn't want to let you say 'Merry Christmas.' You would go around, you'd see department stores that have everything—Red, snow, beautiful ribbons, bows. Everything was there, but they wouldn't say 'Merry Christmas.' They're all saying 'Merry Christmas' again. You remember?

"I went through that, during the campaign: 'They going to say Merry Christmas again.' And they are. That's the least of it, too, because we got a lot of things that they're doing that they weren't doing. And we got to keep the country—We got to keep what we're doing."

Own Presidency/Administration—2019 Tweets

January 1, 2019

8:08 am: HAPPY NEW YEAR TO EVERYONE, INCLUDING THE HATERS AND THE FAKE NEWS MEDIA! 2019 WILL BE A FANTASTIC YEAR FOR THOSE NOT SUFFERING FROM TRUMP DERANGEMENT SYNDROME. JUST CALM DOWN AND ENJOY THE RIDE, GREAT THINGS ARE HAPPENING FOR OUR COUNTRY!

5:51 pm: Washington Examiner—"MAGA list: 205 'historic results' help Trump make case for 2020 re-election." True!

January 4, 2019
8:16 am: How do you impeach a president who has won perhaps the greatest election of all time, done nothing wrong (no Collusion with Russia, it was the Dems that Colluded), had the most successful first two years of any president, and is the most popular Republican in party history 93%?

January 9, 2019

10:25 am: Billions of dollars are sent to the State of California for Forest fires that, with proper Forest Management, would never happen. Unless they get their act together, which is unlikely, I have ordered FEMA to send no more money. It is a disgraceful situation in lives & money!

January 12, 2019

8:09 am: I have been FAR tougher on Russia than Obama, Bush or Clinton. Maybe tougher than any other President. At the same time, & as I have often said, getting along with Russia is a good thing, not a bad thing. I fully expect that someday we will have good relations with Russia again!

10:57 am to 11:07 am: I just watched a Fake reporter from the Amazon Washington Post say the White House is "chaotic, there does not seem to be a strategy for this Shutdown. There is no plan." The Fakes always like talking Chaos, there is NONE. In fact, there's almost nobody in the W.H. but me, and…

…I do have a plan on the Shutdown. But to understand that plan you would have to understand the fact that I won the election, and I promised safety and security for the American people. Part of that promise was a Wall at the Southern Border. Elections have consequences!

January 13, 2019

5:01 pm: Wish I could share with everyone the beauty and majesty of being in the White House and looking outside at the snow filled lawns and Rose Garden. Really is something—SPECIAL COUNTRY, SPECIAL PLACE!

January 14, 2019

7:32 am: Getting ready to address the Farm Convention today in Nashville, Tennessee. Love our farmers, love Tennessee—a great combination! See you in a little while.

January 23, 2019

1:47 pm: The citizens of Venezuela have suffered for too long at the hands of the illegitimate Maduro regime. Today, I have officially recognized the President of the Venezuelan National Assembly, Juan Guaido, as the Interim President of Venezuela.

January 26, 2019

8:51 pm: WITCH HUNT!

January 27, 2019

8:09 pm: After all that I have done for the Military, our great Veterans, Judges (99), Justices (2), Tax & Regulation Cuts, the Economy,

Energy, Trade & MUCH MORE, does anybody really think I won't build the WALL? Done more in first two years than any President! MAKE AMERICA GREAT AGAIN!

January 30, 2019

4:58 pm: Spoke today with Venezuelan Interim President Juan Guaido to congratulate him on his historic assumption of the presidency and reinforced strong United States support for Venezuela's fight to regain its democracy...

February 4, 2019

3:13 pm: I am pleased to announce that David Bernhardt, Acting Secretary of the Interior, will be nominated as Secretary of the Interior. David has done a fantastic job from the day he arrived, and we look forward to having his nomination officially confirmed!

February 10, 2019

1:27 pm to 1:39 pm: The media was able to get my work schedule, something very easy to do, but it should have been reported as a positive, not negative. When the term Executive Time is used, I am generally working, not relaxing. In fact, I probably work more hours than almost any past President...

...The fact is, when I took over as President, our Country was a mess. Depleted Military, Endless Wars, a potential War with North Korea, V.A., High Taxes & too many Regulations, Border, Immigration & HealthCare problems, & much more. I had no choice but to work very long hours!

February 11, 2019

7:43 am: No president ever worked harder than me (cleaning up the mess I inherited)!

February 17, 2019

7:41 am: 52% Approval Rating, 93% in Republican Party (a record)! Pretty amazing considering that 93% (also) of my press is REALLY BAD. The "people" are SMART!

March 1, 2019

8:00 am: Wow, just revealed that Michael Cohen wrote a "love letter to Trump" manuscript for a new book that he was pushing. Written and submitted long after Charlottesville and Helsinki, his phony reasons for going rogue. Book is exact opposite of his fake testimony, which now is a lie!

8:19 am to 8:26 am: Oh' I see! Now that the 2 year Russian Collusion case has fallen apart, there was no Collusion except bye Crooked Hillary and the Democrats, they say, "gee, I have an idea, let's look at Trump's finances and every deal he has ever done. Let's follow discredited Michael Cohen...

...and the fraudulent and dishonest statements he made on Wednesday. No way, it's time to stop this corrupt and illegally brought Witch Hunt. Time to start looking at the other side where real crimes were committed. Republicans have been abused long enough. Must end now!

March 5, 2019

9:12 am: PRESIDENTIAL HARASSMENT!

Republican Approval Rating just hit 93%. Sorry Haters! MAKE AMERICA GREAT AGAIN!

March 8, 2019

11:04 am: Bad lawyer and fraudster Michael Cohen said under sworn testimony that he never asked for a Pardon. His lawyers totally contradicted him. He lied! Additionally, he directly asked me for a pardon. I said NO. He lied again! He also badly wanted to work at the White House. He lied!

March 9, 2019

11:19 am: Will soon be 145 Judges!

March 13, 2019

5:50 am: I greatly appreciate Nancy Pelosi's statement against impeachment, but everyone must remember the minor fact that I never did anything wrong, the Economy and Unemployment are the best ever, Military and Vets are great-and many other successes! How do you impeach...

...a man who is considered by many to be the President with the most successful first two years in history, especially when he has done nothing wrong and impeachment is for "high crimes and misdemeanors"?

6:17 am: MAKE AMERICA GREAT AGAIN!

KEEP AMERICA GREAT!

5:52 pm: I agree with Rand Paul. This is a total disgrace and should NEVER happen to another President!

March 14, 2019

6:22 am: My Administration looks forward to negotiating a large scale Trade Deal with the United Kingdom. The potential is unlimited!

March 18, 2019

5:29 pm: While the press doesn't like writing about it, nor do I need them to, I donate my yearly Presidential salary of $400,000.00 to different agencies throughout the year, this to Homeland Security. If I didn't do it there would be hell to pay from the FAKE NEWS MEDIA!

April 2, 2019

6:33 am: Puerto Rico got 91 Billion Dollars for the hurricane, more money than has ever been gotten for a hurricane before, & all their local politicians do is complain & ask for more money. The pols are

317

grossly incompetent, spend the money foolishly or corruptly, & only take from USA...

April 16, 2019

4:57 pm: The forgotten voters of the 2016 Election are now doing great. The Steel Industry is rebuilding and expanding at a pace that it hasn't seen in decades. Our Country has one of the best Economies in many years, perhaps ever. Unemployment numbers best in 51 years. Wow!

5:39 pm: Just signed a critical bill to formalize drought contingency plans for the Colorado River. Thanks to @SenMcSallyAZ for getting it done. Big deal for Arizona!

April 19, 2019

6:53 am to 3:47 pm: Statements are made about me by certain people in the Crazy Mueller Report, in itself written by 18 Angry Democrat Trump Haters, which are fabricated & totally untrue. Watch out for people that take so-called "notes," when the notes never existed until needed. Because I never...

...agreed to testify, it was not necessary for me to respond to statements made in the "Report" about me, some of which are total bullshit & only given to make the other person look good (or me to look bad). This was an Illegally Started Hoax that never should have happened, a...

...big, fat, waste of time, energy and money—$30,000,000 to be exact. It is now finally time to turn the tables and bring justice to some very sick and dangerous people who have committed very serious crimes, perhaps even Spying or Treason. This should never happen again!

April 21, 2019

6:04 am: Happy Easter! I have never been happier or more content because your Country is doing so well, with an Economy that is the talk of the World and may be stronger than it has ever been before. Have a great day!

April 22, 2019

8:47 am: Only high crimes and misdemeanors can lead to impeachment. There were no crimes by me (No Collusion, No Obstruction), so you can't impeach. It was the Democrats that committed the crimes, not your Republican President! Tables are finally turning on the Witch Hunt!

1:05 pm: My friend Herman Cain, a truly wonderful man, has asked me not to nominate him for a seat on the Federal Reserve Board. I will respect his wishes. Herman is a great American who truly loves our Country!

April 23, 2019

5:27 am: In the "old days" if you were President and you had a good economy, you were basically immune from criticism. Remember, "It's the economy stupid." Today I have, as President, perhaps the greatest economy in history...and to the Mainstream Media, it means NOTHING. But it will!

April 30, 2019

1:23 pm: I am monitoring the situation in Venezuela very closely. The United States stands with the People of Venezuela and their Freedom!

4:09 pm: If Cuban Troops and Militia do not immediately CEASE military and other operations for the purpose of causing death and destruction to the Constitution of Venezuela, a full and complete...

...embargo, together with highest-level sanctions, will be placed on the island of Cuba. Hopefully, all Cuban soldiers will promptly and peacefully return to their island!

May 3, 2019

12:06 pm: Had a long and very good conversation with President Putin of Russia. As I have always said, long before the Witch Hunt started, getting along with Russia, China, and everyone is a good thing, not a bad thing...

...We discussed Trade, Venezuela, Ukraine, North Korea, Nuclear Arms Control and even the "Russian Hoax." Very productive talk!

May 4, 2019

8:49 am: Very good call yesterday with President Putin of Russia. Tremendous potential for a good/great relationship with Russia, despite what you read and see in the Fake News Media. Look how they have misled you on "Russia Collusion." The World can be a better and safer place. Nice!

May 13, 2019

4:34 pm: Under my Administration, we are restoring @NASA to greatness and we are going back to the Moon, then Mars. I am updating my budget to include an additional $1.6 billion so that we can return to Space in a BIG WAY!

4:38 pm: We must protect our Great Lakes, keeping them clean and beautiful for future generations. That's why I am fighting for $300 million in my updated budget for the Great Lakes Restoration Initiative.

4:41 pm: Today, I officially updated my budget to include $18 million for our GREAT @SpecialOlympics, whose athletes inspire us and make our Nation so PROUD!

May 15, 2019

7:53 am: Thank you Joe and remember, the BRAIN is much sharper also!

May 22, 2019

5:03 am: PRESIDENTIAL HARASSMENT!

6:00 am: Without the ILLEGAL Witch Hunt, my poll numbers, especially because of our historically "great" economy, would be at 65%. Too bad! The greatest Hoax in American History.

May 23, 2019

7:11 pm: The U.S. Senate has just approved a 19 Billion Dollar Disaster Relief Bill, with my total approval. Great!

7:19 pm: "Today, at the request and recommendation of the Attorney General of the United States, President Donald J. Trump directed the intelligence community to quickly and fully cooperate with the Attorney General's investigation into surveillance activities...

...during the 2016 Presidential election. The Attorney General has been delegated full and complete authority to declassify information pertaining to this investigation in accordance with the long-established standards for handling classified information...

...Today's action will help ensure that all Americans learn the truth about the events that occurred, and the actions that were taken, during the last Presidential election and will restore confidence in our public institutions." @PressSec

May 24, 2019

1:00 pm: Just spoke to Prime Minister @NarendraModi where I congratulated him on his big political victory. He is a great man and leader for the people of India—they are lucky to have him!

May 29, 2019

7:32 pm: How do you impeach a Republican President for a crime that was committed by the Democrats? WITCH-HUNT!

7:49 pm: I was not informed about anything having to do with the Navy Ship USS John S. McCain during my visit to Japan. Nevertheless, @FLOTUS and I loved being with our great Military Men and Women-what a spectacular job they do!

May 30, 2019

6:21 am: The Greatest Presidential Harassment in history. After spending $40,000,000 over two dark years, with unlimited access, people, resources and cooperation, highly conflicted Robert Mueller would have brought charges, if he had ANYTHING, but there were no charges to bring!

6:57 am: Russia, Russia, Russia! That's all you heard at the beginning of this Witch Hunt Hoax...And now Russia has disappeared because I had nothing to do with Russia helping me to get elected. It was a crime that didn't exist. So now the Dems and their partner, the Fake News Media,...

...say he fought back against this phony crime that didn't exist, this horrendous false accusation, and he shouldn't fight back, he should just sit back and take it. Could this be Obstruction? No, Mueller didn't find Obstruction either. Presidential Harassment!

5:23 pm: The Navy put out a disclaimer on the McCain story. Looks like the story was an exaggeration, or even Fake News—but why not, everything else is!

May 31, 2019

2:12 pm: As we celebrate LGBT Pride Month and recognize the outstanding contributions LGBT people have made to our great Nation, let us also stand in solidarity with the many LGBT people who live in dozens of countries worldwide that punish, imprison, or even execute individuals...

...on the basis of their sexual orientation. My Administration has launched a global campaign to decriminalize homosexuality and invite all nations to join us in this effort!

3:35 pm: I will be announcing my Second Term Presidential Run with First Lady Melania, Vice President Mike Pence, and Second Lady Karen Pence on June 18th in Orlando, Florida, at the 20,000 seat Amway Center. Join us for this Historic Rally!
Tickets: https://t.co/1krDP2oQvG

June 2, 2019

8:41 pm: Kevin Hassett, who has done such a great job for me and the Administration, will be leaving shortly. His very talented replacement will be named as soon as I get back to the U.S. I want to thank Kevin for all he has done—he is a true friend!

June 5, 2019

1:01 am: I kept hearing that there would be "massive" rallies against me in the UK, but it was quite the opposite. The big crowds, which the Corrupt Media hates to show, were those that gathered in support of the USA and me. They were big & enthusiastic as opposed to the organized flops!

June 8, 2019

11:08 pm: I know it is not at all "Presidential" to hit back at the Corrupt Media, or people who work for the Corrupt Media, when they make false statements about me or the Trump Administration. Problem is, if you don't hit back, people believe the Fake News is true. So we'll hit back!

June 10, 2019

6:01 pm: Despite the Phony Witch Hunt, we will continue to MAKE AMERICA GREAT AGAIN! Thank you!!

June 13, 2019

8:23 am: I meet and talk to "foreign governments" every day. I just met with the Queen of England (U.K.), the Prince of Wales, the P.M. of the United Kingdom, the P.M. of Ireland, the President of France and the President of Poland. We talked about "Everything!" Should I immediately...

...call the FBI about these calls and meetings? How ridiculous! I would never be trusted again. With that being said, my full answer is rarely played by the Fake News Media. They purposely leave out the part that matters.

June 13, 2019

3:10 pm: After 3 1/2 years, our wonderful Sarah Huckabee Sanders will be leaving the White House at the end of the month and going home to the Great State of Arkansas…

…She is a very special person with extraordinary talents, who has done an incredible job! I hope she decides to run for Governor of Arkansas—she would be fantastic. Sarah, thank you for a job well done!

4:03 pm: Today we announced vital new actions that we are taking to help former inmates find a job, live a crime-free life, and succeed beyond their dreams…

June 15, 2019

7:05 am: Despite the Greatest Presidential Harassment of all time by people that are very dishonest and want to destroy our Country, we are doing great in the Polls, even better than in 2016, and will be packed at the Tuesday Announcement Rally in Orlando, Florida. KEEP AMERICA GREAT!

June 22, 2019

11:55 am: I am at Camp David working on many things, including Iran! We have a great Economy, Tariffs have been very helpful both with respect to the huge Dollars coming IN, & on helping to make good Trade Deals. The Dow heading to BEST June in 80 years! Stock Market BEST June in 50 years!

June 26, 2019

6:46 pm: Ever since the passage of the Super Predator Crime Bill, pushed hard by @JoeBiden, together with Bill and Crooked Hillary Clinton, which inflicted great pain on many, but especially the African American Community, Democrats have tried and failed to pass Criminal Justice Reform…

…They came to me asking for help, and I got Criminal Justice Reform passed, with help from both Republicans and Democrats.

Many said that nobody but President Trump could have done this. All previous administrations failed. Please ask why THEY failed to the candidates!

June 28, 2019

5:41 pm: 54% in Poll! I would be at 75% (with our great economy, maybe the best ever) if not for the Phony Witch Hunt and the Fake News Media!

June 30, 2019

10:17 pm: So many amazing things happened over the last three days. All, or at least most of those things, are great for the United States. Much was accomplished!

July 2, 2019

5:08 pm: I am pleased to announce that it is my intention to nominate Christopher Waller, Ph. D., Executive VP and Director of Research, Federal Reserve Bank of St. Louis, Missouri, to be on the board of the Federal Reserve...

5:36 pm: I am pleased to announce that it is my intention to nominate Judy Shelton, Ph. D., U.S. Executive Dir, European Bank of Reconstruction & Development to be on the board of the Federal Reserve...

July 3, 2019

9:30 am: The cost of our great Salute to America tomorrow will be very little compared to what it is worth. We own the planes, we have the pilots, the airport is right next door (Andrews), all we need is the fuel. We own the tanks and all. Fireworks are donated by two of the greats. Nice!

July 10, 2019

10:06 am: Word just out that I won a big part of the Deep State and Democrat induced Witch Hunt. Unanimous decision in my favor from The United States Court of Appeals For The Fourth Circuit on the ridiculous Emoluments Case. I don't make money, but lose a fortune for the honor of...

...serving and doing a great job as your President (including accepting Zero salary!)

July 11, 2019

6:37 am: The Pledge of Allegiance to our great Country, in St. Louis Park, Minnesota, is under siege. That is why I am going to win the Great State of Minnesota in the 2020 Election. People are sick and tired of this stupidity and disloyalty to our wonderful USA!

July 12, 2019

9:55 am: Alex Acosta informed me this morning that he felt the constant drumbeat of press about a prosecution which took place under his watch more than 12 years ago was bad for the Administration, which he so strongly believes in, and he graciously tendered his resignation...

...Alex was a great Secretary of Labor and his service is truly appreciated. He will be replaced on an acting basis by Pat Pizzella, the current Deputy Secretary.

July 16, 2019

8:59 am: Those Tweets were NOT Racist. I don't have a Racist bone in my body! The so-called vote to be taken is a Democrat con game. Republicans should not show "weakness" and fall into their trap. This should be a vote on the filthy language, statements and lies told by the Democrat...

...Congresswomen, who I truly believe, based on their actions, hate our Country. Get a list of the HORRIBLE things they have said. Omar is polling at 8%, Cortez at 21%. Nancy Pelosi tried to push them away, but now they are forever wedded to the Democrat Party. See you in 2020!

July 17, 2019

9:30 am: New Poll: The Rasmussen Poll, one of the most accurate in predicting the 2016 Election, has just announced that "Trump" numbers have recently gone up by four points, to 50%. Thank you to the vicious young Socialist Congresswomen. America will never buy your act! #MAGA2020

July 18, 2019

9:54 am: A lot of bad things are happening in Puerto Rico. The Governor is under siege, the Mayor of San Juan is a despicable and incompetent person who I wouldn't trust under any circumstance, and the United States Congress foolishly gave 92 Billion Dollars for hurricane relief, much…

…of which was squandered away or wasted, never to be seen again. This is more than twice the amount given to Texas & Florida combined. I know the people of Puerto Rico well, and they are great. But much of their leadership is corrupt, & robbing the U.S. Government blind!

7:22 pm: I am pleased to announce that it is my intention to nominate Gene Scalia as the new Secretary of Labor. Gene has led a life of great success in the legal and labor field and is highly respected not only as a lawyer, but as a lawyer with great experience…

…working with labor and everyone else. He will be a great member of an Administration that has done more in the first 2 ½ years than perhaps any Administration in history!

July 20, 2019

5:57 am: As you can see, I did nothing to lead people on, nor was I particularly happy with their chant. Just a very big and patriotic crowd. They love the USA! https://t.co/6IVKEffNnq

July 23, 2019

6:25 am: Newest Poll: Only 11% in favor of starting ridiculous impeachment hearings. Well, let's see: We have the Best Economy in

History, the Best Employment Numbers in History, Most People Working in History, Highest Stock Market in History, Biggest Tax and Regulation Cuts in History,…

…Best and Newest Military (almost totally rebuilt from the depleted military I took over) in History, Best V.A. in History (Choice), and MUCH, MUCH MORE. Gee, let's impeach the President. The "Squad" (AOC Plus 3) and other Dems suffer from Trump Derangement Syndrome. Crazy!

6:32 pm: Just got back only to hear of a last minute change allowing a Never Trumper attorney to help Robert Mueller with his testimony before Congress tomorrow. What a disgrace to our system. Never heard of this before. VERY UNFAIR, SHOULD NOT BE ALLOWED. A rigged Witch Hunt!

July 26, 2019

1:17 pm: Great morning at the Pentagon yesterday. Congratulations to our new Defense Secretary, Mark @EsperDoD!

August 8, 2019

5:19 pm: Sue Gordon is a great professional with a long and distinguished career. I have gotten to know Sue over the past 2 years and have developed great respect for her. Sue has announced she will be leaving on August 15, which…

…coincides with the retirement of Dan Coats. A new Acting Director of National Intelligence will be named shortly.

6:12 pm: I am pleased to inform you that the Honorable Joseph Maguire, current Director of the National Counterterrorism Center, will be named Acting Director of National Intelligence, effective August 15th. Admiral Maguire has a long and distinguished…

…career in the military, retiring from the U.S. Navy in 2010. He commanded at every level, including the Naval Special Warfare Command. He has also served as a National Security Fellow at Harvard University. I have no doubt he will do a great job!

6:55 pm: Rod Blagojevich, the former Governor of Illinois, was sentenced to 14 years in prison. He has served 7 years. Many people have asked that I study the possibility of commuting his sentence in that it was a very severe one. White House staff is continuing the review of this matter.

August 10, 2019

9:47 pm: Anthony Scaramucci, who was quickly terminated (11 days) from a position that he was totally incapable of handling, now seems to do nothing but television as the all time expert on "President Trump." Like many other so-called television experts, he knows very little about me...

...other than the fact that this Administration has probably done more than any other Administration in its first 2 1/2 years of existence. Anthony, who would do anything to come back in, should remember the only reason he is on TV, and it's not for being the Mooch!

August 12, 2019

4:26 pm: The United States is learning much from the failed missile explosion in Russia. We have similar, though more advanced, technology. The Russian "Skyfall" explosion has people worried about the air around the facility, and far beyond. Not good!

August 16, 2019

5:52 pm: I donate 100% of my President's salary, $400,000, back to our Country, and feel very good about it!

August 19, 2019

9:51 pm: Nobody ever heard of this dope until he met me. He only lasted 11 days!

August 20, 2019

8:54 am: Just another disgruntled former employee who got fired for gross incompetence!

August 23, 2019

5:49 am: 94% Approval Rating within the Republican Party. Thank you!

August 27, 2019

6:36 pm: Can you believe it? I'm at 94% approval in the Republican Party, and have Three Stooges running against me. One is "Mr. Appalachian Trail" who was actually in Argentina for bad reasons...

...Another is a one-time BAD Congressman from Illinois who lost in his second term by a landslide, then failed in radio. The third is a man who couldn't stand up straight while receiving an award. I should be able to take them!

August 28, 2019

9:45 pm: Puerto Rico is one of the most corrupt places on earth. Their political system is broken and their politicians are either Incompetent or Corrupt. Congress approved Billions of Dollars last time, more than anyplace else has ever gotten, and it is sent to Crooked Pols. No good!...

...And by the way, I'm the best thing that's ever happened to Puerto Rico!

August 29, 2019

3:40 pm: Establishment of the U.S. Space Command!

August 31, 2019

7:52 am: While Madeleine Westerhout has a fully enforceable confidentiality agreement, she is a very good person and I don't think there would ever be reason to use it. She called me yesterday to apologize, had a bad night. I fully understood and forgave her! I love Tiffany, doing great!

7:58 am: ...Yes, I am currently suing various people for violating their confidentiality agreements. Disgusting and foul mouthed Omarosa is one. I gave her every break, despite the fact that she was despised by everyone, and she went for some cheap money from a book. Numerous others also!

September 4, 2019

5:23 pm: This was the originally projected path of the Hurricane in its early stages. As you can see, almost all models predicted it to go through Florida also hitting Georgia and Alabama. I accept the Fake News apologies!

September 5, 2019

10:45 am: After almost 3 years in my Administration, Jason Greenblatt will be leaving to pursue work in the private sector. Jason has been a loyal and great friend and fantastic lawyer.

3:14 pm: Just as I said, Alabama was originally projected to be hit. The Fake News denies it!

3:18 pm: I was with you all the way Alabama. The Fake News Media was not!

September 8, 2019

10:11 pm: I was with you all the way Alabama. The Fake News Media was not!

…A man named @VanJones68, and many others, were profusely grateful (at that time!). I SIGNED IT INTO LAW, no one else did, & Republicans deserve much credit. But now that it is passed, people that had virtually nothing to do with it are taking the praise. Guys like boring…

…musician @johnlegend, and his filthy mouthed wife, are talking now about how great it is—but I didn't see them around when we needed help getting it passed. "Anchor"@LesterHoltNBC doesn't even bring up the subject of President Trump or the Republicans when talking about.

...the importance or passage of Criminal Justice Reform. They only talk about the minor players, or people that had nothing to do with it...And the people that so desperately sought my help when everyone else had failed, all they talk about now is Impeaching President Trump!

September 9, 2019

8:43 am: I know nothing about an Air Force plane landing at an airport (which I do not own and have nothing to do with) near Turnberry Resort (which I do own) in Scotland, and filling up with fuel, with the crew staying overnight at Turnberry (they have good taste!). NOTHING TO DO WITH ME

8:52 am: I had nothing to do with the decision of our great @VP Mike Pence to stay overnight at one of the Trump owned resorts in Doonbeg, Ireland. Mike's family has lived in Doonbeg for many years, and he thought that during his very busy European visit, he would stop and see his family!

9:55 am: The Trump Administration has achieved more in the first 2 1/2 years of its existence than perhaps any administration in the history of our Country. We get ZERO media credit for what we have done, and are doing, but the people know, and that's all that is important!

September 10, 2019

10:58 am: I informed John Bolton last night that his services are no longer needed at the White House. I disagreed strongly with many of his suggestions, as did others in the Administration, and therefore...

...I asked John for his resignation, which was given to me this morning. I thank John very much for his service. I will be naming a new National Security Advisor next week.

September 12, 2019

12:22 pm: In fact, my views on Venezuela, and especially Cuba, were far stronger than those of John Bolton. He was holding me back!

September 13, 2019

7:58 am: How do you impeach a President who has helped create perhaps the greatest economy in the history of our Country? All time best unemployment numbers, especially for Blacks, Hispanics, Asians & Women. More people working today than ever before. Rebuilt Military & Choice for Vets...

...Became Number 1 in World & Independent in Energy. Will soon have record number of Judges, 2 SC Justices. Done more than any President in first 2 1/2 years despite phony & fraudulent Witch Hunt illegally led against him. WIN on Mueller Report, Mueller Testimony & James Comey...

...IG Report, which showed him to be a Disgraced & Dirty Cop. Republicans have unified like never before. You don't impeach Presidents for doing a good (great!) job. No Obstruction, No Collusion, only treasonous crimes committed by the other side, and led by the Democrats. Sad!

September 14, 2019

7:44 am: "A Very Stable Genius!" Thank you.

September 16, 2019

12:59 pm: In a short while I will be presenting the New York @Yankees @MarianoRivera, the greatest relief pitcher (Closer!) of all time, with the Presidential Medal of Freedom in the East Room of the @WhiteHouse!

September 18, 2019

8:23 am: I am pleased to announce that I will name Robert C. O'Brien, currently serving as the very successful Special Presidential Envoy for Hostage Affairs at the State Department, as our new National Security Advisor. I have worked long & hard with Robert. He will do a great job!

333

10:19 am: The Trump Administration is revoking California's Federal Waiver on emissions in order to produce far less expensive cars for the consumer, while at the same time making the cars substantially SAFER. This will lead to more production because of this pricing and safety...

advantage, and also due to the fact that older, highly polluting cars, will be replaced by new, extremely environmentally friendly cars. There will be very little difference in emissions between the California Standard and the new U.S. Standard, but the cars will be...

...far safer and much less expensive. Many more cars will be produced under the new and uniform standard, meaning significantly more JOBS, JOBS, JOBS! Automakers should seize this opportunity because without this alternative to California, you will be out of business.

September 21, 2019

5:47 pm: "Ukraine Foreign Minister disputes reports of any pressure from Trump. This conversation was long, friendly, and it touched on many questions." @NBCNews Correct. If your looking for something done wrong, just look at the tape of Sleepy Joe. He is being protected by the Media!

September 23, 2019

10:29 am: "The very thing that they are accusing President Trump of doing (which I didn't do), was actually done by Joe Biden. Continues to be a double standard." @RepDevinNunes @foxandfriends These people are stone cold Crooked. Also, who is this so-called "whistle-blower" who doesn't.

...know the correct facts. Is he on our Country's side. Where does he come from. Is this all about Schiff & the Democrats again after years of being wrong?

September 24, 2019

1:12 pm: I am currently at the United Nations representing our Country, but have authorized the release tomorrow of the complete, fully declassified and unredacted transcript of my phone conversation with President Zelensky of Ukraine...

...You will see it was a very friendly and totally appropriate call. No pressure and, unlike Joe Biden and his son, NO quid pro quo! This is nothing more than a continuation of the Greatest and most Destructive Witch Hunt of all time!

5:22 pm: Secretary of State Pompeo recieved permission from Ukraine Government to release the transcript of the telephone call I had with their President. They don't know either what the big deal is. A total Witch Hunt Scam by the Democrats!

September 25, 2019

6:24 am: There has been no President in the history of our Country who has been treated so badly as I have. The Democrats are frozen with hatred and fear. They get nothing done. This should never be allowed to happen to another President. Witch Hunt!

September 26, 2019

6:24 am: THE GREATEST SCAM IN THE HISTORY OF AMERICAN POLITICS!

11:43 am: A whistleblower with second hand information? Another Fake News Story! See what was said on the very nice, no pressure, call. Another Witch Hunt!

6:02 pm: The President of Ukraine said that he was NOT pressured by me to do anything wrong. Can't have better testimony than that! As V.P., Biden had his son, on the other hand, take out millions of dollars by strong arming the Ukrainian President. Also looted millions from China. Bad!

September 27, 2019

8:25 am: "IT WAS A PERFECT CONVERSATION WITH UKRAINE PRESIDENT!"

8:42 am: Sounding more and more like the so-called Whistleblower isn't a Whistleblower at all. In addition, all second hand information that proved to be so inaccurate that there may not have even been somebody else, a leaker or spy, feeding it to him or her? A partisan operative?

2:41 pm: I AM DRAINING THE SWAMP!

September 28, 2019

7:34 am: PRESIDENTIAL HARASSMENT!

7:35 am: MAKE AMERICA GREAT AGAIN!

7:35 am: KEEP AMERICA GREAT!

5:00 pm: How do you impeach a President who has created the greatest Economy in the history of our Country, entirely rebuilt our Military into the most powerful it has ever been, Cut Record Taxes & Regulations, fixed the VA & gotten Choice for our Vets (after 45 years), & so much more?…

…The conversation with the new and very good Ukraine President, who told the Fake News, at the United Nations, that HE WAS NOT PRESSURED BY ME IN ANY WAY, SHAPE, OR FORM, should by and of itself bring an end to the new and most recent Witch Hunt. Others ended in ashes!

5:30 pm: The Whistleblower's complaint is completely different and at odds from my actual conversation with the new President of Ukraine. The so-called "Whistleblower" knew practically NOTHING in that those ridiculous charges were far more dramatic & wrong, just like Liddle' Adam Schiff…

…fraudulently and illegally inserted his made up & twisted words into my call with the Ukrainian President to make it look like I did something very wrong. He then boldly read those words to Congress and millions of people, defaming & libeling me. He must resign from Congress!

September 29, 2019

9:20 am: Investigating Corruption is correct!

5:53 pm: Like every American, I deserve to meet my accuser, especially when this accuser, the so-called "Whistleblower," represented a perfect conversation with a foreign leader in a totally inaccurate and fraudulent way. Then Schiff made up what I actually said by lying to Congress…

His lies were made in perhaps the most blatant and sinister manner ever seen in the great Chamber. He wrote down and read terrible things, then said it was from the mouth of the President of the United States. I want Schiff questioned at the highest level for Fraud & Treason.

…In addition, I want to meet not only my accuser, who presented SECOND & THIRD HAND INFORMATION, but also the person who illegally gave this information, which was largely incorrect, to the "Whistleblower." Was this person SPYING on the U.S. President? Big Consequences!

September 30, 2019

6:39 am: The Greatest Witch Hunt in the history of our Country!

7:03 am: The Fake Whistleblower complaint is not holding up. It is mostly about the call to the Ukrainian President which, in the name of transparency, I immediately released to Congress & the public. The Whistleblower knew almost nothing, its 2ND HAND description of the call is a fraud!

7:12 am: Rep. Adam Schiff illegally made up a FAKE & terrible statement, pretended it to be mine as the most important part of my call to the Ukrainian President, and read it aloud to Congress and the American people. It bore NO relationship to what I said on the call. Arrest for Treason?

7:40 am: Again, the President of Ukraine said there was NO (ZERO) PRESSURE PUT ON HIM BY ME. Case closed!

7:44 am: #FakeWhistleblower

8:58 am: Very simple! I was looking for Corruption and also why Germany, France and others in the European Union don't do more for Ukraine. Why is it always the USA that does so much and puts up so much money for Ukraine and other countries? By the way, the Bidens were corrupt!

October 1, 2019

6:09 am: "The congratulatory phone call with the Ukrainian President was PERFECT, unless you heard Liddle' Adam Schiff's fraudulently made up version of the call. This is just another Fake News Media, together with their partner, the Democrat Party, HOAX!

8:19 am: So if the so-called "Whistleblower" has all second hand information, and almost everything he has said about my "perfect" call with the Ukrainian President is wrong (much to the embarrassment of Pelosi & Schiff), why aren't we entitled to interview & learn everything about.

...the Whistleblower, and also the person who gave all of the false information to him. This is simply about a phone conversation that could not have been nicer, warmer, or better. No pressure at all (as confirmed by Ukrainian Pres.). It is just another Democrat Hoax!

6:41 pm: As I learn more and more each day, I am coming to the conclusion that what is taking place is not an impeachment, it is a COUP, intended to take away the Power of the...

...People, their VOTE, their Freedoms, their Second Amendment, Religion, Military, Border Wall, and their God-given rights as a Citizen of The United States of America!

October 3, 2019

3:32 pm: There wasn't ANYTHING said wrong in my conversation with the Ukrainian President. This is a Democrat Scam!

8:04 pm: As the President of the United States, I have an absolute right, perhaps even a duty, to investigate, or have investigated, CORRUPTION, and that would include asking, or suggesting, other Countries to help us out!

October 4, 2019

7:16 am: As President I have an obligation to end CORRUPTION, even if that means requesting the help of a foreign country or countries. It is done all the time. This has NOTHING to do with politics or a political campaign against the Bidens. This does have to do with their corruption!

October 5, 2019

8:58 am: The so-called Whistleblower's account of my perfect phone call is "way off," not even close. Schiff and Pelosi never thought I would release the transcript of the call. Got them by surprise, they got caught. This is a fraud against the American people!

8:17 pm: The first so-called second hand information "Whistleblower" got my phone conversation almost completely wrong, so now word is they are going to the bench and another "Whistleblower" is coming in from the Deep State, also with second hand info. Meet with Shifty. Keep them coming!

October 8, 2019

8:23 am: The first so-called second hand information "Whistleblower" got my phone conversation almost completely wrong, so now word is they are going to the bench and another "Whistleblower" is coming in from the Deep State, also with second hand info. Meet with Shifty. Keep them coming!

...to see. Importantly, Ambassador Sondland's tweet, which few report, stated, "I believe you are incorrect about President Trump's intentions. The President has been crystal clear: no quid pro quo's of any kind."

October 9, 2019

6:10 am: The Whistleblower's facts have been so incorrect about my "no pressure" conversation with the Ukrainian President, and now the conflict of interest and involvement with a Democrat Candidate, that he or she should be exposed and questioned properly. This is no Whistleblower.

7:22 am: The so-called Whistleblower, before knowing I was going to release the exact Transcript, stated that my call with the Ukrainian President was "crazy, frightening, and completely lacking in substance related to national security." This is a very big Lie. Read the Transcript!

7:43 am: ...No Pressure at all said Ukraine! Very congenial, a perfect call. The Whistleblower and others spoke BEFORE seeing the Transcript. Now they must apologize to me and stop this ridiculous impeachment!

11:27 am: Only 25 percent want the President Impeached, which is pretty low considering the volume of Fake News coverage, but pretty high considering the fact that I did NOTHING wrong. It is all just a continuation of the greatest Scam and Witch Hunt in the history of our Country!

10:53 pm: Impeached for what, having created the greatest Economy in the history of our Country, building our strongest ever Military, Cutting Taxes too much?

October 10, 2019

8:08 am: From the day I announced I was running for President, I have NEVER had a good @FoxNews Poll. Whoever their Pollster is, they suck. But @FoxNews is also much different than it used to be in the good old days. With people like Andrew Napolitano, who wanted to be a Supreme.

...Court Justice & I turned him down (he's been terrible ever since), Shep Smith, @donnabrazile (who gave Crooked Hillary the debate questions & got fired from @CNN), & others, @FoxNews doesn't deliver for US anymore. It is so different than it used to be. Oh well, I'm President!

8:39 am: The President of the Ukraine just stated again, in the strongest of language, that President Trump applied no pressure and did absolutely nothing wrong. He used the strongest language possible. That should end this Democrat Scam, but it won't, because the Dems & Media are FIXED!

October 12, 2019

8:49 am: The case of Major Mathew Golsteyn is now under review at the White House. Mathew is a highly decorated Green Beret who is being tried for killing a Taliban bombmaker. We train our boys to be killing machines, then prosecute them when they kill! @PeteHegseth

10:11 am: So now they are after the legendary "crime buster" and greatest Mayor in the history of NYC, Rudy Giuliani. He may seem a little rough around the edges sometimes, but he is also a great guy and wonderful lawyer. Such a one sided Witch Hunt going on in USA. Deep State. Shameful!

October 16, 2019

11:39 pm: I am the only person who can fight for the safety of our troops & bring them home from the ridiculous & costly Endless Wars, and be scorned. Democrats always liked that position, until I took it. Democrats always liked Walls, until I built them. Do you see what's happening here?

October 18, 2019

2:34 pm: I want to thank Secretary of Energy Rick Perry for the outstanding job he has done. He will be leaving at the end of the year to pursue other interests. Rick was a great Governor of Texas and a great Secretary of Energy…

…He is also my friend! At the same time, I am pleased to nominate Deputy Secretary Dan Brouillette to be the new Secretary of Energy.

Dan's experience in the sector is unparalleled. A total professional, I have no doubt that Dan will do a great job!

October 19, 2019

7:32 am: #StopTheCoup

8:18 pm: I thought I was doing something very good for our Country by using Trump National Doral, in Miami, for hosting the G-7 Leaders. It is big, grand, on hundreds of acres, next to MIAMI INTERNATIONAL AIRPORT, has tremendous ballrooms & meeting rooms, and each delegation would have.

October 21, 2019

8:17 am: Doral in Miami would have been the best place to hold the G-7, and free, but too much heat from the Do Nothing Radical Left Democrats & their Partner, the Fake News Media! I'm surprised that they allow me to give up my $400,000 Plus Presidential Salary! We'll find someplace else!

October 22, 2019

6:57 am: 95% Approval Rating in the Republican Party. Thank you!

October 23, 2019

7:40 am: Where's the Whistleblower?

October 24, 2019

8:52 pm: Where is the Whistleblower, and why did he or she write such a fictitious and incorrect account of my phone call with the Ukrainian President? Why did the IG allow this to happen? Who is the so-called Informant (Schiff?) who was so inaccurate? A giant Scam!

October 26, 2019

6:02 am: "General Michael Flynn's attorney is demanding that charges be immediately dropped after they found that FBI Agents manipulated records against him. They say that James Clapper told a reporter to "take a kill shot at Flynn. This has been a complete setup of Michael Flynn...

...They exonerated him completely of being an agent of Russia (Recently Crooked Hillary charged Tulsi Gabbard & Jill Stein with the same thing-SICK), and yet Mr. Comey still runs to the White House on February 14 and conjures up the Obstruction of Justice narrative against...

...the President when Flynn had been cleared of everything long before that. The DOJ is withholding a lot of evidence & information, as are Clapper & Brennan & all of the people who participated in the complete setup of Michael Flynn."(Terrible!) Sidney Powell. This is a disgrace!

October 29, 2019

6:42 am: Why are people that I never even heard of testifying about the call. Just READ THE CALL TRANSCRIPT AND THE IMPEACHMENT HOAX IS OVER! Ukrain said NO PRESSURE.

7:19 am: Where's the Whistleblower? Just read the Transcript, everything else is made up garbage by Shifty Schiff and the Never Trumpers!

7:47 am: How many more Never Trumpers will be allowed to testify about a perfectly appropriate phone call when all anyone has to do is READ THE TRANSCRIPT! I knew people were listening in on the call (why would I say something inappropriate?), which was fine with me, but why so many?

October 30, 2019

7:59 am: Yesterday's Never Trumper witness could find NO Quid Pro Quo in the Transcript of the phone call. There were many people

343

listening to the call. How come they (including the President of Ukraine) found NOTHING wrong with it. Witch Hunt!

October 31, 2019

8:29 am: READ THE TRANSCRIPT!

9:57 am: The Impeachment Hoax is hurting our Stock Market. The Do Nothing Democrats don't care!

10:31 am: The Greatest Witch Hunt In American History!

8:32 pm: 1600 Pennsylvania Avenue, the White House, is the place I have come to love and will stay for, hopefully, another 5 years as we MAKE AMERICA GREAT AGAIN, but my family and I will be making Palm Beach, Florida, our Permanent Residence. I cherish New York, and the people of...

...New York, and always will, but unfortunately, despite the fact that I pay millions of dollars in city, state and local taxes each year, I have been treated very badly by the political leaders of both the city and state. Few have been treated worse. I hated having to make...

...this decision, but in the end it will be best for all concerned. As President, I will always be there to help New York and the great people of New York. It will always have a special place in my heart!

November 1, 2019

8:52 am: "Adam Schiff has taken all of the power for himself. That is very unfair. There were dozens of people on this call, yesterdays witness knew that and had no problems (nor did any of them). Facts matter, and that's why this is not about Impeachment." Guy Lewis, former prosecutor...

...@FoxNews @BillHemmer The public is watching and seeing for themselves how unfair this process is. Corrupt politicians, Pelosi and Schiff, are trying to take down the Republican Party. It will never happen, we will take back the House!

5:48 pm: You can't Impeach someone who hasn't done anything wrong!

6:16 pm: The Whistleblower must come forward to explain why his account of the phone call with the Ukrainian President was so inaccurate (fraudulent?). Why did the Whistleblower deal with corrupt politician Shifty Adam Schiff and/or his committee?

November 2, 2019

3:57 pm: The Whistleblower has disappeared. Where is the Whistleblower?

4:10 pm: A giant Scam!

November 3, 2019

9:33 pm: The Whistleblower got it sooo wrong that HE must come forward. The Fake News Media knows who he is but, being an arm of the Democrat Party, don't want to reveal him because there would be hell to pay. Reveal the Whistleblower and end the Impeachment Hoax!

10:01 am: Walking into Madison Square Garden last night with @danawhite for the big @UFC Championship fight was a little bit like walking into a Trump Rally. Plenty of MAGA & KAG present. Great energy. Fantastic job Dana! Heading to D.C. and then to Kentucky for a big @MattBevin Rally...

11:40 am: Many people listened to my phone call with the Ukrainian President while it was being made. I never heard any complaints. The reason is that it was totally appropriate, I say perfect. Republicans have never been more unified, and my Republican Approval Rating is now 95%!

7:59 pm: False stories are being reported that a few Republican Senators are saying that President Trump may have done a quid pro quo, but it doesn't matter, there is nothing wrong with that, it is not an impeachable event. Perhaps so, but read the transcript, there is no quid pro quo!

November 4, 2019

6:38 am: Great! But how do you know it was a "mistweet?" May be something with deep meaning! https://t.co/00EXMCgQLp

6:53 am: Mark Levin, a great lawyer and scholar, said last night on his @marklevinshow, that all you have to do is read the transcript of the call, you do not need Never Trumpers or other witnesses to say what it means or says. It is plainly and very well stated for all to see. Witch Hunt

7:06 am: What I said on the phone call with the Ukrainian President is "perfectly" stated. There is no reason to call witnesses to analyze my words and meaning. This is just another Democrat Hoax that I have had to live with from the day I got elected (and before!). Disgraceful!

7:50 am: The Whistleblower gave false information & dealt with corrupt politician Schiff. He must be brought forward to testify. Written answers not acceptable! Where is the 2nd Whistleblower? He disappeared after I released the transcript. Does he even exist? Where is the informant? Con!

7:58 am: 95% Approval Rating in the Republican Party. Thank you!

9:22 am: Many people say they know me, claiming to be "best friends" and really close etc., when I don't know these people at all. This happens, I suppose, to all who become President. With that being stated, I don't know, to the best of my knowledge, a man named Michael Esposito…

…I don't like him using my name to build his consulting company, or whatever. Please advise his clients and Administration officials accordingly.

9:51 am: Read the Transcript!

November 6, 2019

12:16 am: Our big Kentucky Rally on Monday night had a massive impact on all of the races. The increase in Governors race was at least

15 points, and maybe 20! Will be in Louisiana for @EddieRispone on Wednesday night. Big Rally!

8:17 am: Thank you to Kurt Volker, U.S. Envoy to Ukraine, who said in his Congressional Testimony, just released, "You asked what conversations did I have about that quid pro quo, et cetra. NONE, because I didn't know there was a quid pro quo." Witch Hunt!

2:10 pm: Just had a meeting with top representatives from Egypt, Ethiopia, and Sudan to help solve their long running dispute on the Grand Ethiopian Renaissance Dam, one of the largest in the world, currently being built. The meeting went well and discussions will continue during the day!

November 7, 2019

7:28 am: Bill Barr did not decline my request to talk about Ukraine. The story was a Fake Washington Post con job with an "anonymous" source that doesn't exist. Just read the Transcript. The Justice Department already ruled that the call was good. We don't have freedom of the press!

8:47 am: Read the Transcript!

9:07 am: Based on the information released last night about the Fake Whistleblowers attorney, the Impeachment Hoax should be ended IMMEDIATELY! There is no case, except against the other side!

10:16 am: It was just explained to me that for next weeks Fake Hearing (trial) in the House, as they interview Never Trumpers and others, I get NO LAWYER & NO DUE PROCESS. It is a Pelosi, Schiff, Scam against the Republican Party and me. This Witch Hunt should not be allowed to proceed!

November 8, 2019

12:19 pm: I will be announcing the winners of the #MAGACHAL-LENGE and inviting them to the @WhiteHouse to meet with me and perform. Good luck!

November 9, 2019

11:15 am: But the Witch Hunt continues. After 3 years of relentless attacks against the Republican Party & me, the Do Nothing Dems are losers for America!

12:49 pm: PRESIDENTIAL HARASSMENT!

2:25 pm: …Whatever happened to the so-called "informer" to Whistleblower #1? Seems to have disappeared after I released the Transcript of the call. Shouldn't he be on the list to testify? Witch Hunt!

2:31 pm: 95% Approval Rating in the Republican Party. Thank you! #MAGA #KAG2020

7:12 pm: A terrible lie. How can she do such a thing? https://t.co/bSvlYI7dqe

10:59 pm: Make America Great Again!

November 10, 2019

2:43 pm: The call to the Ukrainian President was PERFECT. Read the Transcript! There was NOTHING said that was in any way wrong. Republicans, don't be led into the fools trap of saying it was not perfect, but is not impeachable. No, it is much stronger than that. NOTHING WAS DONE WRONG!

November 11, 2019

9:09 am: So with one Rally by me at the end of the campaign, I lift the poll numbers of Kentucky Governor Matt Bevin by 19 points, he just misses, every other Republican in the Commonwealth wins big, and the Fake News blames me for a bad night! OK! By the way, Mississippi won everything!

9:12 am: The lawyer for the Whistleblower takes away all credibility from this big Impeachment Scam! It should be ended and the Whistleblower, his lawyer and Corrupt politician Schiff should be investigared for fraud!

9:30 am: Shifty Adam Schiff will only release doctored transcripts. We haven't even seen the documents and are restricted from (get this) having a lawyer. Republicans should put out their own transcripts! Schiff must testify as to why he MADE UP a statement from me, and read it to all!

3:26 pm: Where is the Whistleblower who gave so much false information? Must testify along with Schiff and others!

3:39 pm: To think I signed the Whistleblower Protection Act!

3:40 pm: Read the Transcript. It is PERFECT!

6:18 pm: Schiff is giving Republicans NO WITNESSES, NO LAWYER & NO DUE PROCESS! It is a totally one sided Witch Hunt. This can't be making the Democrats look good. Such a farce!

6:35 pm: In order to continue being the most Transparent President in history, I will be releasing sometime this week the Transcript of the first, and therefore most important, phone call I had with the President of Ukraine. I am sure you will find it tantalizing!

8:33 pm: Vote for Sean Spicer on Dancing with the Stars. He is a great and very loyal guy who is working very hard. He is in the quarterfinals—all the way with Sean! #MAGA #KAG

10:07 pm: A great try by @seanspicer. We are all proud of you!

November 12, 2019

6:25 am: Why is such a focus put on 2nd and 3rd hand witnesses, many of whom are Never Trumpers, or whose lawyers are Never Trumpers, when all you have to do is read the phone call (transcript) with the Ukrainian President and see first hand? He and others also stated that there was…

…"no pressure" put on him to investigate Sleepy Joe Biden even though, as President, I have an "obligation" to look into corruption, and Biden's actions, on tape, about firing the prosecutor, and his son's taking millions of dollars, with no knowledge or talent, from a…

...Ukrainian energy company, and more millions taken from China, and now reports of other companies and countries also giving him big money, are certainly looking very corrupt (to put it mildly!) to me. Both Bidens should be forced to testify in this No Due Process Scam!

6:31 am: I will be releasing the transcript of the first, and therefore more important, phone call with the Ukrainian President before week's end!

10:41 am: A total Impeachment Scam by the Do Nothing Democrats!

November 13, 2019

8:30 am: NEVER TRUMPERS!

READ THE TRANSCRIPT!

November 14, 2019

10:39 am: Where's the Fake Whistleblower?

11:52 pm: Democrats must apologize to USA: Ukrainian Foreign Minister Vadym Prystaiko said that "United States Ambassador Gordon Sondland did NOT link financial military assistance to a request for Ukraine to open up an investigation into former V.P. Joe Biden & his son, Hunter Biden...

...Ambassador Sondland did not tell us, and certainly did not tell me, about a connection between the assistance and the investigation." THE FAKE IMPEACHMENT INQUIRY IS NOW DEAD!

November 15, 2019

10:01 am: Everywhere Marie Yovanovitch went turned bad. She started off in Somalia, how did that go? Then fast forward to Ukraine, where the new Ukrainian President spoke unfavorably about her in my second phone call with him. It is a U.S. President's absolute right to appoint ambassadors.

...They call it "serving at the pleasure of the President." The U.S. now has a very strong and powerful foreign policy, much different than proceeding administrations. It is called, quite simply, America First! With all of that, however, I have done FAR more for Ukraine than O.

11:21 am: We have vacancies in various departments because we do not want or need as many people as past administrations (and save great cost), and also, the Democrats delay the approval process to levels unprecedented in the history of our Country!

9:39 pm: #NewHoaxSameSwamp

November 17, 2019

12:09 am: Visited a great family of a young man under major surgery at the amazing Walter Reed Medical Center. Those are truly some of the best doctors anywhere in the world. Also began phase one of my yearly physical. Everything very good (great!). Will complete next year.

2:57 pm: Tell Jennifer Williams, whoever that is, to read BOTH transcripts of the presidential calls, & see the just released ststement from Ukraine. Then she should meet with the other Never Trumpers, who I don't know & mostly never even heard of, & work out a better presidential attack!

3:03 pm: The Crazed, Do Nothing Democrats are turning Impeachment into a routine partisan weapon. That is very bad for our Country, and not what the Founders had in mind!!!!

3:08 pm: Republicans & others must remember, the Ukrainian President and Foreign Minister both said that there was no pressure placed on them whatsoever. Also, they didn't even know the money wasn't paid, and got the money with no conditions. But why isn't Germany, France (Europe) paying?

3:12 pm: Where is the Fake Whistleblower?

10:39 pm: "All they do is bring up witnesses who didn't witness anything." @KatrinaPierson @SteveHiltonx Nothing matters except the two transcripts of the presidential calls, and the statement of no pressure put out by Ukraine!

November 18, 2019

3:56 pm: THANK YOU! #MAGA #KAG https://t.co/igO1r1cTHS

4:28 pm: GREAT NEWS! #MAGA #KAG https://t.co/GXDE2IlGGu

6:54 pm: Mark Levin speaking one week after I took office. This was always a planned COUP and the Radical Left Democrats will suffer at the polls in 2020!

November 19, 2019

7:10 pm: I agree, but in the end we will win and save our Country from certain destruction! https://t.co/CPjdxq5hXT

8:06 pm: A great day for Republicans, a great day for our Country!

November 20, 2019

7:22 am: Read the transcripts!

7:27 am: The three year Hoax continues!

1:57 pm: Impeachment Witch Hunt is now OVER! Ambassador Sondland asks U.S. President (me): "What do you want from Ukraine? I keep hearing all these different ideas & theories. What do you want? It was a very abrupt conversation. He was not in a good mood. He (the President) just said,"...

..."I WANT NOTHING! I WANT NOTHING! I WANT NO QUID PRO QUO! TELL PRESIDENT ZELENSKY TO DO THE RIGHT THING!" Later, Ambassador Sondland said that I told him, "Good, go tell the truth!" This Witch Hunt must end NOW. So bad for our Country!

2:04 pm: I WANT NOTHING!

6:38 pm: If this were a prizefight, they'd stop it!

8:22 pm: Poll: Trump leads top 2020 Democrats in Wisconsin

November 21, 2019

7:32 am: The Republican Party, and me, had a GREAT day yesterday with respect to the phony Impeachment Hoax, & yet, when I got home to the White House & checked out the news coverage on much of television, you would have no idea they were reporting on the same event. FAKE & CORRUPT NEWS!

7:58 am: Bob Mueller, after spending two years and 45 million dollars, went over all of my financials, & my taxes, and found nothing. Now the Witch Hunt continues with local New York Democrat prosecutors going over every financial deal I have ever done. This has never happened to a...

...President before. What they are doing is not legal. But I'm clean, and when I release my financial statement (my decision) sometime prior to Election, it will only show one thing—that I am much richer than people even thought—And that is a good thing. Jobs, Jobs, Jobs!

8:01 am: I never in my wildest dreams thought my name would in any way be associated with the ugly word, Impeachment! The calls (Transcripts) were PERFECT, there was NOTHING said that was wrong. No pressure on Ukraine. Great corruption & dishonesty by Schiff on the other side!

8:15 am: Corrupt politician Adam Schiff's lies are growing by the day. Keep fighting tough, Republicans, you are dealing with human scum who have taken Due Process and all of the Republican Party's rights away from us during the most unfair hearings in American History...

...But we are winning big, and they will soon be on our turf.

9:19 am: Read the two Transcripts of Ukrainian calls!

9:27 am: I have been watching people making phone calls my entire life. My hearing is, and has been, great. Never have I been watching a person making a call, which was not on speakerphone, and been able to hear or understand a conversation. I've even tried, but to no avail. Try it live!

November 22, 2019

7:05 am: "Former FBI Employee Accused of Altering FISA Documents." Hello, here we go! @foxandfriends

November 24, 2019

7:34 am: Polls have now turned very strongly against Impeachment, especially in swing states. 75% to 25%. Thank you!

9:43 am: Too bad we didn't have the G-7 here. I offered to pick up the entire cost, would have saved at least $35,000,000 for the USA. Best location. Very stupid people thought I would gain. Wrong! Looking at Camp David. Will announce soon.

2:14 pm: But I did nothing wrong. Read the Transcripts (2)!

2:44 pm: Witch Hunt!

6:32 pm to 6:33 pm: I was not pleased with the way that Navy Seal Eddie Gallagher's trial was handled by the Navy. He was treated very badly but, despite this, was completely exonerated on all major charges. I then restored Eddie's rank. Likewise, large cost overruns from past administration's…

…contracting procedures were not addressed to my satisfaction. Therefore, Secretary of the Navy Richard Spencer's services have been terminated by Secretary of Defense Mark Esper. I thank Richard for his service & commitment. Eddie will retire peacefully with all of the…

…honors that he has earned, including his Trident Pin. Admiral and now Ambassador to Norway Ken Braithwaite will be nominated by me to be the new Secretary of the Navy. A man of great achievement and success, I know Ken will do an outstanding job!

November 25, 2019

7:54 am: Support for Impeachment is dropping like a rock, down into the 20's in some Polls. Dems should now get down to work and finally approve USMCA, and much more!

November 26, 2019

10:43 am: The D.C. Wolves and Fake News Media are reading far too much into people being forced by Courts to testify before Congress. I am fighting for future Presidents and the Office of the President. Other than that, I would actually like people to testify. Don McGahn's respected...

...lawyer has already stated that I did nothing wrong. John Bolton is a patriot and may know that I held back the money from Ukraine because it is considered a corrupt country, & I wanted to know why nearby European countries weren't putting up money also. Likewise, I would...

...love to have Mike Pompeo, Rick Perry, Mick Mulvaney and many others testify about the phony Impeachment Hoax. It is a Democrat Scam that is going nowhere but, future Presidents should in no way be compromised. What has happened to me should never happen to another President!

November 27, 2019

9:45 am: GOD BLESS THE U.S.A.! #MAGA

5:06 pm: People now realize it is a Democrat Hoax!

November 28, 2019

8:21 am: HAPPY THANKSGIVING!

November 30, 2019

6:21 pm: And the Do Nothing Democrats want to impeach President Trump?

6:38 pm: I will be representing our Country in London at NATO, while the Democrats are holding the most ridiculous Impeachment hearings in history. Read the Transcripts, NOTHING was done or said wrong! The Radical Left is undercutting our Country. Hearings scheduled on same dates as NATO!

December 2, 2019

8:53 am: Breaking News: The President of Ukraine has just again announced that President Trump has done nothing wrong with respect to Ukraine and our interactions or calls. If the Radical Left Democrats were sane, which they are not, it would be case over!

9:22 am: The Do Nothing Democrats get 3 Constitutional lawyers for their Impeachment hoax (they will need them!), the Republicans get one. Oh, that sounds fair!

11:43 am: Thank you to Congressman Ben @Cline4Virginia for the Great remarks this morning on the illegitimate Impeachment Hoax. He understands the Do Nothing Democrats very well. Also, and as usual, @RepAndyBiggsAZ was fantastic!

2:27 pm: Thank you to President Zelensky. Case over. The Do Nothing Democrats should finally go back to work!

December 4, 2019

10:50 pm: When I said, in my phone call to the President of Ukraine, "I would like you to do US a favor though because our country has been through a lot and Ukraine knows a lot about it." With the word "us" I am referring to the United States, our Country. I then went on to say that…

…"I would like to have the Attorney General (of the United States) call you or your people…" This, based on what I have seen, is their big point—and it is no point at a all (except for a big win for me!). The Democrats should apologize to the American people!

December 5, 2019

7:20 am: Tremendous things achieved for U.S. on my NATO trip. Proudly for our Country, no President has ever achieved so much in so little time. Without a U.S. increase, other countries have already increased by $130 Billion-with $400 Billion soon. Such a thing has never been done before!

8:01 am: The Do Nothing Democrats had a historically bad day yesterday in the House. They have no Impeachment case and are demeaning our Country. But nothing matters to them, they have gone crazy. Therefore I say, if you are going to impeach me, do it now, fast, so we can have a fair...

...trial in the Senate, and so that our Country can get back to business. We will have Schiff, the Bidens, Pelosi and many more testify, and will reveal, for the first time, how corrupt our system really is. I was elected to "Clean the Swamp," and that's what I am doing!

10:11 am: The Do Nothing, Radical Left Democrats have just announced that they are going to seek to Impeach me over NOTHING. They already gave up on the ridiculous Mueller "stuff," so now they hang their hats on two totally appropriate (perfect) phone calls with the Ukrainian President...

...This will mean that the beyond important and seldom used act of Impeachment will be used routinely to attack future Presidents. That is not what our Founders had in mind. The good thing is that the Republicans have NEVER been more united. We will win!

12:38 pm: Republican Approval Rating = 95%. Thank you!

10:32 pm: Where's the Fake Whistleblower? Where's Whistleblower number 2? Where's the phony informer who got it all wrong?

December 6, 2019

7:23 pm: Fake News @CNN is reporting that I am "still using personal cell phone for calls despite repeated security warnings." This is totally false information and reporting. I haven't had a personal cell phone for years. Only use government approved and issued phones. Retract!

December 7, 2019

3:21 pm: The United States Secret Service Deputy Assistant Director, Anthony Ornato, will become my new Deputy Chief of Staff for Operations. I have worked with Tony for 3 years—he will do a fantastic job! Thank you to Dan Walsh for his great service, and congratulations to Tony!

December 8, 2019

10:21 am: Less than 48 hours before start of the Impeachment Hearing Hoax, on Monday, the No Due Process, Do Nothing Democrats are, believe it or not, changing the Impeachment Guidelines because the facts are not on their side. When you can't win the game, change the rules

3:18 pm: I.G. report out tomorrow. That will be the big story!

11:52 pm: AMERICA FIRST!

December 9, 2019

12:05 am: Witch Hunt!

10:11 am: Witch Hunt!

10:47 am: Read the Transcripts!

December 10, 2019

7:37 am: To Impeach a President who has proven through results, including producing perhaps the strongest economy in our country's history, to have one of the most successful presidencies ever, and most importantly, who has done NOTHING wrong, is sheer Political Madness! #2020Election

9:56 am: Nadler just said that I "pressured Ukraine to interfere in our 2020 Election." Ridiculous, and he knows that is not true. Both the President & Foreign Minister of Ukraine said, many times, that there "WAS NO PRESSURE." Nadler and the Dems know this, but refuse to acknowledge!

WITCH HUNT!

10:10 am: Read the Transcripts! "us" is a reference to USA, not me!

5:36 pm: On my way to Hershey, Pennsylvania for a rally. See everyone soon. I love Hershey chocolate!

5:51 pm: Just had a very good meeting with Foreign Minister Sergey Lavrov and representatives of Russia. Discussed many items including Trade, Iran, North Korea, INF Treaty, Nuclear Arms Control, and Election Meddling. Look forward to continuing our dialogue in the near future!

8:47 pm: THANK YOU PENNSYLVANIA! With your help, your devotion, and your drive, we are going to keep on working, we are going to keep on fighting, and we are going to keep ON WINNING! We are ONE movement, ONE people, ONE family, and ONE GLORIOUS NATION UNDER GOD!

8:55 pm: Day after day, we are exposing the depravity, dishonesty and sickness of the corrupt Washington establishment—and with your help, we are going to complete the mission and DRAIN THE SWAMP! #KAG2020

8:58 pm: After years of rebuilding OTHER NATIONS, we are finally rebuilding OUR NATION. In everything we do, we are putting AMERICA FIRST!

December 11, 2019

10:17 am: Wow! All of our priorities have made it into the final NDAA: Pay Raise for our Troops, Rebuilding our Military, Paid Parental Leave, Border Security, and Space Force! Congress—don't delay this anymore! I will sign this historic defense legislation immediately!

December 12, 2019

7:05 am: No crime!

8:46 am: Very dishonest pols!

10:40 am: Dems Veronica Escobar and Jackson Lee purposely misquoted my call. I said I want you to do us (our Country!) a favor, not me a favor. They know that but decided to LIE in order to make a fraudulent point! Very sad.

11:05 am: I also have constantly asked, "Why aren't Germany, France and other European countries helping Ukraine more? They are the biggest beneficiaries. Why is it always the good ol' United States?" The Radical Left, Do Nothing Democrats, never mention this at their phony hearing!

December 13, 2019

6:51 am: The Republicans House members were fantastic yesterday. It always helps to have a much better case, in fact the Dems have no case at all, but the unity & sheer brilliance of these Republican warriors, all of them, was a beautiful sight to see. Dems had no answers and wanted out!

6:53 am: My Approval Rating in the Republican Party is 95%, a Record. Thank you! #2020Election

7:01 am: Poll numbers have gone through the roof in favor of No Impeachment, especially with Swing States and Independents in Swing States. People have figured out that the Democrats have no case, it is a total Hoax. Even Pelosi admitted yesterday that she began this scam 2 1/2 years ago!

8:42 am: How do you get Impeached when you have done NOTHING wrong (a perfect call), have created the best economy in the history of our Country, rebuilt our Military, fixed the V.A. (Choice!), cut Taxes & Regs, protected your 2nd A, created Jobs, Jobs, Jobs, and soooo much more? Crazy!

7:38 pm: It's not fair that I'm being Impeached when I've done absolutely nothing wrong! The Radical Left, Do Nothing Democrats have become the Party of Hate. They are so bad for our Country!

December 14, 2019

6:26 pm: The last time I spoke to Debbie Dingell was her call thanking me for granting top memorial and funeral service honors for her then just departed husband, long time Congressman John Dingell. Now I watch her ripping me as part of the Democrats Impeachment Hoax. Really pathetic!

8:02 pm: It was my Great Honor to attend the 120th Army-Navy game today in Philadelphia, Pennsylvania! @NavyFB @ArmyWP_Football @ArmyNavyGame

December 15, 2019

1:24 pm: A PERFECT phone call. "Can you do us (not me. Us is referring to our Country) a favor." Then go on to talk about "Country" and "U.S. Attorney General." The Impeachment Hoax is just a continuation of the Witch Hunt which has been going on for 3 years. We will win! #MAGAKAG #2020

2:14 pm: Approval Rating in Republican Party = 95%, a Record! Overall Approval Rating = 51%. Think of where I'd be without the never ending, 24 hour a day, phony Witch Hunt, that started 3 years ago!

7:04 pm: Watch these two great people talk about the Impeachment Hoax. Will be by far the best hour on television!

December 16, 2019

8:54 am: READ THE TRANSCRIPTS! The Impeachment Hoax is the greatest con job in the history of American politics! The Fake News Media, and their partner, the Democrat Party, are working overtime to make life for the United Republican Party, and all it stands for, as difficult as possible!

December 17, 2019

9:51 am: Impeachment Poll numbers are starting to drop like a rock now that people are understanding better what this whole Democrat Scam is all about!

6:48 pm: Democrat "leadership," despite their denials, are putting tremendous pressure on their members to vote yes on this ridiculous

Impeachment. If they vote yes, it will be much easier for Republicans to win in 2020!

10:54 pm: Good marks and reviews on the letter I sent to Pelosi today. She is the worst! No wonder with people like her and Cryin' Chuck Schumer, D.C. has been such a mess for so long—and that includes the previous administration who (and now we know for sure) SPIED on my campaign.

11:10 pm: So, if Comey & the top people in the FBI were dirty cops and cheated on the FISA Court, wouldn't all of these phony cases have to be overturned or dismissed? They went after me with the Fake Dossier, paid for by Crooked Hillary & the DNC, which they illegally presented to FISA…

…They want to Impeach me (I'm not worried!), and yet they were all breaking the law in so many ways. How can they do that and yet impeach a very successful (Economy Plus) President of the United States, who has done nothing wrong? These people are Crazy!

December 18, 2019

7:34 am: Can you believe that I will be impeached today by the Radical Left, Do Nothing Democrats, AND I DID NOTHING WRONG! A terrible Thing. Read the Transcripts. This should never happen to another President again. Say a PRAYER!

December 19, 2019

9:10 am: I got Impeached last night without one Republican vote being cast with the Do Nothing Dems on their continuation of the greatest Witch Hunt in American history. Now the Do Nothing Party want to Do Nothing with the Articles & not deliver them to the Senate, but it's Senate's call!

7:36 pm: The House Democrats were unable to get even a single vote from the Republicans on their Impeachment Hoax. The Republicans have never been so united! The Dem's case is so bad that they don't even want to go to trial!

December 20, 2019

9:12 am: I will be signing our 738 Billion Dollar Defense Spending Bill today. It will include 12 weeks Paid Parental Leave, gives our troops a raise, importantly creates the SPACE FORCE, SOUTHERN BORDER WALL FUNDING, repeals "Cadillac Tax" on Health Plans, raises smoking age to 21! BIG!

4:09 pm: Just had a great call with the President of Brazil, @JairBolsonaro. We discussed many subjects including Trade. The relationship between the United States and Brazil has never been Stronger!

10:30 pm: A total Witch Hunt!

11:46 pm: Plus, never did anything wrong. Read the Transcripts. A Democrat Hoax!

December 21, 2019

2:38 pm: Last night I was so proud to have signed the largest Defense Bill ever. The very vital Space Force was created. New planes, ships, missiles, rockets and equipment of every kind, and all made right here in the USA. Additionally, we got Border Wall (being built) funding. Nice!

3:21 pm: Melania and I send our warmest wishes to Jewish people in the United States, Israel, and across the world as you commence the 8-day celebration of Hanukkah.

5:14 pm: The Democrats and Crooked Hillary paid for & provided a Fake Dossier, with phony information gotten from foreign sources, pushed it to the corrupt media & Dirty Cops, & have now been caught. They spied on my campaign, then tried to cover it up—Just Like Watergate, but bigger!

December 23, 2019

5:13 pm: Nancy Pelosi, who has already lost the House & Speakership once, & is about to lose it again, is doing everything she can to delay the zero Republican vote Articles of Inpeachment. She is trying to take over the Senate, & Cryin' Chuck is trying to take over the trial. No way!…

…What right does Crazy Nancy have to hold up this Senate trial. None! She has a bad case and would rather not have a negative decision. This Witch Hunt must end NOW with a trial in the Senate, or let her default & lose. No more time should be wasted on this Impeachment Scam!

6:25 pm: Wouldn't it be reasonable to assume that Republicans in the Senate should handle the Impeachment Hoax in the exact same manner as Democrats in the House handled their recent partisan scam? Why would it be different for Republicans than it was for the Radical Left Democrats?

7:17 pm: STOCK MARKET CLOSES AT ALL-TIME HIGH! What a great time for the Radical Left, Do Nothing Democrats to Impeach your favorite President, especially since he has not done anything wrong!

December 24, 2019

7:10 am: Everything we're seeing from Speaker Pelosi and Senator Schumer suggests that they're in real doubt about the evidence they've brought forth so far not being good enough, and are very, very urgently seeking a way to find some more evidence. The only way to make this work is to…

…mount some kind of public pressure to demand witnesses, but McConnell has the votes and he can run this trial anyway he wants to. @brithume @foxandfriends

5:32 pm: 187 new Federal Judges have been confirmed under the Trump Administration, including two great new United States Supreme Court Justices. We are shattering every record! Read all about this in "The Long Game," a great new book by @senatemajldr Mitch McConnell. Amazing story!

December 25, 2019

7:26 am: MERRY CHRISTMAS!

5:29 pm: Governor Gavin N has done a really bad job on taking care of the homeless population in California. If he can't fix the problem, the Federal Govt. will get involved!

10:12 pm: Why should Crazy Nancy Pelosi, just because she has a slight majority in the House, be allowed to Impeach the President of the United States? Got ZERO Republican votes, there was no crime, the call with Ukraine was perfect, with "no pressure." She said it must be "bipartisan...

...& overwhelming," but this Scam Impeachment was neither. Also, very unfair with no Due Process, proper representation, or witnesses. Now Pelosi is demanding everything the Republicans weren't alowed to have in the House. Dems want to run majority Republican Senate. Hypocrites!

December 26, 2019

7:18 am: The Radical Left, Do Nothing Democrats said they wanted to RUSH everything through to the Senate because "President Trump is a threat to National Security" (they are vicious, will say anything!), but now they don't want to go fast anymore, they want to go very slowly. Liars!

9:36 am: Despite all of the great success that our Country has had over the last 3 years, it makes it much more difficult to deal with foreign leaders (and others) when I am having to constantly defend myself against the Do Nothing Democrats & their bogus Impeachment Scam. Bad for USA!

December 27, 2019

11:37 am: Thank YOU Indian Country for being such an IMPORTANT part of the American story! I recently signed 3 bills to support tribal sovereignty...

…and native culture—S.216/Spokane Tribe, S.256/Native Languages and NDAA Sec. 2870 officially recognizing Little Shell Tribe of Chippewa Indians. My great honor to do so!

December 28, 2019

8:33 am: California and New York must do something about their TREMENDOUS Homeless problems. They are setting records! If their Governors can't handle the situation, which they should be able to do very easily, they must call and "politely" ask for help. Would be so easy with competence!

3:45 pm: Crazy Nancy Pelosi should spend more time in her her decaying city and less time on the Impeachment Hoax!

December 30, 2019

9:28 am: Thank you to highly respected Jewish leader Dov Hikind for his wonderful statements about me this morning on @foxandfriends.

December 31, 2019

11:51 am: Very good meeting on the Middle East, the Military, and Trade. Heading back to The Southern White House (Mar-a-Lago!). Updates throughout the day.

12:34 pm: Read the Transcripts!

Election Campaign—2017 News Quotes

Response to a question from David Muir of ABC News, January 26, 2017.
Source: https://www.telegraph.co.uk/news/2017/01/26/
full-transcript-president-donald-trumps-interview-abc-news/

"I would've won the popular vote if I was campaigning for the popular vote. I would've gone to California where I didn't go at all. I would've gone to New York, where I didn't campaign at all.

"I would've gone to a couple of places that I didn't go to. And I would've won that much easier than winning the Electoral College. But as you know, the Electoral College is all that matters. It doesn't make any difference. So, I would've won very, very easily. But it's a different form of winning. You would campaign much differently. You would have a totally different campaign.

"So, but, you're just asking a question. I would've easily won the popular vote, much easier, in my opinion, than winning the Electoral College. I ended up going to 19 different states. I went to the state of Maine four times for one. I needed one.

"I went to M—I got it, by the way. But it turned out I didn't need it because we ended up winning by a massive amount, 306. I needed 270. We got 306. You and everybody said, 'There's no way you get to 270.' I mean, your network said and almost everybody said, 'There's no way you can get to.' So, I went to Maine four times. I went to various places. And that's the beauty of the Electoral College. With

367

that being said, if you look at voter registration, you look at the dead people that are registered to vote who vote, you look at people that are registered in two states, you look at all of these different things that are happening with registration. You take a look at those registration for, you're gonna s—Find, and we're gonna do an investigation on it."

Response to a question from David Muir of ABC News, January 26, 2017.
Source: https://www.telegraph.co.uk/news/2017/01/26/
full-transcript-president-donald-trumps-interview-abc-news/

"In fact, I heard one of the other side, they were saying it's not three to five. It's not three to five. I said, 'Well, Mr. Trump is talking about registration, tell.' He said, 'You know we don't wanna talk about registration.' They don't wanna talk about registration.

"You have people that are registered who are dead, who are illegals, who are in two states. You have people registered in two states. They're registered in a New York and a New Jersey. They vote twice. There are millions of votes, in my opinion. Now."

Response to a question from David Muir of ABC News, January 26, 2017.
Source: https://www.telegraph.co.uk/news/2017/01/26/
full-transcript-president-donald-trumps-interview-abc-news/

"Of course, and I want the voting process to be legitimate."

Response to a question from David Muir of ABC News, January 26, 2017.
Source: https://www.telegraph.co.uk/news/2017/01/26/
full-transcript-president-donald-trumps-interview-abc-news/

"We're gonna launch an investigation to find out. And then the next time—And I will say this, of those votes cast, none of 'em come to me. None of 'em come to me. They would all be for the other side. None of 'em come to me. But when you look at the people that are registered: dead, illegal, and two states—And some cases maybe three states, we have a lot to look into."

Response to a question from David Muir of ABC News, January 26, 2017.
Source: https://www.telegraph.co.uk/news/2017/01/26/
full-transcript-president-donald-trumps-interview-abc-news/

"David [Muir of ABC News] and I also say this, if I was going for the popular vote I would've won easily. But I would've been in California and New York. I wouldn't have been in Maine. I wouldn't have been in Iowa. I wouldn't have been in Nebraska and all of those states that I had to win in order to win this. I would've been in New York; I would've been in California. I never even went there."

Response to a question from David Muir of ABC News, January 26, 2017.
Source: https://www.telegraph.co.uk/news/2017/01/26/
full-transcript-president-donald-trumps-interview-abc-news/

"No, no. We're looking at it for the next time. No, no, you have to understand, I had a tremendous victory, one of the great victories ever. In terms of counties I think the most ever or just about the most ever. When you look at a map it's all red. Red meaning us, Republicans.

"One of the greatest victories ever. But, again, I ran for the Electoral College. I didn't run for the popular vote. What I'm saying is if there are these problems that many people agree with me that there might be. Look, Barack Obama, if you look back eight years ago when he first ran, he was running for office in Chicago, for we needed Chicago vote.

"And he was laughing at the system because he knew all of those votes were going to him. You look at Philadelphia, you look at what's going on in Philadelphia. But take a look at the tape of Barack Obama who wrote me, by the way, a very beautiful letter in the drawer of the desk. Very beautiful. And I appreciate it. But look at what he said, it's on tape. Look at what he said about voting in Chicago eight years ago. It's not changed. It hasn't changed, believe me. Chicago. Look what's going on in Chicago. It's only gotten worse.

"But he [Obama] was smiling and laughing about the vote in Chicago. Now, once he became President he didn't do that. All of a sudden it became this is the foundation of our country. So, here's the point, you have a lot of stuff going on possibly. I say probably. But possibly. We're gonna get to the bottom of it.

"And then we're gonna make sure it doesn't happen again. If people are registered wrongly, if illegals are registered to vote, which they are, if dead people are registered to vote and voting, which they do. There are some. I don't know how many. We're gonna try finding that out and the other categories that we talk about, double states where they're registered in two states, we're gonna get to the bottom of it because we have to stop it. Because I agree, so important. But the other side is trying to downplay this. Now, I'll say this—I think that if that didn't happen, first of all, would, would be a great thing if it didn't happen. But I believe it did happen. And I believe a part of the vote would've been much different."

Video clip shown on CBS News, April 30, 2017.

Source: https://www.cbsnews.com/news/face-the-nation-transcript-april-30-2017-president-trump/

"Congratulations to everybody. We all deserve it. This was a tough go, and it was really fun. And I just want to congratulate everybody.

"And now we are going to do a great job for the American people. Thank you."

Response to a question from Peter Baker of *The New York Times*, July 19, 2017.

Source: https://www.nytimes.com/2017/07/19/us/politics/trump-interview-transcript.html

"That's all I did, was make those speeches about her [Hillary Clinton]. I don't think I added anything much different than I had been doing. I've made some very strong speeches about the corrupt emails. The 33,000 emails being deleted and bleached, and all of the things she [Hillary Clinton] was doing. I would make those speeches routinely. There wasn't much I could say about Hillary Clinton that was worse than what I was already saying."

Response to a question from Peter Baker of *The New York Times*, July 19, 2017.

Source: https://www.nytimes.com/2017/07/19/us/politics/trump-interview-transcript.html

"I mean, I was talking about, she [Hillary Clinton] deleted and bleached, which nobody does because of the cost. How she got away with that one, I have no idea. Thirty-three thousand emails. I talked about the back of the plane, I talked about the uranium deal, I talked about the speech that Russia gave Clinton—Five hundred thousand dollars while she was Secretary of State—The husband. I talked about the back of the plane. Honestly, Peter [Baker of *The New York Times*], I mean, unless somebody said that she shot somebody in the back, there wasn't much I could add to my repertoire."

Response to a question from Maggie Haberman of *The New York Times*, July 19, 2017.
Source: https://www.nytimes.com/2017/07/19/us/politics/trump-interview-transcript.html

"You know, you can only say many things. After that it gets boring, OK? How can it be better than deleting emails after you get a subpoena from the United States Congress? Guys go to jail for that, when they delete an email from a civil case. Here, she [Hillary Clinton] gets an email from the United States Congress—[Peter Baker of *The New York Times* interrupts.]"

Election Campaign—2017 Tweets

March 4, 2017

6:35 am: Terrible! Just found out that Obama had my "wires tapped" in Trump Tower just before the victory. Nothing found. This is McCarthyism!

6:52 am: I'd bet a good lawyer could make a great case out of the fact that President Obama was tapping my phones in October, just prior to Election!

March 20, 2017

8:15 am: What about all of the contact with the Clinton campaign and the Russians? Also, is it true that the DNC would not let the FBI in to look?

April 2, 2017

8:34 am: The real story turns out to be SURVEILLANCE and LEAKING! Find the leakers.

April 16, 2017

8:07 am: I did what was an almost an impossible thing to do for a Republican-easily won the Electoral College! Now Tax Returns are brought up again?

8:13 am: Someone should look into who paid for the small organized rallies yesterday. The election is over!

May 2, 2017

9:51 am to 10:06 am: FBI Director Comey was the best thing that ever happened to Hillary Clinton in that he gave her a free pass for many bad deeds! The phony.

…Trump/Russia story was an excuse used by the Democrats as justification for losing the election. Perhaps Trump just ran a great campaign?

May 8, 2017

6:57 am: General Flynn was given the highest security clearance by the Obama Administration—but the Fake News seldom likes talking about that.

5:46 pm: The Russia-Trump collusion story is a total hoax, when will this taxpayer funded charade end?

May 10, 2017

7:56 am: The Roger Stone report on @CNN is false—Fake News. Have not spoken to Roger in a long time—had nothing to do with my decision.

May 11, 2017

3:35 pm: Russia must be laughing up their sleeves watching as the U.S. tears itself apart over a Democrat EXCUSE for losing the election.

May 12, 2017

6:51 am: Again, the story that there was collusion between the Russians & Trump campaign was fabricated by Dems as an excuse for losing the election.

June 15, 2017

5:55 am: They made up a phony collusion with the Russians story, found zero proof, so now they go for obstruction of justice on the phony story. Nice

6:57 am: You are witnessing the single greatest WITCH HUNT in American political history—led by some very bad and conflicted people! #MAGA

June 16, 2017

6:53 am: After 7 months of investigations & committee hearings about my "collusion with the Russians," nobody has been able to show any proof. Sad!

June 22, 2017

8:22 am: By the way, if Russia was working so hard on the 2016 Election, it all took place during the Obama Admin. Why didn't they stop them?

June 26, 2017

7:59 am to 8:05 am: The real story is that President Obama did NOTH-ING after being informed in August about Russian meddling. With 4 months looking at Russia...

under a magnifying glass, they have zero "tapes" of T people colluding. There is no collusion & no obstruction. I should be given apology!

July 9, 2017

6:31 am: I strongly pressed President Putin twice about Russian meddling in our election. He vehemently denied it. I've already given my opinion...

6:50 am to 7:06 am: Putin & I discussed forming an impenetrable Cyber Security unit so that election hacking, & many other negative things, will be guarded...

...and safe. Questions were asked about why the CIA & FBI had to ask the DNC 13 times for their SERVER, and were rejected, still don't...

...have it. Fake News said 17 intel agencies when actually 4 (had to apologize). Why did Obama do NOTHING when he had info before election?

7:45 pm: The fact that President Putin and I discussed a Cyber Security unit doesn't mean I think it can happen. It can't-but a ceasefire can, & did!

July 22, 2017

7:00 am: My son Donald openly gave his e-mails to the media & authorities whereas Crooked Hillary Clinton deleted (& acid washed) her 33,000 e-mails!

7:10 am: In all fairness to Anthony Scaramucci, he wanted to endorse me 1st, before the Republican Primaries started, but didn't think I was running!

July 29, 2017

6:07 am: In other words, Russia was against Trump in the 2016 Election—and why not, I want strong military & low oil prices. Witch Hunt! https://t.co/mMSxj4Su5z

Aug 19, 2017

6:33 am: I want to thank Steve Bannon for his service. He came to the campaign during my run against Crooked Hillary Clinton—it was great! Thanks S

September 22, 2017

5:44 am: The Russia hoax continues, now it's ads on Facebook. What about the totally biased and dishonest Media coverage in favor of Crooked Hillary?

October 19, 2017

6:56 am: Workers of firm involved with the discredited and Fake Dossier take the 5th. Who paid for it, Russia, the FBI or the Dems (or all)?

October 21, 2017

2:59 pm: Officials behind the now discredited "Dossier" plead the Fifth. Justice Department and/or FBI should immediately release who paid for it.

October 25, 2017

6:21 am: "Clinton campaign & DNC paid for research that led to the anti-Trump Fake News Dossier. The victim here is the President." @FoxNews

October 27, 2017

8:33 am: It is now commonly agreed, after many months of COSTLY looking, that there was NO collusion between Russia and Trump. Was collusion with HC!

October 29, 2017

9:48 am: All of this "Russia" talk right when the Republicans are making their big push for historic Tax Cuts & Reform. Is this coincidental? NOT!

October 30, 2017

6:37 am: Report out that Obama Campaign paid $972,000 to Fusion GPS. The firm also got $12,400,000 (really?) from DNC. Nobody knows who OK'd!

9:28 am: …Also, there is NO COLLUSION!

November 2, 2017

7:39 pm to 7:48 pm: Donna Brazile just stated the DNC RIGGED the system to illegally steal the Primary from Bernie Sanders. Bought and paid for by Crooked H…

…This is real collusion and dishonesty. Major violation of Campaign Finance Laws and Money Laundering—where is our Justice Department?

November 3, 2017

9:28 am: Bernie Sanders supporters have every right to be apoplectic of the complete theft of the Dem primary by Crooked Hillary!

9:29 am: I always felt I would be running and winning against Bernie Sanders, not Crooked H, without cheating, I was right.

11:09 am: The rigged Dem Primary, one of the biggest political stories in years, got ZERO coverage on Fake News Network TV last night. Disgraceful!

November 8, 2017

1:17 pm: Congratulations to all of the "DEPLORABLES" and the millions of people who gave us a MASSIVE (304-227) Electoral College landslide victory!

November 29, 2017

8:03 pm: The House of Representatives seeks contempt citations(?) against the JusticeDepartment and the FBI for withholding key documents and an FBI witness which could shed light on surveillance of associates of Donald Trump. Big stuff. Deep State. Give this information NOW! @FoxNews

December 8, 2017

12:41 am: I fulfilled my campaign promise—others didn't! https://t.co/bYdaOHmPVJ

December 12, 2017

7:10 am: Despite thousands of hours wasted and many millions of dollars spent, the Democrats have been unable to show any collusion with Russia—so now they are moving on to the false accusations and fabricated stories of women who I don't know and/or have never met. FAKE NEWS!

Election Campaign—2018 News Quotes

Response to a question from Bret Baier of FOX News, June 12, 2018.
Source: https://www.youtube.com/watch?v=zogD8bnGJu4

"No, I know but he [Russian President Vladimir Putin] didn't respect our leadership. He didn't respect it and so—But this wasn't me. You know people say, 'Well, look what he [Putin] did.' He did it to [then-U.S. President Barack] Obama. Obama should not have allowed that to happen. Even with the voter stuff. Supposedly the FBI went to Obama. They told him about it. He didn't do anything about it."

Remarks at a rally in Tampa, Florida, July 31, 2018.
Source: https://www.tampabay.com/florida-politics/buzz/2018/08/01/
heres-a-full-transcript-of-president-trumps-speech-from-his-tampa-rally/

"We started off; it was a small group. They said it couldn't be done. It was actually done quite easily. We won quite handily. We were never left center stage.

"You know what that means, right? The debates. We never left center stage. And I said, 'I always want odd numbers.' Because I want to be in the center. I didn't want to be tied for the center. Does everybody understand?

"But we never, we never left center stage."

"And I'll tell you. Corey [Lewandowski], David [Bossie], Ivanka, Lara, Eric, Don Jr., all of them, they were fantastic. They were fantastic.

"And I have to say, our First Lady is home watching. Look at all those cameras right there. She's home watching.

"And everybody loves Melania. They love Melania.

"Great. Doing a fantastic thing. She's doing a fantastic job."

Remarks at a rally in Tampa, Florida, July 31, 2018.
Source: https://www.tampabay.com/florida-politics/buzz/2018/08/01/
heres-a-full-transcript-of-president-trumps-speech-from-his-tampa-rally/

"In the past, politicians ran for office pledging to crack down on unfair trade. They never did anything about it. Only to get elected, and they just didn't do anything.

"The United States was allowed to truly get ripped off.

"But we're not going to let that happen. I'm not like other politicians. You've seen what happens. I've kept my promises."

Remarks at a rally in Tampa, Florida, July 31, 2018.
Source: https://www.tampabay.com/florida-politics/buzz/2018/08/01/
heres-a-full-transcript-of-president-trumps-speech-from-his-tampa-rally/

"But we're turning it around. Remember I said it's awfully early to be thinking this, but I always think it, remember the attack on Merry Christmas, they're not attacking it anymore. Everyone is happy to say Merry Christmas, right? Merry Christmas, Merry Christmas, Merry Christmas. That was under siege. You have these big department stores they say, 'Happy Holidays.' I say, 'Where is the Merry Christmas?' Now they're all putting up Merry Christmas again and that's because, only because of our campaign.

"And by the way, the evangelicals and Paula White, Pastor Paula White, the evangelicals have been so amazing to us. They came out and they voted 84% and doubled and tripled the numbers that ever voted in an election before. We love the evangelical Christians."

Response to a question from the Associated Press[24], published October 17, 2018[25].
Source: https://www.cnbc.com/2018/10/17/read-the-transcript-of-aps-interview-with-president-trump.html

"The midterms are very tough for anybody the opposite of President, for whatever reason, nobody has been able to say."

Response to a question from the Associated Press[26], published October 17, 2018[27].
Source: https://www.cnbc.com/2018/10/17/read-the-transcript-of-aps-interview-with-president-trump.html

"No, I think I'm helping people. Look, I'm 48 and 1 in the primaries, and actually it's much higher than that because I endorsed a lot of people that were successful that people don't even talk about. But many of

---

24 AP White House reporters Catherine Lucey, Zeke Miller, and Jonathan Lemire conducted this interview. However, the transcript does not indicate which reporter asked President Trump which question.

25 The interview was conducted by the AP before the midterm elections of October 16, 2018. However, it was published by CNBC on October 17, 2018.

26 AP White House reporters Catherine Lucey, Zeke Miller, and Jonathan Lemire conducted this interview. However, the transcript does not indicate which reporter asked President Trump which question.

27 The interview was conducted by the AP before the midterm elections of October 16, 2018. However, it was published by CNBC on October 17, 2018.

those 48, as you know, were people that had no chance, in some cases. We look at Florida, you look at [Dan] Donovan[28] in Staten Island. He was losing by 10 points, I endorsed him and he won. I could give you a long list of names. Look at Georgia governor of Georgia. And many, many races. And I will say that we have a very big impact. I don't believe anybody's ever had this kind of an impact. They would say that in the old days that if you got the support of a president or if you've got the support of somebody it would be nice to have, but it meant nothing, zero. Like literally zero. Some of the people I've endorsed have gone up 40 and 50 points just on the endorsement."

Response to a question from the Associated Press[29], published October 17, 2018[30].

Source: https://www.cnbc.com/2018/10/17/read-the-transcript-of-aps-interview-with-president-trump.html

"So, I think we're going to do well. Look, it feels to me very much like '16. I was going out and making speeches and I was getting tens of thousands of people. And I was getting literally tens of thousands of people, also, more than Hillary [Clinton] in the same location. And I said, 'Why am I going to lose?' I mean, I go out, I make a speech like I have, you know, 25 times more people than she gets. And I didn't need Beyonce to get them. I didn't have to have, you know, entertainment and entertainers to get them. And then they'd all leave before she made the speech after the entertainer was finished. Honestly, it feels very much like it did in '16. Now, I'm not sure that that's right. And I'm not running. I mean, there are many people that have said to me, 'Sir, I will never ever,' you on the trail when I'm talking to people backstage etcetera, 'I will never ever go and vote in the midterms because you're not running and I don't think you like Congress.' Well, I do like

---

28 At the time of President Trump's speech, Congressman Dan Donovan was a Republican representing New York. He was defeated by Democrat Max Rose in the 2018 election; thus, Donovan's term ended in January 2019.

29 AP White House reporters Catherine Lucey, Zeke Miller, and Jonathan Lemire conducted this interview. However, the transcript does not indicate which reporter asked President Trump which question.

30 The interview was conducted by the AP before the midterm elections of October 16, 2018. However, it was published by CNBC on October 17, 2018.

Congress because I think, and when I say Congress, I like the Republicans that support me in Congress. We've had tremendous support. I mean, we've got the taxes with 100% Republican votes and we don't really have much of a majority. You know when you say majority, I always say, 'If somebody has a cold, we have to delay the vote.'"

Response to a question from the Associated Press[31], published October 17, 2018[32].

Source: https://www.cnbc.com/2018/10/17/read-the-transcript-of-aps-interview-with-president-trump.html

"We have a witch hunt now going on, and I handle it very well, and there was no collusion. Everyone knows it. It's, people laugh. People are laughing at the concept of it."

Response to a question from the Associated Press[33], published October 17, 2018[34].

Source: https://www.cnbc.com/2018/10/17/read-the-transcript-of-aps-interview-with-president-trump.html

"We'll see how that works out. You know that's in process. It's a tremendous waste of time for the President of the United States. To think that I would be even thinking about using Russia to help me win Idaho. We're using Russia to help me win the great state of Iowa or anywhere else is the most preposterous, embarrassing thing. And I will say that the Democrats know it and they wink. They're all laughing. And you know if I often hear that Russia likes to sow discord. The word is sow, an old English term. They like to sow chaos and

---

31 AP White House reporters Catherine Lucey, Zeke Miller, and Jonathan Lemire conducted this interview. However, the transcript does not indicate which reporter asked President Trump which question.

32 The interview was conducted by the AP before the midterm elections of October 16, 2018. However, it was published by CNBC on October 17, 2018.

33 AP White House reporters Catherine Lucey, Zeke Miller, and Jonathan Lemire conducted this interview. However, the transcript does not indicate which reporter asked President Trump which question.

34 The interview was conducted by the AP before the midterm elections of October 16, 2018. However, it was published by CNBC on October 17, 2018.

discord. Well, if that's the case, you gave it to them on a silver platter because this is ridiculous. This was an excuse made by the Democrats for the reason they lost the Electoral College, which gives them a big advantage, a big advantage. Very different than the popular vote. The popular vote would be much easier to win if you were campaigning on it. You know, it's like running the 100-yard dash versus a 10-mile run. You train differently. Nobody explained that to Hillary Clinton, by the way. Someday she'll figure it out. But winning the Electoral College is a tremendous advantage for the Democrats. And this was an excuse for how they lost the election. How they lost an election they should have won. And one of the reasons they lost because I happened to be a great candidate. And another reason they lost is that Hillary forgot to campaign in Wisconsin, Michigan, Pennsylvania. And I guess she needed a lot more time in North Carolina, a lot more time in South Carolina and a lot more time in a place called—A beautiful, sunny, wonderful place called Florida."

Response to a question from Chris Wallace of FOX News, November 18, 2018.

Source: https://www.youtube.com/watch?v=rMgJnnG-Nql

"From the day I announced, I was looked at as a candidate with nothing, no proof, with phony people like [Andrew] McCabe and [Peter] Strzok[35] and his [Strzok's] lover—You had Lisa Page, his lover. These people were looking at me. They wanted an insurance policy just in case I won or Hillary [Clinton] lost, and this was the insurance policy. It's a scam. There was no collusion whatsoever, and the whole thing is a scam."

Response to a question from Chris Wallace of FOX News, November 18, 2018.

Source: https://www.youtube.com/watch?v=rMgJnnG-Nql

"No, no, no, not my team. I'm preparing written answers. My, I, I'm the one that does the answering."

---

35   Andrew McCabe and Peter Strzok were both FBI officials fired by the Trump Administration.

Response to a question from Chris Wallace of FOX News, November 18, 2018.
Source: https://www.youtube.com/watch?v=rMgJnnG-Nql

"I did nothing wrong."

Response to a question from Chris Wallace of FOX News, November 18, 2018.
Source: https://www.youtube.com/watch?v=rMgJnnG-Nql

"Well, there was no obstruction of justice."

Response to a question from Chris Wallace of FOX News, November 18, 2018.
Source: https://www.youtube.com/watch?v=rMgJnnG-Nql

"I think we've wasted enough time on this witch hunt and the answer is probably, we're finished."

Response to a question from Chris Wallace of FOX News, November 18, 2018.
Source: https://www.youtube.com/watch?v=rMgJnnG-Nql

"We gave very, very complete answers to a lot of questions that I shouldn't have even been asked and I think that should solve the problem. I hope it solves the problem. If it doesn't, you know, I'll be told and we'll make a decision at that time. But probably this is the end."

Response to a question from Chris Wallace of FOX News, November 18, 2018.
Source: https://www.youtube.com/watch?v=rMgJnnG-Nql

"Are you ready? I won the Senate, and that's historic too, because if you look at presidents in the White House it's almost never happened where you won a seat. We won, we now have 53 as opposed to 51 and we have 53 great Senators in the U.S. Senate. We won. That's a tremendous victory. Nobody talks about that. That's a far greater victory than it is for the other side. Number two, I wasn't on the ballot. I wasn't."

Response to a question from Chris Wallace of FOX News, November 18, 2018.
Source: https://www.youtube.com/watch?v=rMgJnnG-Nql

"But I have people and you see the polls, how good they are, I have people that won't vote unless I'm on the ballot, OK? And I wasn't on the ballot.

"And almost everybody that I won, I think they said it was 10 out of 11.

"And I won against [former U.S.] President [Barack] Obama and Oprah Winfrey and Michelle Obama in a great state called Georgia for the governor."

Response to a question from Chris Wallace of FOX News, November 18, 2018.
Source: https://www.youtube.com/watch?v=rMgJnnG-Nql

"Look at Florida. I went down to Florida. Rick Scott[36] won, and he won by a lot. I don't know what happened to all those votes that disappeared at the very end. And if I didn't put a spotlight on that election before it got down to the 12,500 votes, he would have lost that election, OK? In my opinion he would have lost. They would have taken that election away from him. Rick Scott won Florida. You'd have to say, excuse me, a man named Ron DeSantis is now your governor, your new governor of Florida.

"A wonderful man named [Mike] DeWine is your governor of the great state of Ohio. Remember what they used to say before my election? You cannot win unless you win Ohio. I won Ohio. We had a tremendous set of victories. You look at the victories."

Response to a question from Chris Wallace of FOX News, November 18, 2018.
Source: https://www.youtube.com/watch?v=rMgJnnG-Nql

"I didn't run. I wasn't running. My name wasn't on the ballot. There are many people that think, 'I don't like Congress,' that like me a lot. I get

---

36 Rick Scott, a Republican, was the governor of Florida from 2011 to 2019; he became a U.S. Senator in 2019.

it all the time, 'Sir, we'll never vote unless you're on the ballot.' I get it all the time. People are saying, 'Sir, I will never vote unless you're on the ballot.' I say, 'No, no, go and vote.' 'Well, what do you mean?' As much as I try and convince people to go vote, I'm not on the ballot."

Election Campaign—2018 Tweets

January 10, 2018

10:14 am: The single greatest Witch Hunt in American history continues. There was no collusion, everybody including the Dems knows there was no collusion, & yet on and on it goes. Russia & the world is laughing at the stupidity they are witnessing. Republicans should finally take control!

January 11, 2018

7:33 am: "House votes on controversial FISA ACT today." This is the act that may have been used, with the help of the discredited and phony Dossier, to so badly surveil and abuse the Trump Campaign by the previous administration and others?

February 3, 2018

7:40 pm to 7:53 pm: "The four page memo released Friday reports the disturbing fact about how the FBI and FISA appear to have been used to influence the 2016 election and its aftermath...The FBI failed to inform the FISA court that the Clinton campaign had funded the dossier...the FBI became...

...a tool of anti-Trump political actors. This is unacceptable in a democracy and ought to alarm anyone who wants the FBI to be a nonpartisan

385

enforcer of the law...The FBI wasn't straight with Congress, as it hid most of these facts from investigators." Wall Street Journal

February 10, 2018

10:20 am: According to the @nytimes, a Russian sold phony secrets on "Trump" to the U.S. Asking price was $10 million, brought down to $1 million to be paid over time. I hope people are now seeing & understanding what is going on here. It is all now starting to come out—DRAIN THE SWAMP!

10:33 am: Peoples lives are being shattered and destroyed by a mere allegation. Some are true and some are false. Some are old and some are new. There is no recovery for someone falsely accused—life and career are gone. Is there no such thing any longer as Due Process?

February 16, 2018

3:18 pm: Russia started their anti-US campaign in 2014, long before I announced that I would run for President. The results of the election were not impacted. The Trump campaign did nothing wrong—no collusion!

February 17, 2018

2:26 pm: "Charges Deal Don A Big Win," written by Michael Goodwin of the @nypost, succinctly states that "the Russians had no impact on the election results." There was no Collusion with the Trump Campaign. "She lost the old-fashioned way, by being a terrible candidate. Case closed."

2:36 pm: Deputy A.G. Rod Rosenstein stated at the News Conference: "There is no allegation in the indictment that any American was a knowing participant in this illegal activity. There is no allegation in the indictment that the charged conduct altered the outcome of the 2016 election.

11:22 pm: General McMaster forgot to say that the results of the 2016 election were not impacted or changed by the Russians and that the only Collusion was between Russia and Crooked H, the DNC and the Dems. Remember the Dirty Dossier, Uranium, Speeches, Emails and the Podesta Company!

February 18, 2018

7:33 am: I never said Russia did not meddle in the election, I said "it may be Russia, or China or another country or group, or it may be a 400 pound genius sitting in bed and playing with his computer." The Russian "hoax" was that the Trump campaign colluded with Russia—it never did!

7:43 am: Now that Adam Schiff is starting to blame President Obama for Russian meddling in the election, he is probably doing so as yet another excuse that the Democrats, lead by their fearless leader, Crooked Hillary Clinton, lost the 2016 election. But wasn't I a great candidate?

8:11 am: If it was the GOAL of Russia to create discord, disruption and chaos within the U.S. then, with all of the Committee Hearings, Investigations and Party hatred, they have succeeded beyond their wildest dreams. They are laughing their asses off in Moscow. Get smart America!

February 27, 2018

7:49 am: WITCH HUNT!

March 17, 2018

7:12 pm: The Mueller probe should never have been started in that there was no collusion and there was no crime. It was based on fraudulent activities and a Fake Dossier paid for by Crooked Hillary and the DNC, and improperly used in FISA COURT for surveillance of my campaign. WITCH HUNT!

March 23, 2018

5:07 am: House Intelligence Committee votes to release final report. FINDINGS: (1) No evidence provided of Collusion between Trump

Campaign & Russia. (2) The Obama Administrations Post election response was insufficient. (3) Clapper provided inconsistent testimony on media contacts.

March 25, 2018

6:40 am to 6:49 am: Many lawyers and top law firms want to represent me in the Russia case...don't believe the Fake News narrative that it is hard to find a lawyer who wants to take this on. Fame & fortune will NEVER be turned down by a lawyer, though some are conflicted. Problem is that a new...

...lawyer or law firm will take months to get up to speed (if for no other reason than they can bill more), which is unfair to our great country—and I am very happy with my existing team. Besides, there was NO COLLUSION with Russia, except by Crooked Hillary and the Dems!

April 15, 2018

6:42 am: Unbelievably, James Comey states that Polls, where Crooked Hillary was leading, were a factor in the handling (stupidly) of the Clinton Email probe. In other words, he was making decisions based on the fact that he thought she was going to win, and he wanted a job. Slimeball!

6:57 am: The big questions in Comey's badly reviewed book aren't answered like, how come he gave up Classified Information (jail), why did he lie to Congress (jail), why did the DNC refuse to give Server to the FBI (why didn't they TAKE it), why the phony memos, McCabe's $700,000 & more?

April 27, 2018

9:04 pm: House Intelligence Committee rules that there was NO COLLUSION between the Trump Campaign and Russia. As I have been saying all along, it is all a big Hoax by the Democrats based on payments and lies. There should never have been a Special Councel appointed. Witch Hunt!

May 1, 2018

5:47 am: So disgraceful that the questions concerning the Russian Witch Hunt were "leaked" to the media. No questions on Collusion. Oh, I see…you have a made up, phony crime, Collusion, that never existed, and an investigation begun with illegally leaked classified information. Nice!

May 18, 2018

5:24 am: "Apparently the DOJ put a Spy in the Trump Campaign. This has never been done before and by any means necessary, they are out to frame Donald Trump for crimes he didn't commit." David Asman @LouDobbs @GreggJarrett Really bad stuff!

8:50 am: Reports are there was indeed at least one FBI representative implanted, for political purposes, into my campaign for president. It took place very early on, and long before the phony Russia Hoax became a "hot" Fake News story. If true—all time biggest political scandal!

May 19, 2018

4:27 pm: If the FBI or DOJ was infiltrating a campaign for the benefit of another campaign, that is a really big deal. Only the release or review of documents that the House Intelligence Committee (also, Senate Judiciary) is asking for can give the conclusive answers. Drain the Swamp!

May 20, 2018

8:04 am: Things are really getting ridiculous. The Failing and Crooked (but not as Crooked as Hillary Clinton) @nytimes has done a long & boring story indicating that the World's most expensive Witch Hunt has found nothing on Russia & me so now they are looking at the rest of the World!

8:11 am to 8:19 am: …At what point does this soon to be $20,000,000 Witch Hunt, composed of 13 Angry and Heavily Conflicted

Democrats and two people who have worked for Obama for 8 years, STOP! They have found no Collussion with Russia, No Obstruction, but they aren't looking at the corruption…

…in the Hillary Clinton Campaign where she deleted 33,000 Emails, got $145,000,000 while Secretary of State, paid McCabes wife $700,000 (and got off the FBI hook along with Terry M) and so much more. Republicans and real Americans should start getting tough on this Scam.

8:29 am: Now that the Witch Hunt has given up on Russia and is looking at the rest of the World, they should easily be able to take it into the Mid-Term Elections where they can put some hurt on the Republican Party. Don't worry about Dems FISA Abuse, missing Emails or Fraudulent Dossier!

8:37 am: What ever happened to the Server, at the center of so much Corruption, that the Democratic National Committee REFUSED to hand over to the hard charging (except in the case of Democrats) FBI? They broke into homes & offices early in the morning, but were afraid to take the Server?

9:04 am: …and why hasn't the Podesta brother been charged and arrested, like others, after being forced to close down his very large and successful firm? Is it because he is a VERY well connected Democrat working in the Swamp of Washington, D.C.?

May 22, 2018

8:13 pm: If the person placed very early into my campaign wasn't a SPY put there by the previous Administration for political purposes, how come such a seemingly massive amount of money was paid for services rendered—many times higher than normal…

…Follow the money! The spy was there early in the campaign and yet never reported Collusion with Russia, because there was no Collusion. He was only there to spy for political reasons and to help Crooked Hillary win—just like they did to Bernie Sanders, who got duped!

May 23, 2018

5:54 am: Look how things have turned around on the Criminal Deep State. They go after Phony Collusion with Russia, a made up Scam, and end up getting caught in a major SPY scandal the likes of which this country may never have seen before! What goes around, comes around!

6:00 am: SPYGATE could be one of the biggest political scandals in history!

6:33 am: "Trump should be happy that the FBI was SPYING on his campaign" No, James Clapper, I am not happy. Spying on a campaign would be illegal, and a scandal to boot!

May 25, 2018

7:04 am: The Democrats are now alluding to the the concept that having an Informant placed in an opposing party's campaign is different than having a Spy, as illegal as that may be. But what about an "Informant" who is paid a fortune and who "sets up" way earlier than the Russian Hoax?

Can anyone even imagine having Spies placed in a competing campaign, by the people and party in absolute power, for the sole purpose of political advantage and gain? And to think that the party in question, even with the expenditure of far more money, LOST!

"Everyone knows there was a Spy, and in fact the people who were involved in the Spying are admitting that there was a Spy...Widespread Spying involving multiple people." Mollie Hemingway, The Federalist Senior Editor But the corrupt Mainstream Media hates this monster story!

May 24, 2018

7:21 am: Clapper has now admitted that there was Spying in my campaign. Large dollars were paid to the Spy, far beyond normal. Starting to look like one of the biggest political scandals in U.S. history. SPYGATE—a terrible thing!

May 26, 2018

2:28 pm: With Spies, or "Informants" as the Democrats like to call them because it sounds less sinister (but it's not), all over my campaign, even from a very early date, why didn't the crooked highest levels of the FBI or "Justice" contact me to tell me of the phony Russia problem?!

2:41 pm: This whole Russia Probe is Rigged. Just an excuse as to why the Dems and Crooked Hillary lost the Election and States that haven't been lost in decades. 13 Angry Democrats, and all Dems if you include the people who worked for Obama for 8 years. #SPYGATE & CONFLICTS OF INTEREST!

May 29, 2018

6:09 am: Why aren't the 13 Angry and heavily conflicted Democrats investigating the totally Crooked Campaign of totally Crooked Hillary Clinton. It's a Rigged Witch Hunt, that's why! Ask them if they enjoyed her after election celebration!

June 2, 2018

12:31 pm: There was No Collusion with Russia (except by the Democrats). When will this very expensive Witch Hunt Hoax ever end? So bad for our Country. Is the Special Councel/Justice Department leaking my lawyers letters to the Fake News Media? Should be looking at Dems corruption instead?

June 15, 2018

5:35 am: FBI Agent Peter Strzok, who headed the Clinton & Russia investigations, texted to his lover Lisa Page, in the IG Report, that "we'll stop" candidate Trump from becoming President. Doesn't get any lower than that!

12:49 pm: I've had to beat 17 very talented people including the Bush Dynasty, then I had to beat the Clinton Dynasty, and now I have to beat a phony Witch Hunt and all of the dishonest people covered in the IG Report…and never forget the Fake News Media. It never ends!

June 17, 2018

9:54 am: WITCH HUNT! There was no Russian Collusion. Oh, I see, there was no Russian Collusion, so now they look for obstruction on the no Russian Collusion. The phony Russian Collusion was a made up Hoax. Too bad they didn't look at Crooked Hillary like this. Double Standard!

June 23, 2018

6:36 am: The Russian Witch Hunt is Rigged!

June 25, 2018

6:28 am: Former Attorney General Michael Mukasey said that President Trump is probably correct that there was surveillance on Trump Tower. Actually, far greater than would ever have been believed!

June 28, 2018

6:25 am: Russia continues to say they had nothing to do with Meddling in our Election! Where is the DNC Server, and why didn't Shady James Comey and the now disgraced FBI agents take and closely examine it? Why isn't Hillary/Russia being looked at? So many questions, so much corruption!

July 14, 2018

4:57 am: …Where is the DNC Server, and why didn't the FBI take possession of it? Deep State?

July 22, 2018

5:49 am: Looking more & more like the Trump Campaign for President was illegally being spied upon (surveillance) for the political gain of Crooked Hillary Clinton and the DNC. Ask her how that worked out—she did better with Crazy Bernie. Republicans must get tough now. An illegal Scam!

5:23 pm: So President Obama knew about Russia before the Election. Why didn't he do something about it? Why didn't he tell our campaign? Because it is all a big hoax, that's why, and he thought Crooked Hillary was going to win!!

July 31, 2018

6:58 am: Collusion is not a crime, but that doesn't matter because there was No Collusion (except by Crooked Hillary and the Democrats)!

August 5, 2018

7:35 am: Fake News reporting, a complete fabrication, that I am concerned about the meeting my wonderful son, Donald, had in Trump Tower. This was a meeting to get information on an opponent, totally legal and done all the time in politics—and it went nowhere. I did not know about it!

7:45 am: …Why aren't Mueller and the 17 Angry Democrats looking at the meetings concerning the Fake Dossier and all of the lying that went on in the FBI and DOJ? This is the most one sided Witch Hunt in the history of our country. Fortunately, the facts are all coming out, and fast!

August 9, 2018

8:22 am: "There has been no evidence whatsoever that Donald Trump or the campaign was involved in any kind of collusion to fix the 2016 election. In fact the evidence is the opposite, that Hillary Clinton & the Democrats colluded with the Russians to fix the 2016 election." @ GrahamLedger

11:02 am: This is an illegally brought Rigged Witch Hunt run by people who are totally corrupt and/or conflicted. It was started and paid for by Crooked Hillary and the Democrats. Phony Dossier, FISA disgrace and so many lying and dishonest people already fired. 17 Angry Dems? Stay tuned!

August 11, 2018

1:28 pm: The big story that the Fake News Media refuses to report is lowlife Christopher Steele's many meetings with Deputy A.G. Bruce Ohr and his beautiful wife, Nelly. It was Fusion GPS that hired Steele to write the phony & discredited Dossier, paid for by Crooked Hillary & the DNC…

1:54 pm: …Do you believe Nelly worked for Fusion and her husband STILL WORKS FOR THE DEPARTMENT OF "JUSTICE." I have never seen anything so Rigged in my life. Our A.G. is scared stiff and Missing in Action. It is all starting to be revealed—not pretty. IG Report soon? Witch Hunt!

August 14, 2018

6:55 am: Bruce Ohr of the "Justice" Department (can you believe he is still there) is accused of helping disgraced Christopher Steele "find dirt on Trump." Ohr's wife, Nelly, was in on the act big time—worked for Fusion GPS on Fake Dossier. @foxandfriends

7:06 am: "They were all in on it, clear Hillary Clinton and FRAME Donald Trump for things he didn't do." Gregg Jarrett on @foxandfriends If we had a real Attorney General, this Witch Hunt would never have been started! Looking at the wrong people.

August 16, 2018

6:45 pm: "While Steele shopped the document to multiple media outlets, he also asked for help with a RUSSIAN Oligarch." Catherine Herridge of @FoxNews @LouDobbs In other words, they were colluding with Russia!

August 19, 2018

6:01 am to 6:15 am: The failing @nytimes wrote a Fake piece today implying that because White House Council Do8n McGahn was giving hours of testimony to the Special Council, he must be a John Dean type "RAT." But I allowed him and all others to testify—I didn't have to. I have nothing to hide…

…and have demanded transparency so that this Rigged and Disgusting Witch Hunt can come to a close. So many lives have been ruined over nothing—McCarthyism at its WORST! Yet Mueller & his gang of Dems refuse to look at the real crimes on the other side—Media is even worse!

7:24 am: Study the late Joseph McCarthy, because we are now in period with Mueller and his gang that make Joseph McCarthy look like a baby! Rigged Witch Hunt!

August 20, 2018

6:48 am: Where's the Collusion? They made up a phony crime called Collusion, and when there was no Collusion they say there was Obstruction (of a phony crime that never existed). If you FIGHT BACK or say anything bad about the Rigged Witch Hunt, they scream Obstruction!

August 22, 2018

8:21 am: I feel very badly for Paul Manafort and his wonderful family. "Justice" took a 12 year old tax case, among other things, applied tremendous pressure on him and, unlike Michael Cohen, he refused to "break"—make up stories in order to get a "deal." Such respect for a brave man!

8:34 am: A large number of counts, ten, could not even be decided in the Paul Manafort case. Witch Hunt!

8:37 am: Michael Cohen plead guilty to two counts of campaign finance violations that are not a crime. President Obama had a big campaign finance violation and it was easily settled!

7:56 pm: The only thing that I have done wrong is to win an election that was expected to be won by Crooked Hillary Clinton and the Democrats. The problem is, they forgot to campaign in numerous states!

August 23, 2018

12:10 am: NO COLLUSION—RIGGED WITCH HUNT!

August 24, 2018

5:17 am: "Department of Justice will not be improperly influenced by political considerations." Jeff, this is GREAT, what everyone wants, so look into all of the corruption on the "other side" including deleted Emails, Comey lies & leaks, Mueller conflicts, McCabe, Strzok, Page, Ohr...

5:28 am: ...FISA abuse, Christopher Steele & his phony and corrupt Dossier, the Clinton Foundation, illegal surveillance of Trump Campaign, Russian collusion by Dems—and so much more. Open up the papers & documents without redaction? Come on Jeff, you can do it, the country is waiting!

August 25, 2018

7:16 am: Michaels Cohen's attorney clarified the record, saying his client does not know if President Trump knew about the Trump Tower meeting (out of which came nothing!). The answer is that I did NOT know about the meeting. Just another phony story by the Fake News Media!

August 29, 2018

8:43 pm to 8:51 pm: "Ohr told the FBI it (the Fake Dossier) wasn't true, it was a lie and the FBI was determined to use it anyway to damage Trump and to perpetrate a fraud on the court to spy on the Trump campaign. This is a fraud on the court. The Chief Justice of the U.S. Supreme Court is in...

...charge of the FISA court. He should direct the Presiding Judge, Rosemary Collier, to hold a hearing, haul all of these people from the DOJ & FBI in there, & if she finds there were crimes committed, and there were, there should be a criminal referral by her..." @GreggJarrett

397

September 1, 2018

8:19 am to 8:27 am: "You have a Fake Dossier, gathered by Steele, paid by the Clinton team to get information on Trump. The Dossier is Fake, nothing in it has been verified. It then filters into our American court system in order to spy on Barrack Obama and Hillary Clinton's political opponent...

@Rasmussen_Poll just came out at 48% approval rate despite the constant and intense Fake News. Higher than Election Day and higher than President Obama. Rasmussen was one of the most accurate Election Day polls!

September 7, 2018

4:39 pm: 14 days for $28 MILLION—$2 MILLION a day, No Collusion. A great day for America!

September 12, 2018

9:06 am: "I can say, as it relates to the Senate Intelligence Committee Investigation, that we have NO hard evidence of Collusion." Richard Burr (R-NC) Senate Intelligence Committee, Chairman

September 16, 2018

9:20 am: The illegal Mueller Witch Hunt continues in search of a crime. There was never Collusion with Russia, except by the Clinton campaign, so the 17 Angry Democrats are looking at anything they can find. Very unfair and BAD for the country. ALSO, not allowed under the LAW!

September 17, 2018

9:23 am: "Lisa Page Testimony—NO EVIDENCE OF COLLUSION BEFORE MUELLER APPOINTMENT." @FoxNews by Catherine Herridge. Therefore, the case should never have been allowed to be brought. It is a totally illegal Witch Hunt!

September 18, 2018

7:42 am to 7:45 am: "What will be disclosed is that there was no basis for these FISA Warrants, that the important information was kept from the court, there's going to be a disproportionate influence of the (Fake) Dossier. Basically you have a counter terrorism tool used to spy on a presidential…

…campaign, which is unprecedented in our history." Congressman Peter King Really bad things were happening, but they are now being exposed. Big stuff!

September 26, 2018

11:47 am: Avenatti is a third rate lawyer who is good at making false accusations, like he did on me and like he is now doing on Judge Brett Kavanaugh. He is just looking for attention and doesn't want people to look at his past record and relationships—a total low-life!

October 16, 2018

10:04 am: "Federal Judge throws out Stormy Danials lawsuit versus Trump. Trump is entitled to full legal fees." @FoxNews Great, now I can go after Horseface and her 3rd rate lawyer in the Great State of Texas. She will confirm the letter she signed! She knows nothing about me, a total con!

10:18 am: "Conflict between Glen Simpson's testimony to another House Panel about his contact with Justice Department official Bruce Ohr. Ohr was used by Simpson and Steele as a Back Channel to get (FAKE) Dossier to FBI. Simpson pleading Fifth." Catherine Herridge. Where is Jeff Sessions?

10:26 am: Is it really possible that Bruce Ohr, whose wife Nellie was paid by Simpson and GPS Fusion for work done on the Fake Dossier, and who was used as a Pawn in this whole SCAM (WITCH HUNT), is still working for the Department of Justice????? Can this really be so?????

November 8, 2018

9:38 pm: Law Enforcement is looking into another big corruption scandal having to do with Election Fraud in #Broward and Palm Beach. Florida voted for Rick Scott!

November 9, 2018

1:20 pm: In the 2016 Election I was winning by so much in Florida that Broward County, which was very late with vote tabulation and probably getting ready to do a "number," couldn't do it because not enough people live in Broward for them to falsify a victory!

November 15, 2018

9:49 pm: Universities will someday study what highly conflicted (and NOT Senate approved) Bob Mueller and his gang of Democrat thugs have done to destroy people. Why is he protecting Crooked Hillary, Comey, McCabe, Lisa Page & her lover, Peter S, and all of his friends on the other side?

November 28, 2018

11:39 pm: So much happening with the now discredited Witch Hunt. This total Hoax will be studied for years!

9:59 pm: The only "Collusion" is that of the Democrats with Russia and many others. Why didn't the FBI take the Server from the DNC? They still don't have it. Check out how biased Facebook, Google and Twitter are in favor of the Democrats. That's the real Collusion!

November 27, 2018

7:42 am to 8:07 am: …The Fake News Media builds Bob Mueller up as a Saint, when in actuality he is the exact opposite. He is doing TRE-MENDOUS damage to our Criminal Justice System, where he is only looking at one side and not the other. Heroes will come of this, and it won't be Mueller

November 28, 2018

11:39 pm: So much happening with the now discredited Witch Hunt. This total Hoax will be studied for years!

November 30, 2018

4:52 am to 4:59 am: Oh, I get it! I am a very good developer, happily living my life, when I see our Country going in the wrong direction (to put it mildly). Against all odds, I decide to run for President & continue to run my business-very legal & very cool, talked about it on the campaign trail...

...Lightly looked at doing a building somewhere in Russia. Put up zero money, zero guarantees and didn't do the project. Witch Hunt!

December 3, 2018

10:48 am: "I will never testify against Trump." This statement was recently made by Roger Stone, essentially stating that he will not be forced by a rogue and out of control prosecutor to make up lies and stories about "President Trump." Nice to know that some people still have "guts!

10:56 am: Bob Mueller (who is a much different man than people think) and his out of control band of Angry Democrats, don't want the truth, they only want lies. The truth is very bad for their mission!

December 8, 2018

8:01 am: AFTER TWO YEARS AND MILLIONS OF PAGES OF DOCUMENTS (and a cost of over $30,000,000), NO COLLUSION!

December 10, 2018

6:46 am to 7:00 am: "Democrats can't find a Smocking Gun tying the Trump campaign to Russia after James Comey's testimony. No Smocking Gun...No Collusion." @FoxNews That's because there was NO COLLUSION. So now the Dems go to a simple private transaction, wrongly call it a campaign contribution,...

which it was not (but even if it was, it is only a CIVIL CASE, like Obama's—but it was done correctly by a lawyer and there would not even be a fine. Lawyer's liability if he made a mistake, not me). Cohen just trying to get his sentence reduced. WITCH HUNT!

December 13, 2018

8:17 am to 8:34 am: I never directed Michael Cohen to break the law. He was a lawyer and he is supposed to know the law. It is called "advice of counsel," and a lawyer has great liability if a mistake is made. That is why they get paid. Despite that many campaign finance lawyers have strongly...

...stated that I did nothing wrong with respect to campaign finance laws, if they even apply, because this was not campaign finance. Cohen was guilty on many charges unrelated to me, but he plead to two campaign charges which were not criminal and of which he probably was not...

...guilty even on a civil bases. Those charges were just agreed to by him in order to embarrass the president and get a much reduced prison sentence, which he did-including the fact that his family was temporarily let off the hook. As a lawyer, Michael has great liability to me!

December 16, 2018

10:20 am: Judge Ken Starr, former Solicitor Generel & Independent Counsel, just stated that, after two years, "there is no evidence or proof of collusion" & further that "there is no evidence that there was a campaign financing violation involving the President." Thank you Judge. @ FoxNews

December 18, 2018

6:28 am: Biggest outrage yet in the long, winding and highly conflicted Mueller Witch Hunt is the fact that 19,000 demanded Text messages between Peter Strzok and his FBI lover, Lisa Page, were purposely & illegally deleted. Would have explained whole Hoax, which is now under protest!

8:32 am: Michael Isikoff was the first to report Dossier allegations and now seriously doubts the Dossier claims. The whole Russian Collusion thing was a HOAX, but who is going to restore the good name of so many people whose reputations have been destroyed?

December 22, 2018

3:28 pm: I won an election, said to be one of the greatest of all time, based on getting out of endless & costly foreign wars & also based on Strong Borders which will keep our Country safe. We fight for the borders of other countries, but we won't fight for the borders of our own!

Election Campaign—2019 News Quotes

Response to an unidentified reporter's question before Marine One departure, March 20, 2019.

Source: https://www.whitehouse.gov/briefings-statements/
remarks-president-trump-marine-one-departure-34/

"I have no idea. No collusion. No collusion. I have no idea when it's [the Mueller report is] going to be released. It's interesting that a man gets appointed by a deputy; he writes a report. You know, never figured that one out. A man gets appointed by a deputy; he writes a report.

"I had the greatest electoral victory, one of them, in the history of our country. Tremendous success. Tens of millions of voters. And now somebody is going to write a report who never got a vote.

"So we'll see what the report says. Let's see if it's fair. I have no idea when it's going to be released."

Response to an unidentified reporter's question before Marine One departure, March 20, 2019.

Source: https://www.whitehouse.gov/briefings-statements/
remarks-president-trump-marine-one-departure-34/

"I don't mind. I mean, frankly, I told the House, 'If you want, let them see it.' Again, I say: A deputy, because of the fact that the Attorney General didn't have the courage to do it himself, a deputy that's appointed appoints another man to write a report. I just won an election with 63 million votes or so. Sixty-three million. I had 206 to 223 in the Electoral College: 306 to 223.

"And I'm saying to myself, wait a minute, I just won one of the greatest elections of all time in the history of this country, and even you will admit that, and now I have somebody writing a report that never got a vote. It's called the Mueller report.

"So explain that, because my voters don't get it. And I don't get it.

"Now, at the same time, let it come out. Let people see it. That's up to the Attorney General. We have a very good Attorney General; he's a very highly respected man. And we'll see what happens.

"But it's sort of interesting that a man, out of the blue, just writes a report. I got 306 electoral votes against 223. That's a tremendous victory. I got 63 million more. I got 63 million votes. And now somebody just writes a report? I think it's ridiculous."

Response to an unidentified reporter's question before Marine One departure, March 20, 2019.

Source: https://www.whitehouse.gov/briefings-statements/
remarks-president-trump-marine-one-departure-34/

"I know nothing about it. I know that he's [Special Counsel Robert Mueller is] conflicted and I know that his best friend is [James] Comey, who's a bad cop. And I know that there are other things, obviously. You know I had a business transaction with him that I've reported many times that you people don't talk about. But I had a nasty business transaction with him and other things. I know that he put 13 highly conflicted and, you know, very angry—I call them angry Democrats in. So, you know—So, what it is.

"Now, let's see whether or not it's legit. You know better than anybody there's no collusion. There was no collusion. There was no obstruction. There was no nothing. But it's sort of an amazing thing that when you have a great victory, somebody comes and does a report out of nowhere, tell me how that makes sense, who never got a vote; who the day before he [Mueller] was retained to become Special Counsel, I told him he wouldn't be working at the FBI. And then the following day, they get him for this. I don't think so. I don't think people get it.

"With all of that being said, I look forward to seeing the [Mueller] report."

Response to a question from Catherine Herridge of FOX News, May 2, 2019.
Source: https://www.foxnews.com/politics/transcript-fox-news-interview-with-president-trump

"Documents, hundreds of people have been interviewed, I've allowed lawyers to be interviewed. I didn't have to do any of that, I could've used presidential privilege, but I've been the most transparent President in history.

"I don't think anybody has been as open as I have, and you know the reason I was? Because I didn't do anything wrong, I didn't do anything with Russia. So I said, 'Give them all the documents you want, give them all the people you want.'

"Somebody told me there was 500 people that were interviewed, I could've stopped all of it. I didn't do that, and now we win with [Special Counsel Robert] Mueller, where they come up very strongly with no collusion, and no obstruction, no nothing. We win very strongly, and now they want to do it all over again?

"Now we won in the House, we won in the Senate because Senator [Richard] Burr said there's been no collusion, so we won…through that. We won here, I mean the Mueller report was a total win. But think of it, we go through this, this is two and a half years now I've been going through the same thing, and the guilt is on the other side, not on our side; the guilt is on the other side."

Response to a question from Catherine Herridge of FOX News, May 2, 2019.
Source: https://www.foxnews.com/politics/transcript-fox-news-interview-with-president-trump

"Well I think they should be satisfied with the findings, they spent $35 million or somebody told me today maybe $40 million on the Mueller report. They had 18 people, most of whom—I think all of whom disliked Donald Trump. They were Democrats, they contributed to the campaign of Hillary Clinton.

"They had conflicts all over the place, and it still came out no collusion. I can't imagine they can keep doing this, this is done just to try and bring me down to a—And I had my highest poll numbers today which is—You'll have to explain that to me, because with all that we do I had my best poll numbers.

"So with—Yes, I think they're treating this very unfairly, I think it's time to get down to business. I want to do infrastructure, I want to do prescription drug pricing, low. I want to do all the other things that we want to do. Nobody's done more. It's an incredible thing, Catherine [Herridge of FOX News].

"Nobody's done more than President Trump and this administration in two and a half years, ever in their first two and a half years. And despite that, I'm wasting time with all of this stuff, it is very unfair. And I think they're treating our attorney general, who is a highly respected man, very unfairly."

Response to a question from Catherine Herridge of FOX News, May 2, 2019.
Source: https://www.foxnews.com/politics/transcript-fox-news-interview-with-president-trump

"But, I don't have to give, I didn't have to give all of this documentation. Probably in the end I would have had to give none.

"I didn't have to get all these testify, I let them all do it because we did nothing wrong, I knew that. They found nothing. With all of this, they spent $35 to $40 million, they found nothing.

"So yes, I think we've been treated very unfairly. And they're doing it not for any legal reason, they're doing it for a political reason because they want to, want—Look, they want to win a race in 2020, and I see what they're up against today."

Response to a question from Catherine Herridge of FOX News, May 2, 2019.
Source: https://www.foxnews.com/politics/transcript-fox-news-interview-with-president-trump

"I think nobody's done more about Russia than I have. [Then-U.S.] President [Barack] Obama in September, before the November election—My November election, if you look he was told by the FBI and others, he did nothing about it."

Response to a question from Catherine Herridge of FOX News, May 2, 2019.
Source: https://www.foxnews.com/politics/transcript-fox-news-interview-with-president-trump

"I think that [Joe] Biden seems to have the lead; I'd be very happy if it were Biden."

Response to a question from Catherine Herridge of FOX News, May 2, 2019.
Source: https://www.foxnews.com/politics/transcript-fox-news-interview-with-president-trump

"Sleepy Joe [Biden]. I think he does—I think he did a bad job; I'd be running against President [Barack] Obama."

Response to a question from Catherine Herridge of FOX News, May 2, 2019.
Source: https://www.foxnews.com/politics/transcript-fox-news-interview-with-president-trump

"I just don't think he'd [Joe Biden would] be a very good candidate. I mean, we'll see what happens. I hope—You know, I wish him well. I'd like him to get it; I'd be happy. I'd be happy with Bernie [Sanders]. I personally think it's those two."

Response to a question from Catherine Herridge of FOX News, May 2, 2019.
Source: https://www.foxnews.com/politics/transcript-fox-news-interview-with-president-trump

"They shouldn't be looking anymore. This is all—It's done. Even my finances, it must've been looked at for $35 million. I assume they looked at my taxes. I assume that [Special Counsel Robert] Mueller looked at my financial statements.

"For $35 million and having 20 people plus 49 FBI agents and all of the staff and all of the money that was spent, they—I assume they looked at my taxes, which are fine. And I assume—Except they are under audit, by the way. I will tell you that officially, because—[Herridge interrupts.]"

Response to a question from Catherine Herridge of FOX News, May 2, 2019.
Source: https://www.foxnews.com/politics/transcript-fox-news-interview-with-president-trump

"Well, she [New York Attorney General Letitia James] campaigned on the fact that 'Oh, I'm going to get Trump. I'm going to get Trump.' So right there, she's precluded from doing anything. I mean can you imagine somebody campaigning who doesn't know anything about me? And she's campaigning on that fact.

"So I assume that, for the $35 million, they've gone through everything—My taxes, my financial statements, which are phenomenal. They've got through everything, and I'm so clean. Think of it. After two and a half years and all of that money spent, nothing. Very few people could have sustained that."

Response to a POLITICO reporter's[37] question, May 10, 2019.
Source: https://www.politico.com/story/2019/05/10/trump-interview-transcript-1317598

"If you remember, from the day I came down the escalator until the end of the primaries, I was in the number one position. I was center stage every debate. And you know, nobody came close. And I had—I mean, I had a big lead pretty much from the beginning, and it got bigger, you know, as it went along, and as people started dropping out."

---

37 POLITICO reporters Andrew Restuccia, Eliana Johnson, and Daniel Lippman conducted the telephone interview with President Trump, but the transcript does not indicate which reporter asked which question.

Response to a POLITICO reporter's[38] question, May 10, 2019.

Source: https://www.politico.com/story/2019/05/10/trump-interview-transcript-1317598

"And [Joe] Biden, for whatever reason, I don't get that, but he seems to be—You know, have some kind of a register. Whether it's name [recognition] or what. And he seems to be doing well. And Bernie [Sanders] seems to be going in the wrong direction. But everyone else is going—I mean almost everybody else seems to be not doing very well. And so I would certainly say—I make it analogous to my race in the sense that, you know, I rode it out. You know, they call it in sports: 'good frontrunner.' I don't know if Biden's a good frontrunner. I heard him talking about [how] he spoke to Margaret Thatcher yesterday. I mean, what he said is he spoke to Margaret Thatcher. I assume he meant Theresa May. So, I don't know, is that a good frontrunner? I don't know. That was a beauty."

Response to a POLITICO reporter's[39] question, May 10, 2019.

Source: https://www.politico.com/story/2019/05/10/trump-interview-transcript-1317598

"Alfred E. Neuman cannot become President of the United States."

Response to a POLITICO reporter's[40] question, May 10, 2019.

Source: https://www.politico.com/story/2019/05/10/trump-interview-transcript-1317598

"Well, the Russian collusion thing has turned out to be a total hoax, and now people are saying it. But I have not given any consideration to any of that at this moment."

---

38 POLITICO reporters Andrew Restuccia, Eliana Johnson, and Daniel Lippman conducted the telephone interview with President Trump, but the transcript does not indicate which reporter asked which question.

39 POLITICO reporters Andrew Restuccia, Eliana Johnson, and Daniel Lippman conducted the telephone interview with President Trump, but the transcript does not indicate which reporter asked which question.

40 POLITICO reporters Andrew Restuccia, Eliana Johnson, and Daniel Lippman conducted the telephone interview with President Trump, but the transcript does not indicate which reporter asked which question.

Remarks at the signing of an executive order protecting and improving Medicare for senior citizens, Ocala, Florida, October 3, 2019.

Source: https://www.whitehouse.gov/briefings-statements/remarks-president-trump-signing-executive-order-protecting-improving-medicare-nations-seniors-ocala-fl/

"Elizabeth 'Pocahontas' Warren. You know, when I used to hit her, I thought she was gone, [Florida Governor] Ron [DeSantis]. I thought she was gone. She came up from the ashes. She emerged. Now, we're probably going to have to do it again, because I don't see Sleepy Joe [Biden] making it, I'll tell you. No, I thought she [Warren] was gone."

Remarks at the signing of an executive order protecting and improving Medicare for senior citizens, Ocala, Florida, October 3, 2019.

Source: https://www.whitehouse.gov/briefings-statements/remarks-president-trump-signing-executive-order-protecting-improving-medicare-nations-seniors-ocala-fl/

"You want to drive them crazy? Don't do 'four more years.' Say 'eight more years.' You'll drive them crazy.

"One of these crazy maniacs on a show was interviewing somebody—Radical Left—And he goes, 'You know he's going to win, don't you?' Big show. And the guy goes, 'No, no. We're going to fight him. We're going to...' 'No, no, no. He's going to win. And you know he's never getting out. You know that don't you?' 'He's not going to get out. You know he's...'

"And I thought, like—You know, he's a comedian. I thought he was like kidding and having fun. He meant it. These people are sick. They meant it.

"Anyway—But, no, if you want to drive them crazy, just say 'eight more years' or 'twelve more years' or 'sixteen.' Sixteen would do it good. They would, you would really drive them into the loony bin.

"And that's why they do the impeachment crap, because they know they can't beat us fairly. That's the only reason they're doing it. They can't win. They can't win. If they won, it would be a sad day for our country. It'll be a sad, sad day for our country if they ever won."

Remarks at a rally in Minneapolis, Minnesota, October 10, 2019.
Source: https://www.twincities.com/2019/10/10/
trump-attacks-joe-biden-ilhan-omar-and-jacob-frey-at-minneapolis-rally/

"He's [Joe Biden's] been part of the Washington swamp for years."

Remarks at a rally in Minneapolis, Minnesota, October 10, 2019.
Source: https://www.twincities.com/2019/10/10/
trump-attacks-joe-biden-ilhan-omar-and-jacob-frey-at-minneapolis-rally/

"The Democrats' brazen attempt to overthrow our government will produce a backlash at the ballot box, the likes of which they've never ever seen before in the history of this country."

Remarks at a rally in Tupelo, Mississippi, November 1, 2019.
Source: https://www.youtube.com/watch?v=0UoOGKYla4Q#action=share

"With the lying, and the spying, and the leaking, and we are kicking their ass, I'll tell you. In the delusional Democrat fantasy, I'm now supposed to be afraid of someone called 1% Joe [Biden]. I used to call him 1% because he could never get 1% percent in the primaries. Then, he got brought out by [Barack] Obama out of the trash heap, became Vice President, but we've now named him very slow sleepy Joe, very slow, he's gotten slower and slower

"I'm afraid if he gets the nomination, he'll be so slow. We'll have the lowest-rated debates in history, as opposed to the highest-rated debates in history, against Crooked Hillary [Clinton]. In fact, I don't even think that Sleepy Joe will get it, but many people are running. So, you know, it's so early. I don't want to talk about their campaign.

"Oh, did you hear Beto[41], Beto? Oh, that poor bastard. Well. Poor, pathetic guy. He was pathetic. Remember the arms are flailing. It's

---

41   Robert Francis "Beto" O'Rourke (D-Texas) was a member of the U.S. House of Representatives from 2013 to 2019. Republican Ted Cruz defeated him in the 2018 election. O'Rourke was a candidate for the 2020 presidential election until he dropped out on November 1, 2019.
Source: https://www.nytimes.com/2019/11/01/us/politics/beto-orourke-drops-out.html

all—Remember that—You know, he ran against Ted Cruz[42]. Ted Cruz won. He spent almost $100 million, and Ted Cruz and I helped Ted, and we campaigned together, and it was good, but I used to watch him.

"Then, when he came on to the really big stage, this crazy stage, I noticed he was flailing with the arms and he was standing on tables, he was standing on countertops. I said, 'Does he ever, like, stand on the floor and speak?' But he's waving his arms and going crazy, and I said, 'What the hell is he doing? What is he on?' And you remember he made the statement that he was born for this.

"Anybody that says he was born for this, they're in trouble. You know, I used to have guys come into my office, 'Sir, I'm the greatest salesman. Nobody can sell—' You know, the truth is, anybody that says they're a great salesman, usually, they're not a very good salesman. It's true. It's those sneaky ones in the back that don't talk, but you don't know about—They're the ones.

"But Beto was nasty and he said that he was born for it. Like he was born from heaven and he came down. And if that's the case, some really bad things happened because he made a total fool out of himself. And he came out of Texas, the great state of Texas. He came out of Texas, a very hot political property and he went back as cold as you can be. So, he was a nasty guy.

"But he had a couple of policies that don't work well in the state of Texas, right? He was against religion, he was against you having a gun—[Audience interrupts with boos.] And he was against oil. So, you come from Texas, you don't like religion, you don't like oil, and you don't have guns. I don't know, that's not a good combination in the state of Texas."

---

42   Ted Cruz (R-Texas) has been a member of the U.S. House of Representatives since 2013. He also ran for the 2016 Republican presidential nomination.

Election Campaign—2019 Tweets

January 5, 2019

8:55 am: Many people currently a part of my opposition, including President Obama & the Dems, have had campaign violations, in some cases for very large sums of money. These are civil cases. They paid a fine & settled. While no big deal, I did not commit a campaign violation!

January 14, 2019

5:19 pm: ...I am doing exactly what I pledged to do, and what I was elected to do by the citizens of our great Country. Just as I promised, I am fighting for YOU!

January 15, 2019

6:58 am: The rank and file of the FBI are great people who are disgusted with what they are learning about Lyin' James Comey and the so-called "leaders" of the FBI. Twelve have been fired or forced to leave. They got caught spying on my campaign and then called it an investigation. Bad!

January 22, 2019

8:15 am: FBI top lawyer confirms "unusual steps." They relied on the Clinton Campaign's Fake & Unverified "Dossier," which is illegal. "That has corrupted them. That has enabled them to gather evidence by UNCONSTITUTIONAL MEANS, and that's what they did to the President." Judge Napolitano

10:53 am: Former FBI top lawyer James Baker just admitted involvement in FISA Warrant and further admitted there were IRREGULARITIES in the way the Russia probe was handled. They relied heavily on the unverified Trump "Dossier" paid for by the DNC & Clinton Campaign, & funded through a...

11:06 am: ...big Crooked Hillary law firm, represented by her lawyer Michael Sussmann (do you believe this?) who worked Baker hard & gave him Oppo Research for "a Russia probe." This meeting, now exposed, is the subject of Senate inquiries and much more. An Unconstitutional Hoax. @FoxNews

January 26, 2019

8:42 am: If Roger Stone was indicted for lying to Congress, what about the lying done by Comey, Brennan, Clapper, Lisa Page & lover, Baker and soooo many others? What about Hillary to FBI and her 33,000 deleted Emails? What about Lisa & Peter's deleted texts & Wiener's laptop? Much more!

January 31, 2019

10:03 pm: Just out: The big deal, very mysterious Don jr telephone calls, after the innocent Trump Tower meeting, that the media & Dems said were made to his father (me), were just conclusively found NOT to be made to me. They were made to friends & business associates of Don. Really sad!

February 7, 2019

9:05 pm: Highly respected Senator Richard Burr, Chairman of Senate Intelligence, said today that, after an almost two year investigation, he saw no evidence of Russia collusion. "We don't have anything that would suggest there was collusion by the Trump campaign and Russia." Thank you!

February 8, 2019

7:23 am: Not only did Senator Burr's Committee find No Collusion by the Trump Campaign and Russia, it's important because they interviewed 200 witnesses and 300,000 pages of documents, & the

Committee has direct access to intelligence information that's Classified. @GreggJarrett

8:41 am: Now we find out that Adam Schiff was spending time together in Aspen with Glenn Simpson of GPS Fusion, who wrote the fake and discredited Dossier, even though Simpson was testifying before Schiff. John Solomon of @thehill

February 13, 2019

5:58 am: The Senate Intelligence Committee: THERE IS NO EVIDENCE OF COLLUSION BETWEEN THE TRUMP CAMPAIGN AND RUSSIA!

February 17, 2019

4:32 pm: "These guys, the investigators, ought to be in jail. What they have done, working with the Obama intelligence agencies, is simply unprecedented. This is one of the greatest political hoaxes ever perpetrated on the people of this Country, and Mueller is a coverup." Rush Limbaugh

6:45 pm: The Mueller investigation is totally conflicted, illegal and rigged! Should never have been allowed to begin, except for the Collusion and many crimes committed by the Democrats. Witch Hunt!

February 24, 2019

11:51 am: The only Collusion with the Russians was with Crooked Hillary Clinton and the Democratic National Committee...And, where's the Server that the DNC refused to give to the FBI? Where are the new Texts between Agent Lisa Page and her Agent lover, Peter S? We want them now!

March 7, 2019

9:24 am: It was not a campaign contribution, and there were no violations of the campaign finance laws by me. Fake News!

March 8, 2019

8:30 am: Both the Judge and the lawyer in the Paul Manafort case stated loudly and for the world to hear that there was NO COLLUSION with Russia. But the Witch Hunt Hoax continues as you now add these statements to House & Senate Intelligence & Senator Burr. So bad for our Country!

March 15, 2019

8:47 am: So, if there was knowingly & acknowledged to be "zero" crime when the Special Counsel was appointed, and if the appointment was made based on the Fake Dossier (paid for by Crooked Hillary) and now disgraced Andrew McCabe (he & all stated no crime), then the Special Counsel...

8:55 am: ...should never have been appointed and there should be no Mueller Report. This was an illegal & conflicted investigation in search of a crime. Russian Collusion was nothing more than an excuse by the Democrats for losing an Election that they thought they were going to win.

8:56 am: ...THIS SHOULD NEVER HAPPEN TO A PRESIDENT AGAIN!

March 16, 2019

11:06 am: On the recent non-binding vote (420-0) in Congress about releasing the Mueller Report, I told leadership to let all Republicans vote for transparency. Makes us all look good and doesn't matter. Play along with the game!

3:46 pm: Spreading the fake and totally discredited Dossier "is unfortunately a very dark stain against John McCain." Ken Starr, Former Independent Counsel. He had far worse "stains" than this, including thumbs down on repeal and replace after years of campaigning to repeal and replace!

March 17, 2019

7:23 am: Report: Christopher Steele backed up his Democrat & Crooked Hillary paid for Fake & Unverified Dossier with information he got from "send in watchers" of low ratings CNN. This is the info that got us the Witch Hunt!

7:41 am: So it was indeed (just proven in court papers) "last in his class" (Annapolis) John McCain that sent the Fake Dossier to the FBI and Media hoping to have it printed BEFORE the Election. He & the Dems, working together, failed (as usual). Even the Fake News refused this garbage!

6:16 pm: What the Democrats have done in trying to steal a Presidential Election, first at the "ballot box" and then, after that failed, with the "Insurance Policy," is the biggest Scandal in the history of our Country!

March 24, 2019

3:42 pm: No Collusion, No Obstruction, Complete and Total EXONERATION. KEEP AMERICA GREAT!

April 1, 2019

7:07 am: Now that the long awaited Mueller Report conclusions have been released, most Democrats and others have gone back to the pre-Witch Hunt phase of their lives before Collusion Delusion took over. Others are pretending that their former hero, Bob Mueller, no longer exists!

April 4, 2019

7:22 am: According to polling, few people seem to care about the Russian Collusion Hoax, but some Democrats are fighting hard to keep the Witch Hunt alive. They should focus on legislation or, even better, an investigation of how the ridiculous Collusion Delusion got started—so illegal!

April 6, 2019

9:22 am: I have not read the Mueller Report yet, even though I have every right to do so. Only know the conclusions, and on the big one, No Collusion. Likewise, recommendations made to our great A.G. who found No Obstruction. 13 Angry Trump hating Dems (later brought to 18) given two...

9:31 am: ...years and $30 million, and they found No Collusion, No Obstruction. But the Democrats, no matter what we give them, will NEVER be satisfied. A total waste of time. As @FrankLuntz has just stated, "Enough, America has had enough. What have you accomplished. Public is fed up."

10:52 am: So, let's get this straight! There was No Collusion and in fact the Phony Dossier was a Con Job that was paid for by Crooked Hillary and the DNC. So the 13 Angry Democrats were investigating an event that never happened and that was in fact a made up Fraud. I just fought back...

10:57 am: ...against something I knew never existed, Collusion with Russia (so ridiculous!)—No Obstruction. This Russia Hoax must never happen to another President, and Law Enforcement must find out, HOW DID IT START?

April 10, 2019

2:45 pm: So, it has now been determined, by 18 people that truly hate President Trump, that there was No Collusion with Russia. In fact, it was an illegal investigation that should never have been allowed to start. I fought back hard against this Phony & Treasonous Hoax!

April 13, 2019

7:21 am: Why should Radical Left Democrats in Congress have a right to retry and examine the $35,000,000 (two years in the making) No Collusion Mueller Report, when the crime committed was by Crooked Hillary, the DNC and Dirty Cops? Attorney General Barr will make the decision!

April 15, 2019

6:15 am: Mueller, and the A.G. based on Mueller findings (and great intelligence), have already ruled No Collusion, No Obstruction. These were crimes committed by Crooked Hillary, the DNC, Dirty Cops and others! INVESTIGATE THE INVESTIGATORS!

8:52 am: THEY SPIED ON MY CAMPAIGN (We will never forget)!

April 18, 2019

6:54 am: The Greatest Political Hoax of all time! Crimes were committed by Crooked, Dirty Cops and DNC/The Democrats.

7:54 am: No Collusion—No Obstruction!

6:28 pm: Anything the Russians did concerning the 2016 Election was done while Obama was President. He was told about it and did nothing! Most importantly, the vote was not affected.

April 24, 2019

8:47 am: No Collusion, No Obstruction—there has NEVER been a President who has been more transparent. Millions of pages of documents were given to the Mueller Angry Dems, plus I allowed everyone to testify, including W.H. counsel. I didn't have to do this, but now they want more...

8:52 am: ...Congress has no time to legislate, they only want to continue the Witch Hunt, which I have already won. They should start looking at The Criminals who are already very well known to all. This was a Rigged System—WE WILL DRAIN THE SWAMP!

11:59 am: As I have been saying all along, NO COLLUSION—NO OBSTRUCTION!

April 20, 2019

6:52 am: Despite the fact that the Mueller Report should not have been authorized in the first place & was written as nastily as possible

419

by 13 (18) Angry Democrats who were true Trump Haters, including highly conflicted Bob Mueller himself, the end result is No Collusion, No Obstruction!

May 1, 2019

8:03 am: NO COLLUSION, NO OBSTRUCTION. Besides, how can you have Obstruction when not only was there No Collusion (by Trump), but the bad actions were done by the "other" side? The greatest con-job in the history of American Politics!

May 3, 2019

7:22 am: Finally, Mainstream Media is getting involved—too "hot" to avoid. Pulitzer Prize anyone? The New York Times, on front page (finally), "Details effort to spy on Trump Campaign." @foxandfriends This is bigger than WATERGATE, but the reverse!

May 12, 2019

6:04 am: Think of it. I became President of the United States in one of the most hard fought and consequential elections in the history of our great nation. From long before I ever took office, I was under a sick & unlawful investigation concerning what has become known as the Russian...

...Hoax. My campaign was being seriously spied upon by intel agencies and the Democrats. This never happened before in American history, and it all turned out to be a total scam, a Witch Hunt, that yielded No Collusion, No Obstruction. This must never be allowed to happen again!

6:10 pm: Ever since the Mueller Report showed No Collusion & No Obstruction, the Dems have been working overtime to damage me and the Republican Party by issuing over 80 demands for documents and testimonies, and with NO REASON. That's all they want to do—don't care about anything else!

6:16 pm: When the Mueller Report came out showing NO Collusion with Russia (of course), it was supposed to be over, back to work for the people. But the Dems have gone "nuts," and it has actually gotten worse! Hope the Republicans win back the House in 2020, or little will get done!

May 17, 2019

6:11 am: My Campaign for President was conclusively spied on. Nothing like this has ever happened in American Politics. A really bad situation. TREASON means long jail sentences, and this was TREASON!

9:35 am: It now seems the General Flynn was under investigation long before was common knowledge. It would have been impossible for me to know this but, if that was the case, and with me being one of two people who would become president, why was I not told so that I could make a change?

May 19, 2019

8:55 am: Never a fan of @justinamash, a total lightweight who opposes me and some of our great Republican ideas and policies just for the sake of getting his name out there through controversy. If he actually read the biased Mueller Report, "composed" by 18 Angry Dems who hated Trump,...

May 21, 2019

4:22 pm: So even though I didn't have to do it with Presidential Privilege, I allowed everyone to testify, including White House Counsel Don McGahn (for over 30 hours), to Robert Mueller and the 18 Angry Trump-Hating Democrats, and they arrived...

...at a conclusion of NO COLLUSION and NO OBSTRUCTION! The Dems were unhappy with the outcome of the $40M Mueller Report, so now they want a do-o

May 24, 2019

7:34 am: I don't know why the Radical Left Democrats want Bob Mueller to testify when he just issued a 40 Million Dollar Report that states, loud & clear & for all to hear, No Collusion and No Obstruction (how do you Obstruct a NO crime?) Dems are just looking for trouble and a Do-Over!

May 29, 2019

10:37 am: Nothing changes from the Mueller Report. There was insufficient evidence and therefore, in our Country, a person is innocent. The case is closed! Thank you.

May 31, 2019

3:35 pm: I will be announcing my Second Term Presidential Run with First Lady Melania, Vice President Mike Pence, and Second Lady Karen Pence on June 18th in Orlando, Florida, at the 20,000 seat Amway Center. Join us for this Historic Rally!
Tickets: https://t.co/1krDP2oQvG

June 5, 2019

3:12 am: House Democrats, fresh off a Republican victory against them (in Federal Court) on the Wall, keep asking people to come and testify regarding the No Collusion Witch Hunt. They are very unhappy with the Mueller Report, especially with his corrective letter, & now want a Do Over!

June 13, 2019

5:21 am: General Michael Flynn, the 33 year war hero who has served with distinction, has not retained a good lawyer, he has retained a GREAT LAWYER, Sidney Powell. Best Wishes and Good Luck to them both!

June 17, 2019

7:07 am: Only Fake Polls show us behind the Motley Crew. We are looking really good, but it is far too early to be focused on that. Much work to do! MAKE AMERICA GREAT AGAIN!

June 26, 2019

4:46 pm: …No Collusion, No Obstruction! Robert Mueller said he was done after his last 9 minute news conference, as later corrected. Now the Dems want to give it another try. Does it ever end

July 2, 2019

6:38 am: As most people are aware, according to the Polls, I won EVERY debate, including the three with Crooked Hillary Clinton, despite the fact that in the first debate, they modulated the sound on me, and got caught. This crew looks somewhat easier than Crooked, but you never know?

9:51 am: Robert Mueller is being asked to testify yet again. He said he could only stick to the Report, & that is what he would and must do. After so much testimony & total transparency, this Witch Hunt must now end. No more Do Overs. No Collusion, No Obstruction. The Great Hoax is dead!

July 23, 2019

7:51 am: In 2016 I almost won Minnesota. In 2020, because of America hating anti-Semite Rep. Omar, & the fact that Minnesota is having its best economic year ever, I will win the State! "We are going to be a nightmare to the President," she say. No, AOC Plus 3 are a Nightmare for America!

July 24, 2019

2:33 pm: TRUTH IS A FORCE OF NATURE!

July 30, 2019

6:26 pm: Wow! A federal Judge in the Southern District of N.Y. completely dismissed a lawsuit brought by the Democratic National Committee against our historic 2016 campaign for President. The Judge said the DNC case was "entirely divorced" from the facts, yet another total & complete...

...vindication & exoneration from the Russian, WikiLeaks and every other form of HOAX perpetrated by the DNC, Radical Democrats and others. This is really big "stuff" especially coming from a highly respected judge who was appointed by President Clinton. The Witch Hunt Ends!

July 31, 2019

9:08 am: Such a great victory in court yesterday on the Russian Hoax, the greatest political scam in the history of our Country. TREASON! Hopefully, the Attorney Generel of the United States, and all of those working with him, will find out, in great detail, what happened. NEVER AGAIN!!!!

9:20 am: If I hadn't won the 2016 Election, we would be in a Great Recession/Depression right now. The people I saw on stage last night, & you can add in Sleepy Joe, Harris, & the rest, will lead us into an economic sinkhole the likes of which we have never seen before. With me, only up!

August 5, 2019

8:33 pm: Check out what @Google is up to for the 2020 election! #KAG2020

August 13, 2019

7:46 pm: No debate on Election Security should go forward without first agreeing that Voter ID (Identification) must play a very strong part in any final agreement. Without Voter ID, it is all so meaningless!

August 15, 2019

9:52 am: Great news! Tonight, we broke the all-time attendance record previously held by Elton John at #SNHUArena in Manchester, New Hampshire!

August 19, 2019

10:52 am: Wow, Report Just Out! Google manipulated from 2.6 million to 16 million votes for Hillary Clinton in 2016 Election! This was put out by a Clinton supporter, not a Trump Supporter! Google should be sued. My victory was even bigger than thought! @JudicialWatch

August 30, 2019

2:12 pm: This should NEVER happen to another President again!

August 31, 2019

8:09 am: MAKE AMERICA GREAT AGAIN, which is happening, and then, KEEP AMERICA GREAT!

September 3, 2019

9:28 am: Based on the IG Report, the whole Witch Hunt against me and my administration was a giant and illegal SCAM. The House of Representatives should now get back to work on drug prices, healthcare, infrastructure and all else. The Mueller Report showed No Collusion, No Obstruction!

September 4, 2019

7:49 pm: "Absolutely nothing is more important than going back & getting to the bottom of the origins of the investigation. We had an administration using America's Spying Apparatus to spy on a political opponent at the height of a presidential election. Those are all known, undisputed...

...facts, and that should terrify every American regardless of their political stripe. The idea that all of that information hasn't already been revealed shows how dastardly these people are, and how terrified they are about what's going to happen when that.

...information does come out." Charlie Hurt, Washington Times @ LouDobbs

September 11, 2019

7:12 am: In a hypothetical poll, done by one of the worst pollsters of them all, the Amazon Washington Post/ABC, which predicted I would lose to Crooked Hillary by 15 points (how did that work out?), Sleepy Joe, Pocahontas and virtually all others would beat me in the General Election...

...This is a phony suppression poll, meant to build up their Democrat partners. I haven't even started campaigning yet, and am constantly fighting Fake News like Russia, Russia, Russia. Look at North Carolina last night. Dan Bishop, down big in the Polls, WINS. Easier than 2016!

September 16, 2019

10:42 pm: We are all united by the same love of Country, the same devotion to family, and the same profound faith that America is blessed by the eternal grace of ALMIGHTY GOD! Bound by these convictions, we will campaign for every vote & we will WIN the Great State of NEW MEXICO in 2020!

10:49 pm: If you want to stop the drug smugglers, human traffickers, and vicious MS-13 gang members from threatening our communities and poisoning our youth, you have only one choice—you must elect more REPUBLICANS! #KAG2020

September 20, 2019

7:02 am: Oh no, really big political news, perhaps the biggest story in years! Part time Mayor of New York City, @BilldeBlasio, who was polling at a solid ZERO but had tremendous room for growth, has shocking dropped out of the Presidential race. NYC is devastated, he's coming home!

September 27, 2019

11:09 pm: Voter I.D. is the best way. Go for it Doug!

October 2, 2019

7:51 am: I won the right to be a presidential candidate in California, in a major Court decision handed down yesterday. It was filed against me by the Radical Left Governor of that State to tremendous Media hoopla. The VICTORY, however, was barely covered by the Fake News. No surprise!

10:48 am: The Do Nothing Democrats should be focused on building up our Country, not wasting everyone's time and energy on BULLSHIT, which is what they have been doing ever since I got overwhelmingly elected in 2016, 223-306. Get a better candidate this time, you'll need it!

6:41 pm: DEMOCRATS WANT TO STEAL THE ELECTION! #KAG2020

October 3, 2019

2:27 pm: ELECTION INTERFERENCE!

3:36 pm: "Trump Fundraising Haul Shows Impeachment Backfiring on Dems"

8:44 pm: This isn't about a Campaign, this is about Corruption on a massive scale!

October 6, 2019

11:42 am: ...And by the way, I would LOVE running against 1% Joe Biden—I just don't think it's going to happen. Sleepy Joe won't get to the starting gate, & based on all of the money he & his family probably "extorted," Joe should hang it up. I wouldn't want him dealing with China & U!

October 8, 2019

9:00 pm: The Greatest Witch Hunt in the history of the USA!

October 9, 2019

9:10 am: Crooked Hillary should try it again!

11:22 am: So why is someone a good or great President if they needed to Spy on someone else's Campaign in order to win (that didn't work out so well), and if they were unable to fill 142 important Federal Judgeships (a record by far), handing them all to me to choose. Will have 182 soon!

October 14, 2019

5:54 am: Former Democrat Senator Harry Reid just stated that Donald Trump is very smart, much more popular than people think, is underestimated, and will be hard to beat in the 2020 Election. Thank you Harry, I agree!

6:41 pm: DEMOCRATS WANT TO STEAL THE ELECTION! #KAG2020

Personal and Business Matters—2017 Web Quotes

Response to Ivanka Trump coming in the room during an interview with *The New York Times* on July 19, 2017.

Source: https://www.nytimes.com/2017/07/19/us/politics/trump-interview-transcript.html

"She's [Ivanka Trump is] great. She speaks fluent Chinese. She's amazing."

Response to his granddaughter Arabella Kushner coming in the room during an interview with *The New York Times* on July 19, 2017.

Source: https://www.nytimes.com/2017/07/19/us/politics/trump-interview-transcript.html

"She's [Arabella Kushner is] unbelievable, huh? Good, smart genes."

Response to a question from Forbes Magazine Editor Randall Lane, October 6, 2017.

Source: https://www.forbes.com/sites/randalllane/2017/10/10/trump-unfiltered/#1ffc406f7a58

"Did you say Trump's not as rich? What?"

Response to a question from Laura Ingraham of FOX News, November 2, 2017.

Source: https://www.youtube.com/watch?v=yTdDH-o_ICM

"Well, I think my family has been treated unfairly. I think that Ivanka has been treated very unfairly, frankly. Melania is really just powering through it. She's been incredible. People love Ivanka. People love Melania and, you know they go through it. But I do think the family's been treated a little bit unfairly."

Personal and Business Matters—2017 Tweets

February 8, 2017

10:51 am: My daughter Ivanka has been treated so unfairly by @Nordstrom. She is a great person—always pushing me to do the right thing! Terrible!

February 11, 2017

6:00 pm: I am so proud of my daughter Ivanka. To be abused and treated so badly by the media, and to still hold her head so high, is truly wonderful!

March 20, 2017

12:15 pm: Congratulations Eric & Lara. Very proud and happy for the two of you!

March 29, 2017

6:58 pm: .@FLOTUS Melania and I were honored to stop by the Women's Empowerment Panel this afternoon at the @WhiteHouse...

April 25, 2017

6:23 am: Proud of @IvankaTrump for her leadership on these important issues. Looking forward to hearing her speak at the W20!

April 26, 2017

9:53 am: HAPPY BIRTHDAY to our @FLOTUS, Melania!

July 10, 2017

6:31 am: When I left Conference Room for short meetings with Japan and other countries, I asked Ivanka to hold seat. Very standard. Angela M agrees!

6:47 am: If Chelsea Clinton were asked to hold the seat for her mother, as her mother gave our country away, the Fake News would say CHELSEA FOR PRES!

July 11, 2017

7:09 am: Marine Plane crash in Mississippi is heartbreaking. Melania and I send our deepest condolences to all!

July 17, 2017

9:07 am: Most politicians would have gone to a meeting like the one Don jr attended in order to get info on an opponent. That's politics!

July 19, 2017

9:33 pm: Melania and I send our thoughts and prayers to Senator McCain, Cindy, and their entire family. Get well soon.

July 25, 2017

5:52 am: Jared Kushner did very well yesterday in proving he did not collude with the Russians. Witch Hunt. Next up, 11 year old Barron Trump!

August 10, 2017

3:18 pm: @IvankaTrump will lead the U.S. delegation to India this fall, supporting women's entrepreneurship globally. #GES2017 @ narendramodi

September 12, 2017

1:41 pm: Congratulations to Eric & Lara on the birth of their son, Eric "Luke" Trump this morning!

November 28, 2017

8:00 am: Melania, our great and very hard working First Lady, who truly loves what she is doing, always thought that "if you run, you will win." She would tell everyone that, "no doubt, he will win." I also felt I would win (or I would not have run)—and Country is doing great!

10:30 pm: Great work Ivanka! https://t.co/AQL4JLvnDh

Personal and Business Matters—2018 Web Quotes

Response to a question from Piers Morgan of ITV, January 29, 2018.
Source: https://www.theguardian.com/us-news/2018/jan/29/donald-trump-interview-piers-morgan-im-very-popular-in-britain-get-a-lot-of-fan-mail

"I eat fine food, really from some of the finest chefs in the world, I eat healthy food, I also have some of that food on occasion. I think I eat actually quite well."

Response to a question from Steve Doocy of FOX News, April 26, 2018.
Source: https://www.bbc.com/news/world-us-canada-43913798

"Michael [Cohen] would represent me on some things, like with this crazy Stormy Daniels deal, and from what I can see he did nothing wrong."

Remarks at the launch of the First Lady's initiatives, May 7, 2018.
Source: https://www.whitehouse.gov/briefings-statements/
remarks-president-trump-launch-first-ladys-initiatives/

"Melania, thank you very much. That was truly a beautiful and heartfelt speech. It's the way she feels, very strongly.

"America is truly blessed to have a First Lady who is so devoted to our country and to our children.

"Over the past 15 months, Melania has visited hospitals, schools, families, who have suffered from the opioid crisis and suffered very deeply.

"Everywhere she has gone, Americans have been touched by her sincerity, moved by her grace, and lifted by her love.

"Melania, your care and compassion for our nation's children, and I have to say this, and I say it to you all the time, inspires us all.

"Today, we pledge to be best, best for our families, best for our communities, and best for our nation. And now, I am proud to sign the 'Be Best Proclamation,' and I think you all know who's going to get the pen. Thank you."

Remarks at a rally in Tampa, Florida, July 31, 2018.
Source: https://www.tampabay.com/florida-politics/buzz/2018/08/01/
heres-a-full-transcript-of-president-trumps-speech-from-his-tampa-rally/

"You know, I told the story the other day, I was probably in Washington in my entire life 17 times. True, 17 times. I don't think I ever stayed overnight. You know what I'm getting at, right? And we have a great cabinet now, a couple of little changes. But we have a great cabinet. We have Mike Pompeo, our Secretary of State.

"So many great people. And we're really getting, we have just incredible people.

"But I made some choices that I wouldn't have made. But I'm riding down Pennsylvania Avenue. Again, I've only been here about 17 times. And probably seven of those times was to check out the hotel I'm building on Pennsylvania Avenue and then I hop on the plane and I go back. So, I've been there 17 times. Never stayed there at night, I don't believe. And then I'm riding down in this beautiful car, picked up at the airport by Secret Service, holding the hand of our great First Lady.

"And I look at her and I say, 'Honey, guess what, I'm President of the United States!' President of the United States.

"And I didn't know anybody in Washington, but now I know everybody in Washington. I know the good ones. I know the bad ones. I know the wonderful people, and I know the scum. And America now is winning again like they haven't won before."

Remarks at a rally in Tampa, Florida, July 31, 2018.
Source: https://www.tampabay.com/florida-politics/buzz/2018/08/01/heres-a-full-transcript-of-president-trumps-speech-from-his-tampa-rally/

"So, I'm sure we all say this about our children, but I have great children. And a couple of them-plus are here tonight. I have Eric Trump, who's been fantastic. He loves this political stuff.

"Eric's wife, Lara, who is so great. I think she singlehandedly won the state of North Carolina for Trump.

"Thank you, Lara. Didn't hurt in Pennsylvania, either. Thank you very much.

"And we have somebody that nobody ever heard of, Ivanka. Ivanka."

Response to a question from Lesley Stahl of *60 Minutes*, October 15, 2018.
Source: https://www.theguardian.com/us-news/2018/oct/15/donald-trumps-60-minutes-interview-eight-takeaways

"I'm not a baby. It's a tough business. This is a vicious place."

Response to a question from Lesley Stahl of *60 Minutes*, October 15, 2018.
Source: https://www.theguardian.com/us-news/2018/oct/15/donald-trumps-60-minutes-interview-eight-takeaways

"I'm President and you're not."

Response to a question from the Associated Press[43], published October 17, 2018[44].

Source: https://www.cnbc.com/2018/10/17/
read-the-transcript-of-aps-interview-with-president-trum

"Oh, absolutely he's lying. And Michael Cohen was a PR person who did small legal work, very small legal work. And what he did was very sad, when you look. By the way, he was in trouble not for what he did for me; he was in trouble for what he did for himself. You do know that? Having to do with loans, mortgages, taxicabs and various other things, if you read the paper. He wasn't in trouble for what he did for me; he was in trouble for what he did for other people. He represented me very little. It's a very low level. And what he was is also a public relations person. And now if he wants to try and get a little bit lighter sentence for what he did. Totally uninvolved. I wasn't involved and he had other clients, number one. And number two, he was a contractor to a large extent. But Michael Cohen, if you take a look at what he did, this had to do with loans, and I guess the taxi industry is something that I have nothing to do with; he did this on his own time."

Response to a question from the Associated Press[45], published October 17, 2018[46].

Source: https://www.cnbc.com/2018/10/17/read-the-transcript-of-aps-interview-with-president-trump.html

"Well, I can say this. I knew nothing about the meeting that you're talking about. My son's a good young guy. He did what every other person in Congress would do if somebody came up to them, said,

---

43 AP White House reporters Catherine Lucey, Zeke Miller, and Jonathan Lemire conducted this interview. However, the transcript does not indicate which reporter asked President Trump which question.

44 The interview was conducted by the AP before the midterm elections of October 16, 2018. However, it was published by CNBC on October 17, 2018.

45 AP White House reporters Catherine Lucey, Zeke Miller, and Jonathan Lemire conducted this interview. However, the transcript does not indicate which reporter asked President Trump which question.

46 The interview was conducted by the AP before the midterm elections of October 16, 2018. However, it was published by CNBC on October 17, 2018.

'Hey, I have information on your opponent.' I don't know of any politician. And I think I can speak for the people in this room that would have said, 'Oh, gee, information on my opponent and it's bad information?' Name me a politician that would have turned that down. There is no such thing as that kind of a politician. So that's what they heard. They heard it was about Hillary Clinton. They had a meeting or he had a meeting with some people. The meeting became about a different subject and they couldn't get out of the meeting fast enough.

"Now, here's the important thing. After the meeting, nothing happened. It was like, 'Hey, let's get together next week. Let's get together tomorrow. Let's get together.' Nothing happened out of that meeting. Absolutely nothing. He did absolutely nothing wrong. And there's nobody harder on my son than I am. And I would tell you, the press has made a fake news deal out of that meeting. If he did something wrong, I would have been livid. I could never really blame him because I've had people come up to me, senators. I've had a lot of political people say, 'Your son didn't do anything wrong. That was just a meeting. It was called oppo research.' A lot of the politicians would call it opposition research. There was nothing wrong with that. But here's more important. Nothing from the day of that meeting. It ended. And if you listen to people, it sounded like it ended like they couldn't get out fast enough. There was nothing wrong with having an opposition research meeting and nothing happened from the meeting. If that meeting went, 'Oh, let's have another meeting next week or let's have a meeting tomorrow or let's start doing this or that or a hundred different things,' that's different. That's totally different depending on what they were going to do. But nothing happened."

Response to a question from Chris Wallace of FOX News, November 18, 2018.
Source: https://www.youtube.com/watch?v=rMgJnnG-Nql

"My wife did a great job in Africa and she was not treated properly by the press; she really worked so hard."

Remarks at the Congressional Ball, December 15, 2018.

Source: https://www.whitehouse.gov/briefings-statements/
remarks-president-trump-congressional-ball/

"This [The White House] is a house that's very exciting. This is a house that we love being in. We love living in it. Look at it tonight in between all of the great food. You know, we have the 'A' team of chefs. We have 'A' teams, 'B' teams, and 'C' teams. The 'C' teams give you a lot. But it's not very good. The 'A' team gives you a lot, and it is very good. So tonight, you have a lot of great food, so enjoy it.

"But look around at the house, because it's an incredible place. It's sort of where it all begins. It starts, it sort of moves along, and then it starts all over again if you don't get it right. And it's been very exciting living in the White House. To me, it's a happy place. You know, a lot of presidents have said it's not a happy place. I find it to be a happy place."

Remarks at the Congressional Ball, December 15, 2018.

Source: https://www.whitehouse.gov/briefings-statements/
remarks-president-trump-congressional-ball/

"I want to thank Melania, our great First Lady, for doing the decorations. As you know, she worked so hard on all of the beautiful decorations. I don't know if you've gotten to see all of them, but upstairs, downstairs, all over, and she's—People love what she did. And I love what she has done. And I'll tell you what, she does it from the heart. She has done a terrific job. People love our First Lady. So, thank you very much, honey. Very nice. Really great."

Remarks at the Congressional Ball, December 15, 2018.

Source: https://www.whitehouse.gov/briefings-statements/
remarks-president-trump-congressional-ball/

"So, look, enjoy yourself, travel around, look at every molding of this house. It's just an incredible place to be. And again, thank you all. Merry Christmas, Happy Hanukkah, have a great New Year. We're going to have an incredible new year for our country, most importantly. And to our First Lady, thank you very much on a job well done. Thank you. Honey?"

Personal and Business Matters—2018 Tweets

January 4, 2018

10:52 am: I authorized Zero access to White House (actually turned him down many times) for author of phony book! I never spoke to him for book. Full of lies, misrepresentations and sources that don't exist. Look at this guy's past and watch what happens to him and Sloppy Steve!

February 20, 2018

10:16 am to 10:29 am: A woman I don't know and, to the best of my knowledge, never met, is on the FRONT PAGE of the Fake News Washington Post saying I kissed her (for two minutes yet) in the lobby of Trump Tower 12 years ago. Never happened! Who would do this in a public space with live security...

...cameras running. Another False Accusation. Why doesn't @washingtonpost report the story of the women taking money to make up stories about me? One had her home mortgage paid off. Only @ FoxNews so reported...doesn't fit the Mainstream Media narrative.

April 21, 2018

7:17 am: The New York Times and a third rate reporter named Maggie Habberman, known as a Crooked H flunkie who I don't speak to and have nothing to do with, are going out of their way to destroy Michael Cohen and his relationship with me in the hope that he will "flip." They use...

...non-existent "sources" and a drunk/drugged up loser who hates Michael, a fine person with a wonderful family. Michael is a businessman for his own account/lawyer who I have always liked & respected. Most people will flip if the Government lets them out of trouble, even if...

...it means lying or making up stories. Sorry, I don't see Michael doing that despite the horrible Witch Hunt and the dishonest media!

May 3, 2018

5:46 am to 6:00 am: Mr. Cohen, an attorney, received a monthly retainer, not from the campaign and having nothing to do with the campaign, from which he entered into, through reimbursement, a private contract between two parties, known as a non-disclosure agreement, or NDA. These agreements are...

...very common among celebrities and people of wealth. In this case it is in full force and effect and will be used in Arbitration for damages against Ms. Clifford (Daniels). The agreement was used to stop the false and extortionist accusations made by her about an affair,...

...despite already having signed a detailed letter admitting that there was no affair. Prior to its violation by Ms. Clifford and her attorney, this was a private agreement. Money from the campaign, or campaign contributions, played no roll in this transaction.

June 14, 2018

10:09 am: The sleazy New York Democrats, and their now disgraced (and run out of town) A.G. Eric Schneiderman, are doing everything they can to sue me on a foundation that took in $18,800,000 and gave out to charity more money than it took in, $19,200,000. I won't settle this case!...

...Schneiderman, who ran the Clinton campaign in New York, never had the guts to bring this ridiculous case, which lingered in their office for almost 2 years. Now he resigned his office in disgrace, and his disciples brought it when we would not settle.

July 21, 2018

7:10 am: Inconceivable that the government would break into a lawyer's office (early in the morning)—almost unheard of. Even more inconceivable that a lawyer would tape a client—totally unheard of

& perhaps illegal. The good news is that your favorite President did nothing wrong!

July 25, 2018

7:34 am: What kind of a lawyer would tape a client? So sad! Is this a first, never heard of it before? Why was the tape so abruptly terminated (cut) while I was presumably saying positive things? I hear there are other clients and many reporters that are taped—can this be so? Too bad!

August 13, 2018

8:50 pm to 8:57 pm: @MarkBurnettTV called to say that there are NO TAPES of the Apprentice where I used such a terrible and disgusting word as attributed by Wacky and Deranged Omarosa. I don't have that word in my vocabulary, and never have. She made it up. Look at her MANY recent quotes saying...

...such wonderful and powerful things about me—a true Champion of Civil Rights—until she got fired. Omarosa had Zero credibility with the Media (they didn't want interviews) when she worked in the White House. Now that she says bad about me, they will talk to her. Fake News!

August 22, 2018

7:44 am: If anyone is looking for a good lawyer, I would strongly suggest that you don't retain the services of Michael Cohen!

September 26, 2018

11:47 am: Avenatti is a third rate lawyer who is good at making false accusations, like he did on me and like he is now doing on Judge Brett Kavanaugh. He is just looking for attention and doesn't want people to look at his past record and relationships—a total low-life!

October 16, 2018

10:04 am: "Federal Judge throws out Stormy Danials lawsuit versus Trump. Trump is entitled to full legal fees." @FoxNews Great, now I can go after Horseface and her 3rd rate lawyer in the Great State of Texas. She will confirm the letter she signed! She knows nothing about me, a total con!

December 3, 2018

10:24 am to 10:29 am: "Michael Cohen asks judge for no Prison Time." You mean he can do all of the TERRIBLE, unrelated to Trump, things having to do with fraud, big loans, Taxis, etc., and not serve a long prison term? He makes up stories to get a GREAT & ALREADY reduced deal for himself, and get...

...his wife and father-in-law (who has the money?) off Scott Free. He lied for this outcome and should, in my opinion, serve a full and complete sentence.

December 19, 2018

9:44 am to 10:05 am: The Trump Foundation has done great work and given away lots of money, both mine and others, to great charities over the years—with me taking NO fees, rent, salaries etc. Now, as usual, I am getting slammed by Cuomo and the Dems in a long running civil lawsuit started by...

...sleazebag AG Eric Schneiderman, who has since resigned over horrific women abuse, when I wanted to close the Foundation so as not to be in conflict with politics. Shady Eric was head of New Yorkers for Clinton, and refused to even look at the corrupt Clinton Foundation...

...In any event, it goes on and on & the new AG, who is now being replaced by yet another AG (who openly campaigned on a GET TRUMP agenda), does little else but rant, rave & politic against me. Will never be treated fairly by these people—a total double standard of "justice."

Personal and Business Matters—2019 Web Quotes

Response to a question from Peter Baker of *The New York Times*, January 31, 2019.

Source: https://www.nytimes.com/2019/02/01/us/politics/trump-interview-transcripts.html

"So let me tell you about, about Trump Tower Moscow. This was a very unimportant deal. This was a very unimportant deal. Number one. Number two, this was a deal, the only thing you heard is through Rudy [Giuliani]. Is that what you heard? Through Rudy?"

Response to a question from Peter Baker of *The New York Times*, January 31, 2019.

Source: https://www.nytimes.com/2019/02/01/us/politics/trump-interview-transcripts.html

"Rudy [Giuliani] was incorrect. Number one, he was incorrect, and we've explained that, he was wrong. Rudy has been wrong. A little bit. But what has happened is this. I didn't care. That deal was not important. It was essentially a letter of intent or an option. I'm not even sure that they had a site. And if you look at where that was sent to, that was a Michael Cohen thing. If you look, I always say, Why don't you bring this up, to Jay Sekulow, good guy. I think it was sent to almost like a public address for Moscow. If you take a look at it. Take a good solid look. The original letter or something was sent. They didn't even have anybody to send it to. But that deal is just like other deals. I was doing other deals. I was running for President, but I was also running a business."

Response to a question from Peter Baker of *The New York Times*, January 31, 2019.

Source: https://www.nytimes.com/2019/02/01/us/politics/trump-interview-transcripts.html

"My point is this—It was a free option to look at a deal, to look at deals. That was not like, 'I'm going to buy a property in Moscow. I'm going to do—Or I'm building a building in Moscow.' Now, I would have had every right to do a deal. That's what I did. That's what I did.

"Rudy [Giuliani] was wrong in that he went—I think what Rudy was looking at, I think, was that in the statement I made to the [Robert] Mueller group, we talked about during that period of a year, up until the election, we talked about that. So he may have been referring to that.

"But the way I view it is early in the year to middle of the year, no interest. I had very little interest in the first place, and again, I viewed it as a free option. It may have been a letter of intent. I don't know exactly what it was called. But it was unimportant. And you know what was very important to me? Running for President. And doing well. But I was running a business. I mean, I would have been allowed to build 20 buildings. I was doing other things. I was doing a lot of other things. I was running a business. Because as you would know, there weren't a lot of people at the time that thought I was going to win. So I don't want to give up a year and a half of my life, not do anything, run for President, then have to go back and say, you know, 'I could have kept running my business.'

"Very interestingly, you know, George Washington ran his business. You can, I guess, you can go long beyond the election, if you wanted to. You know. But I didn't do that."

Response to a question from Maggie Haberman of *The New York Times*, January 31, 2019.

Source: https://www.nytimes.com/2019/02/01/us/politics/trump-interview-transcripts.html

"Well, I will say this: I think people have the right to speak their mind. You know, speaking your mind."

Response to a POLITICO reporter's[47] question, May 10, 2019.

Source: https://www.politico.com/story/2019/05/10/trump-interview-transcript-1317598

"But I know that my son [Donald Trump Jr.] did testify. I know that [Special Counsel Robert] Mueller went over his testimony and very,

---

47   POLITICO reporters Andrew Restuccia, Eliana Johnson, and Daniel Lippman conducted the telephone interview with President Trump, but the transcript does not indicate which reporter asked which question.

very strongly went over his testimony, and found that he did absolutely nothing wrong. That was an oppo research meeting. And I would say that everybody in Washington has had those meetings. You know, your opponent, 'Hey, we have information on your opponent. Would you like to hear?' I mean, you tell me how many politicians would turn that meeting down. And then it turned out she did that—It turned out you didn't have any information."

Remarks at the White House Summit on Child Care and Paid Leave, December 12, 2019.
Source: https://www.whitehouse.gov/briefings-statements/ remarks-president-trump-white-house-summit-child-care-paid-leave/

"Thank you. What a nice group. Thank you very much. Hi, everybody. Hi. Well, thank you very much. And I had a very busy time and a very busy day, and my daughter [Ivanka] said, 'You will be here.' So—That was the end of that busy day, right? When a daughter says, 'You have to be here.' But she's done such an incredible job.

"So I want to thank Ivanka. And from the very beginning—That's true. Yeah. From the very beginning, it's been an extraordinary— She has been so extraordinary, in terms of her advocacy for America's working families. Fourteen million people she's gotten jobs for, where she would go into Walmart, she would go into our great companies and say, 'They really want help. They really want you to teach them.' Because the government can't teach like the companies can teach. And companies would take a half a million people, a million people.

"And her goal when she started it two years ago was 500,000 jobs; she's done over 14 million. So that's really something. And that's on top of everything else, including what we're here for today."

Remarks at a rally in Battle Creek, Michigan, December 18, 2019.
Source: http://www.youtube.com/watch?v=Wjf5EM5MhzQ#action=share

"Thank you very much. And did you notice that everybody is saying Merry Christmas again? Did you notice? Saying Merry Christmas. I remember when I first started this beautiful trip, this beautiful journey, I just said to the First Lady [Melania], 'You're so lucky I took you on this fantastic journey. It's so much fun.'"

Remarks at a rally in Battle Creek, Michigan, December 18, 2019.
Source: http://www.youtube.com/watch?v=Wjf5EM5MhzQ#action=share

"I understand that. I understand that but it's my life, very unfair to my family. I have to say this, very, very unfair to my family. What they put my family through is a disgrace. Me, it's my life. It's fine. I do, but you know what? What they put my family through is a disgrace and they ought to be ashamed, and we should get apologies all over the place."

Remarks at a rally in Battle Creek, Michigan, December 18, 2019.
Source: http://www.youtube.com/watch?v=Wjf5EM5MhzQ#action=share

"They called and complained so much that they changed the headline and took it from positive to negative on a good story. Can you believe it? No, they're among the most dishonest people. But I'll never forget, before I took that great escalator ride down with our First Lady, our First Lady is doing a great job.

"I said, 'First Lady [Melania], you're so lucky I took you on this journey. This wonderful, beautiful journey.' And it is. You know why it's a wonderful, beautiful journey? Because look at we've accomplished—What we've accomplished is unbelievable. It's unprecedented. It is unprecedented, what we've accomplished. We're so lucky."

Personal and Business Matters—2019 Tweets

January 20, 2019

7:50 pm: A truly great First Lady who doesn't get the credit she deserves!

January 24, 2019

7:48 am: So interesting that bad lawyer Michael Cohen, who sadly will not be testifying before Congress, is using the lawyer of Crooked Hillary Clinton to represent him—Gee, how did that happen? Remember July 4th weekend when Crooked went before FBI & wasn't sworn in, no tape, nothing?

10:28 pm: A third rate conman who interviewed me many years ago for just a short period of time has been playing his biggest con of all on Fake News CNN. Michael D'Antonio, a broken down hack who knows nothing about me, goes on night after night telling made up Trump stories. Disgraceful!

February 5, 2019

12:08 pm: Melania and I send our greetings to those celebrating the Lunar New Year. Today, people across the United States and around the world mark the beginning of the Lunar New Year with spectacular fireworks displays, joyful festivals, and family gatherings…

February 7, 2019

4:08 am: Michael Cohen was one of many lawyers who represented me (unfortunately). He had other clients also. He was just disbarred by the State Supreme Court for lying & fraud. He did bad things unrelated to Trump. He is lying in order to reduce his prison time. Using Crooked's lawyer!

March 3, 2019

2:52 pm: My wonderful daughter, Ivanka, will be interviewed tonight by Steve Hilton on "The Next Revolution." @FoxNews 9:00 P.M. She works so hard and has achieved so much for the U.S.A.(and gets so little credit!). Then watch Mark Levin at 10:00 P.M., a great show!

March 7, 2019

5:39 pm: Breaking News @MSNBC: "Cohen's lawyer contradicts Cohen's testimony about never seeking a Presidential Pardon."

March 22, 2019

3:15 pm: Today in Florida, @FLOTUS and I were honored to welcome and meet with leaders from the Bahamas, Dominican Republic, Haiti, Jamaica, and Saint Lucia!

April 22, 2019

2:41 pm: Today, @FLOTUS Melania and I are honored to host the 2019 @WhiteHouse Easter Egg Roll!

May 8, 2019

5:56 am: Real estate developers in the 1980's & 1990's, more than 30 years ago, were entitled to massive write offs and depreciation which would, if one was actively building, show losses and tax losses in almost all cases. Much was non monetary. Sometimes considered "tax shelter,".

…you would get it by building, or even buying. You always wanted to show losses for tax purposes…almost all real estate developers did—and often re-negotiate with banks, it was sport. Additionally, the very old information put out is a highly inaccurate Fake News hit job!

May 20, 2019

6:20 am: The Failing New York Times (it will pass away when I leave office in 6 years), and others of the Fake News Media, keep writing phony stories about how I didn't use many banks because they didn't want to do business with me. WRONG! It is because I didn't need money. Very old…

…fashioned, but true. When you don't need or want money, you don't need or want banks. Banks have always been available to me, they want to make money. Fake Media only says this to disparage, and always uses unnamed sources (because their sources don't even exist).

The Mainstream Media has never been as corrupt and deranged as it is today. FAKE NEWS is actually the biggest story of all and is the true ENEMY OF THE PEOPLE! That's why they refuse to cover the REAL Russia Hoax. But the American people are wise to what is going on…

…Now the new big story is that Trump made a lot of money and buys everything for cash, he doesn't need banks. But where did he get all of that cash? Could it be Russia? No, I built a great business and don't need banks, but if I did they would be there…and DeutscheBank.

…was very good and highly professional to deal with—and if for any reason I didn't like them, I would have gone elsewhere…there was always plenty of money around and banks to choose from. They would be very happy to take my money. Fake News!

June 11, 2019

6:14 am: New book just out, "The Real Deal, My Decade Fighting Battles and Winning Wars With Trump," is really wonderful. It is written by two people who are very smart & know me well, George Sorial & Damian Bates, as opposed to all the books where the author has no clue who I am. ENJOY!

July 1, 2019

9:47 am: Congratulations to legislators in New Jersey for not passing taxes that would have driven large numbers of high end taxpayers out of the state. Many were planning to leave, & will now be staying. New York & others should start changing their thought process on taxes, fast!

11:10 am: It is very hard and expensive to live in New York. Governor Andrew Cuomo uses his Attorney General as a bludgeoning tool for his own purposes. They sue on everything, always in search of a crime. I even got sued on a Foundation which took Zero rent & expenses & gave away...

...more money than it had. Going on for years, originally brought by Crooked Hillary's Campaign Chair, A.G. Eric Schneiderman, until forced to resign for abuse against women. They never even looked at the disgusting Clinton Foundation. Now Cuomo's A.G. is harassing all of my...

...New York businesses in search of anything at all they can find to make me look as bad as possible. So, on top of ridiculously high taxes, my children and companies are spending a fortune on lawyers. No wonder people and businesses are fleeing New York in record numbers!

11:37 am: That's right, The Trump Foundation gave away 100% plus, with Zero rent or expenses charged, and has been being sued by Cuomo and New York State for years—another part of the political Witch Hunt. Just in case anyone is interested—Clinton Foundation never even looked at!

July 11, 2019

6:45 am: The Fake News Media loves the narrative that I didn't use many banks because the banks didn't like me. No, I didn't use many banks because I didn't (don't) need their money (old fashioned, isn't it?). If I did, it would have been very easy for me to get...

...And remember, a bank that I did use years ago, the now badly written about and maligned Deutsche Bank, was then one of the largest and most prestigious banks in the world! They wanted my business, and so did many others!

July 29, 2019

5:30 am: I have known Al for 25 years. Went to fights with him & Don King, always got along well. He "loved Trump!" He would ask me

449

for favors often. Al is a con man, a troublemaker, always looking for a score. Just doing his thing. Must have intimidated Comcast/NBC. Hates Whites & Cops!

6:26 am: Al Sharpton would always ask me to go to his events. He would say, "it's a personal favor to me." Seldom, but sometimes, I would go. It was fine. He came to my office in T.T. during the presidential campaign to apologize for the way he was talking about me. Just a conman at work!

August 5, 2019

11:51 am: The First Lady and I join all Americans in praying and grieving for the victims, their families, and the survivors. We will stand by their side FOREVER!

August 7, 2019

11:20 pm: Just watched a world class loser, Tim O'Brien, who I haven't seen or spoken to in many years, & knows NOTHING about me except that he wrote a failed hit piece book about me 15 years ago. Fired like a dog from other jobs? Saw him on Lyin' Brian Williams Trump Slam Show. Bad TV…

August 20, 2019

8:41 am: Two incredible people. I can't believe they're not working (few work harder)! https://t.co/tsh8KDS8Qs

3:00 pm: CONGRATULATIONS @EricTrump and @LaraLeaTrump, on the birth of Carolina Dorothy Trump. So proud!

August 29, 2019

6:31 am: Crazy Lawrence O'Donnell, who has been calling me wrong from even before I announced my run for the Presidency, even being previously forced by NBC to apologize, which he did while crying, for things he said about me & The Apprentice, was again forced to apologize, this time…

for the most ridiculous claim of all, that Russia, Russia, Russia, or Russian oligarchs, co-signed loan documents for me, a guarantee. Totally false, as is virtually everything else he, and much of the rest of the LameStream Media, has said about me for years. ALL APOLOGIZE!

September 9, 2019

8:43 am: I know nothing about an Air Force plane landing at an airport (which I do not own and have nothing to do with) near Turnberry Resort (which I do own) in Scotland, and filling up with fuel, with the crew staying overnight at Turnberry (they have good taste!). NOTHING TO DO WITH ME

8:52 am: I had nothing to do with the decision of our great @VP Mike Pence to stay overnight at one of the Trump owned resorts in Doonbeg, Ireland. Mike's family has lived in Doonbeg for many years, and he thought that during his very busy European visit, he would stop and see his family!

September 26, 2019

6:06 am: So cute! Her father is under siege, for no reason, since his first day in office! https://t.co/8wtB3H4fth

October 19, 2019

8:18 pm: I thought I was doing something very good for our Country by using Trump National Doral, in Miami, for hosting the G-7 Leaders. It is big, grand, on hundreds of acres, next to MIAMI INTERNATIONAL AIRPORT, has tremendous ballrooms & meeting rooms, and each delegation would have...

...its own 50 to 70 unit building. Would set up better than other alternatives. I announced that I would be willing to do it at NO PROFIT or, if legally permissible, at ZERO COST to the USA. But, as usual, the Hostile Media & their Democrat Partners went CRAZY!

8:52 pm: .Therefore, based on both Media & Democrat Crazed and Irrational Hostility, we will no longer consider Trump National Doral,

Miami, as the Host Site for the G-7 in 2020. We will begin the search for another site, including the possibility of Camp David, immediately. Thank you!

October 20, 2019

5:41 pm: So interesting that, when I announced Trump National Doral in Miami would be used for the hosting of the G-7, and then rescinded due to Do Nothing Democrat/Fake News Anger, very few in Media mentioned that NO PROFITS would be taken, or would be given FREE, if legally permissible!

October 26, 2019

6:21 am: Had a beautiful dinner last night at Camp David in celebration of the 10th Wedding Anniversary of Ivanka and Jared. Attended by a small number of family and friends, it could not have been nicer. Camp David is a special place. Cost of the event will be totally paid for by me!

October 31, 2019

8:32 pm: 1600 Pennsylvania Avenue, the White House, is the place I have come to love and will stay for, hopefully, another 5 years as we MAKE AMERICA GREAT AGAIN, but my family and I will be making Palm Beach, Florida, our Permanent Residence. I cherish New York, and the people of...

...New York, and always will, but unfortunately, despite the fact that I pay millions of dollars in city, state and local taxes each year, I have been treated very badly by the political leaders of both the city and state. Few have been treated worse. I hated having to make...

...this decision, but in the end it will be best for all concerned. As President, I will always be there to help New York and the great people of New York. It will always have a special place in my heart!

November 4, 2019

12:39 pm: My son, @DonaldJTrumpJr is coming out with a new book, "Triggered: How the Left Thrives on Hate and Wants to Silence Us"—available tomorrow, November 5th! A great new book that I highly recommend for ALL to read. Go order it today!

November 9, 2019

10:37 am: Just finished reading my son Donald's just out new book, "Triggered." It is really good! He, along with many of us, was very unfairly treated. But we all fight back, and we always win!

November 16, 2019

12:57 pm: "Triggered," a great book by my son, Don. Now number one on @NYTIMES LIST. Keep it there for a while!

December 12, 2019

7:36 am: I will be there in two weeks, The Southern White House! https://t.co/2djJrzAEfZ

December 27, 2019

11:13 pm: Our great First Lady. She really cares!

December 31, 2019

8:22 pm: Our fantastic First Lady!

Press/Media/Journalists—2017 News Quotes

Response to a question from David Muir of ABC News, January 26, 2017.
Source: https://www.telegraph.co.uk/news/2017/01/26/
full-transcript-president-donald-trumps-interview-abc-news/

"You know, I always talk about the reporters that grovel when they wanna write something that you wanna hear but not necessarily millions of people wanna hear or have to hear."

Response to a question from Tucker Carlson of FOX News, March 15, 2017.
Source: https://www.youtube.com/watch?v=RYGH6ejacNO

"Well, I had been reading about things. I read in, I think it was January 20th, a *New York Times* article where they were talking about wiretapping. There was an article, I think they used that exact term. I read other things.

"I watched your friend Bret Baier, the day previous where he was talking about certain, very complex sets of things happening and wiretapping. I said, 'Wait a minute, there's lot of wiretapping being talked about.'

"I've been seeing a lot of things. Now, for the most part, I am not going to discuss it because we have it before the committee. And we will be submitting things before the committee very soon that has not been submitted as of yet. But it's potentially a very serious situation."

Response to a question from Tucker Carlson of FOX News, March 15, 2017.
Source: https://www.youtube.com/watch?v=RYGH6ejacNO

"Well, because *The New York Times* wrote about it. You know?

"Not that I respect *The New York Times*. I call it the failing *New York Times*, but they did write on January 20th. They're using the word wiretapped."

Response to a question from John Dickerson of CBS News, April 30, 2017.
Source: https://www.cbsnews.com/news/face-the-nation-transcript-april-30-2017-president-trump/

"Well, your show. I love your show. I call it 'Deface the Nation.' But, you know, your show is sometimes not exactly correct."

Response to a question from John Dickerson of CBS News, April 30, 2017.
Source: https://www.cbsnews.com/news/face-the-nation-transcript-april-30-2017-president-trump/

"But when I watch some of the news reports, which are so unfair, and they say we don't cover pre-existing conditions, we cover it beautifully. I'll tell you who doesn't cover pre-existing conditions. Obamacare. You know why? It's dead."

Press/Media/Journalists—2017 Tweets

January 22, 2017

7:47 am: Watched protests yesterday but was under the impression that we just had an election! Why didn't these people vote? Celebs hurt cause badly.

7:51 am: Wow, television ratings just out: 31 million people watched the Inauguration, 11 million more than the very good ratings from 4 years ago!

January 28, 2017

8:04 am: The failing @nytimes has been wrong about me from the very beginning. Said I would lose the primaries, then the general election. FAKE NEWS!

8:08 am to 8:16 am: Thr coverage about me in the @nytimes and the @washingtonpost gas been so false and angry that the times actually apologized to its...

dwindling subscribers and readers. They got me wrong right from the beginning and still have not changed course, and never will. DISHONEST

February 3, 2017

6:34 am: Thank you to Prime Minister of Australia for telling the truth about our very civil conversation that FAKE NEWS media lied about. Very nice!

February 6, 2017

7:01 am: Any negative polls are fake news, just like the CNN, ABC, NBC polls in the election. Sorry, people want border security and extreme vetting

7:07 am: I call my own shots, largely based on an accumulation of data, and everyone knows it. Some FAKE NEWS media, in order to marginalize, lies!

February 10, 2017

8:35 am: The failing @nytimes does major FAKE NEWS China story saying "Mr. Xi has not spoken to Mr. Trump since Nov.14." We spoke at length yesterday!

February 12, 2017

7:14 am: While on FAKE NEWS @CNN, Bernie Sanders was cut off for using the term fake news to describe the network. They said technical difficulties!

February 15, 2017

6:40 am: The fake news media is going crazy with their conspiracy theories and blind hatred. @MSNBC & @CNN are unwatchable. @foxandfriends is great!

February 16, 2017

6:58 am: Leaking, and even illegal classified leaking, has been a big problem in Washington for years. Failing @nytimes (and others) must apologize!

9:10 am: FAKE NEWS media, which makes up stories and "sources," is far more effective than the discredited Democrats—but they are fading fast

February 17, 2017

4:32 pm: The FAKE NEWS media (failing @nytimes, @CNN, @NBC-News and many more) is not my enemy, it is the enemy of the American people. SICK!

February 18, 2017

8:31 am: Don't believe the main stream (fake news) media. The White House is running VERY WELL. I inherited a MESS and am in the process of fixing it.

February 24, 2017

10:09 pm: FAKE NEWS media knowingly doesn't tell the truth. A great danger to our country. The failing @nytimes has become a joke. Likewise @CNN. Sad!

February 25, 2017

8:19 am: The media has not reported that the National Debt in my first month went down by $12 billion vs a $200 billion increase in Obama first mo.

4:53 pm: I will not be attending the White House Correspondents' Association Dinner this year. Please wish everyone well and have a great evening!

February 26, 2017

1:16 pm: Russia talk is FAKE NEWS put out by the Dems, and played up by the media, in order to mask the big election defeat and the illegal leaks!

March 7, 2017

9:14 am: Don't let the FAKE NEWS tell you that there is big infighting in the Trump Admin. We are getting along great, and getting major things done!

March 15, 2017

5:55 am: Does anybody really believe that a reporter, who nobody ever heard of, "went to his mailbox" and found my tax returns? @NBCNews FAKE NEWS!

March 20, 2017

5:35 am: James Clapper and others stated that there is no evidence Potus colluded with Russia. This story is FAKE NEWS and everyone knows it!

March 23, 2017

7:18 am: Just watched the totally biased and fake news reports of the so-called Russia story on NBC and ABC. Such dishonesty!

April 1, 2017

7:43 am: When will Sleepy Eyes Chuck Todd and @NBCNews start talking about the Obama SURVEILLANCE SCANDAL and stop with the Fake Trump/Russia story?

April 3, 2017

5:15 am: Such amazing reporting on unmasking and the crooked scheme against us by @foxandfriends. "Spied on before nomination." The real story.

April 17, 2017

7:17 am: The Fake Media (not Real Media) has gotten even worse since the election. Every story is badly slanted. We have to hold them to the truth!

April 20, 2017

8:48 am: Failing @nytimes, which has been calling me wrong for two years, just got caught in a big lie concerning New England Patriots visit to W.H.

April 24, 2017

7:15 am: The two fake news polls released yesterday, ABC & NBC, while containing some very positive info, were totally wrong in General E. Watch!

April 25, 2017

7:36 am: Don't let the fake media tell you that I have changed my position on the WALL. It will get built and help stop drugs, human trafficking etc.

May 4, 2017

6:02 am: The Fake News media is officially out of control. They will do or say anything in order to get attention—never been a time like this!

May 5, 2017

6:29 pm: Why is it that the Fake News rarely reports Ocare is on its last legs and that insurance companies are fleeing for their lives? It's dead!

May 7, 2017

6:15 am: When will the Fake Media ask about the Dems dealings with Russia & why the DNC wouldn't allow the FBI to check their server or investigate?

May 28, 2017

7:33 am: It is my opinion that many of the leaks coming out of the White House are fabricated lies made up by the #FakeNews media.

7:34 am to 7:35 am: Whenever you see the words 'sources say' in the fake news media, and they don't mention names...

...it is very possible that those sources don't exsist but are made up by fake news writers. #FakeNews is the enemy!

9:43 am: British Prime Minister May was very angry that the info the U.K. gave to U.S. about Manchester was leaked. Gave me full details!

7:20 pm: The Fake News Media works hard at disparaging & demeaning my use of social

media because they don't want America to hear the real story!

May 30, 2017

6:04 am: Russian officials must be laughing at the U.S. & how a lame excuse for why the Dems lost the election has taken over the Fake News.

11:06 pm: Despite the constant negative press covfefe

May 31, 2017

5:09 am: Who can figure out the true meaning of "covfefe" ??? Enjoy!

6:14 am: Kathy Griffin should be ashamed of herself. My children, especially my 11 year old son, Barron, are having a hard time with this. Sick!

June 6, 2017

6:58 am: The FAKE MSM is working so hard trying to get me not to use Social Media. They hate that I can get the honest and unfiltered message out.

June 13, 2017

7:48 am: Fake News is at an all time high. Where is their apology to me for all of the incorrect stories???

June 27, 2017

5:33 am: Wow, CNN had to retract big story on "Russia," with 3 employees forced to resign. What about all the other phony stories they do? FAKE NEWS!

7:47 am: So they caught Fake News CNN cold, but what about NBC, CBS & ABC? What about the failing @nytimes & @washingtonpost? They are all Fake News!

June 29, 2017

7:52 am to 7:58 am: I heard poorly rated @Morning_Joe speaks badly of me (don't watch anymore). Then how come low I.Q. Crazy Mika, along with Psycho Joe, came...

to Mar-a-Lago 3 nights in a row around New Year's Eve, and insisted on joining me. She was bleeding badly from a face-lift. I said no!

July 1, 2017

8:12 am: I am extremely pleased to see that @CNN has finally been exposed as #FakeNews and garbage journalism. It's about time!

8:20 am: Crazy Joe Scarborough and dumb as a rock Mika are not bad people, but their low rated show is dominated by their NBC bosses. Too bad!

July 16, 2017

6:15 am: With all of its phony unnamed sources & highly slanted & even fraudulent reporting, #Fake News is DISTORTING DEMOCRACY in our country!

July 18, 2017

7:53 pm: Fake News story of secret dinner with Putin is "sick." All G 20 leaders, and spouses,

were invited by the Chancellor of Germany. Press knew!

7:59 pm: The Fake News is becoming more and more dishonest! Even a dinner arranged for top 20 leaders in Germany is made to look sinister!

July 22, 2017

5:33 am: A new INTELLIGENCE LEAK from the Amazon Washington Post,this time against A.G. Jeff Sessions.These illegal leaks, like Comey's, must stop!

5:45 am: The Failing New York Times foiled U.S. attempt to kill the single most wanted terrorist,Al-Baghdadi.Their sick agenda over National Security

July 24, 2017

5:40 am: Drain the Swamp should be changed to Drain the Sewer— it's actually much worse than anyone ever thought, and it begins with the Fake News!

9:23 pm: The Amazon Washington Post fabricated the facts on my ending massive, dangerous, and wasteful payments to Syrian rebels fighting Assad...

9:28 pm: So many stories about me in the @washingtonpost are Fake News. They are as bad as ratings challenged @CNN. Lobbyist for Amazon and taxes?

July 29, 2017

6:15 pm: I love reading about all of the "geniuses" who were so instrumental in my election success. Problem is, most don't exist. #Fake News! MAGA

August 6, 2017

8:18 pm: The Fake News refuses to report the success of the first 6 months: S.C., surging economy & jobs, border & military security, ISIS & MS-13 etc.

August 7, 2017

5:58 am to 6:09 am: The Trump base is far bigger & stronger than ever before (despite some phony Fake News polling). Look at rallies in Penn, Iowa, Ohio…

…and West Virginia. The fact is the Fake News Russian collusion story, record Stock Market, border security, military strength, jobs…

… Supreme Court pick, economic enthusiasm, deregulation & so much more have driven the Trump base even closer together. Will never change!

3:15 pm: The Fake News Media will not talk about the importance of the United Nations Security Council's 15-0 vote in favor of sanctions on N. Korea!

August 19, 2017

3:41 pm: Our great country has been divided for decades. Sometimes you need protest in order to heal, & we will heal, & be stronger than ever before!

3:41 pm: I want to applaud the many protestors in Boston who are speaking out against bigotry and hate. Our country will soon come together as one!

August 23, 2017

12:32 am: Not only does the media give a platform to hate groups, but the media turns a blind eye to the gang violence on our streets!

August 30, 2017

8:27 am: After reading the false reporting and even ferocious anger in some dying magazines, it makes me wonder, WHY? All I want to do is #MAGA

September 30, 2017

5:46 pm: Because of #FakeNews my people are not getting the credit they deserve for doing a great job. As seen here, they are ALL doing a GREAT JOB! https://t.co/1ltW2t3rwy

6:24 pm: In analyzing the Alabama Primary race, FAKE NEWS always fails to mention that the candidate I endorsed went up MANY points after endorsement!

October 4, 2017

10:18 am: The @NBCNews story has just been totally refuted by Sec. Tillerson and @VP Pence. It is #FakeNews. They should issue an apology to AMERICA!

October 7, 2017

6:05 am to 6:11 am: Can't believe I finally got a good story in the @washingtonpost. It discusses the enthusiasm of "Trump" voters through campaign...

...contributions. The RNC is taking in far more $'s than the Dems, and much of it by my wonderful small donors. I am working hard for them!

October 10, 2017

8:15 pm to 8:21 pm: The Fake News is at it again, this time trying to hurt one of the finest people I know, General John Kelly, by saying he will soon be...

...fired. This story is totally made up by the dishonest media. The Chief is doing a FANTASTIC job for me and, more importantly, for the USA!

October 11, 2017

7:09 pm: Network news has become so partisan, distorted and fake that licenses must be challenged and, if appropriate, revoked. Not fair to public!

October 12, 2017

7:45 am: The Fake News Is going all out in order to demean and denigrate! Such hatred!

7:12 pm: People are just now starting to find out how dishonest and disgusting (FakeNews) @NBCNews is. Viewers beware. May be worse than even @CNN!

October 15, 2017

8:25 am to 8:46 am: The Failing @nytimes, in a story by Peter Baker, should have mentioned the rapid terminations by me of TPP & The Paris Accord & the fast...

...approvals of The Keystone XL & Dakota Access pipelines. Also, look at the recent EPA cancelations & our great new Supreme Court Justice!

October 18, 2017

10:03 pm: "46% of Americans think the Media is inventing stories about Trump & his Administration." @FoxNews It is actually much worse than this!

October 19, 2017

9:53 pm: The Fake News is going crazy with wacky Congresswoman Wilson(D), who was SECRETLY on a very personal call, and gave a total lie on content!

October 22, 2017

7:08 am: It is finally sinking through. 46% OF PEOPLE BELIEVE MAJOR NATIONAL NEWS ORGS FABRICATE STORIES ABOUT ME. FAKE NEWS, even worse! Lost cred.

October 23, 2017

7:30 am: I had a very respectful conversation with the widow of Sgt. La David Johnson, and spoke his name from beginning, without hesitation!

October 27, 2017

6:38 am: JFK Files are being carefully released. In the end there will be great transparency. It is my hope to get just about everything to public!

November 11, 2017

7:43 pm: Does the Fake News Media remember when Crooked Hillary Clinton, as Secretary of State, was begging Russia to be our friend with the misspelled reset button? Obama tried also, but he had zero chemistry with Putin.

November 14, 2017

3:07 am: One of the most accurate polls last time around. But #FakeNews likes to say we're in the 30's. They are wrong. Some people think numbers could be in the 50's. Together, WE will MAKE AMERICA GREAT AGAIN! https://t.co/YhrwkdObhP

November 25, 2017

5:37 pm: .@FoxNews is MUCH more important in the United States than CNN, but outside of the U.S., CNN International is still a major source of (Fake) news, and they represent our Nation to the WORLD very poorly. The outside world does not see the truth from them!

2:40 pm: Time Magazine called to say that I was PROBABLY going to be named "Man (Person) of the Year," like last year, but I would have to agree to an interview and a major photo shoot. I said probably is no good and took a pass. Thanks anyway!

November 29, 2017

7:16 am: Wow, Matt Lauer was just fired from NBC for "inappropriate sexual behavior in the workplace." But when will the top executives at NBC & Comcast be fired for putting out so much Fake News. Check out Andy Lack's past!

December 1, 2017

3:08 pm: The media has been speculating that I fired Rex Tillerson or that he would be leaving soon—FAKE NEWS! He's not leaving and while we disagree on certain subjects, (I call the final shots) we work well together and America is highly respected again!

December 3, 2017

6:15 am: Congratulations to @ABC News for suspending Brian Ross for his horrendously inaccurate and dishonest report on the Russia, Russia, Russia Witch Hunt. More Networks and "papers" should do the same with their Fake News!

December 9, 2017

8:02 am: Fake News CNN made a vicious and purposeful mistake yesterday. They were caught red handed, just like lonely Brian Ross at ABC News (who should be immediately fired for his "mistake"). Watch to see if @CNN fires those responsible, or was it just gross incompetence?

467

8:21 am: CNN'S slogan is CNN, THE MOST TRUSTED NAME IN NEWS. Everyone knows this is not true, that this could, in fact, be a fraud on the American Public. There are many outlets that are far more trusted than Fake News CNN. Their slogan should be CNN, THE LEAST TRUSTED NAME IN NEWS!

5:01 pm: .@DaveWeigel @WashingtonPost put out a phony photo of an empty arena hours before I arrived @ the venue, w/ thousands of people outside, on their way in. Real photos now shown as I spoke. Packed house, many people unable to get in. Demand apology & retraction from FAKE NEWS WaPo!

December 11, 2017

9:17 am: Another false story, this time in the Failing @nytimes, that I watch 4-8 hours of television a day—Wrong! Also, I seldom, if ever, watch CNN or MSNBC, both of which I consider Fake News. I never watch Don Lemon, who I once called the "dumbest man on television!" Bad Reporting

December 16, 2017

9:52 am: Congratulations to two great and hardworking guys, Corey Lewandowski and David Bossie, on the success of their just out book, "Let Trump Be Trump." Finally people with real knowledge are writing about our wonderful and exciting campaign!

December 24, 2017

8:48 am: The Fake News refuses to talk about how Big and how Strong our BASE is. They show Fake Polls just like they report Fake News. Despite only negative reporting, we are doing well—nobody is going to beat us. MAKE AMERICA GREAT AGAIN!

December 29, 2017

7:46 am: While the Fake News loves to talk about my so-called low approval rating, @foxandfriends just showed that my rating on Dec.

28, 2017, was approximately the same as President Obama on Dec. 28, 2009, which was 47%...and this despite massive negative Trump coverage & Russia hoax!

Press/Media/Journalists—2018 News Quotes

Remarks at a rally in Tampa, Florida, July 31, 2018.
Source: https://www.tampabay.com/florida-politics/buzz/2018/08/01/
heres-a-full-transcript-of-president-trumps-speech-from-his-tampa-rally/

"Of course, if the fake news did a poll, they're called suppression polls.

"You know, polls are fake, just like everything else.

"If the fake news did a poll, it would show that I'm only getting 25% with the 401(k) people, even though they're up 44%. No, we got— We're doing well. We're doing well, and I'm happy you're doing well. They just came out with a poll. Did you hear? The most popular person in the history of the Republican Party is Trump. Can you believe this?

"So, I said, 'Does that include honest Abe Lincoln?' You know, he was pretty good, right? Remember, I said, when I'd be a little bit wild, and we'd have a lot of fun, they'd say, 'He's not acting presidential.' And I'd say, 'Well, it's a lot easier to act presidential than to do what I do.' Anybody can act presidential.

"Ladies and gentlemen of the state of Florida, thank you very much for being here. You are tremendously people, and I will leave now, because I am boring you to death. Thank you.

"No, but I said, 'I can be.' I used to tell them all the time, the fake news, I'd say, 'I can be more presidential than any president in history, except for possibly Abe Lincoln with the big hat.' I, I don't know about that. Abe, Abe looked pretty presidential, right? What do you think? He's tough. He's tough. I admit it. Abe Lincoln is tough. But we love Abe Lincoln.

"One of these guys, when that poll came out, most popular, and it was in the 90s. And one of these guys is on television. You know, can't miss a word. Can't miss a word. Every, they see the poll. 'Oh, my God. Oh, my God. Look at this. Oh, my God.' Yeah, seven more years, seven more.

"Seven more. 'Oh, my God. We've got to find something. We've got to do anything, anything, to get him out. He's doing too well. This is not good.'

"Worst of all, Democrats want to—You know that. They want to open our borders. They want to let crime, tremendous crime into our country. We can't do it."

Response to a question from Lesley Stahl of *60 Minutes*, October 15, 2018.
Source: https://www.theguardian.com/us-news/2018/oct/15/
donald-trumps-60-minutes-interview-eight-takeaways

"So when I won the presidency—The press treats me terribly. I thought very strongly that, you know, the one great thing will happen is the press will start treating me great. Lesley [Stahl of *60 Minutes*], they treat me worse. They got worse instead of better. Very dishonest."

Response to a question from Lesley Stahl of *60 Minutes*, October 15, 2018.
Source: https://www.theguardian.com/us-news/2018/oct/15/
donald-trumps-60-minutes-interview-eight-takeaways

"I regret that the press treats me so badly."

Response to a question from Chris Wallace of FOX News, November 18, 2018.
Source: https://www.youtube.com/watch?v=rMgJnnG-Nql

"Yeah, they're doing them now. I mean, we'll have rules of decorum, you know, you can't keep asking questions. You have, we had a lot of reporters in that room, many, many reporters in that room and they were unable to ask questions because this guy gets up and starts, you know, doing what he's supposed to be doing for him and for CNN and, you know, just shouting out questions. But, but I will say this, look, nobody believes in the First Amendment more than I do and if I think somebody's acting out of sorts, I will leave. I'll say, 'Thank you very much, everybody. I appreciate you coming.' And I will leave. And those reporters will not be too friendly to whoever it is that's acting up."

Response to a question from Chris Wallace of FOX News, November 18, 2018.
Source: https://www.youtube.com/watch?v=rMgJnnG-Nql

"The people that are supporting me in particular, they're very smart people. They're hard working, brilliant, great people. They know when the news is fake, and they get angry when they see all of the fakeness."

Response to a question from Chris Wallace of FOX News, November 18, 2018.
Source: https://www.youtube.com/watch?v=rMgJnnG-Nql

"No, it's not, no. No. I don't mind getting bad news if I'm wrong. If I do something wrong, like, for instance, the cemetery. I was not allowed to go because of the Secret Service. Because they expected to take a helicopter."

Response to a question from Chris Wallace of FOX News, November 18, 2018.
Source: https://www.youtube.com/watch?v=rMgJnnG-Nql

"I'm totally in favor of the media. I'm totally in favor of free press, got to be fair press."

Response to a question from Chris Wallace of FOX News, November 18, 2018.
Source: https://www.youtube.com/watch?v=rMgJnnG-Nql

"I'm only saying it very differently than anyone's ever said it before. I'm saying fake news, false reporting, dishonest reporting, of which there is a lot, and I know it. See, I know it because I'm a subject of it. A lot of people don't know it. But when I explain it to them, they understand it."

Response to a question from Chris Wallace of FOX News, November 18, 2018.
Source: https://www.youtube.com/watch?v=rMgJnnG-Nql

"I am calling fake news, fake reporting, is what's tearing this country apart because people know, people like things that are happening and they're not hearing about it."

Press/Media/Journalists—2018 Tweets

January 2, 2018

8:05 pm: will be announcing THE MOST DISHONEST & COR-RUPT MEDIA AWARDS OF THE YEAR on Monday at 5:00 o'clock. Subjects will cover Dishonesty & Bad Reporting in various categories from the Fake News Media. Stay tuned!

January 4, 2018

10:52 pm: I authorized Zero access to White House (actually turned him down many times) for author of phony book! I never spoke to him for book. Full of lies, misrepresentations and sources that don't exist. Look at this guy's past and watch what happens to him and Sloppy Steve!

January 5, 2018

9:32 am: Well, now that collusion with Russia is proving to be a total hoax and the only collusion is with Hillary Clinton and the FBI/

Russia, the Fake News Media (Mainstream) and this phony new book are hitting out at every new front imaginable. They should try winning an election. Sad!

11:32 pm: Michael Wolff is a total loser who made up stories in order to sell this really boring and untruthful book. He used Sloppy Steve Bannon, who cried when he got fired and begged for his job. Now Sloppy Steve has been dumped like a dog by almost everyone. Too bad!

January 7, 2018

10:15 am: Jake Tapper of Fake News CNN just got destroyed in his interview with Stephen Miller of the Trump Administration. Watch the hatred and unfairness of this CNN flunky!

January 13, 2018

5:08 pm: So much Fake News is being reported. They don't even try to get it right, or correct it when they are wrong. They promote the Fake Book of a mentally deranged author, who knowingly writes false information. The Mainstream Media is crazed that WE won the election!

January 14, 2018

7:58 am to 8:01 am: The Wall Street Journal stated falsely that I said to them "I have a good relationship with Kim Jong Un" (of N. Korea). Obviously I didn't say that. I said "I'd have a good relationship with Kim Jong Un," a big difference. Fortunately we now record conversations with reporters…

…and they knew exactly what I said and meant. They just wanted a story. FAKE NEWS!

February 11, 2018

1:21 pm: So many positive things going on for the U.S.A. and the Fake News Media just doesn't want to go there. Same negative stories over and over again! No wonder the People no longer trust the media, whose approval ratings are correctly at their lowest levels in history! #MAGA

February 22, 2018

7:26 am to 7:40 am: I never said "give teachers guns" like was stated on Fake News @CNN & @NBC. What I said was to look at the possibility of giving "concealed guns to gun adept teachers with military or special training experience—only the best. 20% of teachers, a lot, would now be able to

...immediately fire back if a savage sicko came to a school with bad intentions. Highly trained teachers would also serve as a deterrent to the cowards that do this. Far more assets at much less cost than guards. A "gun free" school is a magnet for bad people. ATTACKS WOULD END!

February 28, 2018

7:02 am: The Heritage Foundation has just stated that 64% of the Trump Agenda is already done, faster than even Ronald Reagan. "We're blown away," said Thomas Binion of Heritage, President Trump "is very active, very conservative and very effective. Huge volume & spectrum of issues.

March 3, 2018

12:33 pm: Mainstream Media in U.S. is being mocked all over the world. They've gone CRAZY!

March 6, 2018

7:55 am: The new Fake News narrative is that there is CHAOS in the White House. Wrong! People will always come & go, and I want strong dialogue before making a final decision. I still have some people that I want to change (always seeking perfection). There is no Chaos, only great Energy!

March 11, 2018

8:41 am to 8:50 am: The Failing New York Times purposely wrote a false story stating that I am unhappy with my legal team on the

Russia case and am going to add another lawyer to help out. Wrong. I am VERY happy with my lawyers, John Dowd, Ty Cobb and Jay Sekulow. They are doing a great job and...

...have shown conclusively that there was no Collusion with Russia... just excuse for losing. The only Collusion was that done by the DNC, the Democrats and Crooked Hillary. The writer of the story, Maggie Haberman, a Hillary flunky, knows nothing about me and is not given access.

April 3, 2018

5:58 am: Check out the fact that you can't get a job at ratings challenged @CNN unless you state that you are totally anti-Trump? Little Jeff Zuker, whose job is in jeopardy, is not having much fun lately. They should clean up and strengthen CNN and get back to honest reporting!

April 12, 2018

5:03 am: If I wanted to fire Robert Mueller in December, as reported by the Failing New York Times, I would have fired him. Just more Fake News from a biased newspaper!

April 18, 2018

5:08 am: A sketch years later about a nonexistent man. A total con job, playing the Fake News Media for Fools (but they know it)!

April 21, 2018

7:17 am: The New York Times and a third rate reporter named Maggie Habberman, known as a Crooked H flunkie who I don't speak to and have nothing to do with, are going out of their way to destroy Michael Cohen and his relationship with me in the hope that he will "flip." They use...

...non-existent "sources" and a drunk/drugged up loser who hates Michael, a fine person with a wonderful family. Michael is a

475

businessman for his own account/lawyer who I have always liked & respected. Most people will flip if the Government lets them out of trouble, even if...

...it means lying or making up stories. Sorry, I don't see Michael doing that despite the horrible Witch Hunt and the dishonest media!

April 21, 2018

2:24 pm: The Washington Post said I refer to Jeff Sessions as "Mr. Magoo" and Rod Rosenstein as "Mr. Peepers." This is "according to people with whom the president has spoken." There are no such people and don't know these characters...just more Fake & Disgusting News to create ill will!

April 22, 2018

7:50 am: Sleepy Eyes Chuck Todd of Fake News NBC just stated that we have given up so much in our negotiations with North Korea, and they have given up nothing. Wow, we haven't given up anything & they have agreed to denuclearization (so great for World), site closure, & no more testing!

3:04 pm: Kim Strassel of the WSJ just said, after reviewing the dumb Comey Memos, "you got to ask, what was the purpose of the Special Counsel? There's no there there." Dan Henninger of the WSJ said Memos would show that this would be one of the weakest obstruction cases ever brought!

April 29. 2018

9:38 pm: The White House Correspondents' Dinner was a failure last year, but this year was

an embarrassment to everyone associated with it. The filthy "comedian" totally bombed (couldn't even deliver her lines-much like the Seth Meyers weak performance). Put Dinner to rest, or start over!

May 9, 2018

5:38 pm: The Failing New York Times criticized Secretary of State Pompeo for being AWOL (missing), when in fact he was flying to North Korea. Fake News, so bad!

May 14, 2018

3:46 pm: The so-called leaks coming out of the White House are a massive over exaggeration put out by the Fake News Media in order to make us look as bad as possible. With that being said, leakers are traitors and cowards, and we will find out who they are!

May 15, 2018

9:08 am: Can you believe that with all of the made up, unsourced stories I get from the Fake News Media, together with the $10,000,000 Russian Witch Hunt (there is no Collusion), I now have my best Poll Numbers in a year. Much of the Media may be corrupt, but the People truly get it!

May 30, 2018

9:35 am: The Failing and Corrupt @nytimes estimated the crowd last night at "1000 people," when in fact it was many times that number— and the arena was rockin'. This is the way they demean and disparage. They are very dishonest people who don't "get" me, and never did!

10:31 am: Bob Iger of ABC called Valerie Jarrett to let her know that "ABC does not tolerate comments like those" made by Roseanne Barr. Gee, he never called President Donald J. Trump to apologize for the HORRIBLE statements made and said about me on ABC. Maybe I just didn't get the call?

May 31, 2018

6:53 am: Iger, where is my call of apology? You and ABC have offended millions of people, and they demand a response. How is Brian

Ross doing? He tanked the market with an ABC lie, yet no apology. Double Standard!

June 1, 2018

6:15 am: Why aren't they firing no talent Samantha Bee for the horrible language used on her low ratings show? A total double standard but that's O.K., we are Winning, and will be doing so for a long time to come!

June 2, 2018

3:57 pm: Why is it that the Wall Street Journal, though well meaning, never mentions the unfairness of the Tariffs routinely charged against the U.S. by other countries, or the many Billions of Dollars that the Tariffs we are now charging are, and will be, pouring into U.S. coffers?

June 15, 2018

5:23 pm: The Fake News Media said that I did not get along with other Leaders at the #G7Summit in Canada. They are once again, WRONG! https://t.co/I6eEKEZV6z

June 17, 2018

7:40 am: Funny how the Fake News, in a coordinated effort with each other, likes to say I gave sooo much to North Korea because I "met." That's because that's all they have to disparage! We got so much for peace in the world, & more is being added in finals. Even got our hostages/remains!

8:26 am: Washington Post employees want to go on strike because Bezos isn't paying them enough. I think a really long strike would be a great idea. Employees would get more money and we would get rid of Fake News for an extended period of time! Is @WaPo a registered lobbyist?

June 23, 2018

8:43 pm: Major Wall Street Journal opinion piece today talking about the Russian Witch Hunt and the disgrace that it is. So many people hurt, so bad for our country—a total sham!

June 25, 2018

7:36 am: Such a difference in the media coverage of the same immigration policies between the Obama Administration and ours. Actually, we have done a far better job in that our facilities are cleaner and better run than were the facilities under Obama. Fake News is working overtime!

June 29, 2018

12:59 pm: Before going any further today, I want to address the horrific shooting that took place yesterday at the Capital Gazette newsroom in Annapolis, Maryland. This attack shocked the conscience of our Nation, and filled our hearts with grief...

July 15, 2018

11:18 am: Heading to Helsinki, Finland—looking forward to meeting with President Putin tomorrow. Unfortunately, no matter how well I do at the Summit, if I was given the great city of Moscow as retribution for all of the sins and evils committed by Russia...

...over the years, I would return to criticism that it wasn't good enough—that I should have gotten Saint Petersburg in addition! Much of our news media is indeed the enemy of the people and all the Dems...

...know how to do is resist and obstruct! This is why there is such hatred and dissension in our country—but at some point, it will heal!

July 19, 2018

5:59 am: The Fake News Media wants so badly to see a major confrontation with Russia, even a confrontation that could lead to war. They are pushing so recklessly hard and hate the fact that I'll probably have a good relationship with Putin. We are doing MUCH better than any other country!

July 20, 2018

4:50 pm: I got severely criticized by the Fake News Media for being too nice to President Putin. In the Old Days they would call it Diplomacy. If I was loud & vicious, I would have been criticized for being too tough. Remember when they said I was too tough with Chairman Kim? Hypocrites!

July 22, 2018

8:15 am: I had a GREAT meeting with Putin and the Fake News used every bit of their energy to try and disparage it. So bad for our country!

July 23, 2018

7:25 am: When you hear the Fake News talking negatively about my meeting with President Putin, and all that I gave up, remember, I gave up NOTHING, we merely talked about future benefits for both countries. Also, we got along very well, which is a good thing, except for the Corrupt Media!

July 29, 2018

2:09 pm: When the media—driven insane by their Trump Derangement Syndrome—reveals internal deliberations of our government, it truly puts the lives of many, not just journalists, at risk! Very unpatriotic! Freedom of the press also comes with a responsibility to report the news...

...accurately. 90% of media coverage of my Administration is negative, despite the tremendously positive results we are achieving, it's no surprise that confidence in the media is at an all time low! I will not allow our great country to be sold out by anti-Trump haters in the...

...dying newspaper industry. No matter how much they try to distract and cover it up, our country is making great progress under my leadership and I will never stop fighting for the American people! As an example, the failing New York Times...

...and the Amazon Washington Post do nothing but write bad stories even on very positive achievements—and they will never change!

August 5, 2018

7:35 am: Fake News reporting, a complete fabrication, that I am concerned about the meeting my wonderful son, Donald, had in Trump Tower. This was a meeting to get information on an opponent, totally legal and done all the time in politics—and it went nowhere. I did not know about it!

August 11, 2018

1:28 pm: The big story that the Fake News Media refuses to report is lowlife Christopher Steele's many meetings with Deputy A.G. Bruce Ohr and his beautiful wife, Nelly. It was Fusion GPS that hired Steele to write the phony & discredited Dossier, paid for by Crooked Hillary & the DNC...

August 19, 2018

6:01 am: The failing @nytimes wrote a Fake piece today implying that because White House Councel Don McGahn was giving hours of testimony to the Special Councel, he must be a John Dean type "RAT." But I allowed him and all others to testify—I didn't have to. I have nothing to hide...

August 26, 2018

5:01 pm: "Mainstream Media tries to rewrite history to credit Obama for Trump accomplishments. Since President Trump took office, the economy is booming. The stronger the economy gets, the more desperate his critics are. O had weakest recovery since Great Depression." @WashTimes

August 28, 2018

4:24 am to 4:34 am: Google search results for "Trump News" shows only the viewing/reporting of Fake New Media. In other words, they have it RIGGED, for me & others, so that almost all stories & news is BAD. Fake CNN is prominent. Republican/Conservative & Fair Media is shut out. Illegal? 96% of...

...results on "Trump News" are from National Left-Wing Media, very dangerous. Google & others are suppressing voices of Conservatives and hiding information and news that is good. They are controlling what we can & cannot see. This is a very serious situation-will be addressed!

4:54 am: "President Trump has done more for minority groups in this country than any president in decades." @LouDobbs

August 29, 2018

7:41 am: When you see "anonymous source," stop reading the story, it is fiction!

7:44 pm: "Lanny Davis admits being anonymous source in CNN Report." @BretBaier Oh well,

so much for CNN saying it wasn't Lanny. No wonder their ratings are so low, it's FAKE NEWS!

August 30, 2018

6:11 am: I just cannot state strongly enough how totally dishonest much of the Media is. Truth doesn't matter to them, they only have their hatred & agenda. This includes fake books, which come out about me all the time, always anonymous sources, and are pure fiction. Enemy of the People!

11:54 am: CNN is working frantically to find their "source." Look hard because it doesn't exist. Whatever was left of CNN's credibility is now gone!

August 31, 2018

1:37 pm: Wow, I made OFF THE RECORD COMMENTS to Bloomberg concerning Canada, and this powerful understanding was BLATANTLY VIOLATED. Oh well, just more dishonest reporting. I am used to it. At least Canada knows where I stand!

9:25 pm: @Rasmussen_Poll just came out at 48% approval rate despite the constant and intense Fake News. Higher than Election Day and higher than President Obama. Rasmussen was one of the most accurate Election Day polls!

9:35 pm: The ABC/Washington Post Poll was by far the least accurate one 2 weeks out from the 2016 Election. I call it a suppression poll—but by Election Day they brought us, out of shame, to about even. They will never learn!

September 4, 2018

9:58 am: NBC FAKE NEWS, which is under intense scrutiny over their killing the Harvey Weinstein story, is now fumbling around making excuses for their probably highly unethical conduct. I have long criticized NBC and their journalistic standards-worse than even CNN. Look at their license?

9:50 pm: Sleepy Eyes Chuck Todd of Fake NBC News said it's time for the Press to stop complaining and to start fighting back. Actually Chuck, they've been doing that from the day I announced for President. They've gone all out, and I WON, and now they're going CRAZY!

10:01 pm: The already discredited Woodward book, so many lies and phony sources, has me calling Jeff Sessions "mentally retarded" and "a dumb southerner." I said NEITHER, never used those terms on anyone, including Jeff, and being a southerner is a GREAT thing. He made this up to divide!

10:32 pm: Jim Mattis Calls Woodward Book 'Fiction': 'Product of Someone's Rich Imagination' https://t.co/HGMDiH98nx via @ BreitbartNews

September 5, 2018

6:33 am: Isn't it a shame that someone can write an article or book, totally make up stories and form a picture of a person that is literally the exact opposite of the fact, and get away with it without retribution or cost. Don't know why Washington politicians don't change libel laws?

6:40 pm: Does the so-called "Senior Administration Official" really exist, or is it just the Failing New York Times with another phony source? If the GUTLESS anonymous person does indeed exist, the Times must, for National Security purposes, turn him/her over to government at once!

September 6, 2018

6:19 am: The Deep State and the Left, and their vehicle, the Fake News Media, are going Crazy—& they don't know what to do. The Economy is booming like never before, Jobs are at Historic Highs, soon TWO Supreme Court Justices & maybe Declassification to find Additional Corruption. Wow!

6:12 pm: Are the investigative "journalists" of the New York Times going to investigate themselves—who is the anonymous letter writer?

September 14, 2018

10:08 pm: When President Obama said that he has been to "57 States," very little mention in Fake News Media. Can you imagine if I said that…story of the year! @IngrahamAngle

September 29, 2018

9:49 pm: NBC News incorrectly reported (as usual) that I was limiting the FBI investigation of Judge Kavanaugh, and witnesses, only to certain people. Actually, I want them to interview whoever they deem appropriate, at their discretion. Please correct your reporting!

October 10, 2018

8:01 am: Despite so many positive events and victories, Media Reseach Center reports that 92% of stories on Donald Trump are negative on ABC, CBS and ABC. It is FAKE NEWS! Don't worry, the Failing New York Times didn't even put the Brett Kavanaugh victory on the Front Page yesterday-A17!

October 14, 2018

8:56 am: NBC News has totally and purposely changed the point and meaning of my story about General Robert E Lee and General Ulysses Grant. Was actually a shoutout to warrior Grant and the great state in which he was born. As usual, dishonest reporting. Even mainstream media embarrassed!

2:54 pm: Thank you to NBC for the correction!

October 17, 2018

7:09 am: AP headline was very different from my quote and meaning in the story. They just can't help themselves. FAKE NEWS!

7:40 am: "Network News gave Zero coverage to the Big Day the Stock Market had yesterday." @foxandfriends

October 21, 2018

5:48 pm: Facebook has just stated that they are setting up a system to "purge" themselves of Fake News. Does that mean CNN will finally be put out of business?

October 22, 2018

2:18 pm: The Fake News Media has been talking about recent approval ratings of me by countries around the world, including the European Union, as being very low...

...I say of course they're low—because for the first time in 50 years I am making them pay a big price for doing business with America. Why should they like me?—But I still like them!

October 25, 2018

6:18 am: A very big part of the Anger we see today in our society is caused by the purposely false and inaccurate reporting of the Mainstream Media that I refer to as Fake News. It has gotten so bad and hateful that it is beyond description. Mainstream Media must clean up its act, FAST!

8:57 am: The New York Times has a new Fake Story that now the Russians and Chinese (glad they finally added China) are listening to all of my calls on cellphones. Except that I rarely use a cellphone, & when I do it's government authorized. I like Hard Lines. Just more made up Fake News!

October 28, 2018

7:12 pm: The Fake News is doing everything in their power to blame Republicans, Conservatives and me for the division and hatred that has been going on for so long in our Country. Actually, it is their Fake & Dishonest reporting which is causing problems far greater than they understand!

October 29, 2018

7:03 am to 7:07 am: There is great anger in our Country caused in part by inaccurate, and even fraudulent, reporting of the news. The Fake News Media, the true Enemy of the People, must stop the open & obvious hostility & report the news accurately & fairly. That will do much to put out the flame...

...of Anger and Outrage and we will then be able to bring all sides together in Peace and Harmony. Fake News Must End!

November 5, 2018

10:18 am: So funny to see the CNN Fake Suppression Polls and false rhetoric. Watch for real results Tuesday. We are lucky CNN's ratings are so low. Don't fall for the Suppression Game. Go out & VOTE. Remember, we now have perhaps the greatest Economy (JOBS) in the history of our Country!

November 7, 2018

7:52 am: To any of the pundits or talking heads that do not give us proper credit for this great Midterm Election, just remember two words—FAKE NEWS!

10:39 am: According to NBC News, Voters Nationwide Disapprove of the so-called Mueller Investigation (46%) more than they Approve (41%). You mean they are finally beginning to understand what a disgusting Witch Hunt, led by 17 Angry Democrats, is all about!

November 13, 2018

12:07 pm: The story in the New York Times concerning North Korea developing missile bases is inaccurate. We fully know about the sites being discussed, nothing new—and nothing happening out of the normal. Just more Fake News. I will be the first to let you know if things go bad!

November 19, 2018

2:20 pm: The Fake News is showing old footage of people climbing over our Ocean Area Fence. This is what it really looks like—no climbers anymore under our Administration!

November 26, 2018

2:47 pm: While CNN doesn't do great in the United States based on ratings, outside of the U.S. they have very little competition. Throughout the world, CNN has a powerful voice portraying the United States in an unfair...

...and false way. Something has to be done, including the possibility of the United States starting our own Worldwide Network to show the World the way we really are, GREAT!

December 6, 2018

7:27 pm: Does the Fake News Media ever mention the fact that Republicans, with the very important help of my campaign Rallies, WON THE UNITED STATES SENATE, 53 to 47? All I hear is that the Open Border Dems won the House. Senate alone approves judges & others. Big Republican Win!

10:08 pm: FAKE NEWS—THE ENEMY OF THE PEOPLE!

December 11, 2018

8:30 am: Fake News has it purposely wrong. Many, over ten, are vying for and wanting the White House Chief of Staff position. Why wouldn't someone want one of the truly great and meaningful jobs in Washington. Please report news correctly. Thank you!

December 13, 2018

12:34 pm: If it was a Conservative that said what "crazed" Mika Brzezinski stated on her show yesterday, using a certain horrible term, that person would be banned permanently from television...

...She will probably be given a pass, despite their terrible ratings. Congratulations to @RichardGrenell, our great Ambassador to Germany, for having the courage to take this horrible issue on!

Press/Media/Journalists—2019 News Quotes

Remarks at the signing of an executive order protecting and improving Medicare for senior citizens, Ocala, Florida, October 3, 2019.
Source: https://www.whitehouse.gov/briefings-statements/remarks-president-trump-signing-executive-order-protecting-improving-medicare-nations-seniors-ocala-fl/

"It'll never end. I'm sorry I smiled. They'll have me; the fake news is back there. Look at all of them. [Audience boos.]

"They'll say, 'It's terrible. It's terrible, the President's smile.' You know, they want me to admonish you. Who said that? 'Lock her up.' Stand up, please. I'm admonishing you. Never ever say that again. That's okay. Sit down. He's admonished, so now they can't do their fake number on us. Thank you."

Remarks at the signing of an executive order protecting and improving Medicare for senior citizens, Ocala, Florida, October 3, 2019.
Source: https://www.whitehouse.gov/briefings-statements/remarks-president-trump-signing-executive-order-protecting-improving-medicare-nations-seniors-ocala-fl/

"You know, to show you how corrupt CNN is, when I used that expression, they said, 'The President wasn't telling the truth. He said they get a Rolls-Royce and they don't.' [Audience laughs.] Ah, they don't get it, do they? They never got it.

"Some idiot at CNN said, 'You can't win without CNN.' I guess we showed them. [Audience laughs and applauds.] I guess we showed them. And their ratings are so low now that they are no longer the big difference at all. They have really bad ratings.

"But you know what is bad for our country? When CNN—So often I go to a foreign country. I go to a country. I meet leaders. And he said, 'Why do they hate your country so much?' I said, 'Who?' You know, CNN outside of the United States is much more important than it is in the United States. And a lot of what you see here is broadcast throughout the world. And we used to have Radio Free—I think

Radio Free Europe and Voice of America. And we did that to build up our country. And that's not working out too well.

"But CNN is a voice that really seems to be the voice out there. And it's a terrible thing for our country. And we ought to start our network and put some real news out there because they are so bad. They are so bad for our country. They are so bad for our country. I go out there and they say, 'Boy, the media hates your country.' And it's just a shame. It's just a shame. And we really are—We are looking at that. We should do something about it, too. Put some really talented people and get a real voice out there, not a voice that's fake."

Press/Media/Journalists—2019 Tweets

January 5, 2019

9:08 am: Looks like Bernie Sanders is history. Sleepy Joe Biden is pulling ahead and think about it, I'm only here because of Sleepy Joe and the man who took him off the 1% trash heap, President O! China wants Sleepy Joe BADLY!

January 7, 2019

9:55 am: The Failing New York Times has knowingly written a very inaccurate story on my intentions on Syria. No different from my original statements, we will be leaving at a proper pace while at the same time continuing to fight ISIS and doing all else that is prudent and necessary!...

January 11, 2019

12:50 pm: The Fake News Media keeps saying we haven't built any NEW WALL. Below is a section just completed on the Border. Anti-climbing feature included. Very high, strong and beautiful! Also, many miles already renovated and in service! https://t.co/UAAGXl5Byr

January 19, 2019

8:50 am: Many people are saying that the Mainstream Media will have a very hard time restoring credibility because of the way they have treated me over the past 3 years (including the election lead-up), as highlighted by the disgraceful Buzzfeed story & the even more disgraceful coverage!

January 21, 2019

9:46 am: Looking like Nick Sandman & Covington Catholic students were treated unfairly with early judgements proving out to be false—smeared by media. Not good, but making big comeback! "New footage shows that media was wrong about teen's encounter with Native American" @TuckerCarlson

January 22, 2019

10:00 am: Last time I went to Davos, the Fake News said I should not go there. This year, because of the Shutdown, I decided not to go, and the Fake News said I should be there. The fact is that the people understand the media better than the media understands them!

January 26, 2019

8:39 pm: CBS reports that in the Roger Stone indictment, data was "released during the 2016 Election to damage Hillary Clinton." Oh really! What about the Fake and Unverified "Dossier," a total phony conjob, that was paid for by Crooked Hillary to damage me and the Trump Campaign? What...

8:49 pm: ...about all of the one sided Fake Media coverage (collusion with Crooked H?) that I had to endure during my very successful presidential campaign. What about the now revealed bias by Facebook and many others. Roger Stone didn't even work for me anywhere near the Election!

January 28, 2019

9:28 pm: In the beautiful Midwest, windchill temperatures are reaching minus 60 degrees, the coldest ever recorded. In coming days, expected to get even colder. People can't last outside even for minutes. What the hell is going on with Global Waming? Please come back fast, we need you!

January 31, 2019

4:40 pm: Just concluded a great meeting with my Intel team in the Oval Office who told me that what they said on Tuesday at the Senate Hearing was mischaracterized by the media—and we are very much in agreement on Iran, ISIS, North Korea, etc. Their testimony was distorted press…

…I would suggest you read the COMPLETE testimony from Tuesday. A false narrative is so bad for our Country. I value our intelligence community. Happily, we had a very good meeting, and we are all on the same page!

February 8, 2019

8:48 am: The mainstream media has refused to cover the fact that the head of the VERY important Senate Intelligence Committee, after two years of intensive study and access to Intelligence that only they could get, just stated that they have found NO COLLUSION between "Trump" & Russia…

8:59 am: …It is all a GIANT AND ILLEGAL HOAX, developed long before the election itself, but used as an excuse by the Democrats as to why Crooked Hillary Clinton lost the Election! Someday the Fake News Media will turn honest & report that Donald J. Trump was actually a GREAT Candidate!

February 19, 2019

10:22 am: The Washington Post is a Fact Checker only for the Democrats. For the Republicans, and for your all time favorite President, it is a Fake Fact Checker!

March 2, 2019

7:34 pm: The brand new manuscript for a new book by failed lawyer Michael Cohen shows his testimony was a total lie! Pundits should only use it.

March 3, 2019

10:44 am: …said was a total lie, but Fake Media won't show it. I am an innocent man being persecuted by some very bad, conflicted & corrupt people in a Witch Hunt that is illegal & should never have been allowed to start—And only because I won the Election! Despite this, great success!

March 6, 2019

7:02 pm: Wall Street Journal: "More migrant families crossing into the U.S. illegally have been arrested in the first five months of the federal fiscal year than in any prior full year." We are doing a great job at the border, but this is a National Emergency!

7:05 pm: Democrats just blocked @FoxNews from holding a debate. Good, then I think I'll do the same thing with the Fake News Networks and the Radical Left Democrats in the General Election debates!

March 17, 2019

6:59 am: It's truly incredible that shows like Saturday Night Live, not funny/no talent, can spend all of their time knocking the same person (me), over & over, without so much of a mention of "the other side." Like an advertisement without consequences. Same with Late Night Shows…

March 19, 2019

7:24 am: The Fake News Media has NEVER been more Dishonest or Corrupt than it is right now. There has never been a time like this in American History. Very exciting but also, very sad! Fake News is the absolute Enemy of the People and our Country itself!

8:57 am: Facebook, Google and Twitter, not to mention the Corrupt Media, are sooo on the side of the Radical Left Democrats. But fear not, we will win anyway, just like we did before! #MAGA

March 25, 2019

5:25 am: "Breaking News: Mueller Report Finds No Trump-Russia Conspiracy." @MSNBC

March 27, 2019

2:38 pm: Just met with @SundarPichai, President of @Google, who is obviously doing quite well. He stated strongly that he is totally committed to the U.S. Military, not the Chinese Military…

…Also discussed political fairness and various things that @Google can do for our Country. Meeting ended very well!

April 12, 2019

10:33 pm: Another Fake Story on @NBCNews that I offered Pardons to Homeland Securiy personnel in case they broke the law regarding illegal immigration and sanctuary cities. Of course this is not true. Mainstream Media is corrupt and getting worse, if that is possible, every day!

April 13, 2019

6:38 pm: …When I won the Election in 2016, the @nytimes had to beg their fleeing subscribers for forgiveness in that they covered the Election (and me) so badly. They didn't have a clue, it was pathetic. They even apologized to me. But now they are even worse, really corrupt reporting!

April 19, 2019

4:23 pm: The Washington Post and New York Times are, in my opinion, two of the most dishonest media outlets around. Truly, the Enemy of the People!

April 20, 2019

7:02 am: The Fake News Media is doing everything possible to stir up and anger the pols and as many people as possible seldom mentioning the fact that the Mueller Report had as its principle conclusion the fact that there was NO COLLUSION WITH RUSSIA. The Russia Hoax is dead!

April 21, 2019

6:40 am: Do you believe this? The New York Times Op-Ed: MEDIA AND DEMOCRATS OWE TRUMP AN APOLOGY. Well, they got that one right!

April 23, 2019

4:59 am: Paul Krugman, of the Fake News New York Times, has lost all credibility, as has the Times itself, with his false and highly inaccurate writings on me. He is obsessed with hatred, just as others are obsessed with how stupid he is. He said Market would crash, Only Record Highs!

5:08 am: I wonder if the New York Times will apologize to me a second time, as they did after the 2016 Election. But this one will have to be a far bigger & better apology. On this one they will have to get down on their knees & beg for forgiveness-they are truly the Enemy of the People!

April 29, 2019

10:20 am: The New York Times has apologized for the terrible Anti-Semitic Cartoon, but they haven't apologized to me for this or all of the Fake and Corrupt news they print on a daily basis. They have reached the lowest level of "journalism," and certainly a low point in @nytimes history!

May 4, 2019

7:34 am: When will the Radical Left Wing Media apologize to me for knowingly getting the Russia Collusion Delusion story so wrong? The real story is about to happen! Why is @nytimes, @washingtonpost, @CNN, @MSNBC allowed to be on Twitter & Facebook. Much of what they do is FAKE NEWS!

May 13, 2019

5:56 am: Also, congratulations to @OANN on the great job you are doing and the big ratings jump ("thank you President Trump")!

May 15, 2019

2:10 pm: The Fake News Washington Post, and even more Fake News New York Times, are writing stories that there is infighting with respect to my strong policy in the Middle East. There is no infighting whatsoever...

...Different opinions are expressed and I make a decisive and final decision—it is a very simple process. All sides, views, and policies are covered. I'm sure that Iran will want to talk soon.

May 17, 2019

11:53 am: With all of the Fake and Made Up News out there, Iran can have no idea what is actually going on!

May 19, 2019

4:15 pm: Hard to believe that @FoxNews is wasting airtime on Mayor Pete, as Chris Wallace likes to call him. Fox is moving more and more to the losing (wrong) side in covering the Dems. They got dumped from the Democrats boring debates, and they just want in. They forgot the people...

who got them there. Chris Wallace said, "I actually think, whether you like his opinions or not, that Mayor Pete has a lot of substance... fascinating biography." Gee, he never speaks well of me—I like Mike Wallace better...and Alfred E. Newman will never be President!

May 20, 2019

6:20 am: The Failing New York Times (it will pass away when I leave office in 6 years), and others of the Fake News Media, keep writing phony stories about how I didn't use many banks because they didn't want to do business with me. WRONG! It is because I didn't need money. Very old

.fashioned, but true. When you don't need or want money, you don't need or want banks. Banks have always been available to me, they want to make money. Fake Media only says this to disparage, and always uses unnamed sources (because their sources don't even exist).

The Mainstream Media has never been as corrupt and deranged as it is today. FAKE NEWS is actually the biggest story of all and is the true ENEMY OF THE PEOPLE! That's why they refuse to cover the REAL Russia Hoax. But the American people are wise to what is going on...

...Now the new big story is that Trump made a lot of money and buys everything for cash, he doesn't need banks. But where did he get all of that cash? Could it be Russia? No, I built a great business and don't need banks, but if I did they would be there...and DeutscheBank.

...was very good and highly professional to deal with—and if for any reason I didn't like them, I would have gone elsewhere...there was always plenty of money around and banks to choose from. They would be very happy to take my money. Fake News!

May 23, 2019

10:19 pm: Wow! CNN Ratings are WAY DOWN, record lows. People are getting tired of so many Fake Stories and Anti-Trump lies. Chris Cuomo was rewarded for lowest morning ratings with a prime time spot—which is failing badly and not helping the dumbest man on television, Don Lemon!

May 29, 2019

7:46 pm: Great show tonight @seanhannity, you really get it(9:00 P.M.@FoxNews), that's why you're Number One (by far)!Also, please tell Mark Levin congrats on having the Number One book!

June 2, 2019

7:44 am: I never called Meghan Markle "nasty." Made up by the Fake News Media, and they got caught cold! Will @CNN, @nytimes and others apologize? Doubt it!

June 3, 2019

5:37 am: Just arrived in the United Kingdom. The only problem is that @CNN is the primary source of news available from the U.S. After watching it for a short while, I turned it off. All negative & so much Fake News, very bad for U.S. Big ratings drop. Why doesn't owner @ATT do something?

5:50 am: I believe that if people stoped using or subscribing to @ATT, they would be forced to make big changes at @CNN, which is dying in the ratings anyway. It is so unfair with such bad, Fake News! Why wouldn't they act. When the World watches @CNN, it gets a false picture of USA. Sad!

June 4, 2019

7:30 pm: Washed up psycho @BetteMidler was forced to apologize for a statement she attributed to me that turned out to be totally fabricated by her in order to make "your great president" look really bad. She got caught, just like the Fake News Media gets caught. A sick scammer!

June 8, 2019

10:54 pm: Little @DonnyDeutsch, whose show, like his previous shoe-biz tries, is a disaster, has been saying that I had been a friend of his. This is false. He, & separately @ErinBurnett, used to BEG me to be on episodes of the Apprentice (both were bad), but that was it. Hardly knew him,…

…other than to know he was, and is, a total Loser. When he makes statements about me, they are made up, he knows nothing!

11:08 pm: I know it is not at all "Presidential" to hit back at the Corrupt Media, or people who work for the Corrupt Media, when they make false statements about me or the Trump Administration. Problem is, if you don't hit back, people believe the Fake News is true. So we'll hit back!

June 9, 2019

8:26 am: If President Obama made the deals that I have made, both at the Border and for the Economy, the Corrupt Media would be hailing them as Incredible, & a National Holiday would be immediately declared. With me, despite our record setting Economy and all that I have done, no credit!

June 10, 2019

6:09 am: When will the Failing New York Times admit that their front page story on the the new Mexico deal at the Border is a FRAUD and nothing more than a badly reported "hit job" on me, something that has been going on since the first day I announced for the presidency! Sick Journalism

1:17 pm: Can't believe they are bringing in John Dean, the disgraced Nixon White House Counsel who is a paid CNN contributor. No Collusion—No Obstruction! Democrats just want a do-over which they'll never get!

June 12, 2019

7:46 am: The Fake News has never been more dishonest than it is today. Thank goodness we can fight back on Social Media. Their new weapon of choice is Fake Polling, sometimes referred to as Suppression Polls (they suppress the numbers). Had it in 2016, but this is worse…

...The Fake (Corrupt) News Media said they had a leak into polling done by my campaign which, by the way and despite the phony and never ending Witch Hunt, are the best numbers WE have ever had. They reported Fake numbers that they made up & don't even exist. WE WILL WIN AGAIN!

June 14, 2019

2:15 pm: The dishonest media will NEVER keep us from accomplishing our objectives on behalf of our GREAT AMERICAN PEOPLE! #MAGA

June 15, 2019

2:04 pm: The Corrupt News Media is totally out of control—they have given up and don't even care anymore. Mainstream Media has ZERO CREDIBILITY—TOTAL LOSERS!

7:51 pm: I enjoyed my interview with @GStephanopoulos on @ABC. So funny to watch the Fake News Media try to dissect & distort every word in as negative a way as possible. It will be aired on Sunday night at 8:00 P.M., and is called, "President Trump: 30 Hours" (which is somewhat...

...misleading in that I personally spent only a small fraction of that time doing interviews. I do have a few other things to do, you know!). Think I will do many more Network Interviews, as I did in 2016, in order to get the word out that no President has done what I have in...

...the first 2 1/2 years of his Presidency, including the fact that we have one of the best Economies in the history of our Country. It is called Earned Media. In any event, enjoy the show!

8:15 pm: Do you believe that the Failing New York Times just did a story stating that the United States is substantially increasing Cyber Attacks on Russia. This is a virtual act of Treason by a once great paper so desperate for a story, any story, even if bad for our Country...

...ALSO, NOT TRUE! Anything goes with our Corrupt News Media today. They will do, or say, whatever it takes, with not even the slightest thought of consequence! These are true cowards and without doubt, THE ENEMY OF THE PEOPLE!

June 16, 2019

8:39 am: A poll should be done on which is the more dishonest and deceitful newspaper, the Failing New York Times or the Amazon (lobbyist) Washington Post! They are both a disgrace to our Country, the Enemy of the People, but I just can't seem to figure out which is worse? The good...

...news is that at the end of 6 years, after America has been made GREAT again and I leave the beautiful White House (do you think the people would demand that I stay longer? KEEP AMERICA GREAT), both of these horrible papers will quickly go out of business & be forever gone!

4:23 pm: Almost 70% in new Poll say don't impeach. So ridiculous to even be talking about this subject when all of the crimes were committed by the other side. They can't win the election fairly!

June 17, 2019

9:13 pm: The story in the @nytimes about the U.S. escalating attacks on Russia's power grid is Fake News, and the Failing New York Times knows it. They should immediately release their sources which, if they exist at all, which I doubt, are phony. Times must be held fully accountable!

June 18, 2019

12:10 am: Only a few people showed up for the so-called Impeachment rallies over the weekend. The numbers were anemic, no spirit, no hope. More importantly, No Collusion, No Obstruction!

June 21, 2019

7:19 am: Just revealed that the Failing and Desperate New York Times was feeding false stories about me, & those associated with me, to the

FBI. This shows the kind of unprecedented hatred I have been putting up with for years with this Crooked newspaper. Is what they have done legal?…

June 29, 2019

7:07 pm: The highly respected Farm Journal has just announced my Approval Rating with our great Farmers at 74%, and that despite all of the Fake & Corrupt News that they are forced to endure. Farmers have been unfairly treated for many years—and that is turning around FAST!

July 7, 2019

10:17 pm: Impossible to believe that @FoxNews has hired @donnabrazile, the person fired by @CNN (after they tried to hide the bad facts, & failed) for giving Crooked Hillary Clinton the questions to a debate, something unimaginable. Now she is all over Fox, including Shep Smith, by far…

…their lowest rated show. Watch the @FoxNews weekend daytime anchors, who are terrible, go after her big time. That's what they want—but it sure is not what the audience wants!

July 9, 2019

8:30 pm: A truly great, patriotic & charitable man, Bernie Marcus, the co-founder of Home Depot who, at the age of 90, is coming under attack by the Radical Left Democrats with one of their often used weapons. They don't want people to shop at those GREAT stores because he contributed…

…to your favorite President, me! These people are vicious and totally crazed, but remember, there are far more great people ("Deplorables") in this country, than bad. Do to them what they do to you. Fight for Bernie Marcus and Home Depot!

July 19, 2019

7:16 am: It is amazing how the Fake News Media became "crazed" over the chant "send he back" by a packed Arena (a record) crowd in the Great State of North Carolina, but is totally calm & accepting of the most vile and disgusting statements made by the three Radical Left Congresswomen...

...Mainstream Media, which has lost all credibility, has either officially or unofficially become a part of the Radical Left Democrat Party. It is a sick partnership, so pathetic to watch! They even covered a tiny staged crowd as they greeted Foul Mouthed Omar in Minnesota, a...

...State which I will win in #2020 because they can't stand her and her hatred of our Country, and they appreciate all that I have done for them (opening up mining and MUCH more) which has led to the best employment & economic year in Minnesota's long and beautiful history!

7:34 am: Thomas "the Chin" Friedman, a weak and pathetic sort of guy, writes columns for The New York Times in between rounds of his favorite game, golf. Two weeks ago, while speaking to a friend on his cell phone, I unfortunately ended up speaking to Friedman. We spoke for a while and...

...he could not have been nicer or more respectful to your favorite President, me. Then I saw the column he wrote, "Trump Will Be Re-elected, Won't He?" He called me a Racist, which I am not, and said Rhode Island went from economically bad to great in 5 years because the...

...Governor of the State did a good job. That may be true but she could not have done it without the tremendous economic success of our Country & the turnaround that my Administration has caused. Really Nasty to me in his average I.Q. Columns, kissed my a... on the call. Phony!

July 22, 2019

7:31 am: The Amazon Washington Post front page story yesterday was total Fake News. They said "Advisors wrote new talking points and

handed him reams of opposition research on the four Congresswomen."
Now really, does that sound like me? What advisors, there were no
talking points,...

7:38 am: Fake News Equals the Enemy of the People!

July 30, 2019

7:11 am: Wow! Morning Joe & Psycho ratings have really crashed. Very
small audience. People are tired of hearing Fake News delivered with
an anger that is not to be believed. Sad, when the show was sane, they
helped get me elected. Thanks! Was on all the time. Lost all of its juice!

8:52 am: Just reminded my staff that Morning Joe & Psycho were with
me in my room, at their request, the night I won New Hampshire.
Likewise, followed me to other states...

...Don't watch show, but heard Mika said I asked to preside over their
marriage. Not true—does anyone really believe that? They were married by Elijah, King of Baltimore!

July 31, 2019

10:31 am: CNN's Don Lemon, the dumbest man on television, insinuat-
ed last night while asking a debate "question" that I was a racist, when in
fact I am "the least racist person in the world." Perhaps someone should
explain to Don that he is supposed to be neutral, unbiased & fair,...

August 5, 2019

6:32 am: The Media has a big responsibility to life and safety in our
Country. Fake News has contributed greatly to the anger and rage that
has built up over many years. News coverage has got to start being fair,
balanced and unbiased, or these terrible problems will only get worse!

August 6, 2019

12:51 pm: .@sundarpichai of Google was in the Oval Office working very hard to explain how much he liked me, what a great job the

Administration is doing, that Google was not involved with China's military, that they didn't help Crooked Hillary over me in the 2016 Election, & that they...

... are NOT planning to illegally subvert the 2020 Election despite all that has been said to the contrary. It all sounded good until I watched Kevin Cernekee, a Google engineer, say terrible things about what they did in 2016 and that they want to "Make sure that Trump losses...

...in 2020." Lou Dobbs stated that this is a fraud on the American public. @peterschweizer stated with certainty that they suppressed negative stories on Hillary Clinton, and boosted negative stories on Donald Trump. All very illegal. We are watching Google very closely!

August 7, 2019

2:48 pm: Just left Dayton, Ohio, where I met with the Victims & families, Law Enforcement, Medical Staff & First Responders. It was a warm & wonderful visit. Tremendous enthusiasm & even Love. Then I saw failed Presidential Candidate (0%) Sherrod Brown & Mayor Whaley totally...

...misrepresenting what took place inside of the hospital. Their news conference after I left for El Paso was a fraud. It bore no resemblance to what took place with those incredible people that I was so lucky to meet and spend time with. They were all amazing!

2:55 pm: Watching Fake News CNN is better than watching Shepard Smith, the lowest rated show on @FoxNews. Actually, whenever possible, I turn to @OANN!

11:20 pm: ...I am so amazed that MSNBC & CNN can keep putting on, over and over again, people that have no idea what I am all about, and yet they speak as experts on "Trump." Same people since long before the 2016 Election, and how did that work out for the Haters and Losers. Not well!

August 9, 2019

1:44 pm: Liberal Hollywood is Racist at the highest level, and with great Anger and Hate! They like to call themselves "Elite," but they are not Elite. In fact, it is often the people that they so strongly oppose that are actually the Elite. The movie coming out is made in order...

...to inflame and cause chaos. They create their own violence, and then try to blame others. They are the true Racists, and are very bad for our Country!

August 10, 2019

6:40 am: Maggie Haberman of the Failing @nytimes reported that I was annoyed by the lack of cameras inside the hospitals in Dayton & El Paso, when in fact I was the one who stated, very strongly, that I didn't want the Fake News inside & told my people NOT to let them in. Fake reporting!

7:07 am: Never has the press been more inaccurate, unfair or corrupt! We are not fighting the Democrats, they are easy, we are fighting the seriously dishonest and unhinged Lamestream Media. They have gone totally CRAZY. MAKE AMERICA GREAT AGAIN!

4:48 pm: Got to see, by accident, wacko comedian Bill Maher's show— So many lies. He said patients in El Paso hospital didn't want to meet with me. Wrong! Had really great meetings with numerous patients. Said I was on vacation. Wrong! Long planned fix up of W.H., stay here rather than.

...cause big disruption by going to Manhattan. Working almost all of the time, including evenings. Don't have to be in W.H. to do that... And sooo many other false statements. He is right about one thing, though. I will win again in 2020. Otherwise, he pays 95% in taxes!

August 13, 2019

7:38 am: I thought Chris was Fredo also. The truth hurts. Totally lost it! Low ratings @CNN

August 18, 2019

6:57 pm: The New York Times will be out of business soon after I leave office, hopefully in 6 years. They have Zero credibility and are losing a fortune, even now, especially after their massive unfunded liability. I'm fairly certain they'll endorse me just to keep it all going!

August 20, 2019

8:26 am: The New York Times will be out of business soon after I leave office, hopefully in 6 years. They have Zero credibility and are losing a fortune, even now, especially after their massive unfunded liability. I'm fairly certain they'll endorse me just to keep it all going!

10:33 am: The LameStream Media is far beyond Fake News, they are treading in very dangerous territory!

August 21. 2019

6:34 am: "Thank you to Wayne Allyn Root for the very nice words. "President Trump is the greatest President for Jews and for Israel in the history of the world, not just America, he is the best President for Israel in the history of the world...and the Jewish people in Israel love him...

...like he's the King of Israel. They love him like he is the second coming of God...But American Jews don't know him or like him. They don't even know what they're doing or saying anymore. It makes no sense! But that's OK, if he keeps doing what he's doing, he's good for...

...all Jews, Blacks, Gays, everyone. And importantly, he's good for everyone in America who wants a job." Wow! @newsmax @foxandfriends @OANN

August 23, 2019

10:58 pm: The New York Times will be out of business soon after I leave office, hopefully in 6 years. They have Zero credibility and are losing a fortune, even now, especially after their massive unfunded liability. I'm fairly certain they'll endorse me just to keep it all going!

August 24, 2019

10:00 am: When I looked up to the sky and jokingly said "I am the chosen one," at a press conference two days ago, referring to taking on Trade with China, little did I realize that the media would claim that I had a "Messiah complex." They knew I was kidding, being sarcastic, and just...

...having fun. I was smiling as I looked up and around. The MANY reporters with me were smiling also. They knew the TRUTH...And yet when I saw the reporting, CNN, MSNBC and other Fake News outlets covered it as serious news & me thinking of myself as the Messiah. No more trust!

10:15 am: "Face It, You Probably Got A Tax Cut!" This was a New York Times headline, and it is very true. If Republicans take back the House, and keep the Senate and Presidency, one of our first acts will be to approve a major middle income Tax Cut! Democrats only want to raise your taxes!

August 25, 2019

12:41 am: Before I arrived in France, the Fake and Disgusting News was saying that relations with the 6 others countries in the G-7 are very tense, and that the two days of meetings will be a disaster. Just like they are trying to force a Recession, they are trying to "will" America into.

...bad Economic times, the worse the better, anything to make my Election more difficult to win. Well, we are having very good meetings, the Leaders are getting along very well, and our Country, economically, is doing great—the talk of the world!

12:45 am: Such False and Inaccurate reporting thus far on the G-7. The Fake News knows this but they can't help themselves! Leaving now to have breakfast with Boris J.

August 26, 2019

4:25 am: The story by Axios that President Trump wanted to blow up large hurricanes with nuclear weapons prior to reaching shore is ridiculous. I never said this. Just more FAKE NEWS!

August 27, 2019

9:45 am: The G-7 was a great success for the USA and all. LameStream Media coverage bore NO relationship to what actually happened in France—FAKE NEWS. It was GREAT!

10:23 pm: A made up Radical Left Story about Doral bedbugs, but Bret Stephens is loaded up with them! Been calling me wrong for years, along with the few remaining Never Trumpers—All Losers!

4:46 pm: The G7 in France was so successful, and yet when I came back and read the Corrupt and Fake News, and watched numerous networks, it was not even recognizable from what actually took place at the Great G7 event!

4:49 pm: It is amazing that I can be at 51% with Zogby when the Fake & Corrupt News is almost 100% against me. Great job Mr. President!

August 28, 2019

6:22 am: "The infestation of bedbugs at The New York Times office" @OANN was perhaps brought in by lightweight journalist Bret Stephens, a Conservative who does anything that his bosses at the paper tell him to do! He is now quitting Twitter after being called a "bedbug." Tough guy!

8:57 am: Just watched @FoxNews heavily promoting the Democrats through their DNC Communications Director, spewing out whatever she wanted with zero pushback by anchor, @SandraSmithFox. Terrible considering that Fox couldn't even land a debate, the Dems give them NOTHING! @CNN & @MSNBC...

...are all in for the Open Border Socialists (or beyond). Fox hires "give Hillary the questions" @donnabrazile, Juan Williams and low ratings Shep Smith. HOPELESS & CLUELESS! They should go all the way LEFT and I will still find a way to Win—That's what I do, Win. Too Bad!.

2:06 pm: Another totally Fake story in the Amazon Washington Post (lobbyist) which states that if my Aides broke the law to build the

Wall (which is going up rapidly), I would give them a Pardon. This was made up by the Washington Post only in order to demean and disparage—FAKE NEWS

7:21 pm: The Amazon Washington Post and @CNN just did a Fake Interview on Pardons for Aids on the Wall, and that I didn't think the Wall on the Southern Border was that important to stop Illegals wanting to come into our Country. WRONG, vitally important. Will make a BIG impact. So bad!

7:35 pm: There has never been a time in the history of our Country that the Media was so Fraudulent, Fake, or Corrupt! When the "Age of Trump" is looked back on many years from now, I only hope that a big part of my legacy will be the exposing of massive dishonesty in the Fake News!

August 29, 2019

6:31 am: Crazy Lawrence O'Donnell, who has been calling me wrong from even before I announced my run for the Presidency, even being previously forced by NBC to apologize, which he did while crying, for things he said about me & The Apprentice, was again forced to apologize, this time…

for the most ridiculous claim of all, that Russia, Russia, Russia, or Russian oligarchs, co-signed loan documents for me, a guarantee. Totally false, as is virtually everything else he, and much of the rest of the LameStream Media, has said about me for years. ALL APOLOGIZE!

September 2, 2019

7:09 am: The Amazon Washington Post did a story that I brought racist attacks against the "Squad." No, they brought racist attacks against our Nation. All I do is call them out for the horrible things they have said. The Democrats have become the Party of the Squad!

6:16 pm: Such a phony hurricane report by lightweight reporter @ jonkarl of @ABCWorldNews. I suggested yesterday at FEMA that, along with Florida, Georgia, South Carolina and North Carolina, even Alabama could possibly come into play, which WAS true. They made a big deal about this…

September 4, 2019

4:08 pm: 8 FACTS that #FakeNewsCNN will ignore in tonight's "Climate Forum"

1. Which country has the largest carbon emission reduction? AMERICA! 2. Who has dumped the most carbon into the air? CHINA! 3. 91% of the world's population are exposed to air pollution above the World Health Organization's suggested level. NONE ARE IN THE U.S.A.!

4. The U.S. now leads the world in energy production… BUT… 5. Who's got the world's cleanest and safest air and water? AMERICA!

6. The Democrats' destructive "environmental" proposals will raise your energy bill and prices at the pump. Don't the Democrats care about fighting American poverty?

7. The badly flawed Paris Climate Agreement protects the polluters, hurts Americans, and cost a fortune. NOT ON MY WATCH! 8. I want crystal clean water and the cleanest and the purest air on the planet—we've now got that!

September 5, 2019

6:48 am: In the early days of the hurricane, when it was predicted that Dorian would go through Miami or West Palm Beach, even before it reached the Bahamas, certain models strongly suggested that Alabama & Georgia would be hit as it made its way through Florida & to the Gulf…

…Instead it turned North and went up the coast, where it continues now. In the one model through Florida, the Great State of Alabama would have been hit or grazed. In the path it took, no. Read my FULL FEMA statement. What I said was accurate! All Fake News in order to demean!

8:39 am: Alabama was going to be hit or grazed, and then Hurricane Dorian took a different path (up along the East Coast). The Fake News knows this very well. That's why they're the Fake News!

9:29 am: The Fake News Media was fixated on the fact that I properly said, at the beginnings of Hurricane Dorian, that in addition to Florida & other states, Alabama may also be grazed or hit. They went Crazy, hoping against hope that I made a mistake (which I didn't). Check out maps...

...This nonsense has never happened to another President. Four days of corrupt reporting, still without an apology. But there are many things that the Fake News Media has not apologized to me for, like the Witch Hunt, or SpyGate! The LameStream Media and their Democrat.

...partner should start playing it straight. It would be so much better for our Country!

September 7, 2019

6:08 am: The Washington Post's @PhilipRucker (Mr. Off the Record) & @AshleyRParker, two nasty lightweight reporters, shouldn't even be allowed on the grounds of the White House because their reporting is so DISGUSTING & FAKE. Also, add the appointment of MANY Federal Judges this Summer!

3:44 pm: The Failing New York Times stated, in an article written by Obama flunky Peter Baker (who lovingly wrote Obama book),"Even after the President forecast the storm to include Alabama." THIS IS NOT TRUE. I said, VERY EARLY ON, that it MAY EVEN hit Alabama. A BIG DIFFERENCE.

...FAKE NEWS. I would like very much to stop referring to this ridiculous story, but the LameStream Media just won't let it alone. They always have to have the last word, even though they know they are defrauding & deceiving the public. The public knows that the Media is corrupt!

September 9, 2019

12:49 pm: A lot of Fake News is being reported that I overruled the VP and various advisers on a potential Camp David meeting with the Taliban. This Story is False! I always think it is good to meet and talk, but in this case I decided not to. The Dishonest Media likes to create…

…the look of turmoil in the White House, of which there is none. I view much of the media as simply an arm of the Democrat Party. They are corrupt, and they are extremely upset at how well our Country is doing under MY Leadership, including…

…the Economy, where there is NO Recession, much to the regret of the LameStream Media! They are working overtime to help the Democrats win in 2020, but that will NEVER HAPPEN, Americans are too smart!

September 10, 2019

9:23 am: ABC/Washington Post Poll was the worst and most inaccurate poll of any taken prior to the 2016 Election. When my lawyers protested, they took a 12 point down and brought it to almost even by Election Day. It was a Fake Poll by two very bad and dangerous media outlets. Sad!

9:31 am: One of the greatest and most powerful weapons used by the Fake and Corrupt News Media is the phony Polling Information they put out. Many of these polls are fixed, or worked in such a way that a certain candidate will look good or bad. Internal polling looks great, the best ever!

September 11, 2019

7:12 am: In a hypothetical poll, done by one of the worst pollsters of them all, the Amazon Washington Post/ABC, which predicted I would lose to Crooked Hillary by 15 points (how did that work out?), Sleepy Joe, Pocahontas and virtually all others would beat me in the General Election

.This is a phony suppression poll, meant to build up their Democrat partners. I haven't even started campaigning yet, and am constantly fighting Fake News like Russia, Russia, Russia. Look at North Carolina last night. Dan Bishop, down big in the Polls, WINS. Easier than 2016!

7:19 am: If it weren't for the never ending Fake News about me, and with all that I have done (more than any other President in the first 2 1/2 years!), I would be leading the "Partners" of the LameStream Media by 20 points. Sorry, but true!

September 14, 2019

8:04 am: Who the hell is Joy-Ann Reid? Never met her, she knows ZERO about me, has NO talent, and truly doesn't have the "it" factor needed for success in showbiz. Had a bad reputation, and now works for the Comcast/NBC losers making up phony stories about me. Low Ratings. Fake News!

September 15, 2019

1:20 pm: I am fighting the Fake (Corrupt) News, the Deep State, the Democrats, and the few remaining Republicans In Name Only (RINOS, who are on mouth to mouth resuscitation), with the help of some truly great Republicans, and others. We are Winning big (150th Federal Judge this week)!

1:41 pm: Can't believe the @washingtonpost wrote a positive front page story, "Unity Issue Has Parties Pointing To Trump. GOP Goes All In, While Democrats Clash Over Ideology & Tactics. Mr. President, We Are With You The Entire Way. REPUBLICANS Have...Coalesced Around Trump.".

6:02 pm: The Fake News is saying that I am willing to meet with Iran, "No Conditions." That is an incorrect statement (as usual!).

September 16, 2019

5:40 pm: I call for the Resignation of everybody at The New York Times involved in the Kavanaugh SMEAR story, and while you're at it, the Russian Witch Hunt Hoax, which is just as phony! They've taken the Old Grey Lady and broken her down, destroyed her virtue and ruined her reputation…

…She can never recover, and will never return to Greatness, under current Management. The Times is DEAD, long live The New York Times!

September 17, 2019

10:12 am: The New York Times is at its lowest point in its long and storied history. Not only is it losing a lot of money, but it is a journalistic disaster, being laughed at even in the most liberal of enclaves. It has become a very sad joke all all over the World. Witch Hunt hurt them…

6:58 pm: The New York Times is now blaming an editor for the horrible mistake they made in trying to destroy or influence Justice Brett Kavanaugh. It wasn't the editor, the Times knew everything. They are sick and desperate, losing in so many ways!

September 18, 2019

8:42 pm: All Polls, and some brand new Polls, show very little support for impeachment. Such a waste of time, especially with sooo much good that could be done, including prescription drug price reduction, healthcare, infrastructure etc.

September 19, 2019

9:47 am: Another Fake News story out there—It never ends! Virtually anytime I speak on the phone to a foreign leader, I understand that there may be many people listening from various U.S. agencies, not to mention those from the other country itself. No problem!

…Knowing all of this, is anybody dumb enough to believe that I would say something inappropriate with a foreign leader while on such a potentially "heavily populated" call. I would only do what is right anyway, and only do good for the USA!

September 21, 2019

7:31 am: The Fake News Media and their partner, the Democrat Party, want to stay as far away as possible from the Joe Biden demand that the Ukrainian Government fire a prosecutor who was investigating his son, or they won't get a very large amount of U.S. money, so they fabricate a…

…story about me and a perfectly fine and routine conversation I had with the new President of the Ukraine. Nothing was said that was in any way wrong, but Biden's demand, on the other hand, was a complete and total disaster. The Fake News knows this but doesn't want to report!

September 22, 2019

7:03 pm: Now the Fake News Media says I "pressured the Ukrainian President at least 8 times during my telephone call with him." This supposedly comes from a so-called "whistleblower" who they say doesn't even have a first hand account of what was said. More Democrat/Crooked Media con…

…Breaking News: The Ukrainian Government just said they weren't pressured at all during the "nice" call. Sleepy Joe Biden, on the other hand, forced a tough prosecutor out from investigating his son's company by threat of not giving big dollars to Ukraine. That's the real story!

September 23, 2019

2:37 pm: This is the real corruption that the Fake News Media refuses to even acknowledge!

6:24 pm: "@FoxNews bombshell information reports that the so-called Whistleblower did not have firsthand knowledge of that phone conversation with Ukraine's President." Wow! @HARRISFAULKNER It is all a Democrat/Adam Schiff Scam! Doing this for 3 years now, and found NOTHING!

September 30, 2019

9:03 am: The Fake News Media wants to stay as far away as possible from the Ukraine and China deals made by the Bidens. A Corrupt Media is so bad for our Country! In actuality, the Media may be even more Corrupt than the Bidens, which is hard to do!

October 2, 2019

10:02 am: Now the press is trying to sell the fact that I wanted a Moat stuffed with alligators and snakes, with an electrified fence and sharp spikes on top, at our Southern Border. I may be tough on Border Security, but not that tough. The press has gone Crazy. Fake News!

October 3, 2019

8:35 pm: We are simultaneously fighting the Fake News Media and their partner, the Democrat Party. Always tough to beat the "Press," but people are beginning to see how totally CORRUPT they are, and it makes our job a whole lot easier!

October 4, 2019

9:12 am: "I think it's outrages that a Whistleblower is a CIA Agent." Ed Rollins @FoxNews

October 6, 2019

6:05 pm: Good job, I must say, by Bob Woodward on "Deface the Nation." The CBS no name host(ess), and other guest, Peter Baker of The Failing New York Times, were totally biased, boring and wrong (as usual), but Woodward was cool, calm and interesting. Thank you Bob!

6:25 pm: Sleepy Eyes Chuck Todd of "Meet the Press" had a total meltdown in his interview with highly reaspected Senator @RonJohnsonWI. Seems that a not very bright Chuck just wasn't getting the answers he was looking for in order to make me look as bad as possible. I did NOTHING wrong!

6:35 pm: Gerry Baker of @WSJatLarge "Do you think what you've seen rises to the level of impeachment?" Ken Starr, Clinton Special Prosecutor. "I don't!"

October 19, 2019

2:16 pm: Just another FAKE SUPPRESSION POLL, this time from @ FoxNews, of course!

November 2, 2019

11:26 am: A great new book by Howie Carr, "What Really Happened, How Donald J. Trump Saved America From Hillary Clinton," is on sale now. Howie is a talented New England force who was there at the very beginning!

November 3, 2019

11:25 am: Thank you to @OANN for the absolutely incredible Special Report narrated by @PearsonSharp. Seldom do the American people get to see journalistic work of this quality. Now it would be great if the legitimate sections of law enforcement would study your SMEARS, SPIES AND LIES...

...and FEDERAL CONTRACTOR SPIES stories. The finest law enforcement on the planet could not have shown a ROADMAP like that which was produced by you. @OANN should be VERY proud of this great work. I wish more people were seeking the facts and the truth. Keep it up!

11:45 am: Fake News!

3:05 pm: The Fake News Media is working hard so that information about the Whistleblower's identity, which may be very bad for them and their Democrat partners, never reaches the Public.

November 7, 2019

12:06 am: Years ago, when Media was legitimate, people known as "Fact Checkers" would always call to check and see if a story was accurate. Nowadays they don't use "Fact Checkers" anymore, they just write whatever they want!

12:08 am: The story in the Amazon Washington Post, of course picked up by Fake News CNN, saying "President Trump asked for AG Barr to host a news conference clearing him on Ukraine," is totally untrue and just another FAKE NEWS story with anonymous sources that don't exist...

...The LameStream Media, which is The Enemy of the People, is working overtime with made up stories in order to drive dissension and distrust!

8:46 am: The degenerate Washington Post MADE UP the story about me asking Bill Barr to hold a news conference. Never happened, and there were no sources!

10:27 am: The Amazon Washington Post and three lowlife reporters, Matt Zapotosky, Josh Dawsey, and Carol Leonnig, wrote another Fake News story, without any sources (pure fiction), about Bill Barr & myself. We both deny this story, which they knew before they wrote it. A garbage newspaper!

10:41 am: The Radical Left Dems and LameStream Media are just trying to make it hard for Republicans and me to win in 2020. The new Impeachment Hoax is already turning against them!

November 9, 2019

6:41 am: Fake News is reporting that I am talking to Mark Burnett about doing a big show, perhaps The Apprentice, after the presidency, which I would assume they mean in 5 years. This is not true, never had such a conversation, don't even have time to think about it. False reporting!

10:44 am: Bringing the word "Nationalism" back into the mainstream—great job by Rich Lowry! Very important book.

November 10, 2019

11:12 am: ABC is as bad as the rest of them. Journalistic standards are nonexistent today. The press is so dishonest that we no longer have Freedom of the Press!

6:02 pm: .@NikkiHaley is out with a new book, "With All Due Respect" this week. Make sure you order your copy today, or stop by one of her book tour stops to get a copy and say hello. Good luck Nikki!

9:25 pm: A great new book just out, "The Plot Against the President. The True Story Of How Congressman Devin Nunes Uncovered the Biggest Political Scandal In U.S. History." Shows very bad and corrupt people on the other side. Check it out!

November 17, 2019

9:09 am: M Dowd never understood the pulse of the Republican Party, present or past. He's just a 3rd rate hit job for Fake News @ABC!

11:51 am: Joe Ricketts, one of our Country's most successful businessmen, including being the owner of the Chicago Cubs, has just written a great new book, THE HARDER YOU WORK, THE LUCKIER YOU GET. So true! Much can be learned from Joe. Go get the book!

12:43 pm: Paul Krugman has called me wrong from day one. People at the Failing New York Times are very angry at him for having "missed" by soooo much. Paul, match over!

2:49 pm: Paul Krugman of @nytimes has been wrong about me from the very beginning. Anyone who has followed his "words of wisdom" has lost a great deal of money. Paul, just concede the game, say I was right, and lets start a brand new game!

November 21, 2019

7:26 am: Why do @ShannonBream & @FoxNews waste airtime on Democrat Rep. Eric Swalwell, who recently left the Presidential Primaries having attained a grand number of ZERO in the polls. I don't even know how that is possible. Fox should stay with the people that got them there, not losers!

November 28, 2019

8:25 pm: I thought Newsweek was out of business?

November 30, 2019

6:11 pm: Thank you to @BuckMcNeely1 and Oliver North for the nice words and thoughts in an excellent interview. Best wishes!

December 2, 2019

2:21 am: Great writer and historian, Doug Wead, has written a true (not Fake News) account of what is going on in Washington and the White House. His new book, INSIDE TRUMP'S WHITE HOUSE, is an incredible description of a very exciting and successful time in our Country's history. Buy it!

6:11 pm: Mini Mike Bloomberg has instructed his third rate news organization not to investigate him or any Democrat, but to go after President Trump, only. The Failing New York Times thinks that is O.K., because their hatred & bias is so great they can't even see straight. It's not O.K.!

December 4, 2019

7:03 pm: Just read the best Maureen Dowd column, in the New York Times, EVER (although she treated me great before politics), but it was written by her brother, Kevin. Someone in the News Media should hire her wonderful, talented, and very smart brother!

December 5, 2019

7:43 am: Do not believe any article or story you read or see that uses "anonymous sources" having to do with trade or any other subject. Only accept information if it has an actual living name on it. The Fake News Media makes up many "sources say" stories. Do not believe them!

December 8, 2019

2:42 pm: Don't get why @FoxNews puts losers on like @RepSwalwell (who got ZERO as presidential candidate before quitting), Pramila Jayapal, David Cicilline and others who are Radical Left Haters? The Dems wouldn't let @FoxNews get near their bad ratings debates, yet Fox panders. Pathetic!

6:20 pm: .CNN is a ratings disaster. Lost all credibility!

December 11, 2019

2:06 pm: The News Media in our Country is FAKE and in many cases, totally CORRUPT!

December 12, 2019

6:59 am: It's great to have a wonderful subject, President Trump. Fake News like CNN & MSNBC are dying. If they treated me fairly, they would do well. Have Zero credibility!

7:22 am: So ridiculous. Greta must work on her Anger Management problem, then go to a good old fashioned movie with a friend! Chill Greta, Chill!

December 13, 2019

7:54 am: Congratulations to @foxandfriends on being named, BY FAR, the Number One Rated cable news show. CNN and MSNBC have totally tanked, their ratings are terrible. They have zero credibility!

9:06 am: The Wall Street Journal story on the China Deal is completely wrong, especially their statement on Tariffs. Fake News. They should find a better leaker!

December 14, 2019

7:10 pm: Hard to believe that @FoxNews will be interviewing sleaze-bag & totally discredited former FBI Director James Comey, & also corrupt politician Adam "Shifty" Schiff. Fox is trying sooo hard to be politically correct, and yet they were totally shut out from the failed Dem debates!

7:47 pm: Hard to believe that @FoxNews will be interviewing sleaze-bag & totally discredited former FBI Director James Comey, & also corrupt politician Adam "Shifty" Schiff. Fox is trying sooo hard to be politically correct, and yet they were totally shut out from the failed Dem debates!

December 15, 2019

12:12 pm: Schiff's correcting the record memo has turned out to be totally wrong (based on the I.G. Report)! A very big lie. @MariaBartiromo And @DevinNunes has turned out to be completely right. Congratulations to Devin. The Fake News Media should apologize to all!

December 20, 2019

7:12 am: A far left magazine, or very "progressive," as some would call it, which has been doing poorly and hasn't been involved with the Billy Graham family for many years, Christianity Today, knows nothing about reading a perfect transcript of a routine phone call and would rather...

...have a Radical Left nonbeliever, who wants to take your religion & your guns, than Donald Trump as your President. No President has done more for the Evangelical community, and it's not even close. You'll not get anything from those Dems on stage. I won't be reading ET again!

1:18 pm: I guess the magazine, "Christianity Today," is looking for Elizabeth Warren, Bernie Sanders, or those of the socialist/communist bent, to guard their religion. How about Sleepy Joe? The fact is, no President has ever done what I have done for Evangelicals, or religion itself!

3:59 pm: Thank you to Franklin Graham for stating that his father, the late great Billy Graham, voted for me in the 2016 Election. I know how pleased you are with the work we have all done together!

December 26, 2019

7:07 pm: The movie will never be the same! (just kidding) https://t.co/FogquK1ei7

December 27, 2019

8:48 am: Academy Award winning actor (and great guy!) @jonvoight is fantastic in the role of Mickey Donovan in the big television hit, Ray Donovan. From Midnight Cowboy to Deliverance to The Champ (one of the best ever boxing movies), & many others, Jon delivers BIG. Also, LOVES THE USA!

9:28 pm: @OANN is doing incredible reporting. If Lamestream Media did the same, they would get respect back. At All-Time Low!

9:41 pm: He made same prediction in 2016. Nobody ever said Michael was stupid!

9:43 pm: Come on Crazy Nancy, do it! https://t.co/skuSBDdwW1

December 28, 2019

4:06 pm: I want to thank Rush Limbaugh for the tremendous support he has given to the MAKE AMERICA GREAT AGAIN Movement and our KEEP AMERICA GREAT Agenda! He is a major star who never wavered despite the Fake News Hits he has had to endure. His voice is far bigger than theirs!

December 30, 2019

5:23 pm: He is Fake News, will always be Fredo to us. I should release some of his dishonest interviews? Coupled with bad ratings, he'd be out! https://t.co/eEk6pdSRnV

December 31, 2019

5:11 pm: The Fake News said I played golf today, and I did NOT! I had meeting in various locations, while closely monitoring the U.S. Embassy situation in Iraq, which I am still doing. The Corrupt Lamestream Media knew this but, not surprisingly, failed to report or correct!

8:03 pm: Thank you to the @dcexaminer Washington Examiner. The list is growing every day.

Social Media/Twitter—2017 News Quotes

Response to a question from Tucker Carlson of FOX News, March 15, 2017.
Source: https://www.youtube.com/watch?v=RYGH6ejacNO

"Well, let me say this about tweeting, I think that maybe I would not be here if it wasn't for Twitter. Because I get such a fake press, such a dishonest press.

"I mean, if you look at—And I'm not including FOX because I think FOX has been fair to me. But if you look at CNN and if you look at these other networks, NBC.

"I made a fortune for NBC with *The Apprentice*. I had a top show where they were doing horribly. And I had one of the most successful reality shows of all time. And I was on for 14 seasons. And you see what happens when I am not on. You saw what happened and the show was a disaster. I was on. I was very good to NBC and they are despicable, despicable in their coverage.

"CBS, ABC, you take a look at what is going on. I call it the fake press, the fake media. It is a disgrace what is happening. So, let me—[Carlson interrupts.]"

Response to a question from Tucker Carlson of FOX News, March 15, 2017.
Source: https://www.youtube.com/watch?v=RYGH6ejacNO

"And when I have close to 100 million people watching me on Twitter, including Facebook, including all of the—Instagram, including POTUS,

526

including lots of things. But we have, you know, I guess pretty close to 100 million people. I have my own form of media. So, you know, if I tweet two or three or four or five times a day, and if most of them are good; I really want them all to be good, but if I make one mistake in a month, this one, I don't think is going to prove to be a mistake at all."

Response to a question from Tucker Carlson of FOX News, March 15, 2017.
Source: https://www.youtube.com/watch?v=RYGH6ejacNO

"But just on Twitter, if I do not do that, I won't get my word out.

"Because when I tell, when I say things, the press does not cover it accurately. They cover it very inaccurately. Much of the press. Some of the press. By the way, some of the finest people I know are reporters. Reporters are wonderful. I'm talking about the fake media, the fake news. And there is a lot of fake news.

"So, if I am not going to—If they are not going to do me the honor or the public the honor of spreading my word accurately as it was meant, and you know exactly what I'm talking about, because there's been nobody in history that got more dishonest media than I've gotten. You look at some of the stories in *The New York Times.* You look at some of the stories in *The Washington Post.* Take a look at what is going on with CBS, and NBC in particular. And ABC. Take a look at CNN. It's a complete hit job. No matter what you do, no matter how good, no matter how great it is, they don't report it in a positive fashion.

"So, when I can reach, whether it's 90 million or 100 million or 80 million—However many people that may turn out to be when you add everything up. And then of course it gets disseminated from there, when I can reach that many people.

"Twitter is a wonderful thing for me, because I get the word out."

Response to a question from Tucker Carlson of FOX News, March 15, 2017.
Source: https://www.youtube.com/watch?v=RYGH6ejacNO

"Sometimes I'll have something, and I'll say, 'What do you think about this?'

527

"A lot of times my staff comes to me and they say, 'Could you do a tweet of this or that, because it's not being shown correctly.' I mean, they'll come to me a lot. And they'll say, 'Could you do—?'

"I probably wouldn't be—I'm not talking about Twitter because it's really Twitter, Facebook, and lots of other things. Okay?

"But I might not be here talking to you right now as President if I didn't have an honest way of getting the word out."

Social Media/Twitter—2017 Tweets

July 1, 2017

5:41 pm: My use of social media is not Presidential—it's MODERN DAY PRESIDENTIAL. Make America Great Again!

August 1, 2017

8:55 am: Only the Fake News Media and Trump enemies want me to stop using Social Media (110 million people). Only way for me to get the truth out!

September 22, 2017

5:44 am: The Russia hoax continues, now it's ads on Facebook. What about the totally biased and dishonest Media coverage in favor of Crooked Hillary?

September 27, 2017

8:36 am to 8:41 am: Facebook was always anti-Trump. The Networks were always anti-Trump hence,Fake News, @nytimes(apologized) & @WaPo were anti-Trump. Collusion?

...But the people were Pro-Trump! Virtually no President has accomplished what we have accomplished in the first 9 months-and economy roaring

October 21, 2017

4:21 pm: Crooked Hillary Clinton spent hundreds of millions of dollars more on Presidential Election than I did. Facebook was on her side, not mine!

November 3, 2017

5:51 am: My Twitter account was taken down for 11 minutes by a rogue employee. I guess the word must finally be getting out-and having an impact.

December 30. 2017

5:36 pm: I use Social Media not because I like to, but because it is the only way to fight a VERY dishonest and unfair "press," now often referred to as Fake News Media. Phony and non-existent "sources" are being used more often than ever. Many stories & reports a pure fiction!

Social Media/Twitter—2018 News Quote

Response to a question from Piers Morgan of ITV, January 29, 2018.
Source: https://www.theguardian.com/us-news/2018/jan/29/
donald-trump-interview-piers-morgan-im-very-popular-in-britain-get-a-lot-of-fan-mail

"If I don't have that form of communication [Twitter], I can't defend myself. I get a lot of fake news, a lot of news that is very false or made up."

Social Media/Twitter—2018 Tweets

February 17, 2018

3:16 pm: "I have seen all of the Russian ads and I can say very definitively that swaying the election was *NOT* the main goal." Rob Goldman Vice President of Facebook Ads

July 6, 2018

8:21 am: Twitter is getting rid of fake accounts at a record pace. Will that include the Failing New York Times and propaganda machine for Amazon, the Washington Post, who constantly quote anonymous sources that, in my opinion, don't exist—They will both be out of business in 7 years!

July 26, 2018

6:46 am: Twitter "SHADOW BANNING" prominent Republicans. Not good. We will look into this discriminatory and illegal practice at once! Many complaints.

August 18, 2018

6:23 am to 6:40 am: Social Media is totally discriminating against Republican/Conservative voices. Speaking loudly and clearly for the Trump Administration, we won't let that happen. They are closing down the opinions of many people on the RIGHT, while at the same time doing nothing to others...

...Censorship is a very dangerous thing & absolutely impossible to police. If you are weeding out Fake News, there is nothing so Fake as CNN & MSNBC, & yet I do not ask that their sick behavior be removed. I get used to it and watch with a grain of salt, or don't watch at all...

...Too many voices are being destroyed, some good & some bad, and that cannot be allowed to happen. Who is making the choices, because I can already tell you that too many mistakes are being made. Let everybody participate, good & bad, and we will all just have to figure it out!

August 24, 2018

6:34 am: Social Media Giants are silencing millions of people. Can't do this even if it means we must continue to hear Fake News like CNN, whose ratings have suffered gravely. People have to figure out what is real, and what is not, without censorship!

August 29, 2018

3:55 pm: #StopTheBias https://t.co/xqz599iQZw

October 21, 2018

5:48 pm: Facebook has just stated that they are setting up a system to "purge" themselves of Fake News. Does that mean CNN will finally be put out of business?

October 26, 2018

9:05 am: Twitter has removed many people from my account and, more importantly, they have seemingly done something that makes it much harder to join—they have stifled growth to a point where it is obvious to all. A few weeks ago it was a Rocket Ship, now it is a Blimp! Total Bias?

November 3, 2018

4:05 pm: Rumor has it that Senator Joe Donnelly of Indiana is paying for Facebook ads for his so-called opponent on the libertarian ticket. Donnelly is trying to steal the election? Isn't that what Russia did!

December 18, 2018

7:26 am: Facebook, Twitter and Google are so biased toward the Dems it is ridiculous! Twitter, in fact, has made it much more difficult for people to join @realDonaldTrump. They have removed many names & greatly slowed the level and speed of increase. They have acknowledged-done NOTHING

Social Media/Twitter—2019 News Quotes

Response to an unidentified reporter's question before Marine One departure, March 20, 2019.
Source: https://www.whitehouse.gov/briefings-statements/
remarks-president-trump-marine-one-departure-34/

"I think that Twitter is a way that I get out the word when we have a corrupt media. And it is corrupt and it's fake. So Twitter is a way that I can get out the word. Because our media is so dishonest, a lot of it, the mainstream. A lot of it. They don't report the facts. They don't report—As an example that I just showed you, they don't want to report this, so I figure I might as well show it.

"So when I do Twitter statements, I get out the word from a fake and corrupt media."

Response to an unidentified reporter's question before Marine One departure, March 20, 2019.
Source: https://www.whitehouse.gov/briefings-statements/
remarks-president-trump-marine-one-departure-34/

"On five sites, I have over 100 million people, and that includes Facebook and Instagram and Twitter and everything. And it's a way that I can get honesty out, because there's tremendous dishonesty with respect to the fake news media."

Social Media/Twitter—2019 Tweets

March 18, 2019

8:32 pm: Rep. Devin Nunes Files $250M Defamation Lawsuit Against Twitter, Two Anonymous Twitter Accounts

March 19, 2019

8:57 am: Facebook, Google and Twitter, not to mention the Corrupt Media, are sooo on the side of the Radical Left Democrats. But fear not, we will win anyway, just like we did before! #MAGA

April 23, 2019

6:26 am to 6:32 am: "The best thing ever to happen to Twitter is Donald Trump." @MariaBartiromo So true, but they don't treat me well as a Republican. Very discriminatory, hard for people to sign on.

Constantly taking people off list. Big complaints from many people. Different names-over 100 M...

...But should be much higher than that if Twitter wasn't playing their political games. No wonder Congress wants to get involved—and they should. Must be more, and fairer, companies to get out the WORD!

3:43 pm: Great meeting this afternoon at the @WhiteHouse with @ Jack from @Twitter. Lots of subjects discussed regarding their platform, and the world of social media in general. Look forward to keeping an open dialogue!

May 3, 2019

5:55 pm: I am continuing to monitor the censorship of AMERICAN CITIZENS on social media platforms. This is the United States of America—and we have what's known as FREEDOM OF SPEECH! We are monitoring and watching, closely!!

6:23 pm: The wonderful Diamond and Silk have been treated so horribly by Facebook. They work so hard and what has been done to them is very sad—and we're looking into. It's getting worse and worse for Conservatives on social media!

6:25 pm: So surprised to see Conservative thinkers like James Woods banned from Twitter, and Paul Watson banned from Facebook!

May 4, 2019

1:31 pm: How can it be possible that James Woods (and many others), a strong but responsible Conservative Voice, is banned from Twitter? Social Media & Fake News Media, together with their partner, the Democrat Party, have no idea the problems they are causing for themselves. VERY UNFAIR!

May 12, 2019

12:12 pm: Big attacks on Republicans and Conservatives by Social Media. Not good!

May 23, 2019

10:29 pm: When is Twitter going to allow the very popular Conservative Voices that it has so viciously shut down, back into the OPEN? IT IS TIME!

June 9, 2019

7:45 am: Twitter should let the banned Conservative Voices back onto their platform, without restriction. It's called Freedom of Speech, remember. You are making a Giant Mistake!

June 12, 2019

7:46 am: The Fake News has never been more dishonest than it is today. Thank goodness we can fight back on Social Media. Their new weapon of choice is Fake Polling, sometimes referred to as Suppression Polls (they suppress the numbers). Had it in 2016, but this is worse...

July 11, 2019

5:39 am: The White House will be hosting a very big and very important Social Media Summit today. Would I have become President without Social Media? Yes (probably)! At its conclusion, we will all go to the beautiful Rose Garden for a News Conference on the Census and Citizenship.

9:01 am: Will be a big and exciting day at the White House for Social Media!

10:52 am: A big subject today at the White House Social Media Summit will be the tremendous dishonesty, bias, discrimination and suppression practiced by certain companies. We will not let them get away with it much longer. The Fake News Media will also be there, but for a limited period...

...The Fake News is not as important, or as powerful, as Social Media. They have lost tremendous credibility since that day in November,

2016, that I came down the escalator with the person who was to become your future First Lady. When I ultimately leave office in six...

...years, or maybe 10 or 14 (just kidding), they will quickly go out of business for lack of credibility, or approval, from the public. That's why they will all be Endorsing me at some point, one way or the other. Could you imagine having Sleepy Joe Biden, or Alfred E. Newman...

...or a very nervous and skinny version of Pocahontas (1/1024th), as your President, rather than what you have now, so great looking and smart, a true Stable Genius! Sorry to say that even Social Media would be driven out of business along with, and finally, the Fake News Media!

6:01 pm: Today, I am directing my Administration to explore all regulatory and legislative solutions to protect the free speech rights of ALL AMERICANS. We hope to see more transparency, more accountability, and more FREEDOM! #SocialMediaSummit

7:15 pm: ...Similarly, Facebook Libra's "virtual currency" will have little standing or dependability. If Facebook and other companies want to become a bank, they must seek a new Banking Charter and become subject to all Banking Regulations, just like other Banks, both National...

September 19, 2019

7:03 pm: Nice meeting with Mark Zuckerberg of @Facebook in the Oval Office today.

Taxes—2017 News Quotes

At the Signing of an Executive Order to Reorganize the Executive Branch, March 13, 2017.
Source: https://www.whitehouse.gov/presidential-actions/
remarks-president-signing-executive-order-reorganize-executive-branch/

"Today there is duplication and redundancy everywhere. Billions and billions of dollars are being wasted on activities that are not delivering results for hardworking American taxpayers, and not even coming close."

Response to a question from Tucker Carlson of FOX News, March 15, 2017.
Source: https://www.youtube.com/watch?v=RYGH6ejacNO

"And we have saved a tremendous amount of money in government already. And that's just the beginning. I will tell you. People are paying too high a tax."

Response to a question from Tucker Carlson of FOX News, March 15, 2017.
Source: https://www.youtube.com/watch?v=RYGH6ejacNO

"And we are just starting. We are just starting. So, there is great optimism about the economy. But we have to get the taxes reduced."

Response to a question from Tucker Carlson of FOX News, March 15, 2017.
Source: https://www.youtube.com/watch?v=RYGH6ejacNO

"I'm going to try and get the 15% [tax] level if we can for the business. I think it will probably be a little bit higher than that, but we're going to try and get the 15% level."

Response to a question from Laura Ingraham of FOX News, November 2, 2017.
Source: https://www.youtube.com/watch?v=yTdDH-o_ICM

"Well, and the most important thing that we're going to be doing is tax cuts. Tax cuts. If we get this through, and I think we will, you're going to see this economy take off like a rocket ship."

Taxes—2017 Tweets

April 22, 2017

11:15 am: Big TAX REFORM AND TAX REDUCTION will be announced next Wednesday.

May 28, 2017

7:07 pm: The massive TAX CUTS/REFORM that I have submitted is moving along in the process very well, actually ahead of schedule. Big benefits to all!

September 13, 2017

6:28 am: The approval process for the biggest Tax Cut & Tax Reform package in the history of our country will soon begin. Move fast Congress!

September 27, 2017

8:55 pm: It is time to take care of OUR people, to rebuild OUR NA-TION, and to fight for OUR GREAT AMERICAN WORKERS! #TaxReform #USA

September 28, 2017

6:55 am: Democrats don't want massive tax cuts—how does that win elections? Great reviews for Tax Cut and Reform Bill.

October 11, 2017

6:28 pm: We need a tax system that is FAIR to working families & that encourages companies to STAY in America, GROW in America, and HIRE in America

October 12, 2017

8:18 pm: It is time to take care of OUR COUNTRY, to rebuild OUR COMMUNITIES, and to protect our GREAT AMERICAN WORK-ERS! #TaxReform

October 20, 2017

5:11 am to 5:15 am: The Budget passed late last night, 51 to 49. We got ZERO Democrat votes with only Rand Paul (he will vote for Tax Cuts) voting against...

...This now allows for the passage of large scale Tax Cuts (and Reform), which will be the biggest in the history of our country!

October 23, 2017

6:42 am: There will be NO change to your 401(k). This has always been a great and popular middle class tax break that works, and it stays!

October 25, 2017

6:35 am: Working hard on the biggest tax cut in U.S. history. Great support from so many sides. Big winners will be the middle class, business & JOBS

8:47 pm: This will be the biggest TAX CUT in the history of our country—and we need it! #TaxReform
Read more: https://t.co/o3W9bJkz5k https://t.co/JYckXWEmLu

October 31, 2017

7:21 am: I hope people will start to focus on our Massive Tax Cuts for Business (jobs) and the Middle Class (in addition to Democrat corruption)!

November 1, 2017

9:59 am to 10:03 am: Wouldn't it be great to Repeal the very unfair and unpopular Individual Mandate in ObamaCare and use those savings for further Tax Cuts...

...for the Middle Class. The House and Senate should consider ASAP as the process of final approval moves along. Push Biggest Tax Cuts EVER

November 2, 2017

7:05 pm: Great Tax Cut rollout today. The lobbyists are storming Capital Hill, but the Republicans will hold strong and do what is right for America!

November 13, 2017

9:21 pm: Excited to be heading home to see the House pass a GREAT Tax Bill with the middle class getting big TAX CUTS! #MakeAmericaGreatAgain

November 15, 2017

9:14 pm: Big vote tomorrow in the House. Tax cuts are getting close!

November 16, 2017

3:16 pm: Congratulations to the House of Representatives for passing the #TaxCutsandJobsAct—a big step toward fulfilling our promise to deliver historic TAX CUTS for the American people by the end of the year!

9:57 pm: Big win today in the House for GOP Tax Cuts and Reform, 227-205. Zero Dems, they want to raise taxes much higher, but not for our military!

November 19, 2017

9:21 pm: Republican Senators are working very hard to get Tax Cuts and Tax Reform approved. Hopefully it will not be long and they do not want to disappoint the American public!

November 22, 2017

9:06 pm: ...And it will get even better with Tax Cuts!
https://t.co/75wozGJQoP

November 26, 2017

8:47 pm: Back in D.C., big week for Tax Cuts and many other things of great importance to our Country. Senate Republicans will hopefully come through for all of us. The Tax Cut Bill is getting better and better. The end result will be great for ALL!

November 27, 2017

9:24 am: The Tax Cut Bill is coming along very well, great support. With just a few changes, some mathematical, the middle class and job producers can get even more in actual dollars and savings and the pass through provision becomes simpler and really works well!

9:50 pm: Thank you Rand! https://t.co/NvPeleVmub

November 29, 2017

6:29 pm: A vote to CUT TAXES is a vote to PUT AMERICA FIRST. It is time to take care of OUR WORKERS, to protect OUR COMMUNITIES, and to REBUILD OUR GREAT COUNTRY! https://t.co/wW3QNxcCHf https://t.co/sRL2yRK6k2

7:40 pm: Now, we have a once in a lifetime opportunity to RESTORE AMERICAN PROSPERITY—and RECLAIM AMERICA'S DESTINY. But in order to achieve this bright and glowing future, the SENATE MUST PASS TAX CUTS—and bring Main Street roaring back to life! https://t.co/jMNwEMrbbr https://t.co/3Niu0thp1D

8:09 pm: The only people who don't like the Tax Cut Bill are the people that don't understand it or the Obstructionist Democrats that know how really good it is and do not want the credit and success to go to the Republicans!

December 2, 2017

2:49 am: We are one step closer to delivering MASSIVE tax cuts for working families across America. Special thanks to @SenateMajLdr Mitch McConnell and Chairman @SenOrrinHatch for shepherding our bill through the Senate. Look forward to signing a final bill before Christmas!

7:54 am: Biggest Tax Bill and Tax Cuts in history just passed in the Senate. Now these great Republicans will be going for final passage. Thank you to House and Senate Republicans for your hard work and commitment!

December 4, 2017

7:03 am: With the great vote on Cutting Taxes, this could be a big day for the Stock Market—and YOU!

December 14, 2017

12:05 pm: As a candidate, I promised we would pass a massive tax cut for the everyday, working Americans. If you make your voices heard, this moment will be forever remembered as a great new beginning— the dawn of a brilliant American future shining with PATRIOTISM, PROSPERITY AND PRIDE! https://t.co/exsBzrlCdw

December 16, 2017

3:05 pm: TAX CUTS will increase investment in the American economy and in U.S. workers, leading to higher growth, higher wages, and more JOBS!

December 17, 2017

12:01 pm: As a candidate, I promised we would pass a massive TAX CUT for the everyday working American families who are the backbone and the heartbeat of our country. Now, we are just days away...

December 18, 2017

3:40 pm: As a candidate, I promised we would pass a massive TAX CUT for the everyday working American families who are the backbone and the heartbeat of our country. Now, we are just days away...

December 20. 2017

1:09 am: The United States Senate just passed the biggest in history Tax Cut and Reform Bill. Terrible Individual Mandate (ObamaCare) Repealed. Goes to the House tomorrow morning for final vote. If approved, there will be a News Conference at The White House at approximately 1:00 P.M.

1:09 pm: We are delivering HISTORIC TAX RELIEF for the American people! #TaxCutsandJobsAct https://t.co/lLgATrCh5o

December 21, 2017

7:21 am: The Massive Tax Cuts, which the Fake News Media is desperate to write badly about so as to please their Democrat bosses, will soon be kicking in and will speak for themselves. Companies are already making big payments to workers. Dems want to raise taxes, hate these big Cuts!

December 22, 2017

10:07 am: Will be signing the biggest ever Tax Cut and Reform Bill in 30 minutes in Oval Office. Will also be signing a much needed 4 billion dollar missile defense bill.

11:46 am: 95% of Americans will pay less or, at worst, the same amount of taxes (mostly far less). The Dems only want to raise your taxes!

3:47 pm: Today, it was my great honor to sign the largest TAX CUTS and reform in the history of our country.
Full remarks: https://t.co/kMxoxEB68G https://t.co/OeAoA0sLfx

December 24, 2017

3:35 pm: The Tax Cut/Reform Bill, including Massive Alaska Drilling and the Repeal of the highly unpopular Individual Mandate, brought it all together as to what an incredible year we had. Don't let the Fake News convince you otherwise...and our insider Polls are strong!

December 30, 2017

4:12 pm: On Taxes: "This is the biggest corporate rate cut ever, going back to the corporate income tax rate of roughly 80 years ago. This is a huge pro-growth stimulus for the economy. Every year the Obama WH overstated how the economy would grow. Now real economics and jobs." @WSJ Report

Taxes—2018 News Quotes

Remarks before Marine One departure, January 5, 2018.

Source: https://www.whitehouse.gov/briefings-statements/
remarks-president-trump-marine-one-departure-5/

"The tax cuts are really kicking in far beyond what anyone thought."

Response to a question from Bret Baier of FOX News, June 12, 2018.

Source: https://www.youtube.com/watch?v=zogD8bnGJu4

"I think it's a whole different ball game. I think the economy is so good. I think the tax cuts have been incredible, far greater than even I thought they would be. The regulation cuts have been great. I mean I've done more in 500 days than any president has ever done in their first 500 days. There's nobody close, and that's not—That's a lot of people saying that. People that would rather not say it are saying it. And I really think that we are going to do very good. Now, history is against me because history for whatever reason, you win the election and then you lose lots of seats. I think we are going to do very well; I really do. The economy is doing so well. We are doing so well as a nation. I think we are going to surprise people and if you look at the numbers and if you look at the kind of turnouts like Texas, how many people showed up to vote as an example, how many Republicans showed up to vote— People were very surprised."

Remarks at a rally in Tampa, Florida, July 31, 2018.

Source: https://www.tampabay.com/florida-politics/buzz/2018/08/01/
heres-a-full-transcript-of-president-trumps-speech-from-his-tampa-rally/

"We passed the biggest tax cuts and reform in American history, biggest cuts in history. More than 100 utilities have slashed rates for consumers, including right here from Duke Energy and Tampa Electric. Your rates have gone down.

"Over $300 billion poured back into the United States in the first quarter, and we expect to be taking back because of our new tax cut and reform plan that passed bigger than anything ever in our country. We expect to be taking back from overseas over $4 trillion. That's a lot of money, could never have come back before.

"And if our opponent had won and the Democrats had won, they would've put more regulations on. They would've raised your taxes. They would've opened your borders, gotten rid of law enforcement. They would not have helped your military. And you know what? Our country would be going to hell.

"And instead of going up, the market would be half of what it was if we're lucky, because frankly the tax cuts were incredible to what we've done. But maybe even more important are the cuts in these horrible regulations that didn't allow anybody to do anything, job-killing regulations. We've gotten rid of more regulations than any president in the history of the United States. And that's done in less than two years. I withdrew the United States from the unfair, one-sided, very, very expensive job-killing Paris Climate Accord."

Taxes—2018 Tweets

January 2, 2018

8:49 am: Companies are giving big bonuses to their workers because of the Tax Cut Bill. Really great!

January 3, 2018

9:07 pm: "Some 40 U.S. companies have responded to President Trump's tax cut and reform victory in Congress last year by handing out bonuses up to $2,000, increases in 401k matches and spending on charity, a much higher number than previously known."

January 11, 2018

10:37 am: Great news, as a result of our TAX CUTS & JOBS ACT!

February 2, 2018

1:05 pm: With 3.5 million Americans receiving bonuses or other benefits from their employers as a result of TAX CUTS, 2018 is off to great start! ✓Unemployment rate at 4.1%. ✓Average earnings up 2.9% in the last year. ✓200,000 new American jobs. ✓#MAGA

February 5, 2018

3:42 pm: Thanks to the historic TAX CUTS that I signed into law, your paychecks are going way UP, your taxes are going way DOWN, and America is once again OPEN FOR BUSINESS!

February 11, 2018

2:15 am: 4.2 million hard working Americans have already received a large Bonus and/or Pay Increase because of our recently Passed Tax Cut & Jobs Bill...and it will only get better! We are far ahead of schedule.

April 5, 2018

3:12 pm: Thanks to our historic TAX CUTS, America is open for business, and millions of American workers are seeing more take-home pay through higher wages, salaries and bonuses!

April 12, 2018

12:13 pm: Just had an Agricultural Roundtable with memembers of Congress and Governors. I will be making remarks on the large scale

TAX CUTS given to American families and workers at 1:45 P.M. from the Rose Garden. Join me live: https://t.co/XAchZ3zUSe https://t.co/Dqe8QhpDAZ

April 17, 2018

7:24 am: So many people are seeing the benefits of the Tax Cut Bill. Everyone is talking, really nice to see!

April 20, 2018

5:50 am: Nancy Pelosi is going absolutely crazy about the big Tax Cuts given to the American People by the Republicans…got not one Democrat Vote! Here's a choice. They want to end them and raise your taxes substantially. Republicans are working on making them permanent and more cuts!

June 21, 2018

3:25 pm: "The real big story that affects everybody in America is the success of @POTUS's TAX CUT package and what it's done for our economy…" @Varneyco

3:46 am: Big Supreme Court win on internet sales tax—about time! Big victory for fairness and for our country. Great victory for consumers and retailers.

June 29, 2018

1:06 pm: Six months after our TAX CUTS, more than 6 MILLION workers have received bonuses, pay raises, and retirement account contributions. #TaxCutsandJobsAct

July 18, 2018

6:03 am: Just had an Agricultural Roundtable with memembers of Congress and Governors. I will be making remarks on the large scale

TAX CUTS given to American families and workers at 1:45 P.M. from the Rose Garden. Join me live: https://t.co/XAchZ3zUSe https://t.co/Dqe8QhpDAZ

October 4, 2018

5:17 pm: Congressman Bishop is doing a GREAT job! He helped pass tax reform which lowered taxes for EVERYONE! Nancy Pelosi is spending hundreds of thousands of dollars on his opponent because they both support a liberal agenda of higher taxes and wasteful spending!

Taxes—2019 News Quotes

From State of the Union address, February 5, 2019.
Source: https://www.whitehouse.gov/briefings-statements/president-donald-j-trumps-state-union-address-2/

"We passed a massive tax cut for working families and doubled the child tax credit.

"We virtually ended the estate, or death, tax on small businesses, ranches, and family farms.

"We eliminated the very unpopular Obamacare individual mandate penalty, and to give critically ill patients access to lifesaving cures, we passed right to try.

"My administration has cut more regulations in a short time than any other administration during its entire tenure. Companies are coming back to our country in large numbers thanks to historic reductions in taxes and regulations."

Remarks at the signing of H.R. 3401, July 1, 2019
Source: https://www.whitehouse.gov/briefings-statements/
remarks-president-trump-signing-h-r-3401/

"We just finished a signing, a very important signing, of the Taxpayer First Bill, the IRS Taxpayer First, which is a tremendous thing for our citizens, having to do with the IRS. It streamlines, and so many other changes made. So, that was just done and signed, and it's been made into law. So we're all set on that."

Remarks at the signing of H.R. 3401, July 1, 2019
Source: https://www.whitehouse.gov/briefings-statements/
remarks-president-trump-signing-h-r-3401/

"Because of the tax cuts, our economy is the hottest in the world. If we didn't have them—We were paying up—Companies were paying the highest tax rates in the world, just about. In many cases, the highest. And now we have them at the low level. Not the lowest, but we have them at the low level, at 21%. And because of that, they're coming in. New companies are being formed."

Taxes—2019 Tweets

May 8, 2019

5:56 am: Real estate developers in the 1980's & 1990's, more than 30 years ago, were entitled to massive write offs and depreciation which would, if one was actively building, show losses and tax losses in almost all cases. Much was non monetary. Sometimes considered "tax shelter,".

...you would get it by building, or even buying. You always wanted to show losses for tax purposes...almost all real estate developers did—

and often re-negotiate with banks, it was sport. Additionally, the very old information put out is a highly inaccurate Fake News hit job

May 11, 2019

1:32 pm: I won the 2016 Election partially based on no Tax Returns while I am under audit (which I still am), and the voters didn't care. Now the Radical Left Democrats want to again relitigate this matter. Make it a part of the 2020 Election!

July 1, 2019

9:47 am: Congratulations to legislators in New Jersey for not passing taxes that would have driven large numbers of high end taxpayers out of the state. Many were planning to leave, & will now be staying. New York & others should start changing their thought process on taxes, fast!

July 7, 2019

8:03 am: Sleepy Joe Biden just admitted he worked with segregation-ists and separately, has already been very plain about the fact that he will be substantially raising everyone's taxes if he becomes president. Ridiculously, all Democrats want to substantially raise taxes!